Motor Sport

PHOTOGRAPHY

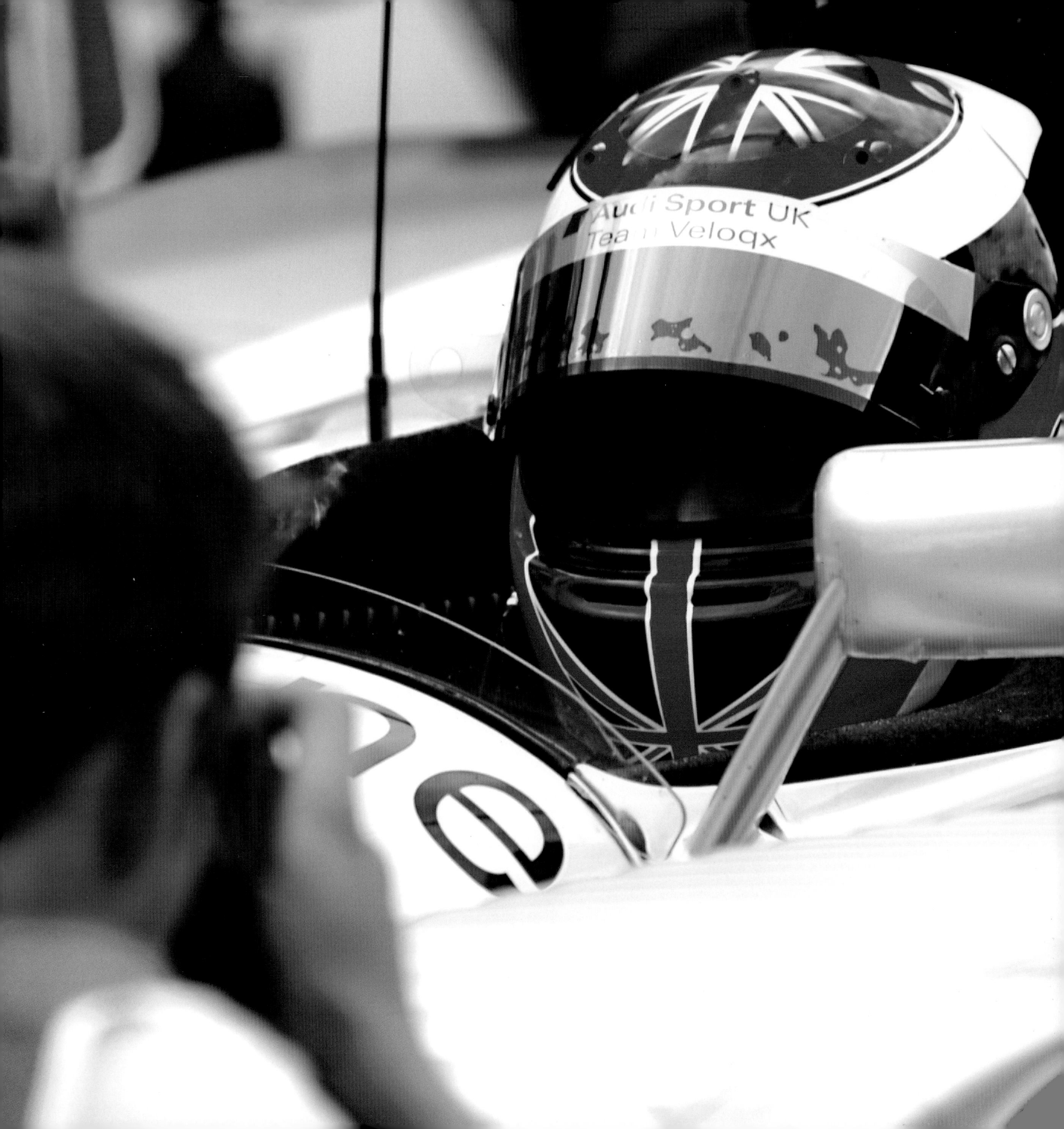
Audi Sport UK

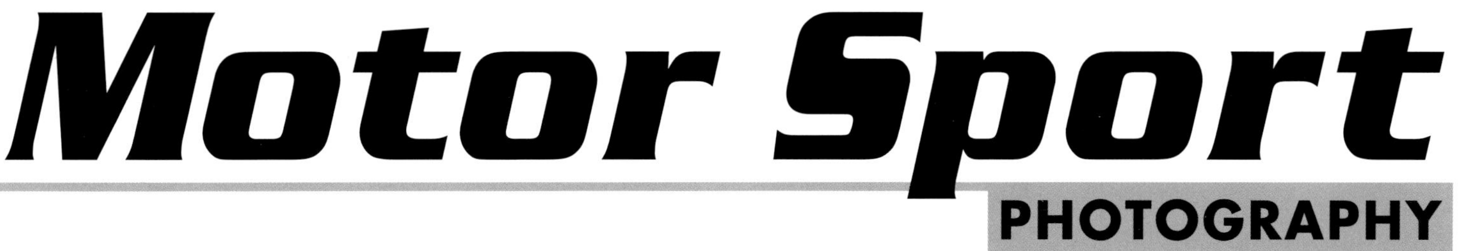

Tony Pleavin

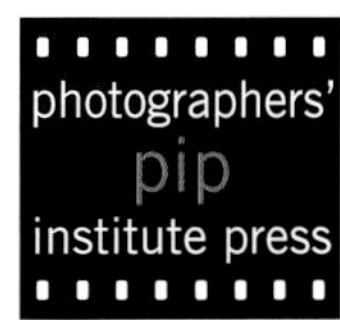

PHOTOGRAPHERS' INSTITUTE PRESS

First published 2005 by
Photographers' Institute Press / PIP
an imprint of The Guild of Master Craftsman Publications Ltd
Castle Place, 166 High Street,
Lewes, East Sussex BN7 1XU

ISBN 1 86108 399 8

A catalogue record for this book is available from the British Library.

Managing Editor: Gerrie Purcell
Production Manager: Hilary MacCallum
Project Editor: Stephen Haynes
Designer: Christopher Halls at Mind's Eye Design, Lewes

Set in Renault Light and Serpentine D

Colour origination by Masterpiece, London
Printed and bound in Singapore by Kyodo Printing Co Ltd

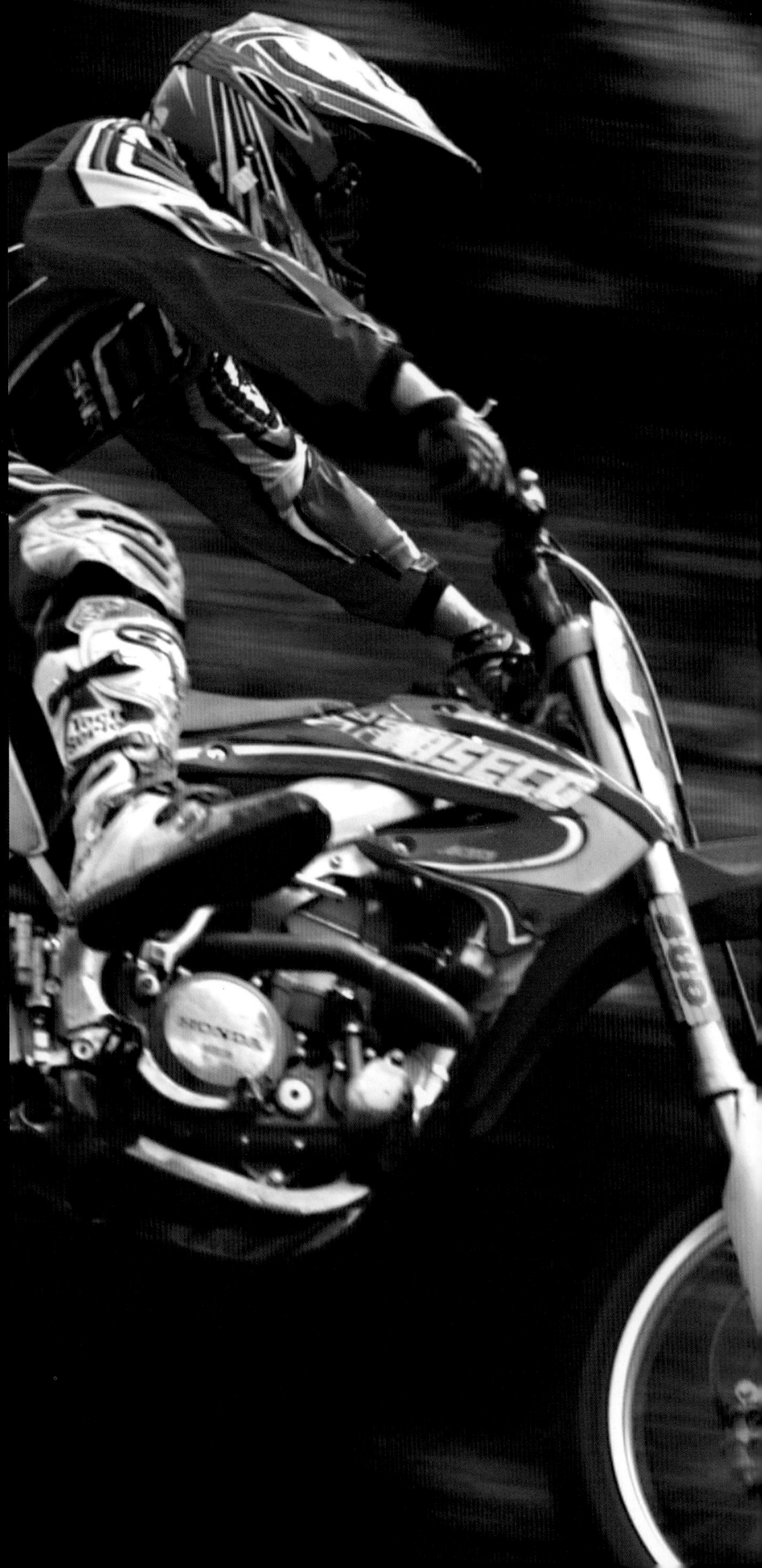

Contents

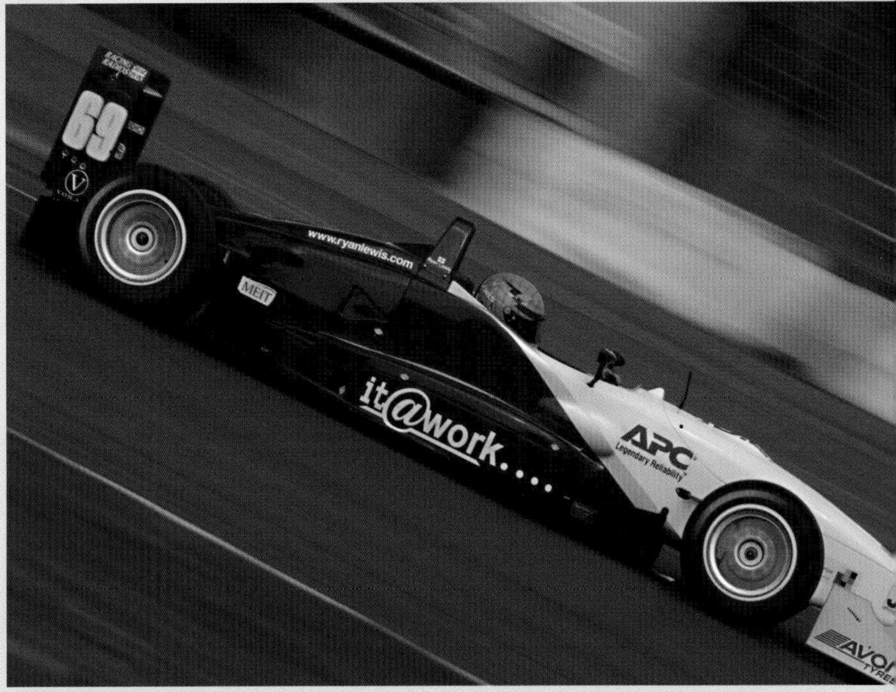

To the memory of my father, John Pleavin, who passed away during the production of this book.

Also to Jenni, for her unwavering support and for mowing the lawns every weekend while I'm away photographing motor sports.

Acknowledgements

I would like to thank all at PIP, most notably Stephen Haynes, Gerrie Purcell and James Beattie. Thanks also to Steven Tee of LAT Photographic, Chris Halls at Mind's Eye Design, Andy Bothwell at MotorSport Vision, Jeff Carter at Rockingham Motor Speedway, Dave Fern at Donington Park, Jonathan Lord at RSAC Ltd, Helen Lovell at Mallory Park, and Katie Tyler at Silverstone Circuit.

A note on focal lengths

Many of the pictures in this book were taken with a digital camera, using lenses which were originally designed for 35mm film-based cameras. Most digital cameras have a sensor area which is less than that of a 35mm film frame, which means that the same lens produces an effect of greater magnification when used on the digital camera. For the benefit of 35mm users, lens focal lengths in the captions are therefore given in two forms: for example, '200mm (35mm equivalent: 300mm)' means that the picture was actually taken with a 200mm lens, but a 300mm lens would be needed to give the same field of view on a 35mm camera.

Foreword

When Tony mentioned he was writing a book on the mechanics of motor sport photography, I had no hesitation in agreeing to write the foreword.

For as long as I can remember I always wanted to be a motor sport photographer, fusing my love of motor racing, photography and travel. I now do just that – but I had a lot of help along the way. When I started to look seriously at how to realize this ambition, there were no books available for guidance – let alone a comprehensive 'how-to' textbook like this. It would have been very useful to have had this book on hand at my college interview, to counter the blank stares I was faced with when I outlined my intended photographic path.

Even though I have now spent 20 years shooting Formula 1, I am still learning, and I am sure I always will be. I firmly believe that being surrounded by talented contemporaries, who bounce ideas off each other and are constantly looking for new ways of doing things, is the best way of improving your own work. So if this book makes it easier for readers to take part in this process, and ultimately helps them follow the same path, then it is an important tool, and Tony should be applauded for his part in creating the next generation of motor sport photographers.

Steven Tee
Managing Director, LAT Photographic *November 2004*

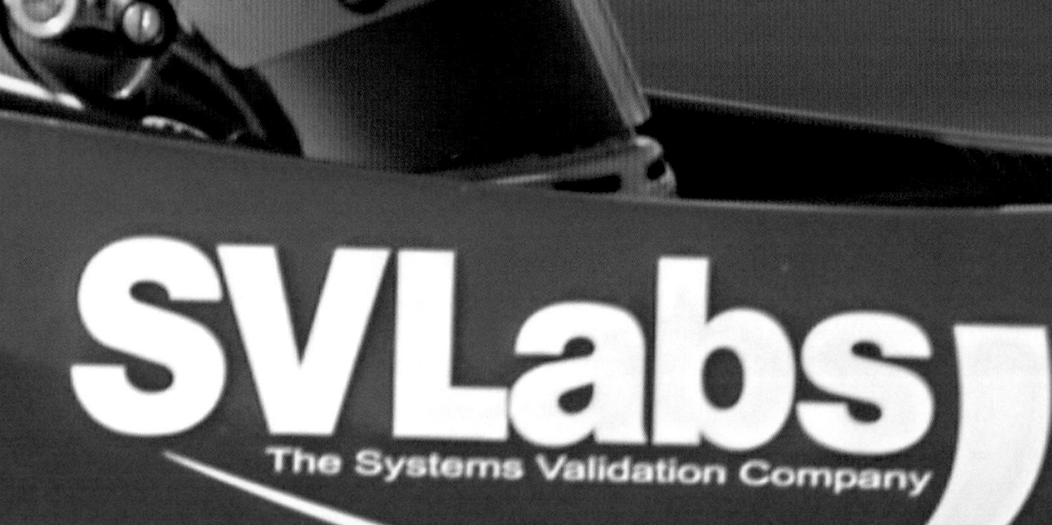
SVLabs
The Systems Validation Company
EXEN
TRUCK TECHNOLOGY
port.co.uk

Introduction

Not so long ago, I was a keen enthusiast of motor sport photography, who visited race meetings to take photographs for personal pleasure. Now I make a significant part of my livelihood by selling my images. If you share my enthusiasm, this book is for you. By adopting a methodical, creative and commonsense approach, you can improve your images to a point where they are comparable with those produced by the full-time professionals.

The techniques of motor sport photography are not difficult to learn, and once you have grasped them you will be in a better position to achieve the pictures you see in your mind's eye. Throughout my transition from enthusiastic amateur to semi-pro, my love of photography has always been the main motivator.

You do not need expensive equipment or privileged access in order to take good motor sport images. Many of my best pictures were taken from public access areas, and similar results are therefore within reach of any amateur photographer. Whether you aspire to become a professional in the future, or are content with taking images for your own pleasure, I sincerely hope this book can help you to realize your goal.

Having visited many motor racing meetings over the years, I am aware of the large numbers of amateur photographers who attend such events and am greatly encouraged to see that our chosen hobby is as popular as ever. If this book helps you to improve your picture-taking and get more enjoyment and fulfilment from it, I will have done what I set out to do.

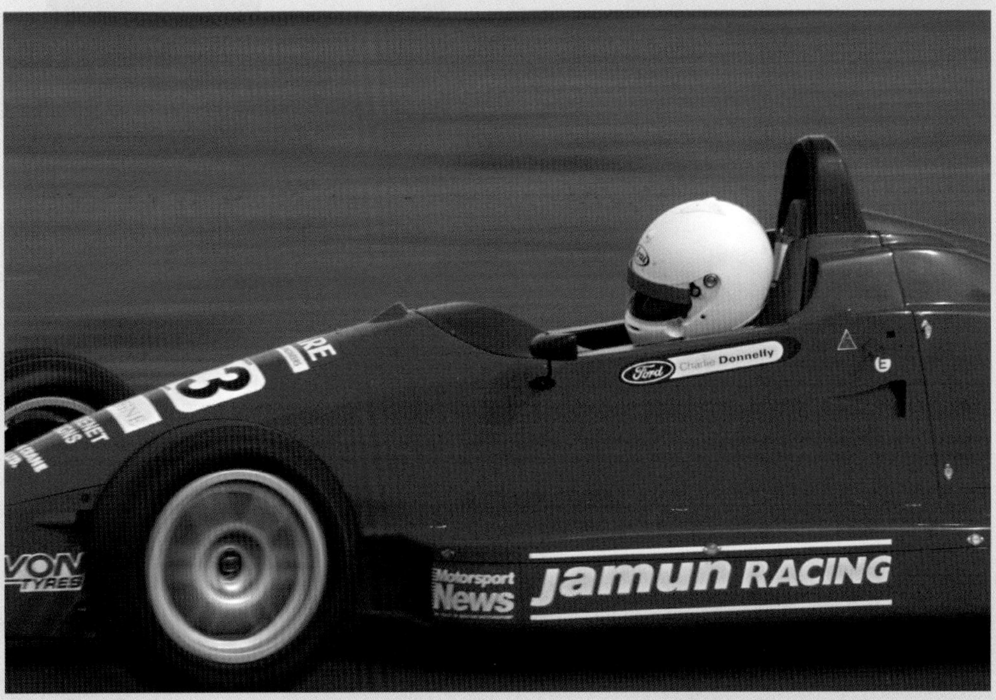

Camera	***Pentax *ist D***
Focal length	***200mm (35mm equivalent: 300mm)***
Exposure	***1/90sec at f/19***
ISO setting	***200***

There are many factors that combine to make an effective motor racing image. A methodical approach, combined with a willingness to learn and keep learning, will allow you to see your images improve.

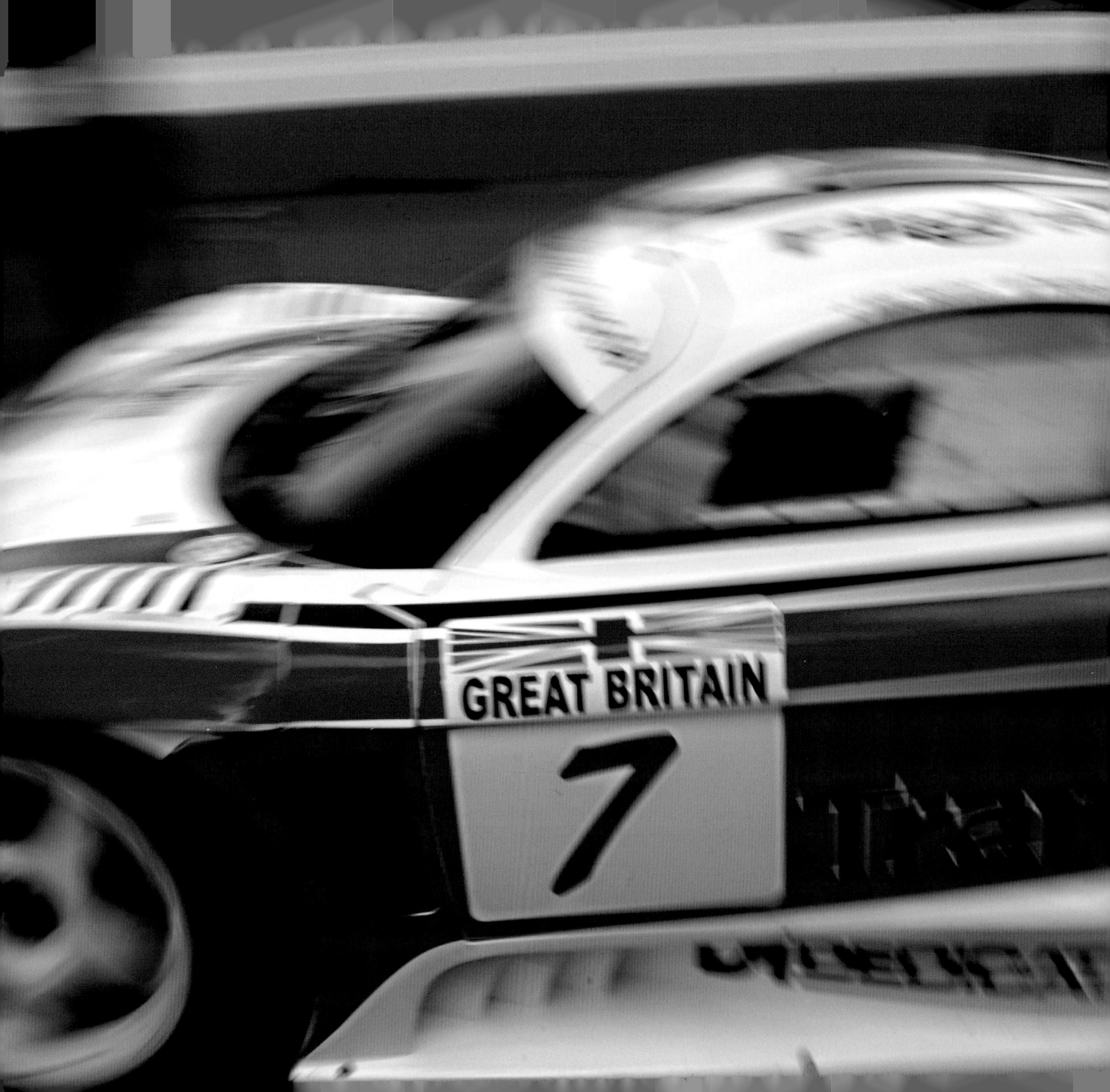
GREAT BRITAIN
7

CHAPTER 1

Equipment

Deciding what kind of camera system to use for photographing motor sport is easy: the flexibility provided by a single-lens reflex (SLR), either 35mm or digital, is unchallenged by any other format in terms of image quality, ease of use, lens choice and availability of film or storage media. That's not to say that you cannot produce quality results with other systems, but over a race weekend the digital or 35mm SLR comes out top.

If you watch professional photographers at race meetings you will see that they usually carry at least two digital camera bodies, with an imposing set of lenses that carry a total price comparable to that of a new small car. Don't be put off by this – having the best equipment for the job in hand is always a benefit, but there is no reason why you can't produce images of a professional standard with more modest equipment. If you already own an SLR, the obvious choice is to stick with that – though you may need to add a couple more lenses to your camera bag in order to be ready to start photographing racing events. (We'll talk about lens choice on pages 22–31.)

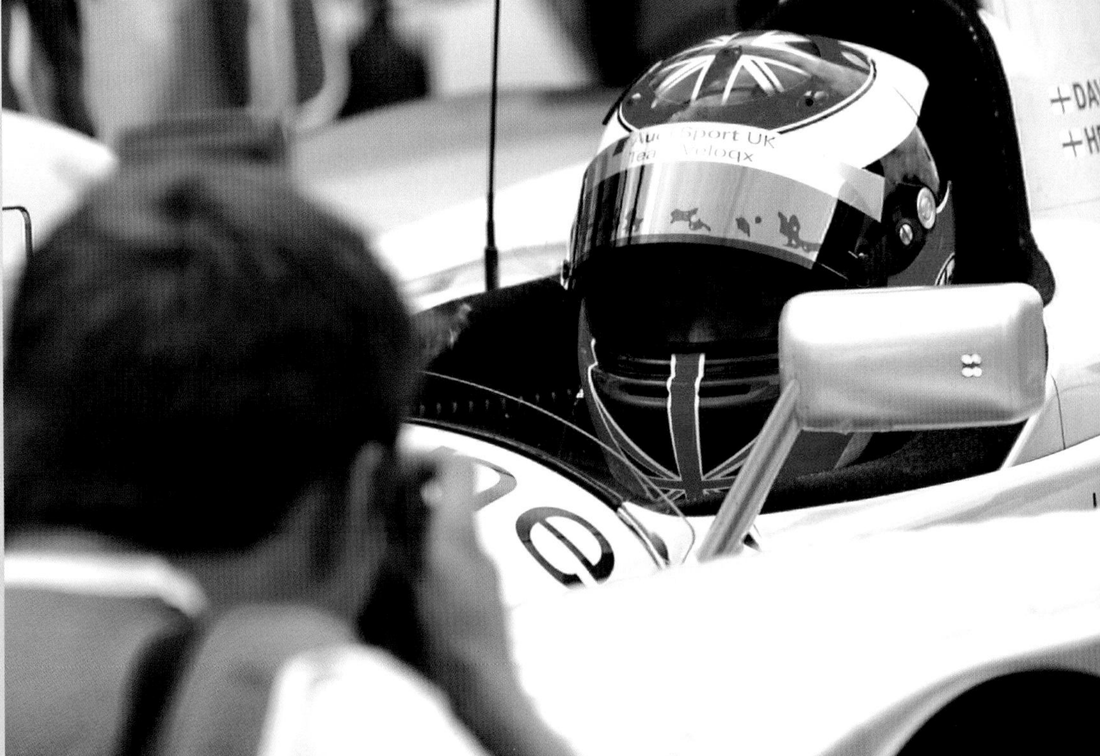

Camera	Pentax *ist D
Focal length	200mm (35mm equivalent: 300mm)
Exposure	1/500sec at f/5.6
ISO setting	200

Professional motor sport photographers often have the sort of equipment that amateurs can only dream of. Though having the best kit does make your life easier, don't imagine that you can't take good quality images without it.

Cameras

When you look at the vast array of cameras available today, selecting the right one for you may seem a daunting prospect. The most important thing is to consider what features you really need. Modern cameras come with a huge range of technical functions that you may *think* you need, but most of the time you will probably only use 20% of these. Try not to get too hung up on having the latest, most technically advanced kit. All the equipment in the world will not make you a better photographer if you don't understand how best to use it.

Camera features

As long as your camera has a decent metering system, can shoot at least 2.5 frames per second, is fairly robust and accepts a wide range of compatible lenses, you have enough to get started. Most modern cameras offer a choice of metering modes, but a model with centre-weighted and multi-segment metering will be adequate. (Metering is discussed on pages 76–85.) In terms of exposure modes you will probably only need three: manual, shutter priority and aperture priority. (These are explained on pages 76–81.) Forget about automated 'program' modes – most consumer-level cameras have them but you don't need them, so they should not influence your buying decision. A mid-range 35mm film body from any of the top manufacturers should give you everything you need.

A digital body may cost around three times as much as a comparable film body, but prices are coming down all the time. The digital SLR (D-SLR) market is constantly evolving: each new development brings higher specifications at ever more competitive prices, which ultimately means that whatever D-SLR you buy will inevitably become obsolete when a new model is brought out to replace it. Some people see this as a problem; but any D-SLR with a sensor capable of producing an image of 6 megapixels (6Mp) or larger will give results of comparable quality to 35mm film.

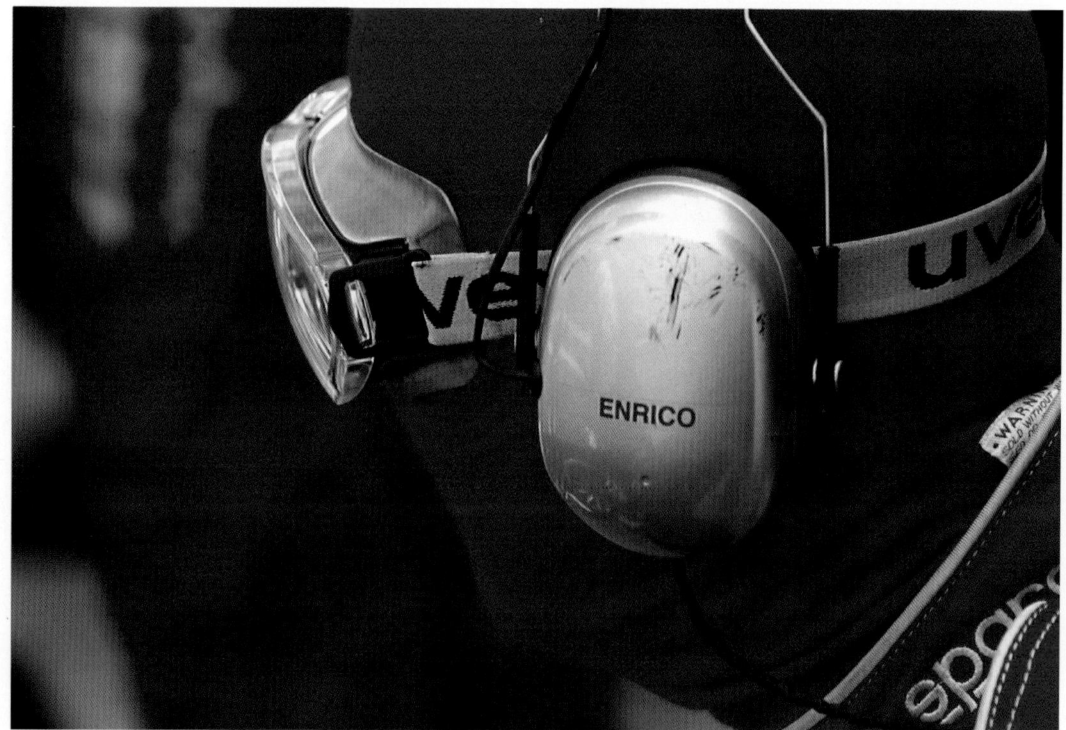

Camera	Pentax *ist D
Focal length	210mm (35mm equivalent: 315mm)
Exposure	1/500sec at f/4.5
ISO setting	200

Understanding the various features of your camera and what they do will make it much easier for you to get the effects you want. By selecting a wide aperture while using my camera in Aperture Priority mode I was able to produce very shallow depth of field, thus throwing the background out of focus and emphasizing the main subject of this image.

Another consideration when buying digital equipment is the length of burst that a camera is capable of. This refers to the number of frames a camera can capture before having to stop in order to transfer the data from the image buffer to the memory card; the camera 'locks out' and becomes inoperable during this process. This is an important issue if you want to capture action sequences, as it is the burst size that will determine how many shots you can take before lockout occurs. The burst length available varies between camera models, but in most situations an ideal burst size would be about 9 or 10 images. My camera has a burst length of 6 images, and though I have only exceeded this on a couple of occasions it is very frustrating to know you have lost a good action sequence because of it.

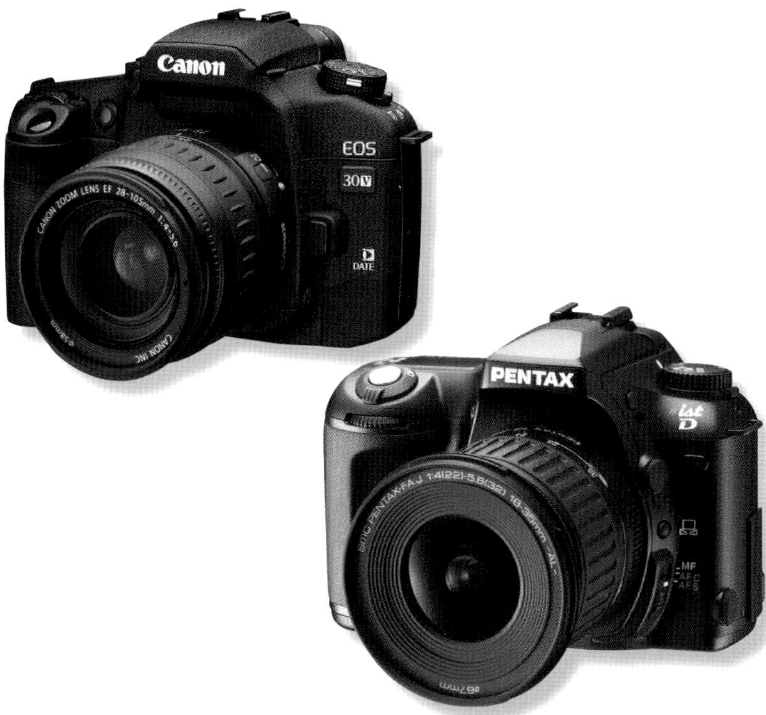

An SLR for 35mm film, the Canon EOS 30V Date (by courtesy of Canon UK Ltd).

A digital SLR, the Pentax *ist D (by courtesy of Pentax UK Ltd).

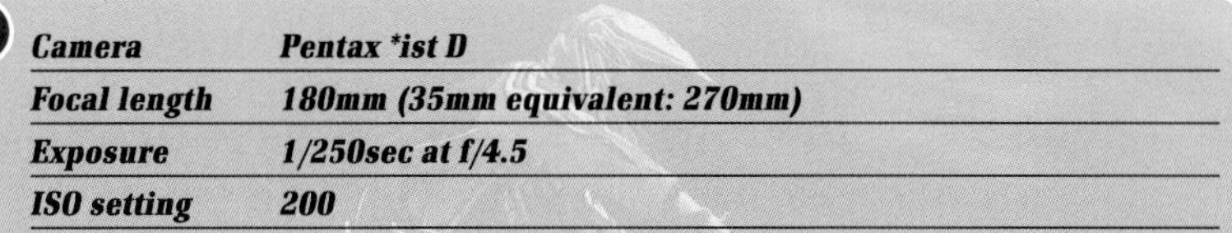

Camera	***Pentax *ist D***
Focal length	***180mm (35mm equivalent: 270mm)***
Exposure	***1/250sec at f/4.5***
ISO setting	***200***

If you are planning to buy a digital SLR, consider the burst length that it produces. Some photographers like to shoot multiple frames for action shots like this, so that they can choose the best from a sequence – in which case your camera must have an adequate burst size to prevent 'lock-out' while you're still shooting. Think carefully before buying cheap memory cards, which may be slow to write images from the memory buffer.

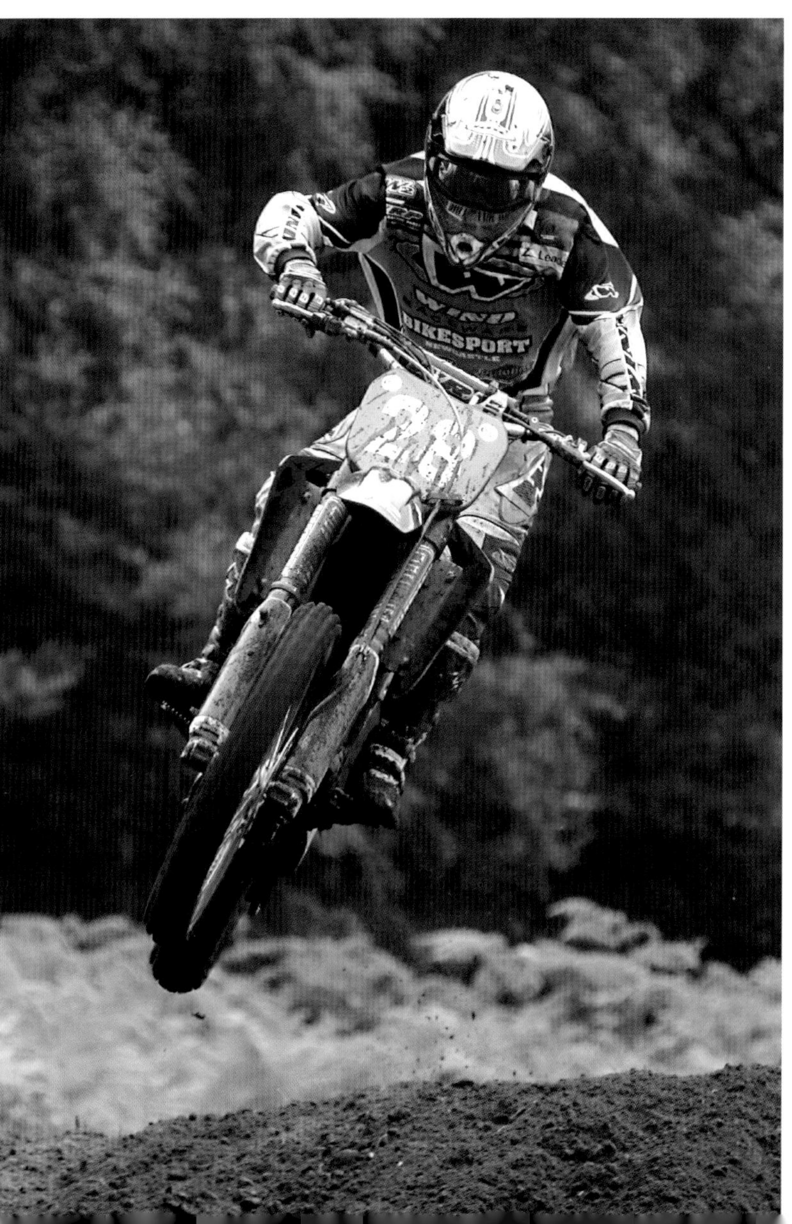

Lens availability

Whether you already have the kit you need or are planning to buy new gear, the most important consideration is the availability of lenses and accessories for your particular brand. It pays to research carefully what is available from each camera manufacturer – or from independent lens manufacturers – before you make your decision. If you're looking to build up a system from scratch for photographing motor sports, both Canon and Nikon have excellent system back-up in terms of the number of lenses and accessories available; they also have an excellent range of D-SLRs to complement their film-based line-up. But this is not to say that you can't get equally good results with other makes. I chose a Pentax *ist D as my first D-SLR because it allows me to use my existing lenses (I have used Pentax film cameras for years), so I didn't have to fork out for a whole new system to go with the camera. I have found this to be a very cost-effective way of moving from film to digital.

Camera	**Pentax *ist D**
Focal length	**200mm (35mm equivalent: 300mm)**
Exposure	**1/250sec at f/8**
ISO setting	**200**

Racing drivers often take the same line through a corner on each lap, which gives you the chance to anticipate the action and to make several attempts at the same shot. Pre-focusing on the track just after the kerb, I took a number of shots of this driver as he cut the corner, throwing up dirt from his rear wheels. The digital camera allowed me to review my shots immediately, ensuring that focusing was pin-sharp and that I had captured the flying dirt. I have previously taken such shots using 35mm film, but with digital I can make sure that I have the image I want and therefore maximize every opportunity.

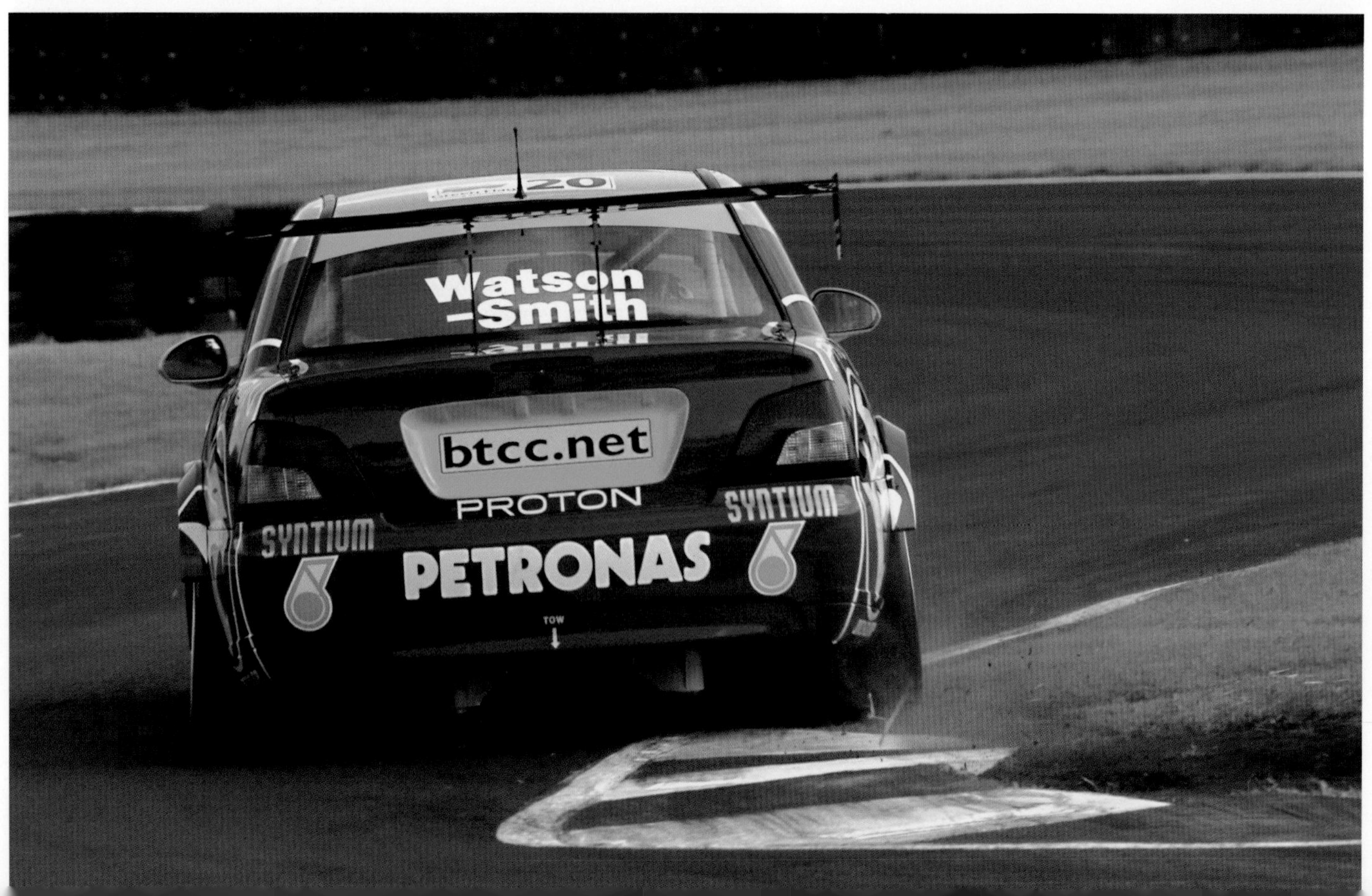

Conventional lenses and digital cameras

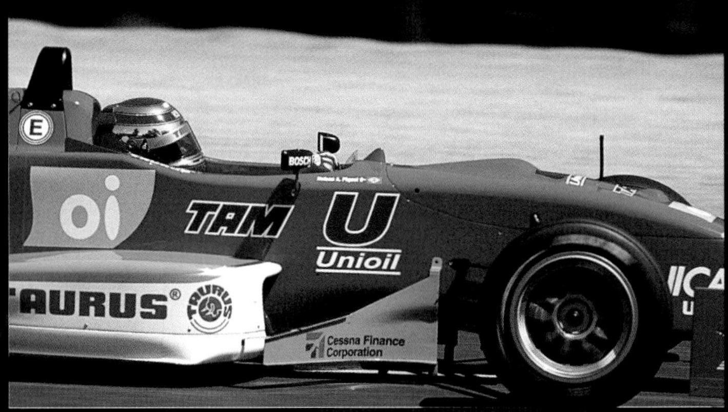

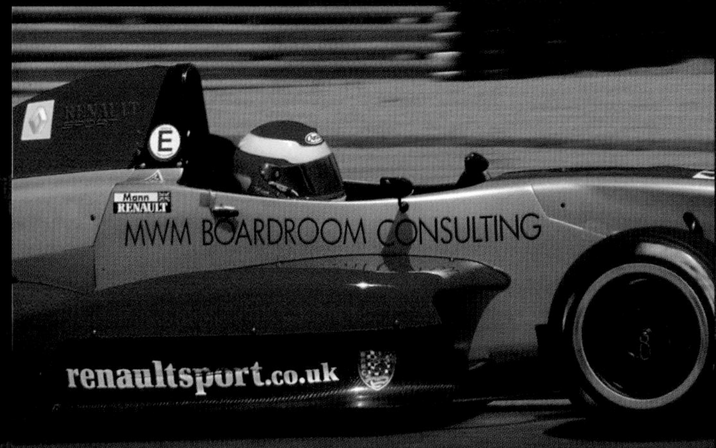

Camera	Pentax *ist D
Focal length	200mm (35mm equivalent: 300mm)
Exposure	1/180sec at f/19
ISO setting	200

These two images were shot at the same corner one year apart; one was taken on 35mm film, the other with a digital SLR. The quality of images produced by modern D-SLRs is now at least as good as, if not better than, 35mm film. Lenses were chosen to give the same image magnification on the two different cameras.

Camera	Pentax Super A
Focal length	300mm
Exposure	1/125sec at f/16
Film	Fuji Velvia 50

If you already have a 35mm system and are thinking of buying a digital camera from the same manufacturer, it's worth finding out whether you can use your existing lenses on the digital body – this could save you having to buy new lenses as well. It is important that you check this carefully with the manufacturer, because even if your existing lenses fit a digital body their functionality could be reduced in certain metering modes. (Some lenses may also suffer from quality fall-off towards the edge of the frame, but I have not experienced this.)

One plus point of using 35mm lenses on digital bodies is that the image magnification may be increased due to the smaller size of the sensor on most D-SLRs compared to 35mm film. For example, the sensor on my digital camera provides an effective increase in the focal length of 1.5 times when using a lens designed for a 35mm film camera body. Therefore a lens with a focal length of 200mm has the effect of a 300mm lens (1.5 x 200mm), although the focal length does not actually change – the sensor is simply recording a smaller area of the image.

In the captions to the digital images in this book, we give both the actual focal length of the lens used, and the 35mm equivalent: for example, '200mm (35mm equivalent: 300mm)' means that the digital camera was fitted with a 200mm lens, but that a 300mm lens would be needed to give the same field of view on a 35mm camera.

For more on focal lengths, see pages 23–7.

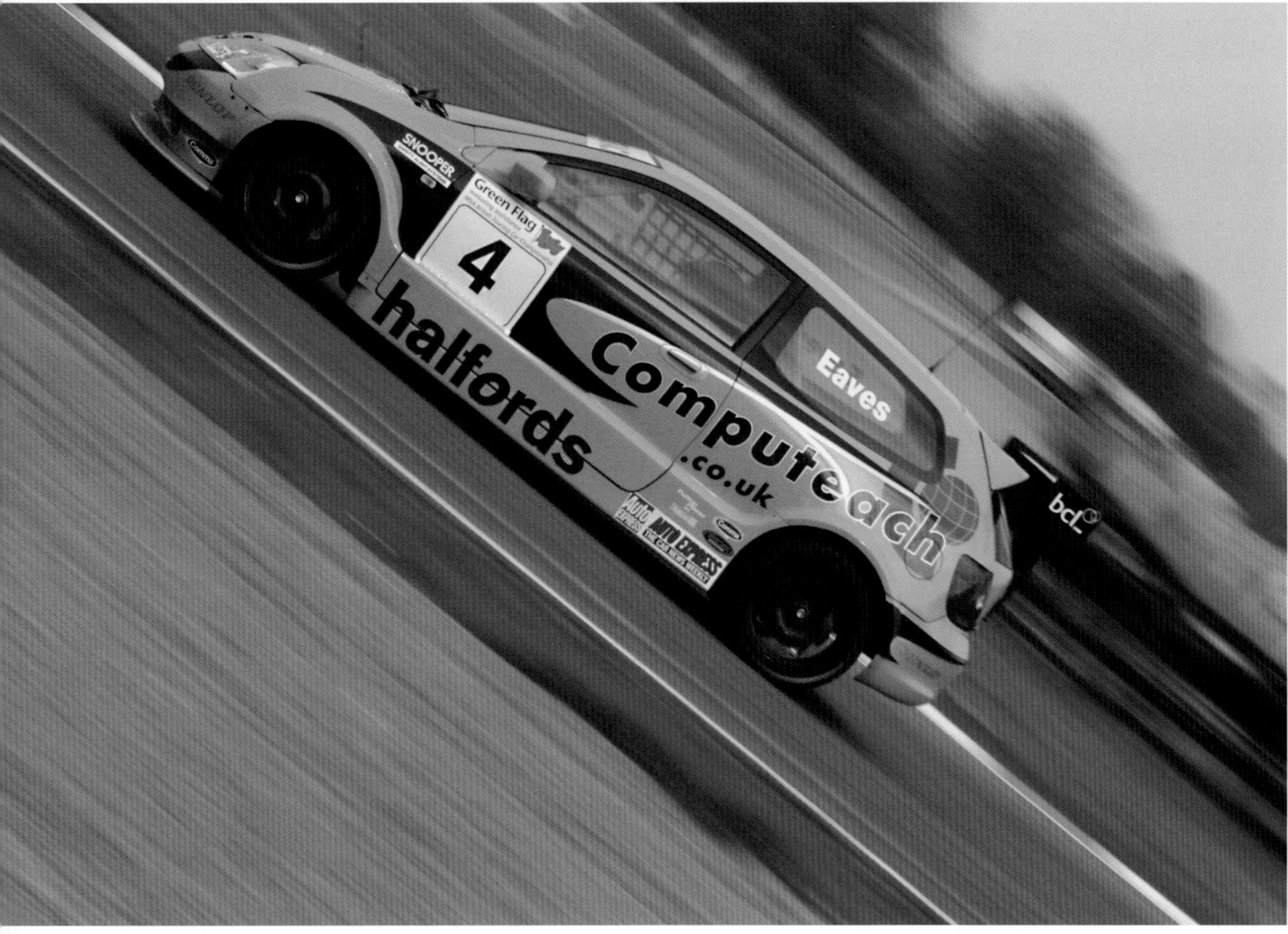

Camera	Pentax *ist D
Focal length	135mm (35mm equivalent: 200mm)
Exposure	1/125sec at f/13
ISO setting	200

Shooting digitally allows me to try out more adventurous approaches. Once I knew I had captured an image from this viewpoint with the car in a conventional horizontal position, I was then able to alter the composition by tilting the camera to produce what I think is a more pleasing result. There is nothing to stop you doing the same with a film camera, but I find that the immediacy of the digital format gives me greater confidence to experiment.

Digital advantages

Unless you have been living on another planet you will have been unable to avoid hearing about the advances made in digital technology and the options they provide for photographers. The film versus digital debate has been raging for a while now, and like most photographers I have been watching the developments in this field, often wondering when I would make the decision to 'go digital'. There are pros and cons with both technologies, but the major issue has to be the quality of the end result, not whether it was captured on film or digitally. When I started planning this book I had not even used an autofocus SLR, let alone a digital one – but with the introduction of a greater range of D-SLRs at more affordable prices I decided it was time to make the leap. My main reason was that the quality of image produced from a 6Mp SLR is at least comparable to that of 35mm professional slide film, if not better. Ally this to the convenience of digital over film in terms of cost, flexibility and immediacy, and, for me, digital wins hands down.

That's not to say film is obsolete – I still take my 35mm gear to every event I attend, but I find that more often than not I return home without having taken it out of my bag. I might consider using it in very low temperatures, as these conditions severely impair battery efficiency, and digital cameras are completely reliant on batteries.

If you are still uncertain and have reservations about moving over to the digital format, let me give you some facts.

Digital files for publication

For this type of photography the majority of publishers accept, if not prefer, digital files. When I shoot on 35mm film I usually scan the transparencies in order to be able to make prints from my PC and email images to editors for consideration – so my 35mm image becomes a digital one in any case, albeit one that has been scanned and has lost some quality in the process. The photo-library through which I sell my pictures will only accept files on CD, and though this is not yet a requirement with all such agencies, I'm sure it will be before too long. For more on presenting images for publication, see Chapter 6.

Camera	*Pentax *ist D*
Focal length	*200mm (35mm equivalent: 300mm)*
Exposure	*1/180sec at f/5.6*
ISO setting	*200*

Shooting digitally provides many advantages over traditional film formats, especially when you consider how an image can be manipulated post capture by using computer programs such as PhotoShop® – though I choose to restrict my use of such programs to basic adjustments in order to stay as true to the original as possible.

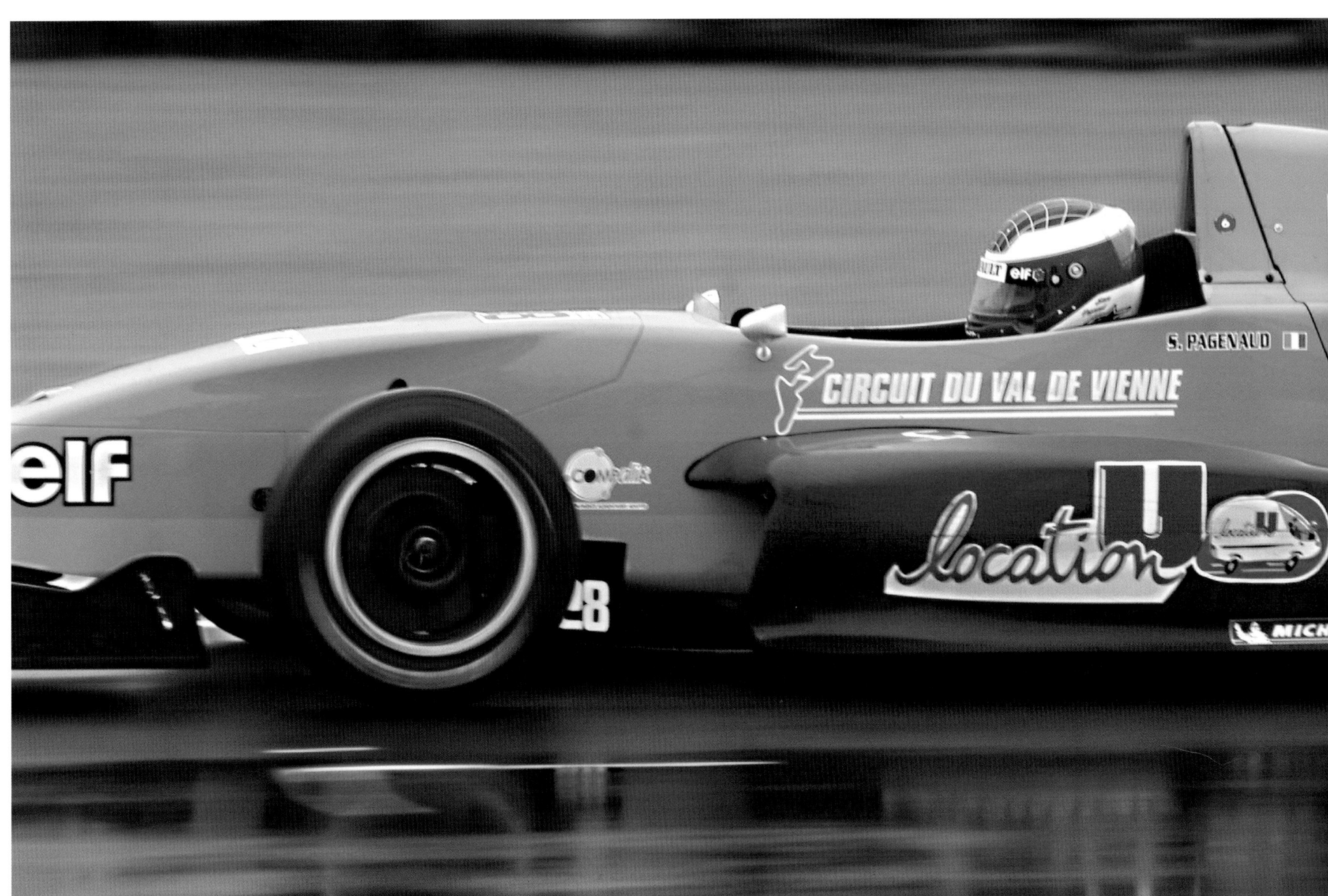

Instant review of images

Lighting conditions and focusing requirements can often be tricky, and the opportunity to review your shots instantly can save a lot of time and heartache. Some might call this cheating, but I see it as a benefit that helps me to learn more quickly: I can correct mistakes on the spot rather than having to wait until my next shoot. I check both the image itself (sometimes zooming in on screen to check the focus) and the histogram, which displays information on the tonal range and is helpful in assessing exposure. Shooting digitally allows me to make the most of every situation by reducing errors and providing a greater number of shots to choose from at the end of the day.

Camera	***Pentax *ist D***
Focal length	***170mm (35mm equivalent: 250mm)***
Exposure	***1/125sec at f/6.7***
ISO setting	***200***

This rider looks as if he is about to catapult off the front of his bike; he is in fact stretching his legs as he begins a practice session. As I was shooting digitally I was able to review the image immediately to see if I had captured the moment. Except in exceptional circumstances, I try to avoid reviewing every image; I prefer to concentrate on the action and just check every now and again to make sure my exposures are OK. Checking too often reduces battery life.

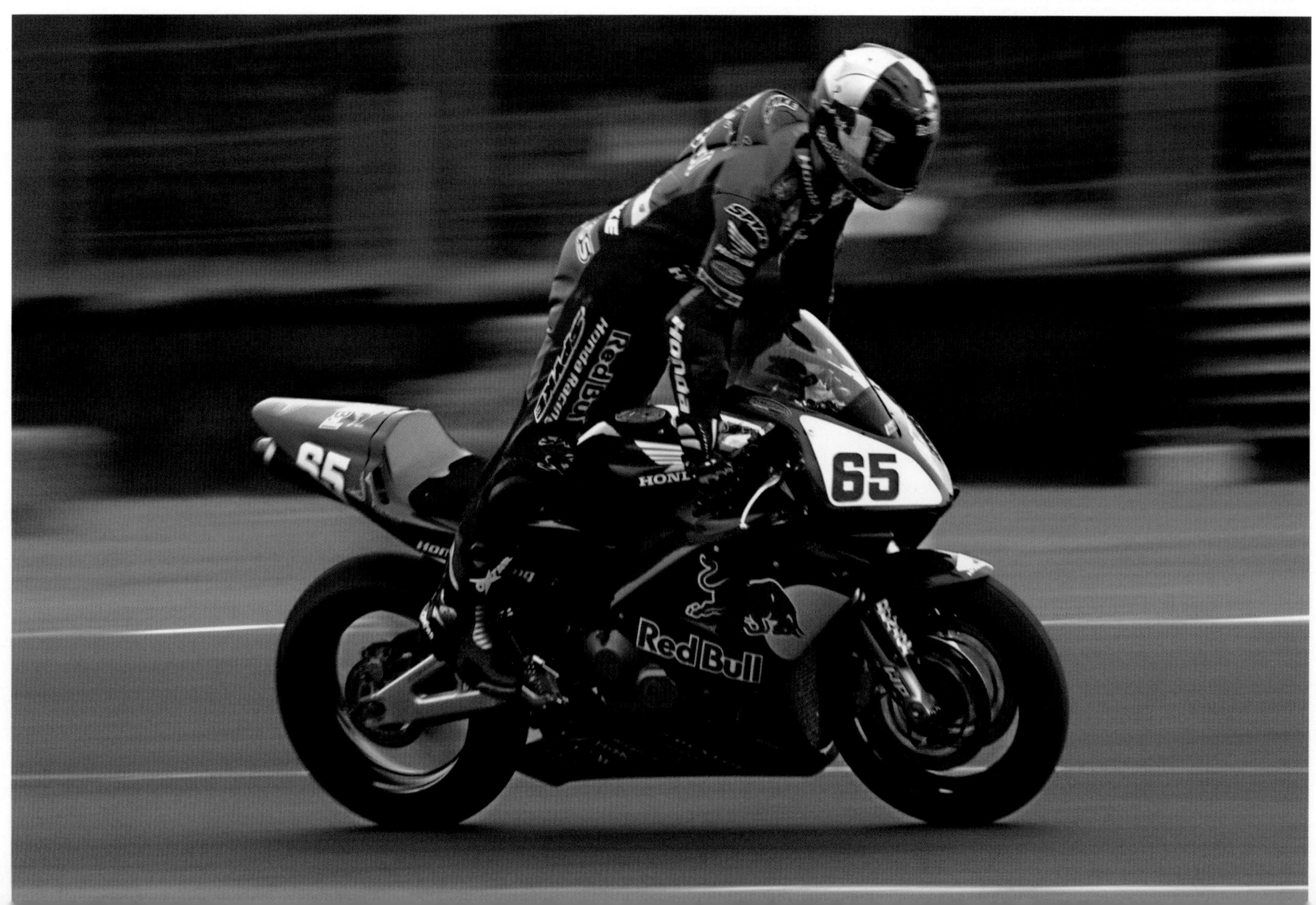

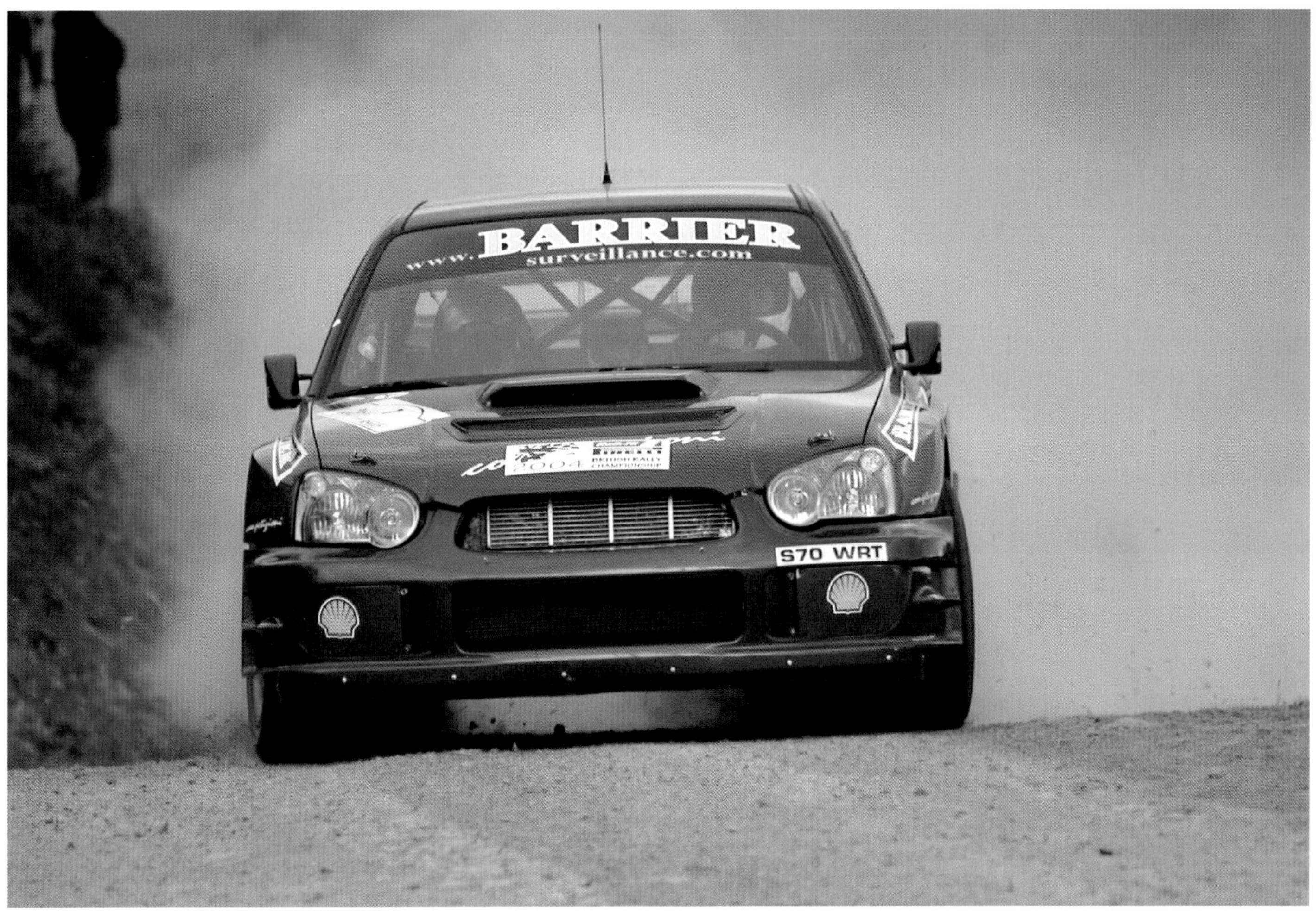

Adjusting to changing light

Another strong benefit of the D-SLR is that you can alter the ISO setting – the digital equivalent of film speed (see pages 36 and 39) – at any time. When shooting in changeable lighting conditions using film, you have to change rolls in order to use a faster or slower emulsion; you also have to carry a range of films to allow for this. With digital you simply alter the setting and keep on shooting. Carrying a few extra films may not seem like an issue, but when you're photographing motor sports you will often find yourself in remote locations, so the amount of kit you carry is important and any weight saving you can make is a bonus.

Camera	***Pentax *ist D***
Focal length	***200mm (35mm equivalent: 300mm)***
Exposure	***1/180sec at f/4.5***
ISO setting	***400***

This rally shot was taken in the evening when light levels were falling. By altering the ISO setting on my digital camera I was just able to use a shutter speed fast enough to capture the image. Had I been using my 35mm camera I would have had to use an ISO 400 film, which I prefer not to do as the amount of grain in faster films affects the quality of the image. Instead, I would probably have chosen a different composition and opted for a panned shot (see Chapter 4), which would have allowed me to use slower shutter speeds in the failing light.

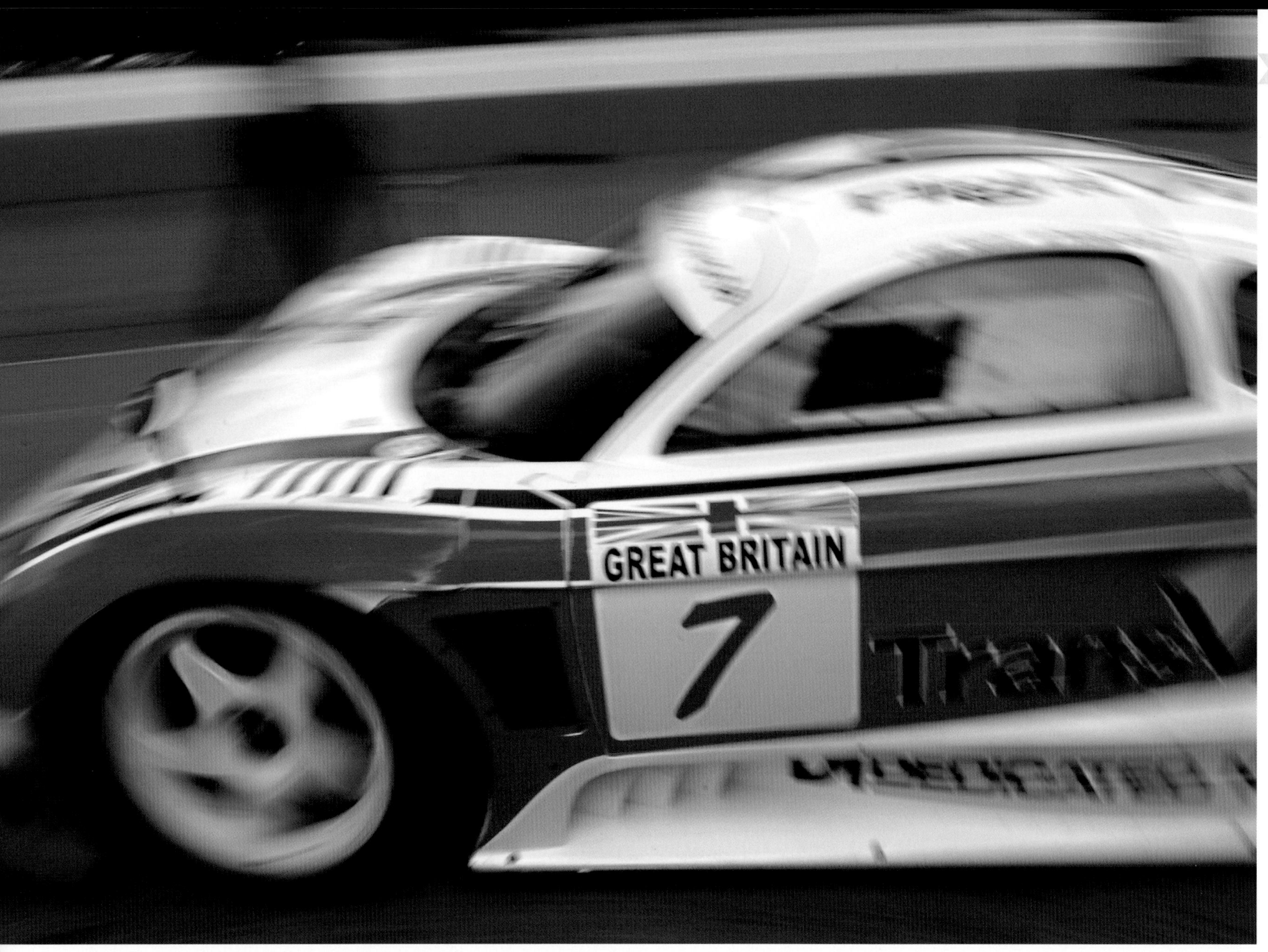

Cost

If you take a lot of images, the lower running costs are a significant advantage of shooting digitally, once you have all the equipment needed – but be careful not to overlook the fact that you will need at least a computer, software and printer in order to process and print your digital images. Printer ink cartridges are very expensive, so if you intend printing all your images you should think carefully before deciding that digital is the medium for you. Prior to 'going digital' I already had a desktop computer,

Camera	***Pentax *ist D***
Focal length	***18mm (35mm equivalent: 28mm)***
Exposure	***1/20sec at f/22***
ISO setting	***200***

Another example of how experimenting with shutter speeds can produce results: by choosing a slow shutter speed and panning with the car I was able to inject movement into this shot.

laptop and good-quality printer, so the set-up costs for me were relatively low. (Actually, I rarely use the printer as I can present my images on my laptop.)

For those like me who shoot over 300 exposures per day, the financial advantages of digital photography over film cannot be ignored. The cost of 35mm films, developing and scanning can mount up, and I estimate that over a year I will save thousands. Even though going digital means that you will initially have to buy a number of memory cards, and will inevitably need more CDs in order to archive your images, the cost benefits of digital for the hard-working photographer are substantial. However, if you are a less regular photographer you may find the arguments not so clear-cut; it is important to consider all these points from the outset.

A related point that is far more important to me is that I can afford to experiment much more – I am now able to try out ideas that I probably wouldn't have done on film because of the expense. In my opinion this is one of the biggest benefits of digital photography. I can experiment with exposure times, apertures and composition, and by reviewing the results instantly I can hone my ideas until I am satisfied. Not only does this improve the breadth and style of my photography, but it is helping me to learn more techniques so that I have a wider range of options for images.

In short, going digital has provided me with a number of benefits, and although I am in many ways a film purist and still use film for other types of photography, I can't really argue against the digital case for motor sport. So, if you're not shooting digital yet, you should certainly be thinking about it, because in a year or so you will be – and you'll wonder why it took you so long to switch.

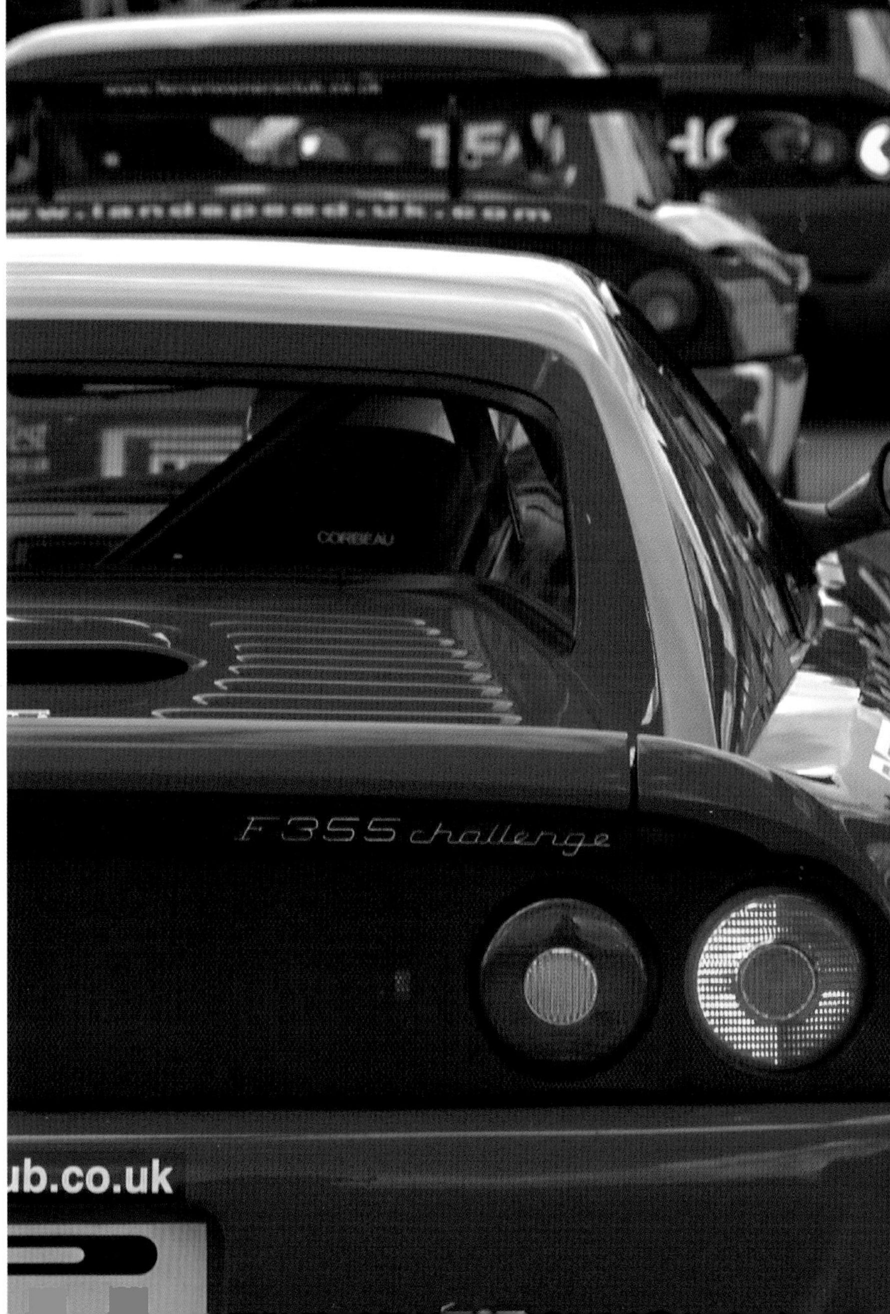

Camera	***Pentax *ist D***
Focal length	***135mm (35mm equivalent: 200mm)***
Exposure	***1/90sec at f/8***
ISO setting	***200***

Whether you shoot on film or use digital equipment, what matters is your ability to understand and use the creative controls provided in order to represent the image as you saw it in your mind's eye. By selecting a moderate aperture for this shot I was able to control the depth of field (see page 99) so that the cars in the top of the image are recognizable and add to the main focal point of the car in the foreground.

Lenses

In my opinion the lenses you have in your camera bag are of greater importance than the camera itself – after all, it is the lens that allows you to reproduce the image you have in your mind. We will talk more about composition and the use of lenses in Chapter 4, but there are a few key requirements.

Camera	**Pentax *ist D**
Focal length	**18mm (35mm equivalent: 28mm)**
Exposure	**1/750sec at f/5.6**
ISO setting	**200**

Many motor sport subjects require telephoto lenses to allow you to fill the frame with your subject; however, wideangle lenses are just as necessary. For this shot I chose to use a moderately wide 18mm lens (equivalent to 28mm on a 35mm camera) from very close to the wheel rather than a longer lens from further away, as the perspective of the wideangle lens at close quarters emphasizes the curve of the wheel.

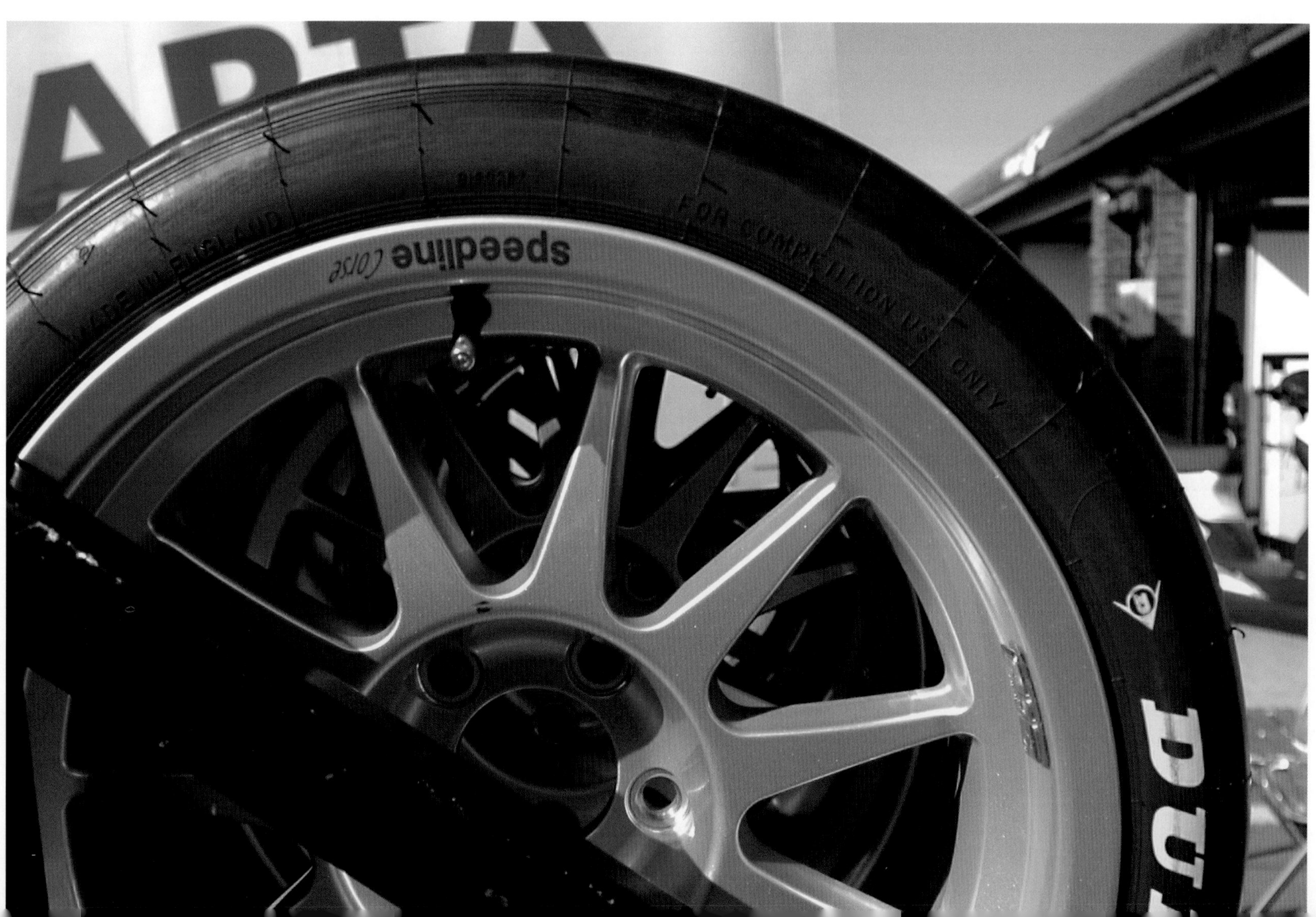

Focal lengths

Until recently most 35mm SLRs were supplied with a 'standard' 50mm lens; this focal length is called 'standard' because the perspective of thc image it produces is the nearest to that seen by the human eye. Lenses of shorter focal length, known as wideangle lenses, appear to lengthen the perspective and provide a wider angle of view, so that objects that are close to the photographer seem smaller and further away, and the distances between nearer and further objects in the frame are exaggerated. Longer focal lengths have the opposite effect: the longer the lens, the more compressed the perspective and the narrower the field of view. Objects appear magnified and closer than they really are, as through a telescope. These longer focal-length lenses are referred to as telephoto lenses, and generally range from 70mm up to 400mm and beyond.

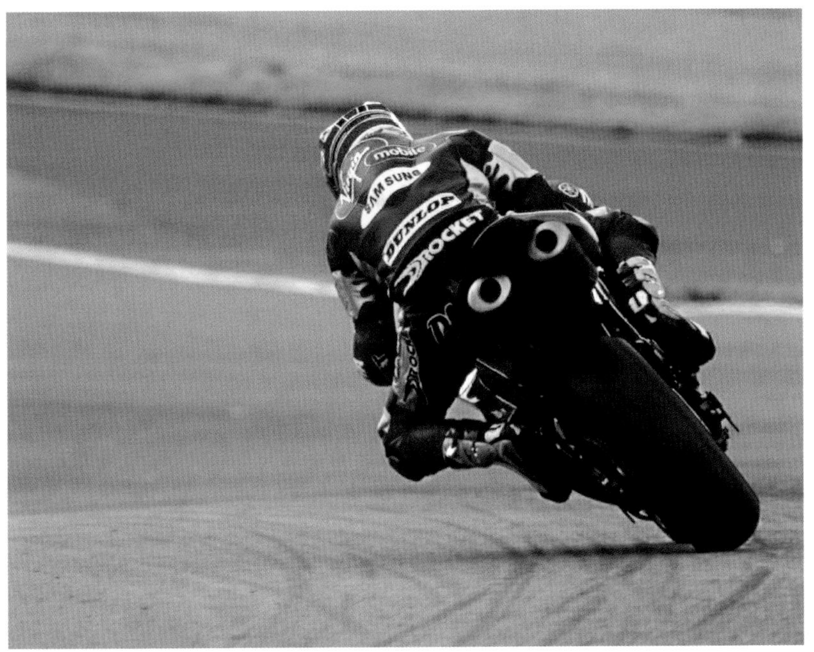

Camera	*Pentax *ist D*
Focal length	*300mm (35mm equivalent: 450mm)*
Exposure	*1/500sec at f/5.6*
ISO setting	*200*

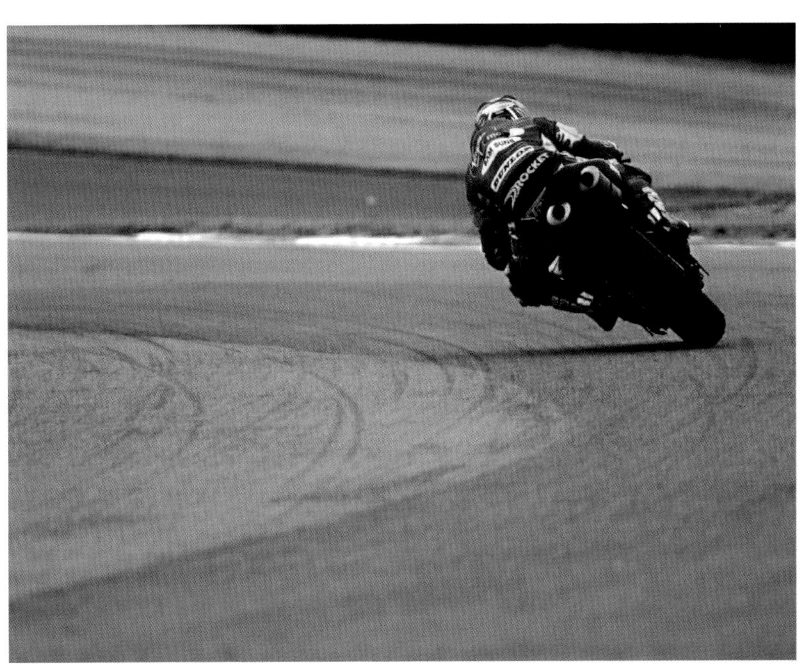

Camera	*Pentax *ist D*
Focal length	*200mm (35mm equivalent: 300mm)*
Exposure	*1/1000sec at f/4*
ISO setting	*200*

These two shots were taken from the same position with different lenses. Even though the shot where the rider appears larger was taken from a slightly closer viewpoint, it is easy to see the difference that focal length has on the resultant image. I actually prefer the shot where the rider is more distant: the composition conveys the idea that, even though the circuit is full of spectators and the rider has a team of people supporting him, there is a certain degree of solitude once a competitor gets onto the track.

Prime and zoom lenses

Prime lenses have a fixed focal length (such as 28, 50, 135 or 200mm), whereas zoom lenses are able to move between focal lengths (typical ranges include 28–80, 70–210 and 100–300mm). A camera lens is made up of a series of concave and convex pieces of glass (called lens 'elements') arranged in groups within the casing of the lens. Prime lenses generally contain fewer elements, which means they are able to let in more light; they can have a wider maximum aperture or f-stop (see page 28), and are therefore said to be 'faster' than zoom lenses. Zoom lenses, though generally a little 'slower' than primes, offer the ability to alter the focal length without changing lenses. It is therefore possible to have three zoom lenses which cover focal lengths all the way from 28mm wideangle up to 400mm telephoto – whereas to get anywhere near to covering this range with prime lenses you would need at least seven lenses, which is a considerable weight to carry!

Camera	***Pentax *ist D***
Focal length	***210mm (35mm equivalent: 315mm)***
Exposure	***1/750sec at f/4.5***
ISO setting	***200***

The characteristics of telephoto lenses allow the photographer to exploit depth of field to great effect. Shooting from the rear of the car in the pit lane, I deliberately included part of the bodywork to fill in the area below the wing mirror. A wide aperture provides very shallow depth of field, highlighting the driver in the mirror.

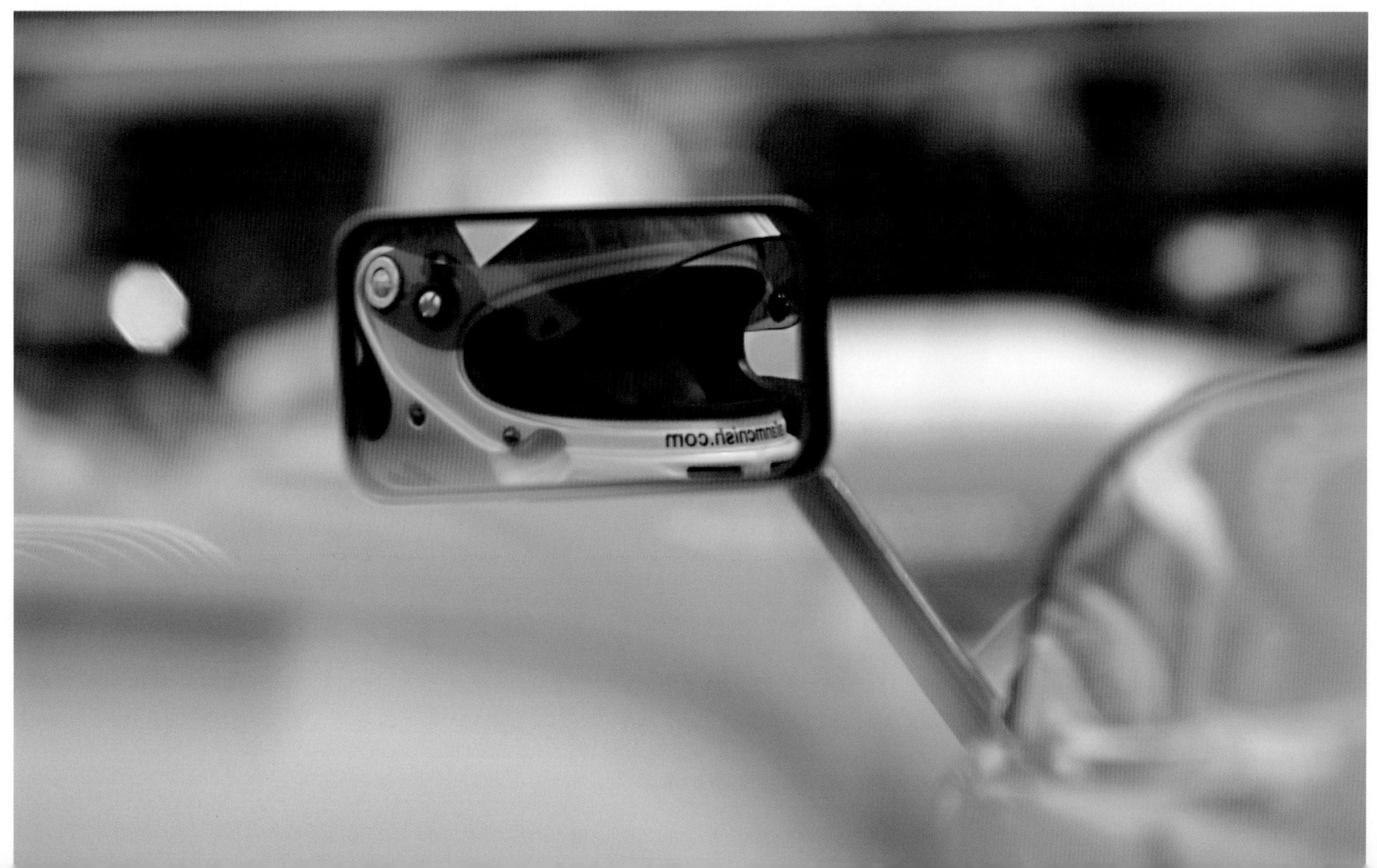

Primes vs. zooms

Though I often use zoom lenses because of their flexibility, I prefer to use prime lenses – not for any technical or even practical reasons (although prime lenses often produce crisper images due to their simpler construction), but simply because I like the immediacy of prime lenses and the way in which they make me work. Using a prime lens makes me 'look' for a picture more – I find that when choosing a place to take photographs my mind's eye works in terms of prime-lens focal lengths, and I feel this adds to the composition of my images. This is, of course, totally subjective – zoom lenses offer greater flexibility and reduced weight in my backpack, but using primes works for me.

Camera	*Pentax *ist D*
Focal length	*135mm (35mm equivalent: 200mm)*
Exposure	*1/750sec at f/4*
ISO setting	*200*

Using telephoto lenses to get good detail shots is an important part of motor sport photography, whether you choose to use fixed focal-length or zoom lenses.

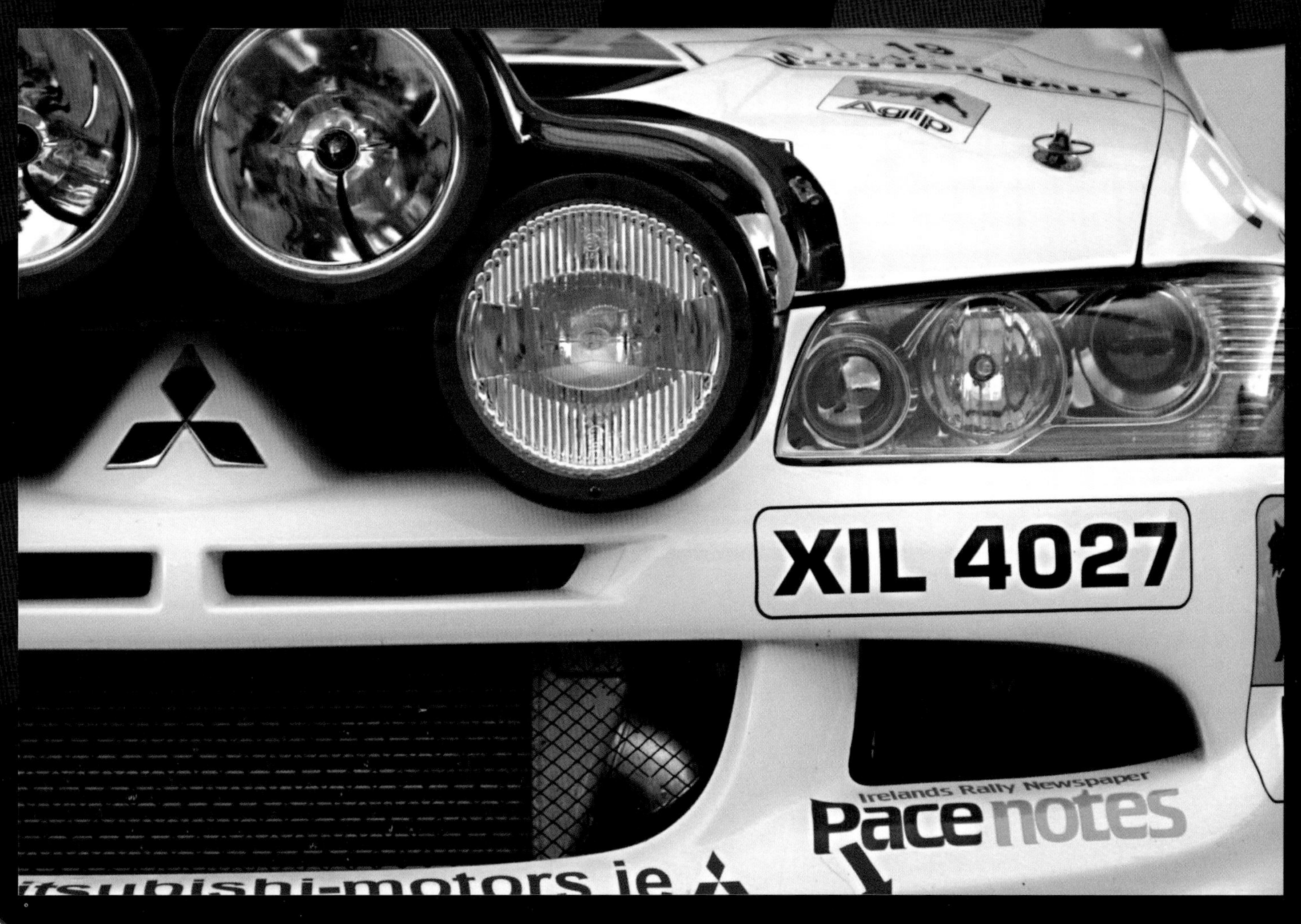

What do you need?

You don't need a bagful of lenses, and you may well have most of what you need already. Those listed in the panel below cover most of my needs; although I prefer to use prime lenses rather than zooms, it is easier to carry four lenses than the five or six I would need if I didn't use a zoom. I also take a bag of lenses that I leave in my car 'just in case', but I can't remember ever having to return and get one.

A basic set of lenses

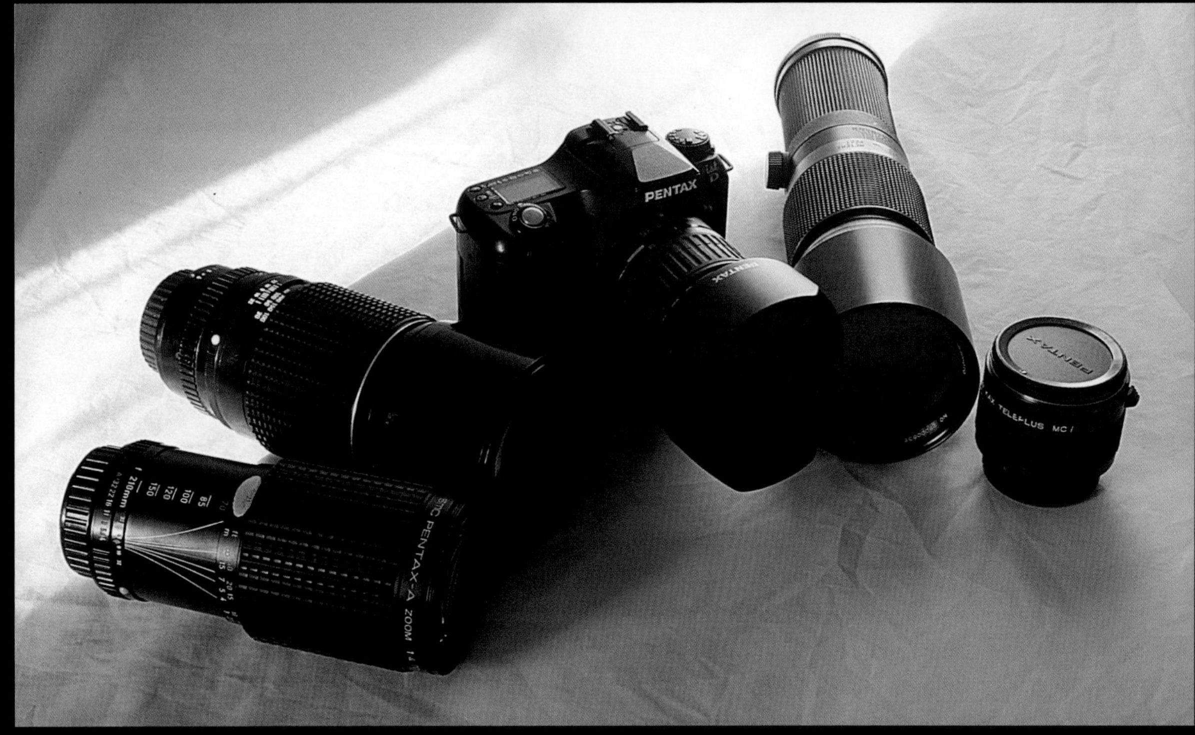

The basic kit that I take with me to all race meetings: digital body, two prime and two zoom lenses, and teleconverter.

For every event I attend, I take with me:

- **a 70–210mm zoom for picking out detail or for medium-range subjects**
- **a 28–50mm zoom for wideangle scenes and for occasions when I can get very close to the subject**
- **300 and 400mm telephoto lenses for very tight detail shots or where subjects are far away.**

I also carry a 1.5x teleconverter, which is a supplementary unit that can be fitted between camera body and lens in order to multiply the focal length by 1.5, thus giving an overall focal length of 450mm when used with a 300mm lens, for example. There are drawbacks to using teleconverters, and they may not be compatible with all lenses; consult the manufacturer's literature if in doubt. By adding more elements to your lens they

As with cameras, there is a vast range of lenses available. In addition to those made by the camera manufacturers themselves, a number of independent firms produce lenses which are compatible with the leading makes of camera. I would always recommend you go for quality – the old adage 'You get what you pay for' is particularly relevant when it comes to optics. A poor-quality lens will always produce poor-quality results, no matter how expensive the camera it is attached to.

reduce its effective speed (that is, its maximum aperture). They work better with prime lenses – I would avoid using them with zooms if possible – and even then they tend to perform better with the longer focal lengths. They can make focusing problematic, especially with some autofocus lenses. I avoid using mine unnecessarily, but it is a useful tool to keep in your bag.

Remember that the effective focal length of a lens designed for 35mm cameras will also be increased when it is used on a digital camera whose sensor is smaller than a 35mm frame (see panel on page 15).

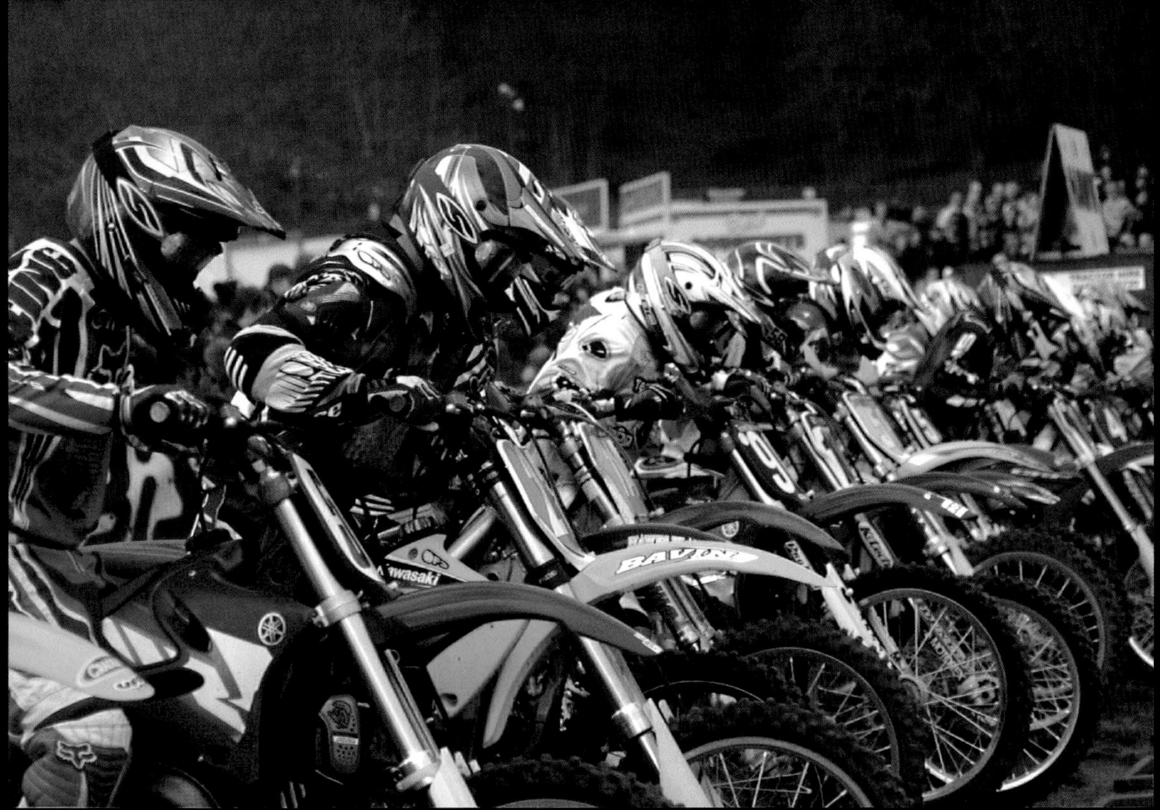

Camera	*Pentax *ist D*
Focal length	*90mm (35mm equivalent: 135mm)*
Exposure	*1/350sec at f/5.6*
ISO setting	*200*

Telephoto lenses flatten perspective, making the distance between foreground and background appear shallower, while wideangle lenses lengthen perspective and make distances seem greater. Using a short telephoto lens for this shot allowed me to include all the riders, while the flattened perspective and a fairly large aperture help to pick out the rider second from left as the main focal point of the image.

Lens speed

The most important considerations when buying a lens for motor sport photography are the aperture range and the optical quality. Buy a lens with as big a maximum aperture setting as you can afford; these are often termed 'fast' lenses, because the bigger the maximum aperture, the more light the lens can let in and the faster the shutter speeds you can use. This may not seem so relevant on a summer's day, when there is plenty of light and you can choose your aperture and shutter speed with ease. However, imagine how frustrating it would be to have driven a couple of hundred miles to a rally in the gloom of winter and then walked two or three miles with all your gear to get to the stage, only to find that the lens of your choice does not allow enough light in to provide you with a fast enough exposure. So what is the best solution?

Understanding aperture

The aperture is an opening in the lens whose diameter can be altered to increase or decrease the amount of light that can pass through to the film or digital sensor. The size of this hole is measured in f-stops, a large number such as f/22 representing a small aperture while a small number such as f/1.4 represents a large aperture. A smaller aperture reduces the amount of light that can pass through it and therefore requires the shutter to be open longer in order to compensate for the smaller opening. Conversely, a larger aperture allows more light to pass through the lens and can therefore be used in conjunction with a faster shutter speed.

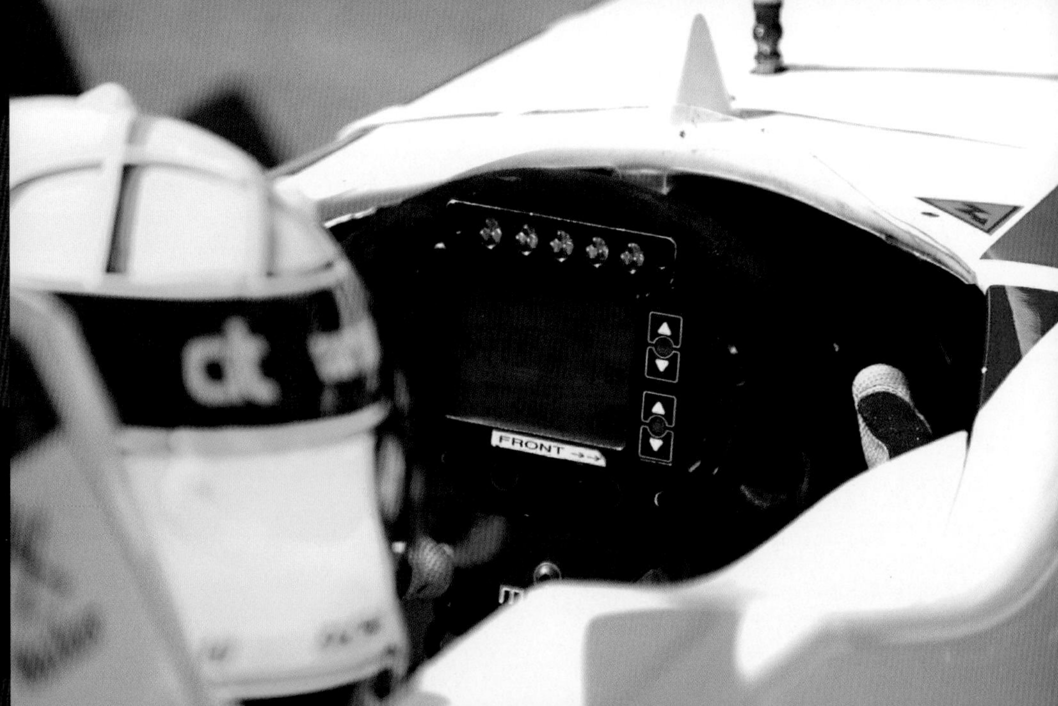

Camera	***Pentax *ist D***
Focal length	***200mm (35mm equivalent: 300mm)***
Exposure	***1/1000sec at f/4***
ISO setting	***200***

This shot demonstrates the very narrow depth of field available when a wide aperture is used with a long telephoto lens; this concentrates the eye on the steering wheel as this driver waits to go out on track.

In an ideal world all your lenses would have maximum apertures of f/2.8 or wider. You will find this fairly affordable at the smaller focal lengths (28–80mm), but once you get above 200mm the costs begin to rise – a 300mm f/2.8 lens will cost more than a top-end camera body. Unless you are lucky enough to have this kind of money to spend, the alternative is to buy a lens with a smaller maximum aperture, say f/4. This will only let in half the light provided by an f/2.8 lens (in other words, it is one stop slower), so it is a compromise – but these lenses are considerably more affordable and are still capable of producing good-quality results. Try to avoid buying lenses with smaller maximum apertures than f/4 – it can prove to be a false economy, and it becomes frustrating when you can't achieve the shutter speeds you want. One photographer I spoke to at a motor racing venue disagreed with this: he uses a 300mm lens with a maximum aperture of f/5.6, and simply uses faster film to compensate. It is true that this will give you the exposures you require, but the faster the film you use, the poorer the quality of the image (see page 36), so I'm sticking to my guns.

Camera	***Pentax *ist D***
Focal length	***200mm (35mm equivalent: 300mm)***
Exposure	***1/125sec at f/9.5***
ISO setting	***200***

Long telephoto lenses can be an expensive purchase, but they are vital if you want to fill the frame with your subject. If you are on a tight budget it is preferable to spend your money on good-quality lenses and buy a lower-specification camera.

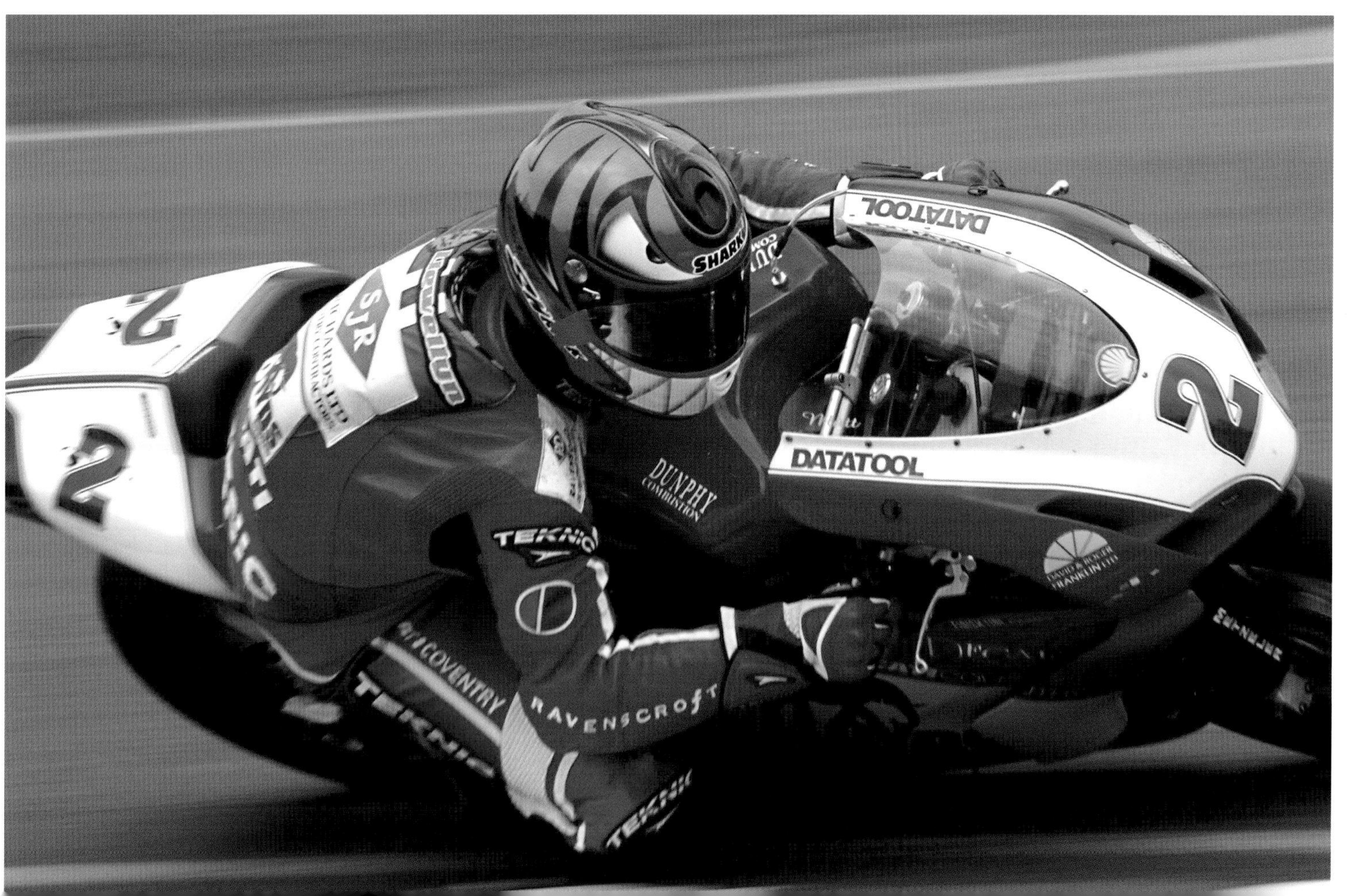

Camera	Pentax *ist D
Focal length	300mm (35mm equivalent: 450mm)
Exposure	1/2000sec at f/4
ISO setting	200

Even when using long telephoto lenses, you don't always have to fill the frame with your subject. Using the curving 'S' of the track to lead the eye through this image, and a wide enough aperture to throw both foreground and background out of focus, I was able to place the motorcyclist in the perfect position.

Cutting the cost

You can make good savings on lenses if you are prepared to buy second-hand, as long as you buy from a reputable dealer. Some dealers give a warranty of up to 12 months, so you should be fairly safe. I have often bought lenses this way, and I would rather have a good-quality used lens with good optics and aperture range than a new one of similar price that may be one or two stops slower. There must be no marks or scratches on the glass, and the electrical contacts must be in good order; the condition of the lens barrel is less important. Buying second-hand means that you aren't utilizing the latest autofocus and optical technologies; older lenses may be heavier, and may lack some of the newer features such as the various types of anti-vibration technology. This can be a drawback; but if you are working to a budget, buying used lenses can be a good way of building a system that provides you with the tools you need.

Another option, for a lens that is only needed occasionally, is to hire one. Some professional photographic retailers hire out lenses on a daily or weekly basis. You will need to leave a deposit, but you can rent a 300mm f/2.8 lens for quite a reasonable sum. This is not a bad way of getting hold of the lens you want without having to shell out a large amount of money.

Protecting your lenses

As a final point, whatever you do, make sure you fit a protective filter to all your lenses when you're attending events that involve flying mud and stones. A skylight or 1A filter will protect the lens's front element without losing too much light; both of these will also help to cut out unwanted ultraviolet light. It's a lot cheaper to replace a filter broken by a stone thrown up by a passing rally car than to replace a lens which didn't have one.

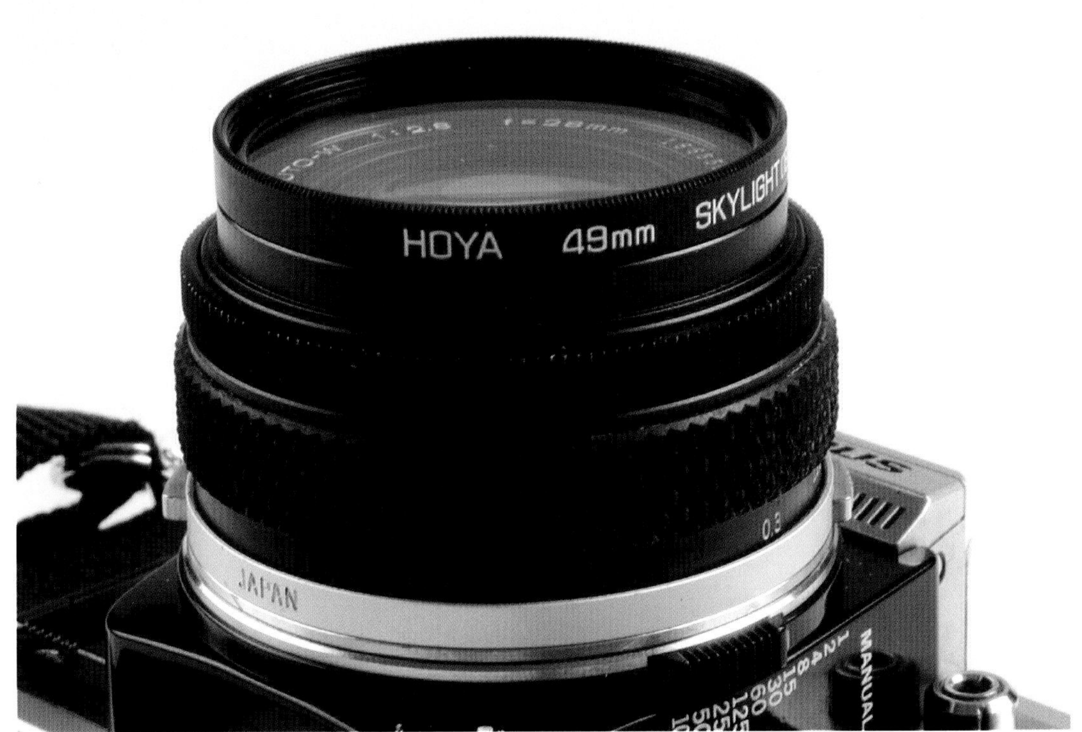

An inexpensive skylight or similar filter attached to the front of your valuable lens will protect it from airborne debris (photo: GMC/Anthony Bailey).

Camera accessories

Once you've got your camera and lenses, the only other pieces of equipment you'll really need are a flash unit, and possibly a motor drive if you are using film. You have the choice of an automatic flash, whose output is controlled by a sensor in the flash unit, or one that is 'dedicated' to your camera and controlled by sensors in the camera itself – many of these units have auto and manual modes as well. Both varieties have their pros and cons, which are discussed on page 109. Whatever

Camera	Pentax *ist D
Focal length	135mm (35mm equivalent: 200mm)
Exposure	1/125sec at f/8
ISO setting	200

Even for outdoor work, a good flash gun is an essential part of your camera kit. Without a burst of fill-in flash (see page 108) this driver's eyes would be in the shadow of his helmet and the shot would not be as effective.

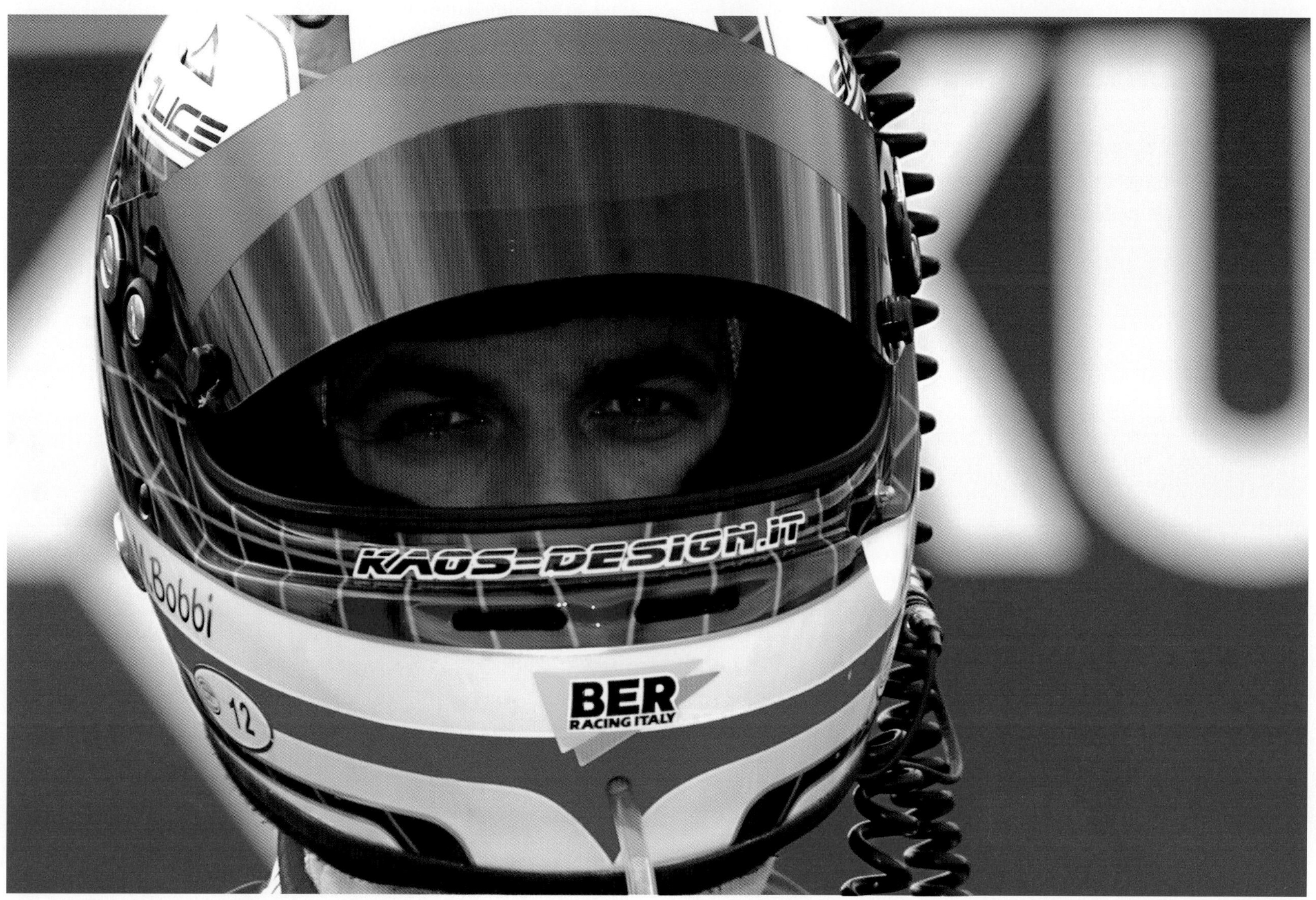

flash you choose, make sure it has a tilting head so that you can adjust the angle of the flash's burst. Flash is not only for low light: it can be used in bright conditions to add highlights to your subject, to fill in unwanted shadows or to light a subject which is cast into shadow by the sun.

Depending on your choice of camera, you may need to purchase a motor drive in order to shoot action sequences; the minimum speed you will need is 2.5 frames per second. Most modern 35mm cameras have a built-in winder; you may find this fast enough, but often you can buy separate add-on units to boost the speed.

With digital cameras, of course, film winding is not an issue, but I would advise buying an additional battery pack which is attached to the camera in a similar way to a motor drive; this provides much-needed back-up power. It also improves the handling of the camera, allowing for much easier shooting when holding it in the upright or 'portrait' position – especially if the camera itself does not have a secondary shutter release for upright use.

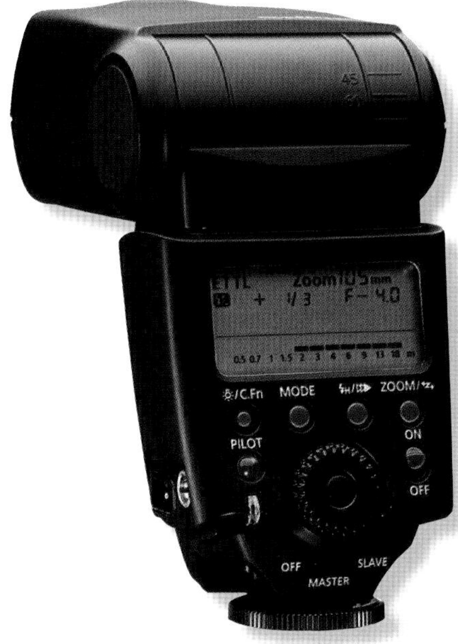

The Canon Speedlite 580 EX, a flashgun suitable for both conventional and digital cameras (by courtesy of Canon UK Ltd).

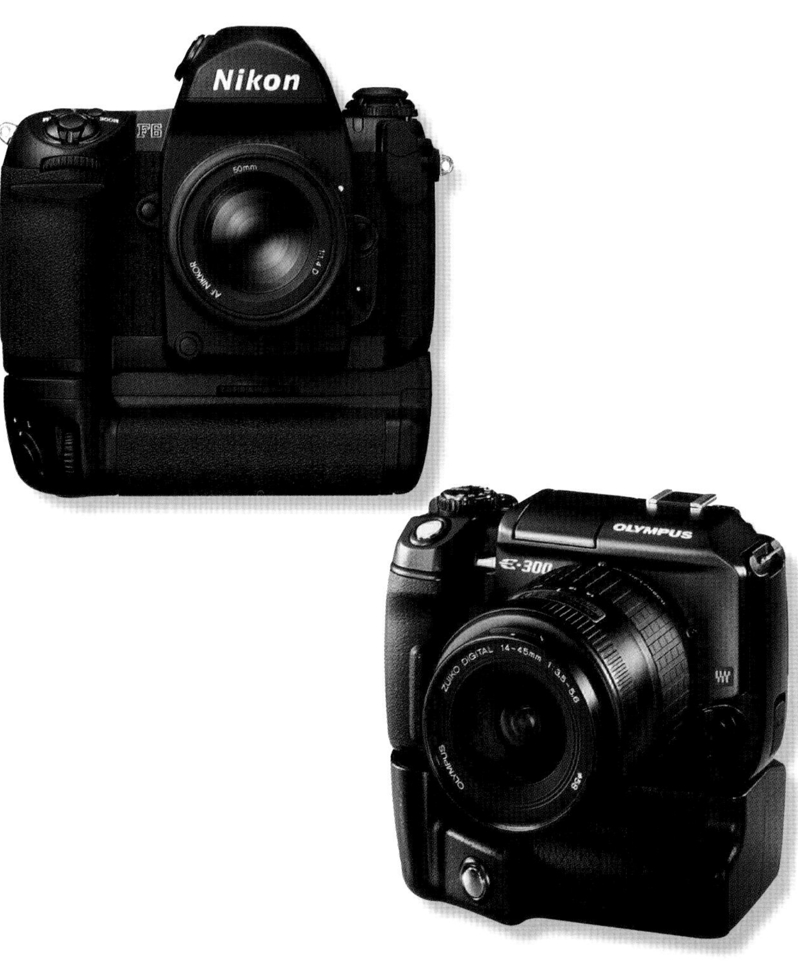

The Nikon F6 35mm SLR fitted with its optional motor drive (by courtesy of Nikon UK Ltd).

The Olympus E-300 digital SLR with its auxiliary battery pack (by courtesy of Olympus UK Ltd).

Film

Although I shoot almost exclusively on digital equipment (only using film as a back-up or when clients request it), there are still many photographers who shoot on film. Different films can be used to produce differing results; understanding the differences between film types will help you to achieve the results you want.

Slide vs. print film

The first choice you need to make is between print film, which produces negatives for printing, and slide film (also known as transparency or reversal film), which produces positive transparencies that can be either scanned, projected or reproduced on paper in various ways. I use slide film because:

- **it gives better colour saturation and generally more predictable colours than print film**
- **it's much easier to store transparencies**
- **very few publishers or picture libraries are willing to accept negatives or prints.**

Slide films generally have a narrower exposure latitude than print film, meaning that with slide film exposure is more critical. However, the improved colour saturation allows colours to be more vibrant than with negative film. Slide film produces a positive result that can be viewed on an illuminated panel (a lightbox), whereas print film gives a negative image which can only be appraised properly when printed. A positive image provides a good reference point as to the true colours when it comes to printing, and for this reason is preferred by publishers.

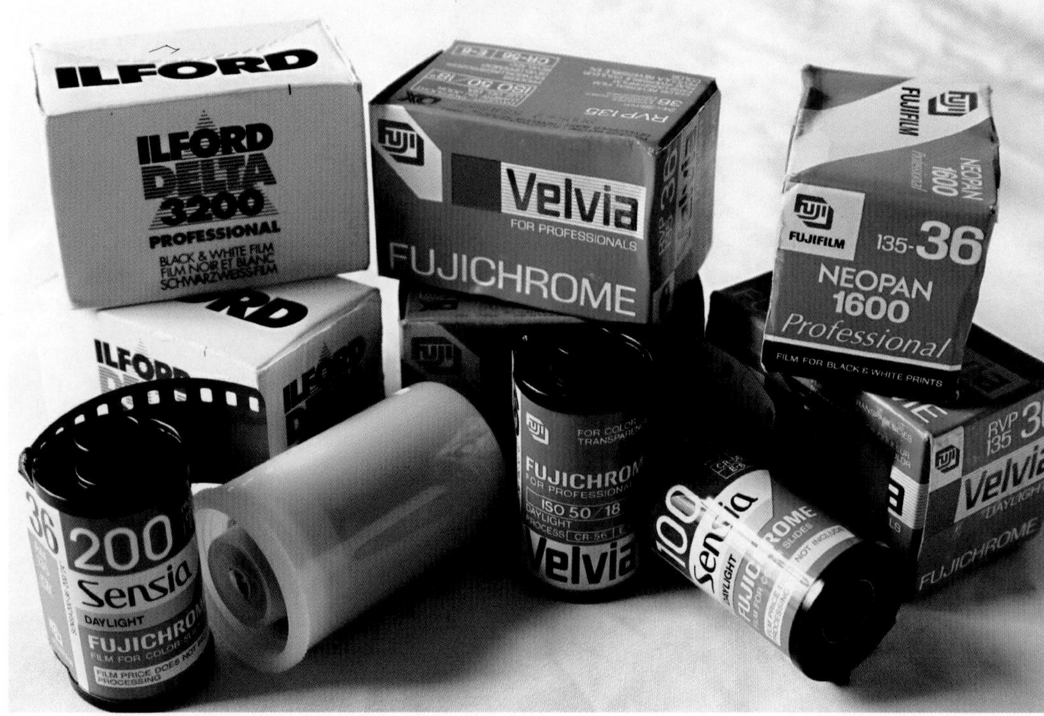

A selection of colour transparency and black and white print films. Despite the digital revolution, a wide range of 35mm films is still available.

Camera	Pentax Super A
Focal length	300mm
Exposure	1/500sec at f/8
Film	Fuji Velvia 50

Though slide film generally has less exposure latitude than print film – necessitating more accurate exposures – it makes up for this by providing better colour saturation.

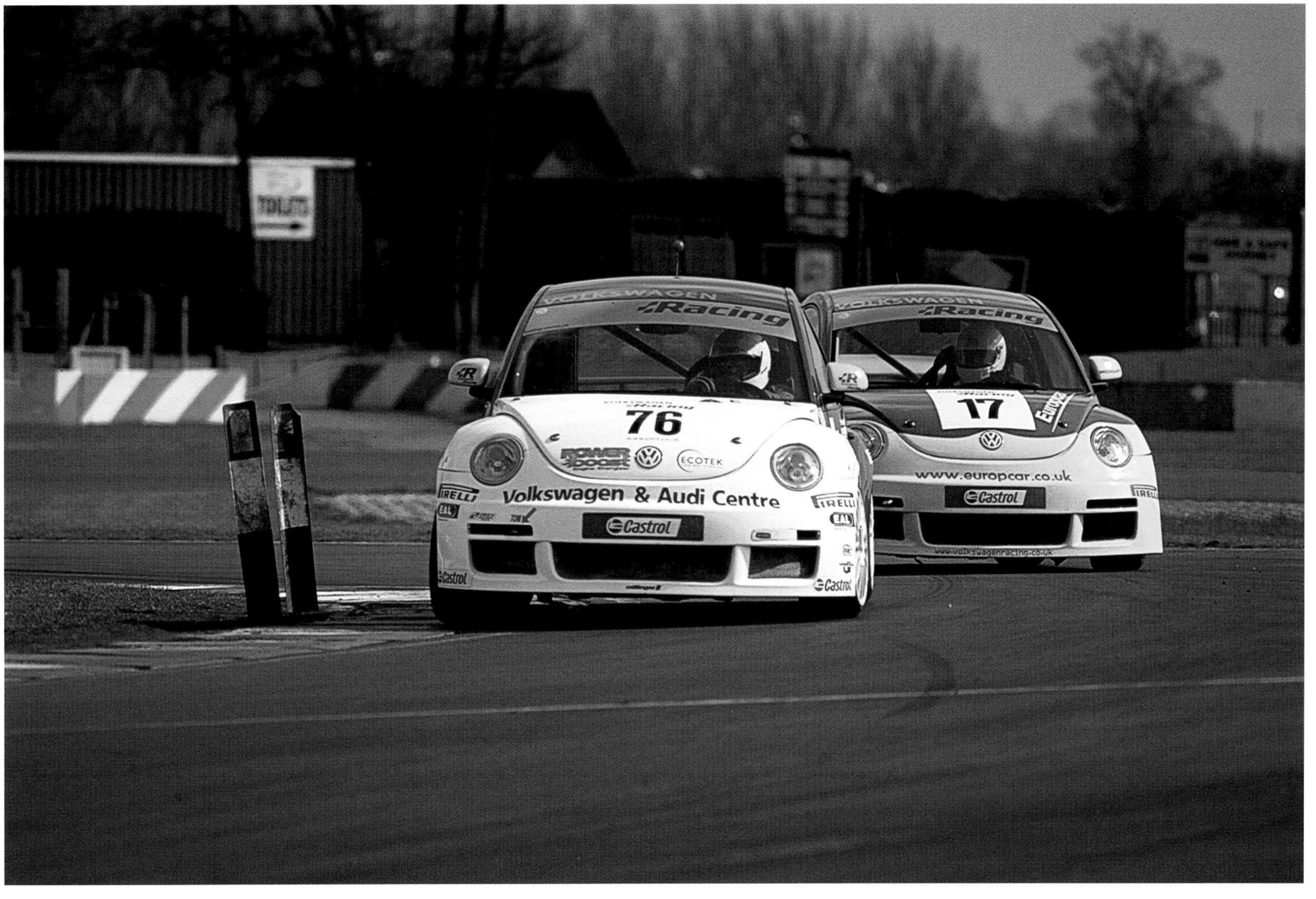

Film speed

The 'speed' of a film – a measure of its sensitivity to light – is a crucial factor when deciding which type to use. Film speeds are identified by an ISO (International Standards Organization) rating; ISO 12 is a very slow speed by present-day standards, while ISO 3200 is very fast. The slower the film, the more exposure it requires, but the less grain it will show. Grain is a common characteristic of faster films, and appears as dots or speckles in the final image; these are magnified when an image is enlarged, and are usually avoided in published work.

Just because the action is fast, it doesn't follow that the film should be as well. When shooting film, I use ISO 50 colour transparency almost exclusively. The reason for this is the same as in any other area of photography: the slower the film, the less grain it produces and the better the image quality – especially when you start enlarging. Also, the colour saturation of moderately slow slide films gives particularly vivid results.

In low light conditions, ISO 50 film may not be fast enough to achieve the shutter speeds or apertures you need to capture fast-moving subjects, and in this case you have four choices:

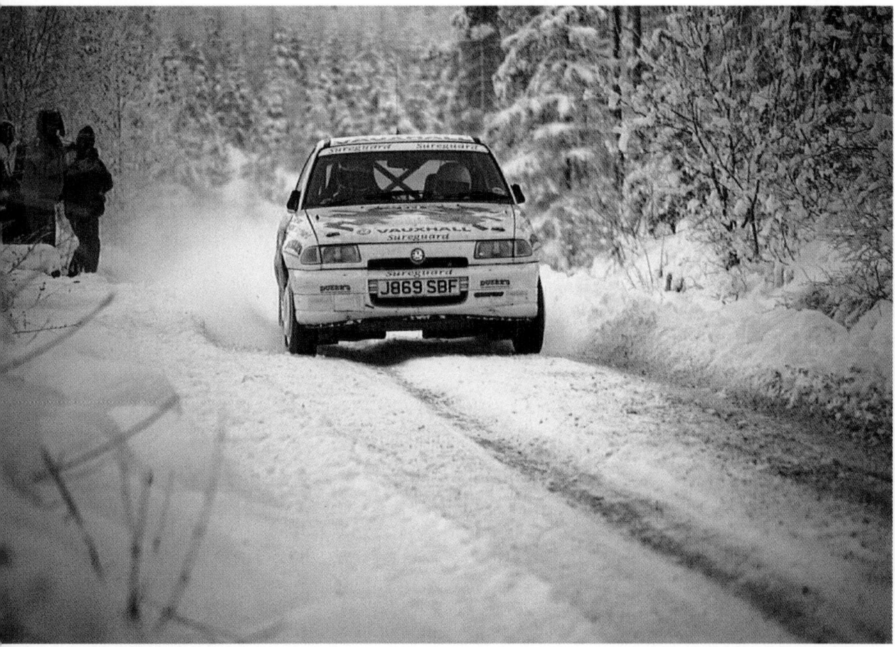

- **You can use slower shutter speeds than usual, so as to blur the subject and highlight its movement. This can give a more creative image, but is not always appropriate.**
- **You can use a faster film that will allow you to use faster shutter speeds. I would generally only use ISO 100 or very occasionally 200, as the increase in grain for films of this speed is fairly negligible. I never use ISO 400 films, as I feel they are too grainy when compared to ISO 50 or 100, yet not enough to make the graininess a 'feature' of the image – in short, they are too much of a compromise. With a very fast, grainy film of perhaps ISO 800 or even 1600 you could compose images to make a feature of the grain; I have rarely done this, as I feel the genre does not really lend itself to heavily grained 'arty' shots, but you should give it a try some time, if only for experiment's sake.**
- **You could 'push' the film. This is done by increasing the film's ISO rating to give the shutter speeds you require; doubling the ISO value, e.g. from 100 to 200, counts as a 'one-stop' push. You will then have to instruct a professional processing lab to 'push-process' the film to compensate for this. You can only push a whole film – if you decide to push a film when it is already half-used, the first half of your film will be overdeveloped. Some films lend themselves to pushing better than others; there may be increased grain and unwelcome colour casts.**

Camera	***Praktica MTL***
Focal length	***200mm***
Exposure	***1/250sec at f/5.6***
Film	***ISO 800***

This image is one of my very earliest, and although I can't remember what brand of film I used, you can easily see the grain in the original slide; in a moderate-sized print it would be very evident. Light levels were low, and I made the wrong decision by using a fast film to combat this, rather than electing to change the type of shot and stick with a slower, less grainy film.

- **A final option is to use flash (see pages 107–13); however, you will often find yourself too far away from your subject to make this feasible.**

When flash is not practical and you can't get the shutter speeds needed by changing to a faster-ISO film, your only real option is to change your style of shooting and utilize slower shutter speeds. This is discussed on pages 86–97.

Camera	***Pentax K1000***
Focal length	***210mm***
Exposure	***1/125sec at f/11***
Film	***Fuji Velvia 50***

Using films with slow ISO ratings does reduce the shutter speeds available to you, but the benefits of increased colour saturation and fine grain more than make up for this. If you are faced with a low-light situation, simply changing to a faster film is not the best solution, as it will degrade your pictures by increasing the grain. It is far better to change to a type of shot where slower shutter speeds are acceptable (such as a panning shot) than to compromise the quality of your images by using fast films.

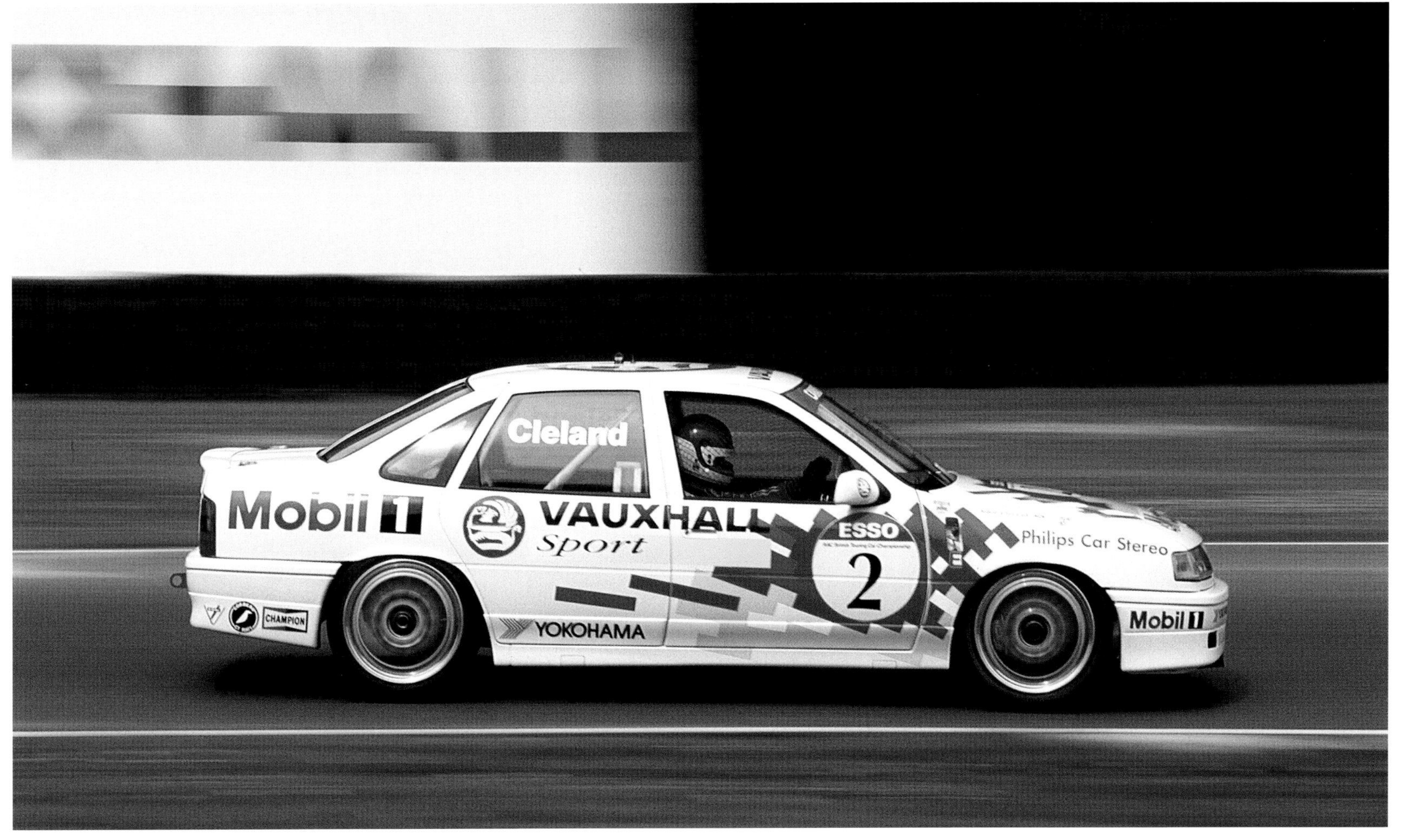

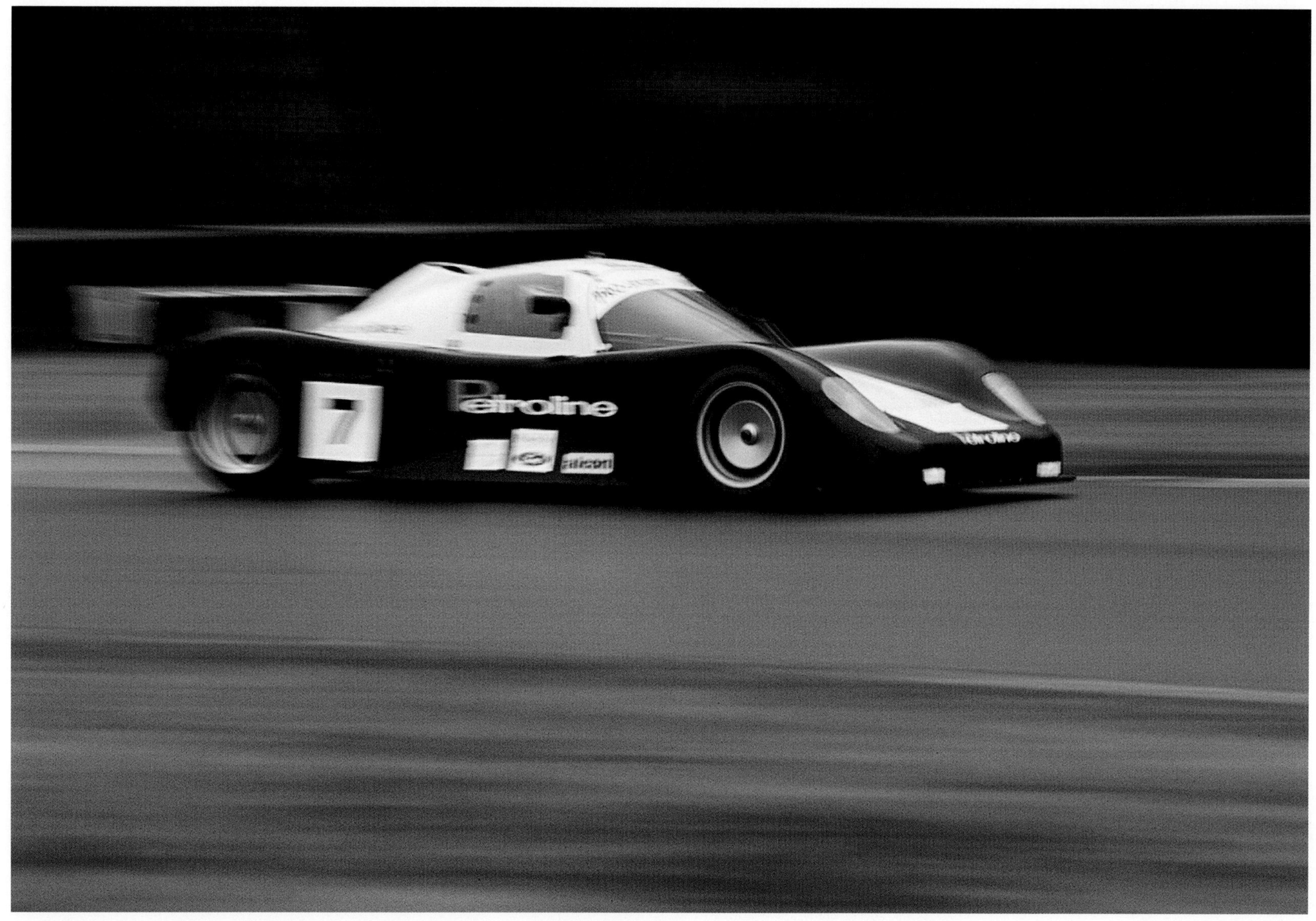

Camera	Pentax Program A
Focal length	135mm
Exposure	1/90sec at f/4
Film	Fuji Velvia 50

This shot was taken on a drizzly, overcast day. Rather than opt for a faster film, I decided to use a slow shutter speed and inject some motion into the image. Using slow film will force you to think creatively about how you can capture good images in poorly lit environments.

Digital image capture

ISO values and noise

Digital SLRs provide a range of ISO speed settings which are equivalent to the film speeds used in conventional cameras. Since there is no film and therefore no grain to contend with, you might think you can simply change to a faster ISO setting and shoot away. However, digital images do suffer from a similar degradation effect, which is called noise. While increasing the ISO setting will allow you to use faster shutter speeds, it will also increase the amount of noise the image will contain.

Whereas the grain of a fast film can be used to creative effect, noise is nowhere near as attractive and should be avoided. Having said this, the current range of 6Mp-plus D-SLRs cope very well with noise and you should experience very little drop-off in image quality between ISO settings of 100 and 400 – so in low-light situations digital cameras provide you with much more flexibility than film. However, noise can increase dramatically above ISO 400. Noise-reduction software, applied in post-capture manipulation, can help with noise resulting from long exposures, but not with that caused by high ISO settings.

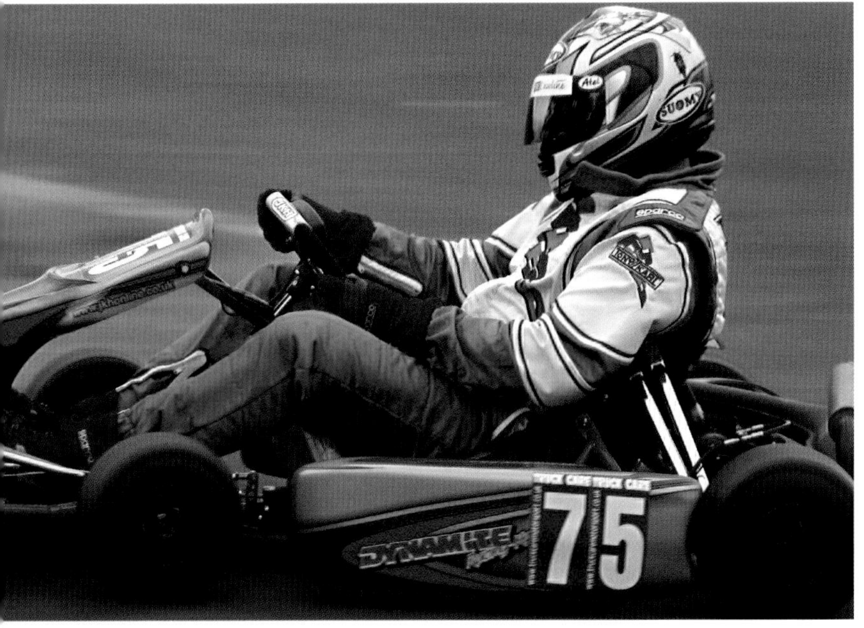

Memory cards

Of the various storage media available for digital cameras, the most popular for D-SLRs is the CF or CompactFlash® card. These are available with varying storage capacity, from 64Mb to over 100 times this amount. There are other types of storage media available, such as the IBM Microdrive®. Personally, I would recommend that you buy a few medium-capacity cards – either 256 or 512Mb – rather than one large-capacity card. The main reason is that cards can get damaged and fail once in a while, and it is better to lose 256Mb of images than over 1.0Gb. That said, it is more convenient shooting on a larger card, as this reduces the number of times you need to change cards in locations where dust or rain might get into the camera. The size of the card you choose will also depend on the size of the files your camera produces: if you're shooting in RAW mode or have a camera that generates large file sizes, you will need a large-capacity card in order to store a reasonable number of images. Really the choice is yours – but whatever card size you opt for, you should get used to downloading your images to a workstation or other storage device on a regular basis.

Another absolute must is to store your cards safely in a protective pouch or wallet: this keeps them free from dust, and preserves them when you inadvertently place one in a back pocket and later sit down!

Camera	***Pentax *ist D***
Focal length	***180mm (35mm equivalent: 270mm)***
Exposure	***1/125sec at f/8***
ISO setting	***200***

Digital cameras allow the user to select from a range of file-capture sizes, notably small, medium or large JPEGs, and RAW files (specific to each make of camera), which are much larger. I generally shoot large JPEG files, which can safely be printed up to A3 size (520 x 297mm).

Downloading your images

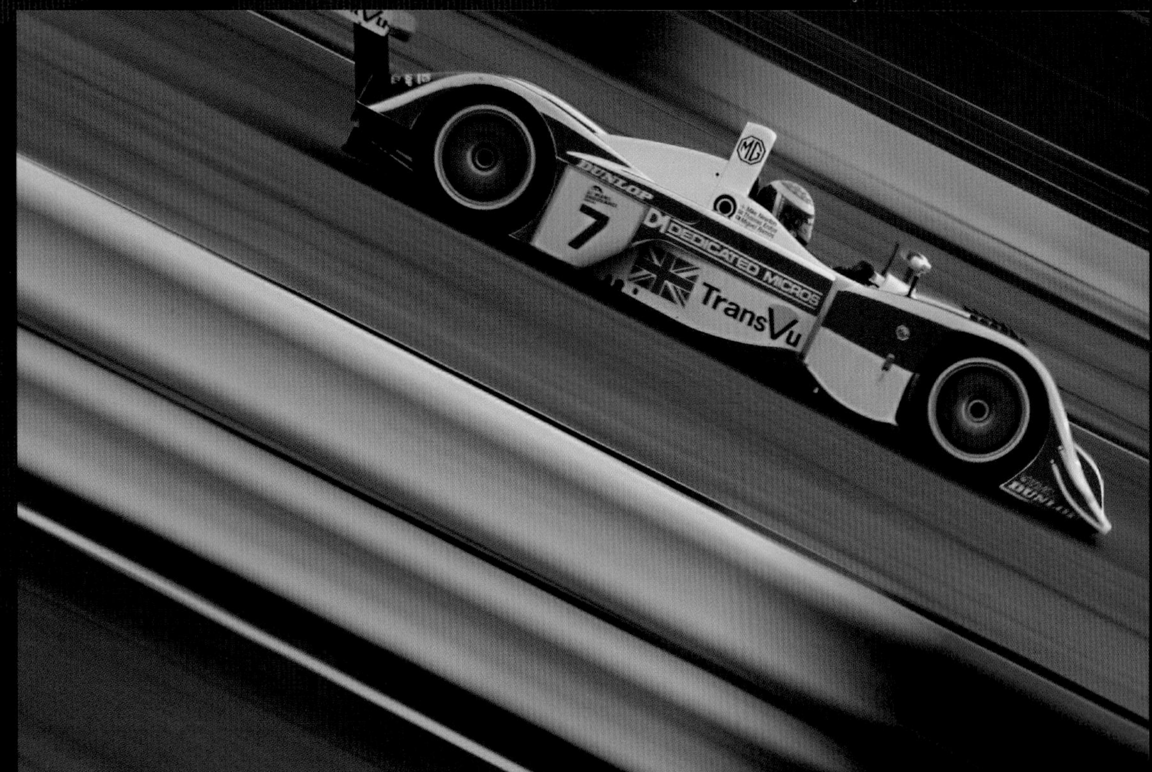

Camera	Pentax *ist D
Focal length	200mm (35mm equivalent: 300mm)
Exposure	1/45sec at f/19
ISO setting	200

By regularly downloading images from memory card to laptop I am able to check the quality of the shots taken so far. While the display on the back of the camera can be used for quick checks, only when you see the image on a decent-sized screen will you know if it is good enough to pass the editing process. By checking my images midway through a day's shooting I can often reshoot a particular composition if I have not got it exactly right.

I always use any breaks in the action to download the images from my camera's memory card to my laptop computer. (Other storage devices are available, but I already owned a laptop.) This allows me to review the images I have taken and helps me plan the rest of my day; it also frees up space on my memory cards so I can start shooting again. I never discard any images at this point, as I prefer to leave all editing for when I get home and have the time to go through each image carefully. This method of image back-up is all well and good if you have a place where you can safely store a laptop computer at a venue – I leave mine locked away in the media centre, but this option is only available if you have a press pass. A better solution might be to use a portable storage device, which is a hand-held hard drive with a small screen to allow basic editing functions. These can be bought at very competitive prices, and are much easier on the back than carrying a laptop around with you. Remember that power is an important issue with all storage devices: no matter what you choose, you will need to ensure that the batteries are fully charged before you leave home, as power supplies are very limited at racing events.

Camera supports

You will only get a sharp image when the camera is steady. When you are using a heavy telephoto lens it is all too easy to experience camera shake, especially if you are using slowish shutter speeds or have been standing in the same position for a length of time. To combat this I will usually try to brace myself as well as I can against some stationary object. However, there are times when the best option is to use a monopod to support the camera. If you've never used one before, they do take some getting used to; and they are difficult to use when panning, as they restrict your movement in the vertical plane – however, they are a big help when a subject is coming towards you, and will prevent your images suffering from camera shake.

I have seen some photographers attempting to use tripods to support their camera at racing events, and I often wonder how their images will turn out. In my experience it's pretty much impossible to use a tripod for motor sports, as they restrict movement far too much and prevent you following your subject.

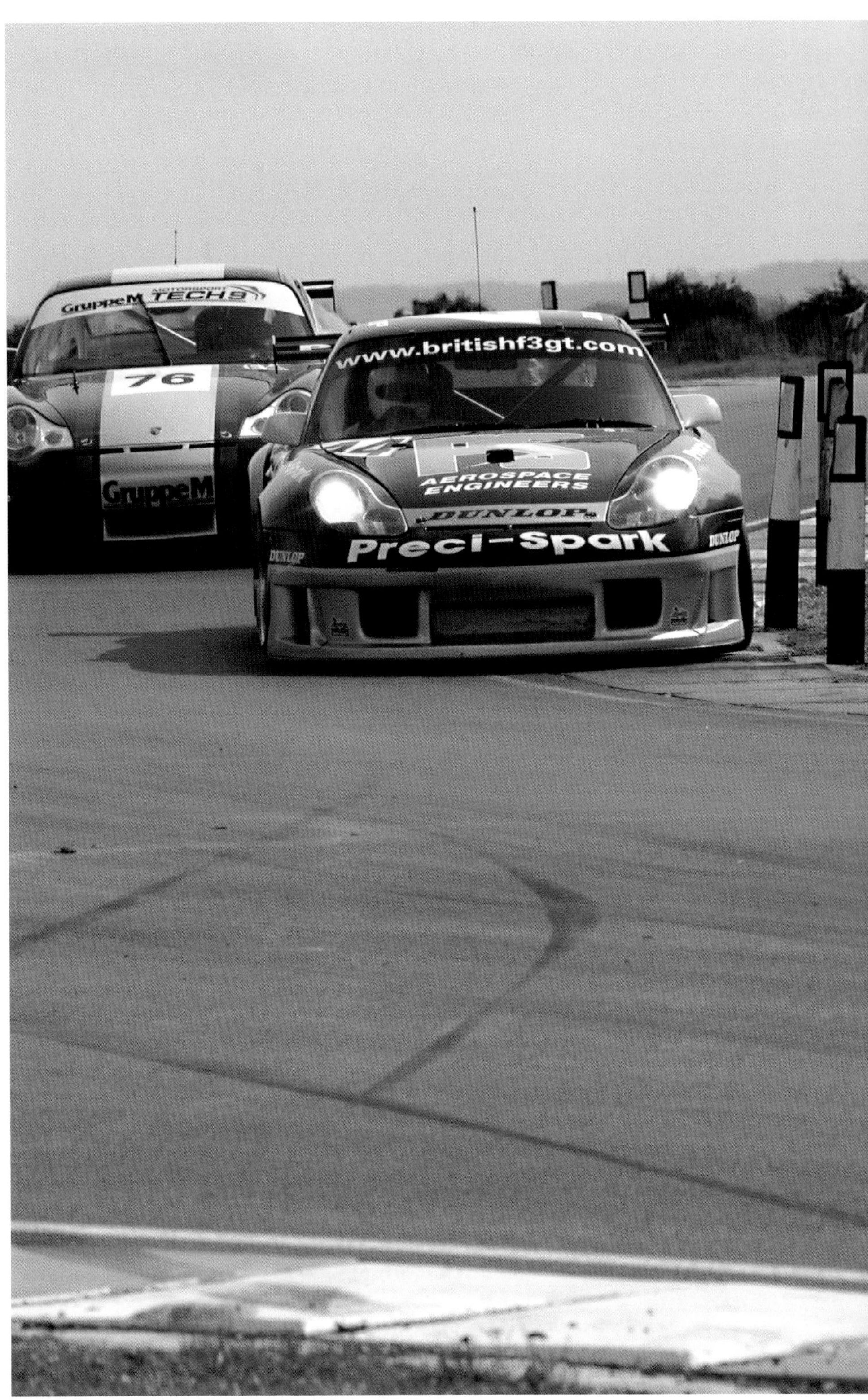

Camera	***Pentax *ist D***
Focal length	***200mm (35mm equivalent: 300mm)***
Exposure	***1/500sec at f/9.5***
ISO setting	***200***

Long telephoto lenses are heavy, and hand-holding such a lens for any period of time can produce camera shake even when you are using fast shutter speeds. A monopod attached to the lens will support the weight and reduce camera shake; I found it took some practice to get used to using one, but it is well worth considering and will save you a lot of backache.

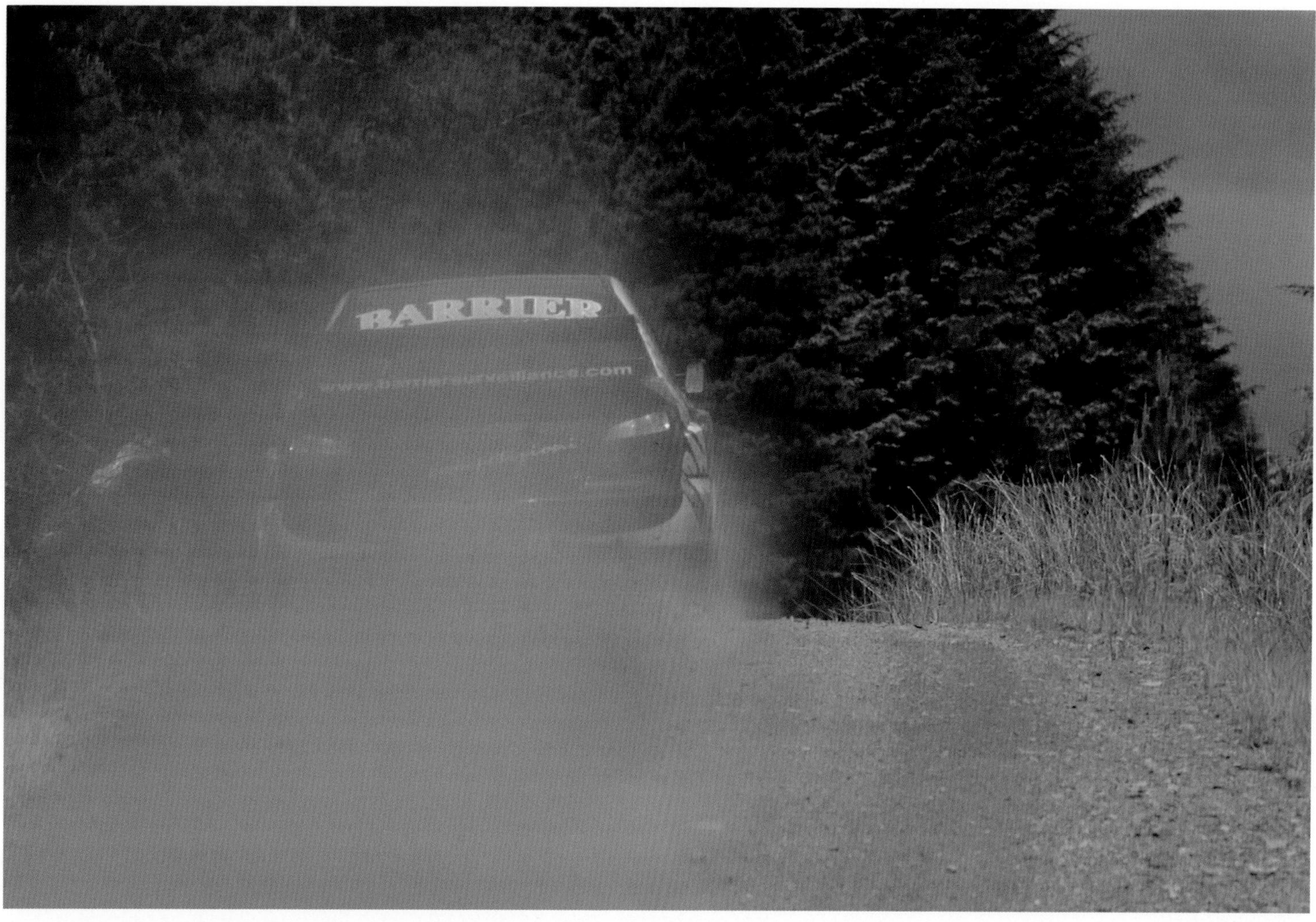

Bags and other essentials

Aside from your camera kit, there are a few items that you will find absolutely essential. Bear in mind that photographing motor sports often involves a lot of walking; you will be standing up all day, and you will usually be away from your car so will have to carry your gear with you, often for considerable distances. It is therefore essential to consider carefully what you need to take and how to carry it. When I started I would carry pretty much all my kit 'just in case'. This was very heavy, and I only ever used 30% of the gear I was carrying. I have now got used to carrying the bare minimum that I will need.

Camera	***Pentax *ist D***
Focal length	***150mm (35mm equivalent: 225mm)***
Exposure	***1/500sec at f/8***
ISO setting	***200***

To get this dusty shot I had to walk a fair distance into the forest stage. In circumstances like this it is important that you carry only the equipment you really need: the aim is to travel as light as possible while still leaving room for non-photographic essentials such as water.

For carrying lenses, flash, film or memory cards, and spare batteries, I use pouches that strap onto my belt so that I can access them easily. If I'm going to be some distance from my car I also take a small photo backpack which holds sundry accessories (spare batteries, memory cards, etc.) plus a few non-photographic essentials:

- a chamois leather, which is essential for covering and drying kit when it rains
- a compact, scrunchable poncho that provides excellent cover in the rain and allows me to keep my gear dry between shots in a way that a coat cannot
- my mobile phone
- a bottle of water – if you're trekking out into a forest stage for a rally there are very few grocery stores along the way
- when attending circuit races, I often put a small set of steps in the car – you never know when you will need a little extra height to capture an image.

Camera	*Pentax *ist D*
Focal length	*170mm (35mm equivalent: 255mm)*
Exposure	*1/125sec at f/6.7*
ISO setting	*200*

The weather plays a big part in motor sport photography; if you are well prepared you will find it much easier to concentrate on taking pictures. When it's raining I wear an inexpensive poncho which acts as a miniature tent to keep myself and my camera dry between shots; this makes it much easier to take photographs in bad weather.

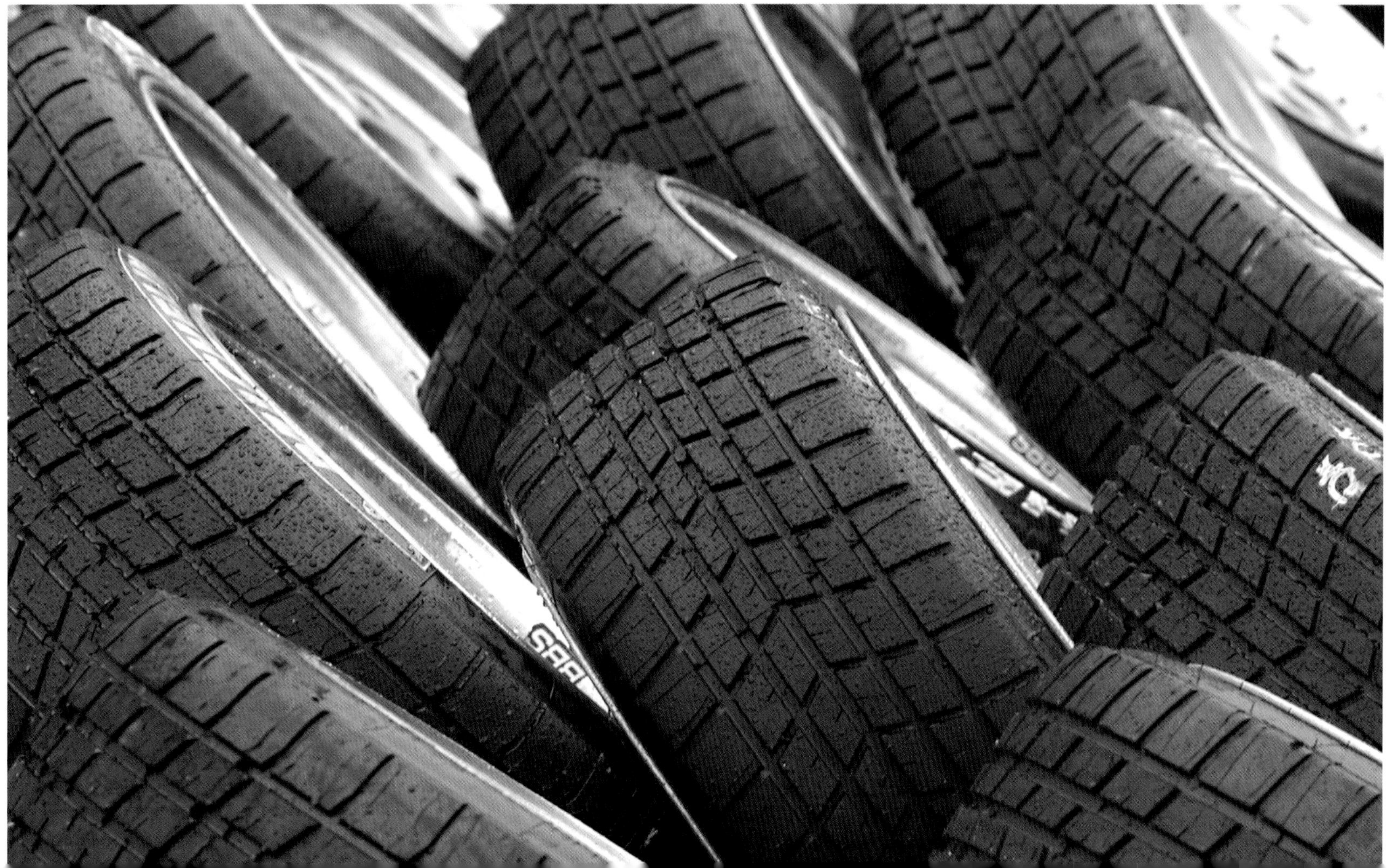

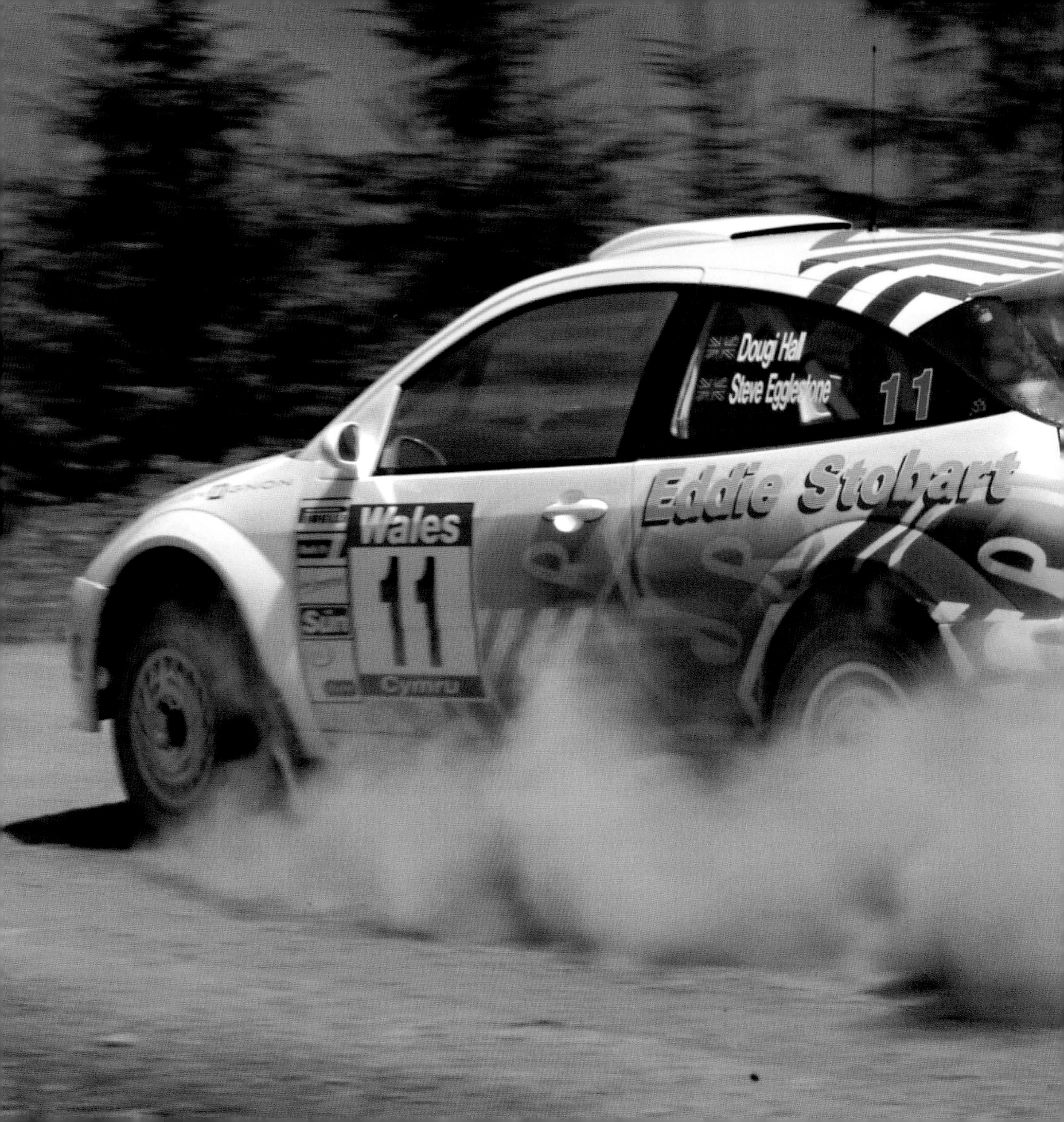
Dougi Hall
Steve Egglestone
11
Eddie Stobart
Wales
11
Cymru

CHAPTER 2

Knowing your subject

Understanding the various disciplines of racing is an important part of taking good motor sport images – unless you have some knowledge of the nature of an event, it will be difficult to predict where and how the best action will happen. A basic understanding of each type of racing – the competitors, the track and the characteristics of the vehicles involved – will help you to plan your shots well before you attend an event. I'm not suggesting that you have to be a complete petrol-head, but it certainly helps if you know where the most dramatic action is likely to be seen, and what type of images you can expect to capture.

Access

No matter what discipline of racing you want to photograph, it is generally fair to say that the more high-profile an event, the more challenging it is to photograph if you do not have press access. More popular events attract greater crowds, and so basic things – like finding a good position with space to work and a clear view of the track – become more problematic. By attending less prestigious events you will find it easier to get a good vantage point, and you will have more freedom to move to different parts of the circuit without having to contend with hundreds of other people. These races often lack the glamour and spectacle of the higher-profile events, but the racing itself is no less dramatic.

Camera	**Pentax *ist D**
Focal length	**135mm (35mm equivalent: 200mm)**
Exposure	**1/250sec at f/4**
ISO setting	**200**

Understanding the basic principles of the various disciplines of motor sport is crucial to getting the shots you want. The start is a key part of any race - this is especially true in the case of motocross, where all the riders line up alongside each other in a starting gate. By arriving in plenty of time I was able to capture this close study of a rider as he prepares for the race to start.

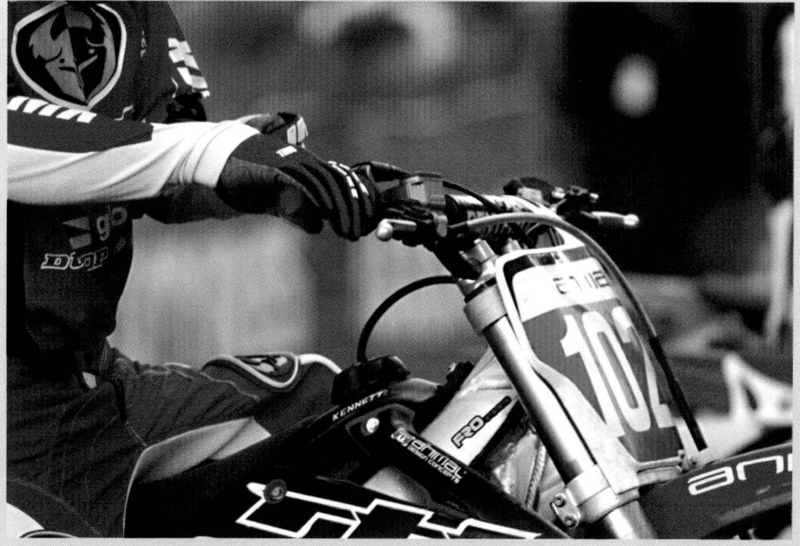

But even the big events need not be entirely out of reach. For example, most major circuit races take place on a Sunday, while the Saturday before (and sometimes also the Friday) is used for testing and qualifying. These are good times to attend a circuit, as the crowds will be much less than on the race day itself, so you will have greater flexibility in the range of shots available to you.

Circuit racing

Circuit racing incorporates a wide variety of racing disciplines, from Formula 1 and Moto GP all the way down to local club events and track days, but the basic characteristics of circuit races are pretty similar, no matter which of these disciplines you are watching. Action usually takes place at the corners: overtaking can occur under braking on the way into a corner or under acceleration out of it, and competitors may lose control and spin off at the entry, middle or exit of a corner. This isn't to say that you should only concentrate on corners – there are opportunities for photographers all round a racing circuit – but the corners are usually a safe bet.

Recent years have seen much improvement in both spectator and competitor safety, the net result of which is the increase in trackside barriers and fences, along with larger run-off areas and gravel traps for the competitors. This means that public viewing points are often further from the action, or screened

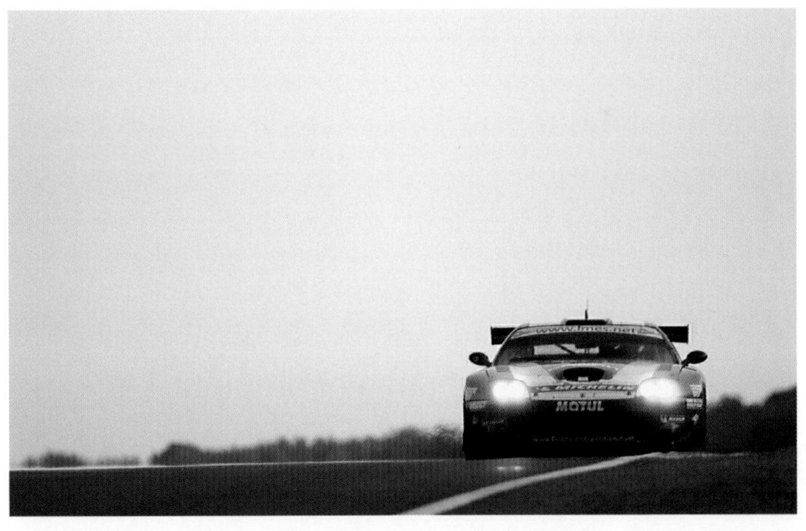

Camera	***Pentax *ist D***
Focal length	***200mm (35mm equivalent: 300mm)***
Exposure	***1/750sec at f/4***
ISO setting	***200***

International events such as the European Le Mans series attract large crowds, which can make it difficult to find a good position from which to take photographs unless you have a press pass. During the practice and qualifying sessions preceding the race day there will be fewer spectators, and you will have better access to good viewpoints.

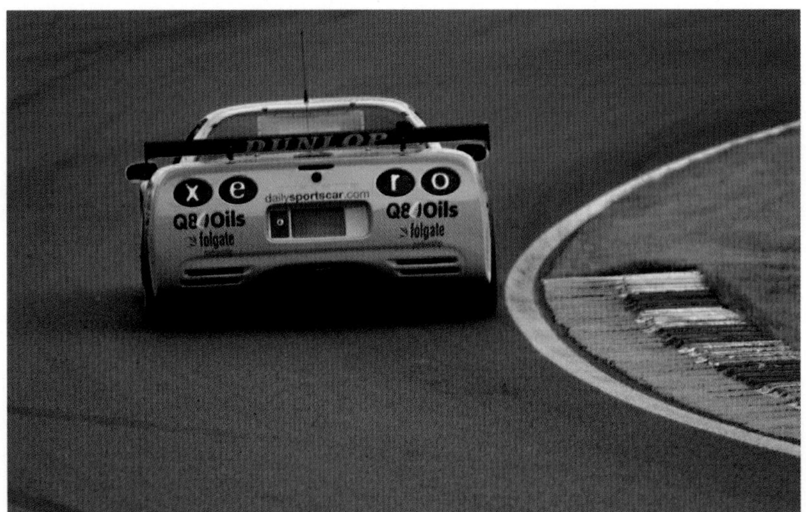

Camera	***Pentax *ist D***
Focal length	***200mm (35mm equivalent: 300mm)***
Exposure	***1/1500sec at f/5.6***
ISO setting	***200***

On racing circuits most action occurs at corners – either under braking on the approach, going through the corner, or under acceleration on the exit. When focusing manually, trackside kerbs and bollards can provide useful focusing points: you can get your images pin-sharp by focusing on them, then fire the shutter as the subject arrives.

behind large wire fences, both of which present obstacles for the keen amateur photographer. It is possible to take photographs through wire fences by standing close to the fence, using a long lens and a wide aperture to blur the fence out (see the explanation of depth of field on page 99), but this is less than ideal. Circuits that are regularly used for international events usually have more safety measures than those which host national championship races, where I feel you can often get better photographic opportunities and yet still see professional racing teams in action.

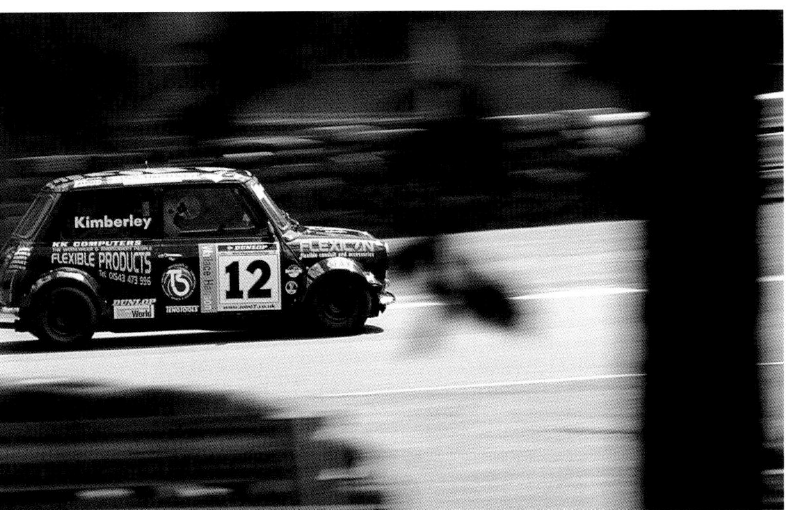

Camera	Pentax Super A
Focal length	200mm
Exposure	1/125sec at f/16
Film	Fuji Velvia 50

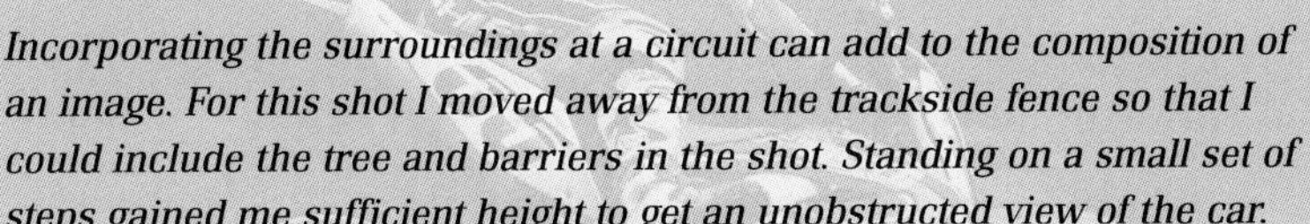

Incorporating the surroundings at a circuit can add to the composition of an image. For this shot I moved away from the trackside fence so that I could include the tree and barriers in the shot. Standing on a small set of steps gained me sufficient height to get an unobstructed view of the car.

Categories of motor sport

The different disciplines of motor sport can be divided into two main sectors – tarmac and off-road racing – which can then be further subdivided into events for cars and motorbikes. There is a vast array of differing types and classes of racing, so the list given here is not exhaustive. There is space in this chapter to discuss only a few of the main types, but this should be enough to alert you to the kinds of factors you need to consider.

Cars: Tarmac

- circuit racing
- karting
- sprints and hillclimbs
- tarmac rallies
- oval racing
- drag racing

Cars: Off-road

- rallying
- stock cars (UK)
- banger racing
- rallycross
- off-road racing

Motorcyles: Tarmac

- circuit racing
- drag racing
- supermoto
- road racing

Motorcycles: Off-road

- motocross
- speedway
- grass track
- trials
- supercross

Tin-tops and slicks-'n'-wings

Just as motorcycle racing is divided into solo bikes and sidecar outfits, so car racing can be split into two distinct categories, each of which has differing characteristics when it comes to the way that they race. Generally, racing cars that are based on road-going machines are more robust than cars that are designed exclusively for racing; this allows for a different style of driving and so provides a different spectacle for the photographer. Road-car-based racers are often known as 'tin-tops', which refers to the fact that the driver is enclosed in a caged shell and the wheels are covered by bodywork. Specialized track-racing cars often have the driver sitting in an open cockpit, and wheels unprotected by bodywork; these are referred to as 'slicks-'n'-wings' cars.

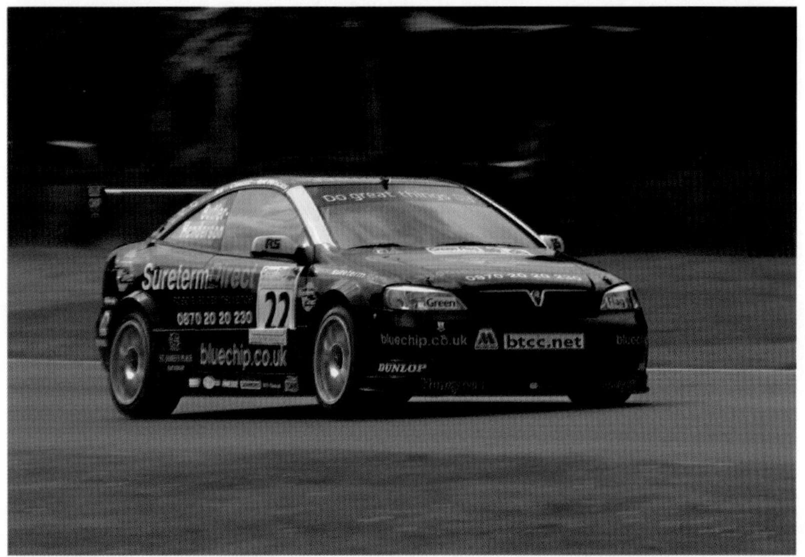

Camera	Pentax *ist D
Focal length	210mm (35mm equivalent: 315mm)
Exposure	1/180sec at f/11
ISO setting	200

This 'tin-top' car has front-wheel drive and possesses different handling characteristics from a rear-wheel-drive car. Which wheels are driven can determine how or when a car loses traction or control; an understanding of this can be useful when you are choosing a place to stand in order to capture dramatic slides or moments of lost traction, especially in wet or slippery conditions.

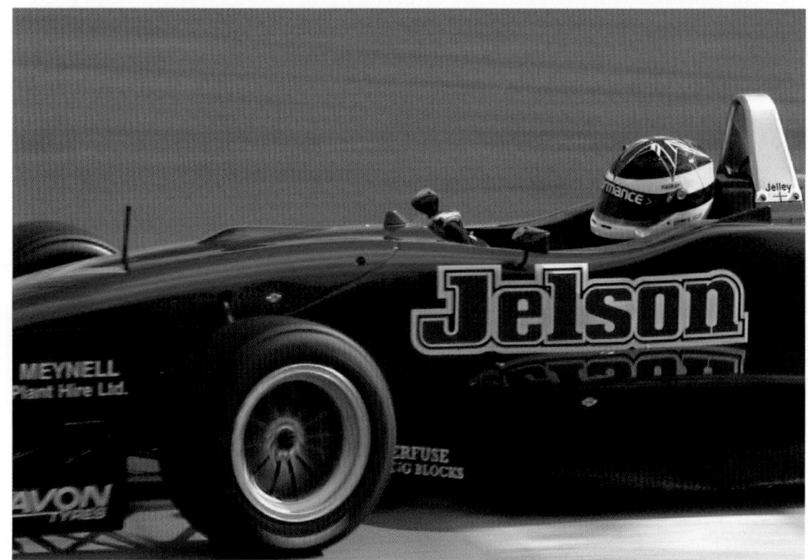

Camera	Pentax *ist D
Focal length	200mm (35mm equivalent: 300mm)
Exposure	1/180sec at f/11
ISO setting	200

Cars that have been designed specifically for racing bear little resemblance to road cars: aerodynamic bodywork and aerofoil-type wings improve the efficiency and handling of these 'slicks-'n'-wings' cars. Because of their more fragile construction and exposed wheels, this type of racing often involves less contact between competitors - although when contact does occur it is often more dramatic than with tin-tops.

The very nature of these two types of car has an impact on the type of action photographs you can take. Tin-top racing often has more thrills and spills, because the bodywork protects the car from potential race-finishing damage – the drivers can afford to make contact with other competitors and can often be seen 'leaning', 'rubbing' or giving a 'love touch' to other cars. The relatively fragile construction of slicks-'n'-wings cars means that any contact with another car brings the risk of performance-inhibiting damage or retirement from the race, so contact in this genre is generally avoided – although accidents do happen.

Camera	*Pentax *ist D*
Focal length	*190mm (35mm equivalent: 285mm)*
Exposure	*1/180sec at f/11*
ISO setting	*200*

This shot shows a Porsche receiving a 'love touch' from the pursuing Ferrari. This is a common sight during 'tin-top' racing, and had no effect on the outcome of the race. Had this incident occurred during a 'slicks-'n'-wings' race it would almost certainly have resulted in one of the cars needing to retire to the pits to repair the damage. Understanding the nature of a particular discipline is an important factor when you are planning the type of shots you want to take.

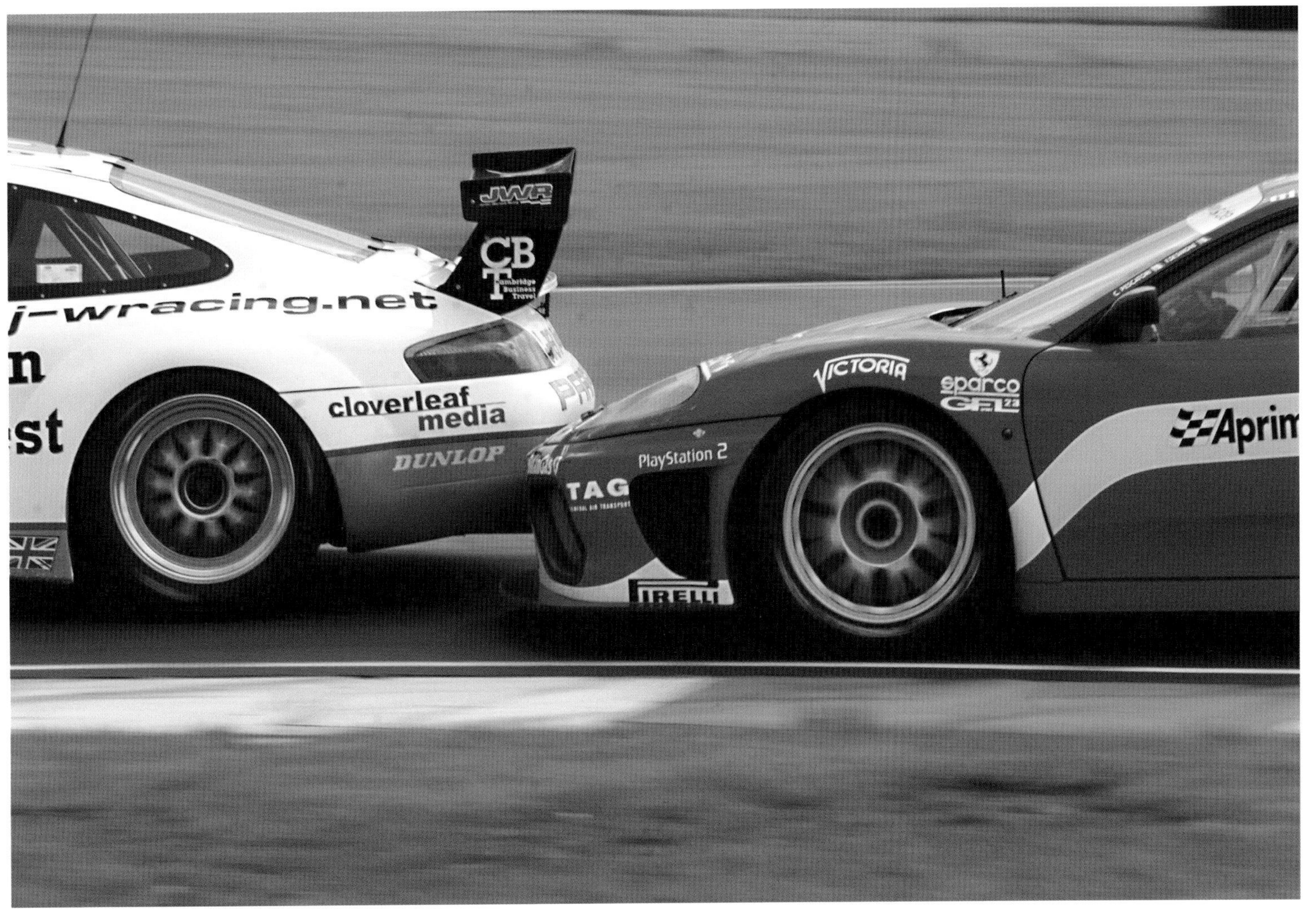

Motorcycles

In my opinion motorcycle circuit racing is more challenging to photograph than cars – the principles are much the same in terms of technique, but bike racing is often more frantic and action-packed. Due to their small size in relation to the width of a circuit, bikes can choose from a number of racing lines, whereas cars usually have only one clear line to take through a corner. This is an important consideration if you are pre-focusing manually on a piece of track (see pages 90–3) – you may have to fine-tune your focusing in a split second in order to keep the subject pin-sharp. However, this can be a bit hit and miss, so where possible I prefer to choose a point to pre-focus on and then wait for the bike to come to me. Bikes also accelerate faster than cars, and generally reach higher top speeds in most disciplines (Formula 1 is an exception), so I would recommend you hone your photographic technique on cars before moving on to bikes.

Camera	***Pentax *ist D***
Focal length	***210mm (35mm equivalent: 315mm)***
Exposure	***1/750sec at f/4***
ISO setting	***200***

Photographing motorcycles is more challenging than taking images of cars. Due to their smaller size they are able to take a number of differing lines through a corner, so it is advisable to use your lens in manual and pre-focus on a selected piece of track, firing the camera's shutter a split second before the subject comes into focus. Even less powerful bikes such as the 125cc machine seen in this shot can travel at high speed, requiring quick reflexes from the photographer.

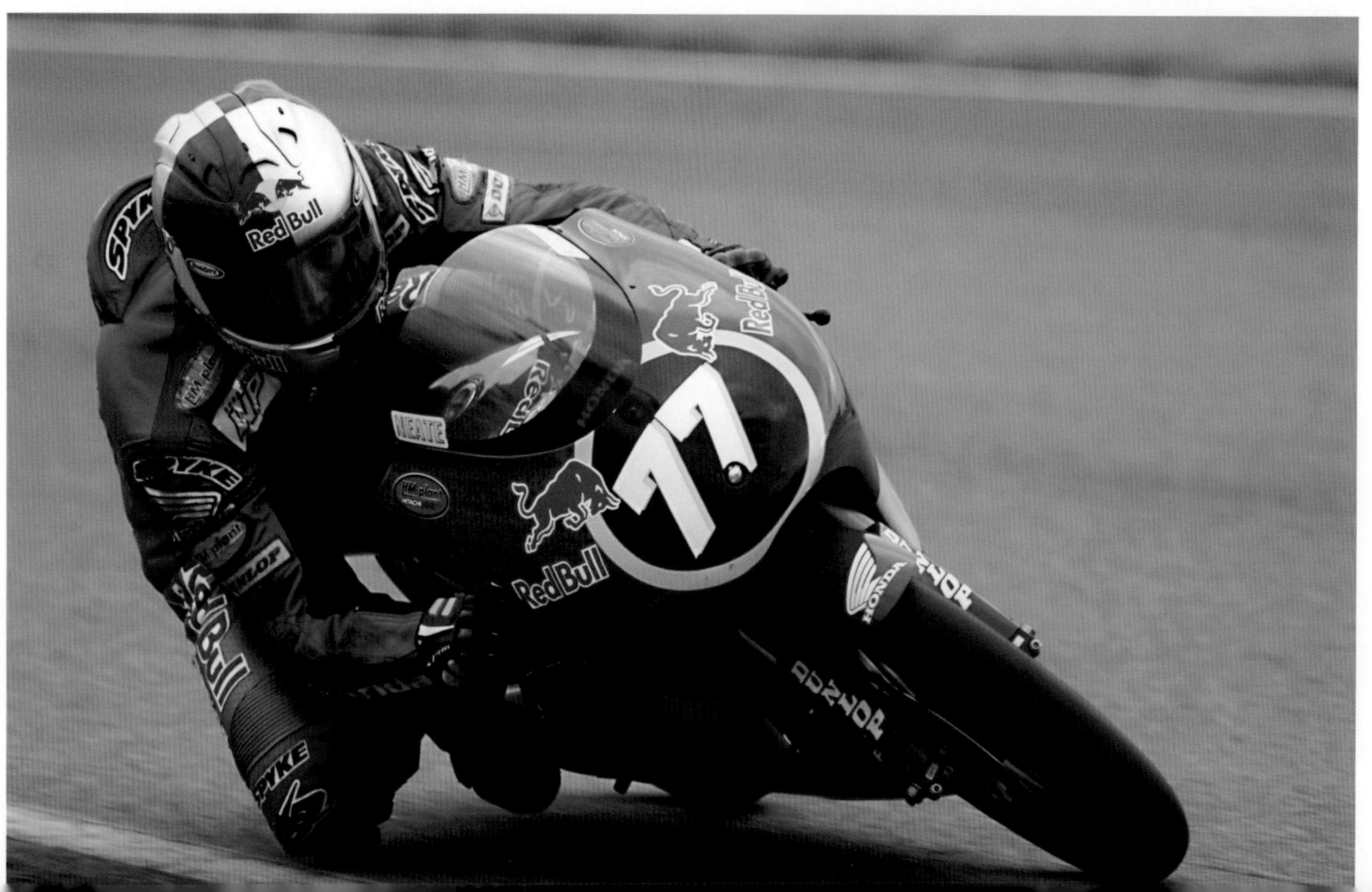

Oval racing

The American discipline of oval racing is worth experiencing if you want to add some variety to your motor sport portfolio. I haven't attended many of these races, because I live in the UK, where there is only one venue for this sport. The cars are low on technology but high on speed, and many races are interrupted by high-speed crashes as competitors connect with each other and with the concrete wall that lines the circuit. Due to the nature and speed of oval racing there are large fences all around the outside of the circuit, so it is a challenge to get good conventional shots from these events. Having said that, there are higher vantage points available, such as the pit garage roof; this doubles as a spectator viewing area, providing a great position from which to photograph pit-lane action.

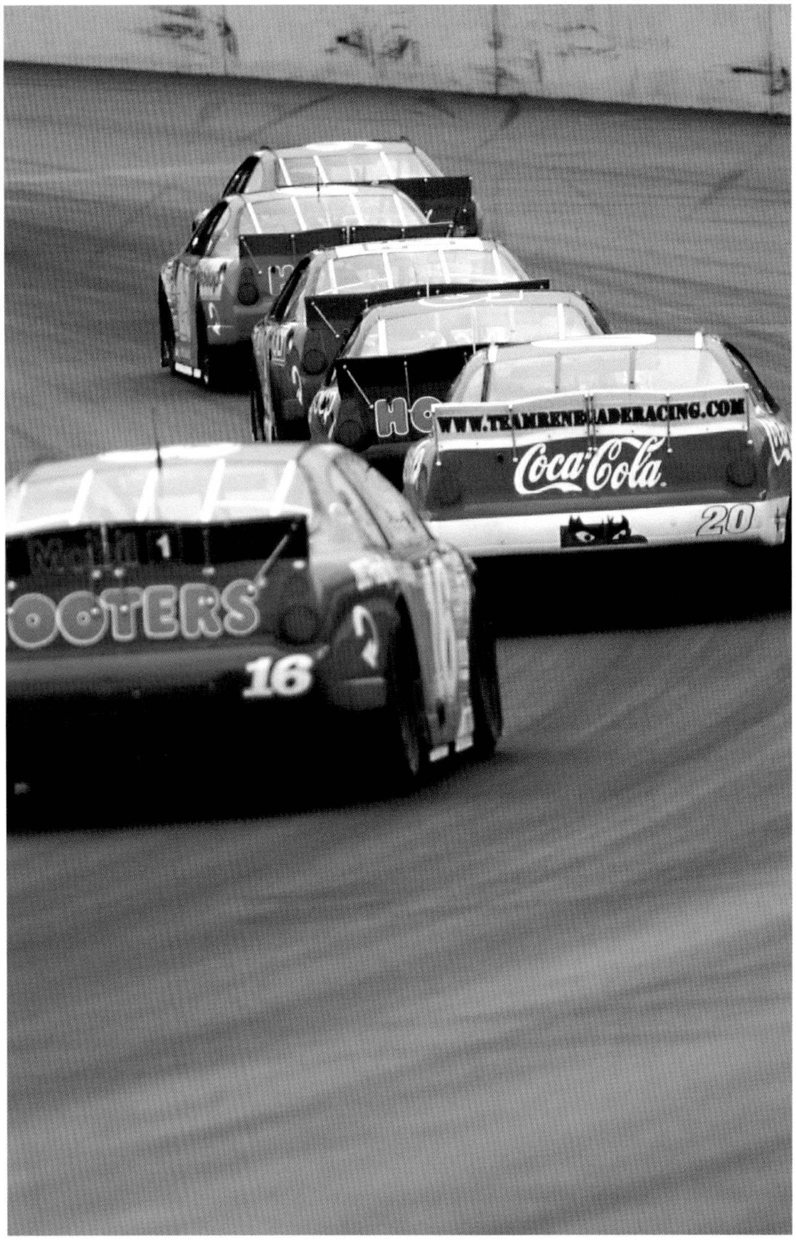

Camera	***Pentax *ist D***
Focal length	***300mm (35mm equivalent: 450mm)***
Exposure	***1/750sec at f/5.6***
ISO setting	***200***

Oval racing is a very different proposition from traditional circuit racing. With only four corners on the circuit, a lot of the overtaking takes place as a result of a driver carrying more speed through a corner, allowing him to 'draft' past the car in front on the straight. Understanding the nuances of the discipline you are shooting is a key part of taking good racing images.

Karting

Karting is another form of circuit racing that provides great action shots for the photographer. Races are held on bespoke kart tracks that are much shorter than those used for car racing; there are generally fewer fences to contend with, and you can get much closer to the action. Many current Formula 1 drivers began in karts at an early age, and this discipline can be a good learning ground for the photographer as well. Karting may not have the glamour of larger circuit racing, but it more than makes up for that with close encounters and plenty of spills. Drivers vary widely in age and experience, with some competitors as young as 8. Racing is always very close and there is generally much more overtaking than in some of the higher-profile circuit races.

Camera	***Pentax *ist D***
Focal length	***170mm (35mm equivalent: 255mm)***
Exposure	***1/750sec at f/4***
ISO setting	***200***

Karting provides an excellent opportunity to refine your photographic skills. Race heats are run so that all the drivers take turns to begin a race from the front, middle and back of the pack. This ensures plenty of overtaking action as the faster drivers fight their way through the pack.

Rallying

Rallying presents fantastic opportunities for the motor sport photographer. Events are run on both tarmac and gravel, and the action can be very dramatic indeed. Here the competitors race each other against the clock through a number of timed stages which are held over two or three days. Events take place in all seasons and are usually held in remote rural locations, so planning and preparation are especially important with this type of event.

Exciting images can be taken at almost any point on a rally stage, as the action is frantic from start to finish. Corners are always a good place to capture dramatic shots of sideways action, but there are also often jumps or water splashes that can be equally impressive.

Camera	***Pentax *ist D***
Focal length	***200mm (35mm equivalent: 300mm)***
Exposure	***1/1500sec at f/6.7***
ISO setting	***200***

The weather can play a major part in rallying; as events are run throughout the year, you can expect to be out in all conditions. In the dry summer months cars throw up huge clouds of dust as they pass by, so it is important to protect your camera once the car has passed – stashing it inside your jacket is a good solution.

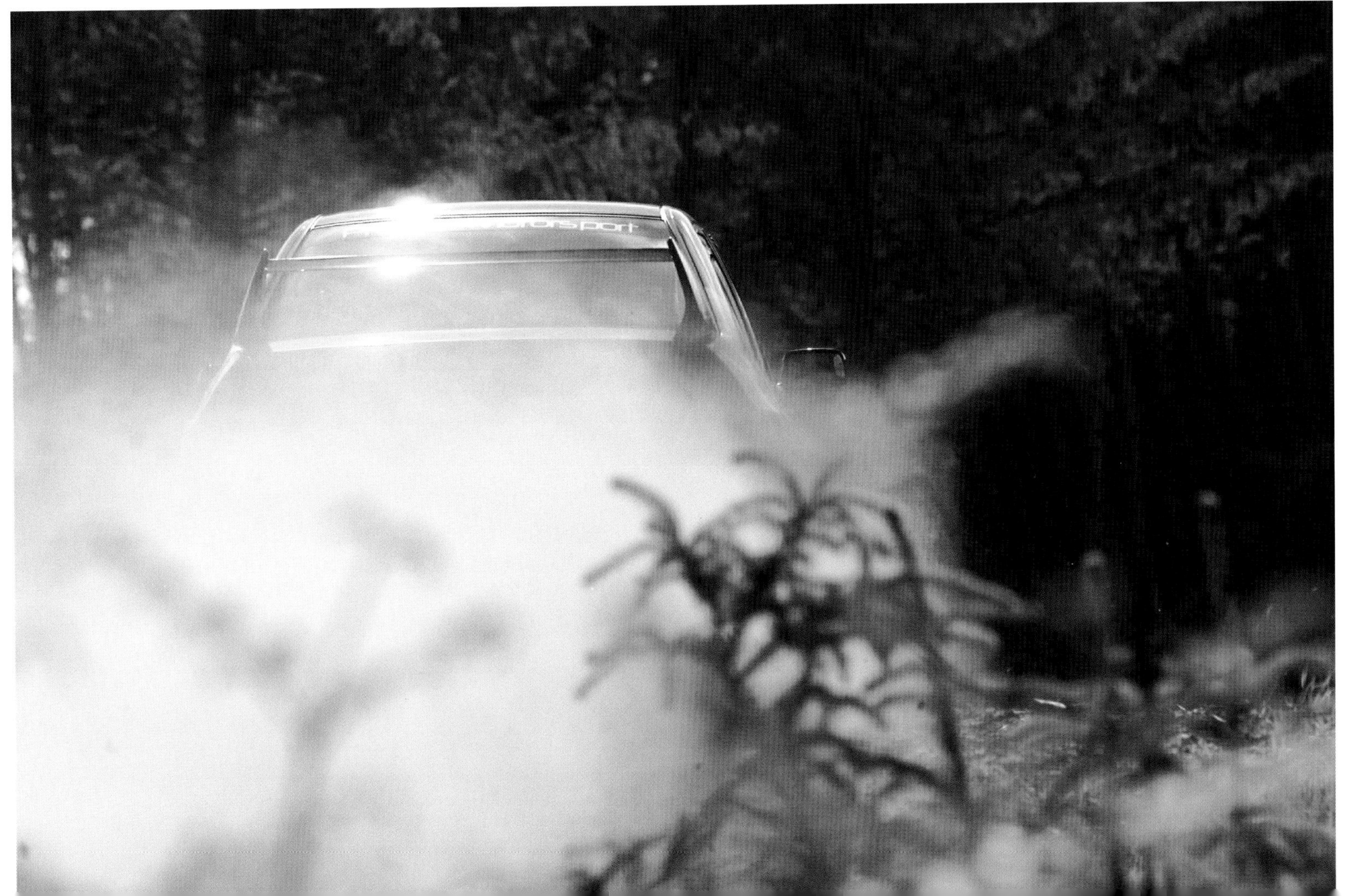

Rally safety

Unlike circuit racing, there are no safety barriers or wire fences between you and the competitors. This means that amateur photographers can have much the same access as accredited professionals, but it also means that you have to be far more aware of safety issues. Stages may be run over a number of miles, and although there will be event marshals at regular intervals you are far more responsible for your own safety. Getting a good photograph is not the only consideration when choosing where to stand on a rally stage: if a driver takes too much speed into a corner and loses control, he will generally leave the road on the outside of the corner. As there are no gravel traps to stop the car, it is up to the scenery to do that job – make sure you're not part of it! Never stand on the outside of a bend unless you are well past the apex of the

Camera	***Pentax *ist D***
Focal length	***135mm (35mm equivalent: 200mm)***
Exposure	***1/180sec at f/22***
ISO setting	***200***

In rallying you can often get as close to the action as you want. Rallies are run in 'stages', often on forest tracks over many miles. Although the surface is often gravel, modern rally cars travel at mind-boggling speeds. The close access means that you must be far more aware of your own safety and that of those around you. Don't stand on the exit of a corner, and never turn your back on a car until it has passed you. If you are in any doubt as to the safety of your chosen position, move somewhere else.

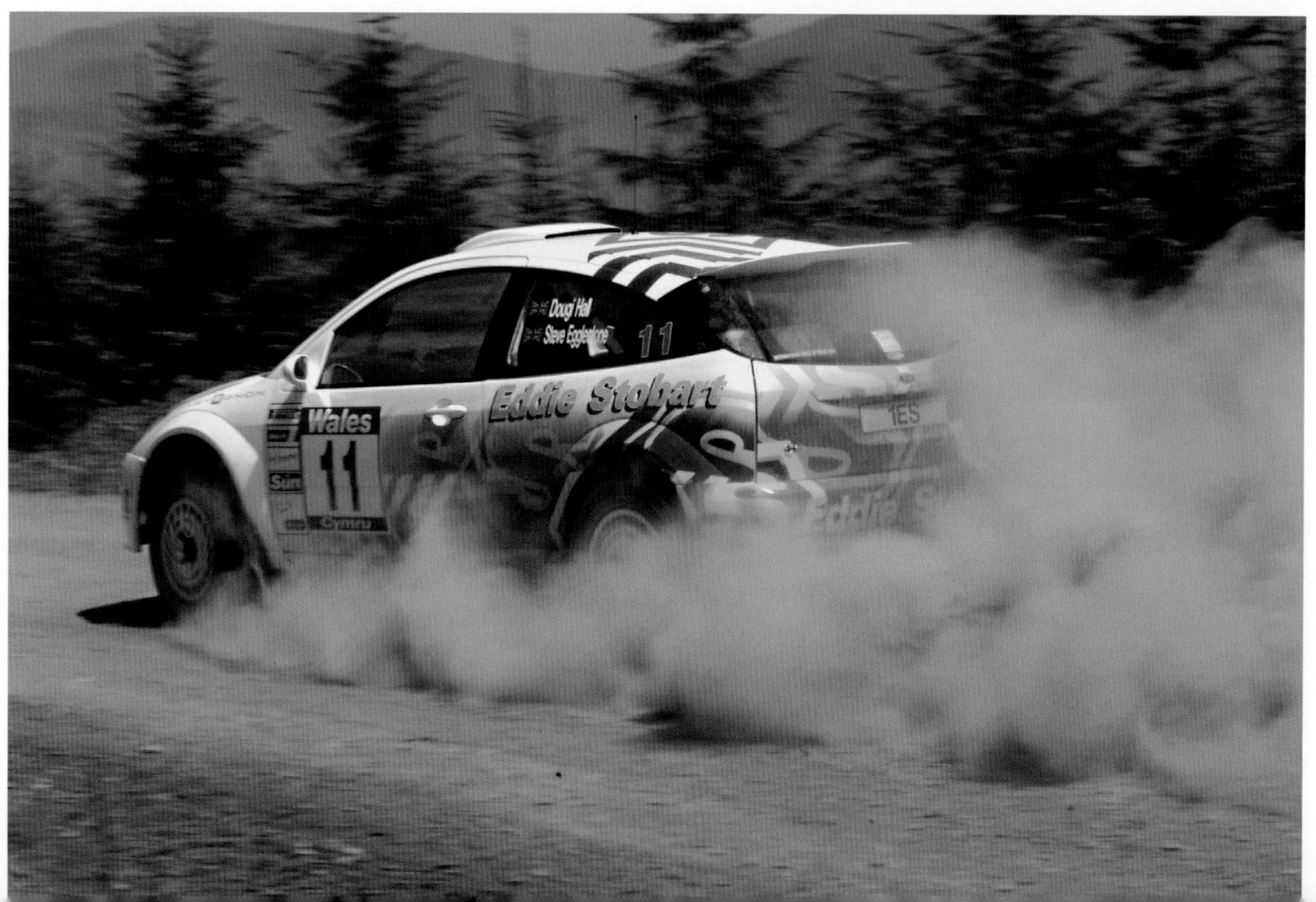

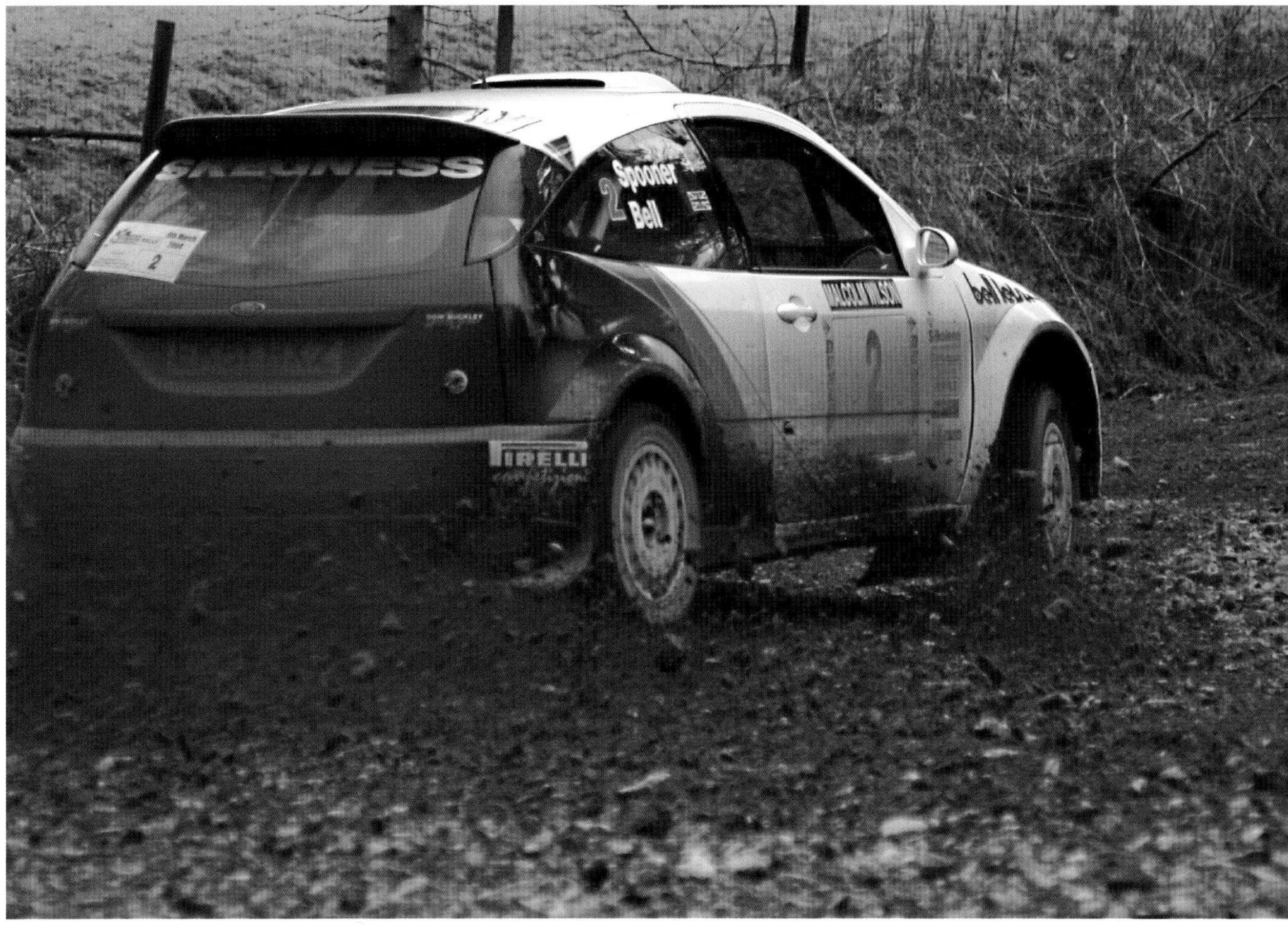

Camera	Pentax *ist D
Focal length	120mm (35mm equivalent: 180mm)
Exposure	1/125sec at f/9.5
ISO setting	200

Modern rally cars have terrific levels of grip, thanks mainly to the use of four-wheel-drive systems. Stones and dirt thrown from the wheels provide good photographic material, but be careful not to get hit by flying debris. Turning your back once you are sure a car has passed – not before – is advisable to protect both yourself and your camera.

corner; even then you should be very careful, and if you are in any doubt at all, move to somewhere safer. You need to keep your wits about you, as cars run at one- or two-minute intervals; so, if you are wanting to change your viewpoint to get a different shot while the stage is still running, you will have to do so in small stages, moving a short distance and then getting to a safe position before the next car passes by.

No matter how many rallies I attend, I am still amazed by the speed that top-level competitors drive at on gravel roads. Modern rally cars often have four-wheel drive, and although they are not geared for high top speeds the levels of acceleration are very impressive.

As each car exits the corner and the driver gets back onto the throttle, stones and loose gravel will be thrown from the wheels; so, once you are sure the car has passed you safely, it's advisable to turn your back to protect your face and your camera. **Never turn your back on a car until it has passed: there are no barriers or gravel traps to stop cars if they leave the road.**

In dry weather dust can be a major problem on forest rallies, covering you and your gear once a car has passed by, and it's wise to wear a jacket so you can quickly tuck your camera inside it to prevent it getting covered in dust.

Motocross

Motocross is one of my favourite photographic subjects. With high-octane action, ultra-competitive racing and easy access to the circuit, the sport provides great opportunities for action shots.

The riders race around a dirt circuit that includes purpose-built jumps of varying sizes, so that for a great deal of each lap the rider is flying through the air. When the bikes are not airborne they throw great 'roosters' of dirt from their rear wheels as they accelerate round the track. Though top speeds are not particularly high, it is still quite a challenge to photograph motocross effectively, as the lines the riders take vary greatly – and picking points to focus on in mid-air is quite tricky!

Camera	***Pentax Super A***
Focal length	***300mm***
Exposure	***1/500sec at f/5.6***
Film	***Fuji Velvia 50***

Motocross action occurs all around the track, so finding a satisfactory viewpoint is rarely a problem. This rider is using his body weight to control the bike as he opens the throttle on the exit from a corner. By follow-focusing as he came towards me (see page 107) I was able to capture this strong action shot.

After a period of relative unpopularity motocross is starting to regain some of its stature and crowds are on the increase. However, it's still pretty easy to get as close to the action as you want, so I've never felt the need to try and get a press pass for these events.

Motocross circuits are usually pretty twisty and don't have long straights as race tracks do, so the action happens all around the circuit. It's not so important to have detailed knowledge of this discipline, as you can get good action shots from pretty much anywhere on the circuit; but it is important to have a well-practised technique – the action is fast and very furious, so you have to be able to react very quickly.

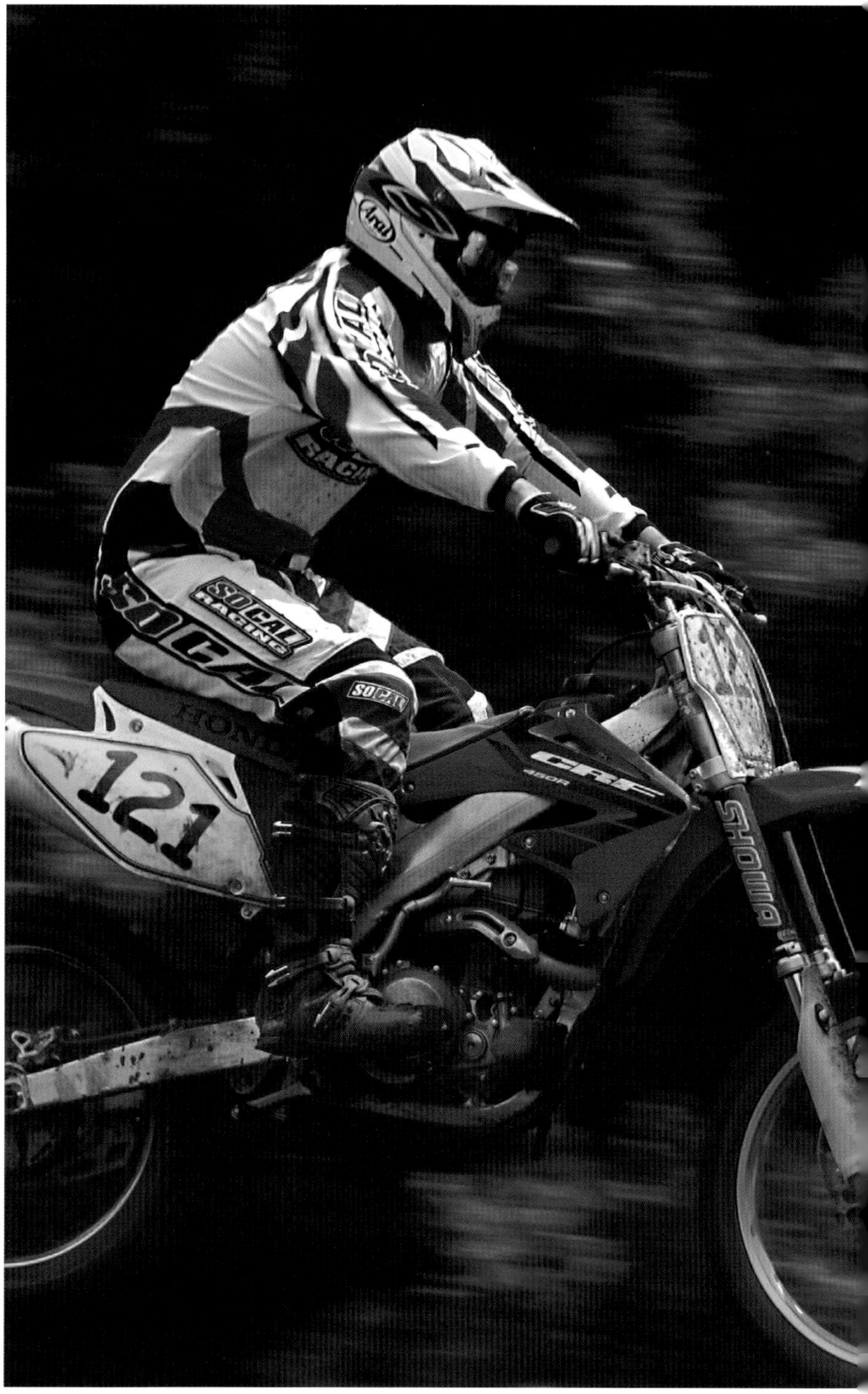

Camera	***Pentax *ist D***
Focal length	***200mm (35mm equivalent: 300mm)***
Exposure	***1/125sec at f/11***
ISO setting	***200***

Selecting a composition that made use of the trees in the background, I chose a bike and rider whose colours complemented the green of the leaves. As the rider is in the air, I opted to focus on the track beneath him, and waited for the rider to become sharp before firing the shutter.

Test days

Racing teams don't just turn up on Saturday, race on Sunday and then go home until the next race meeting. Many teams across all disciplines go testing during the week in order to improve their machinery ready for a race weekend. If you are able to get time off work during the week, it is worth seeing whether your local circuit is holding any test days. These are a great way to practise and perfect your photographic technique; and there are no crowds to contend with, so you won't have to worry about getting a decent viewpoint.

Camera	***Pentax *ist D***
Focal length	***120mm (35mm equivalent: 180mm)***
Exposure	***1/125sec at f/11***
ISO setting	***200***

Recent years have seen the introduction and growing popularity of 'track days' where private car owners can drive their road cars around a racing circuit. These are often held on weekdays, and provide a crowd-free environment for you to hone your photographic skills.

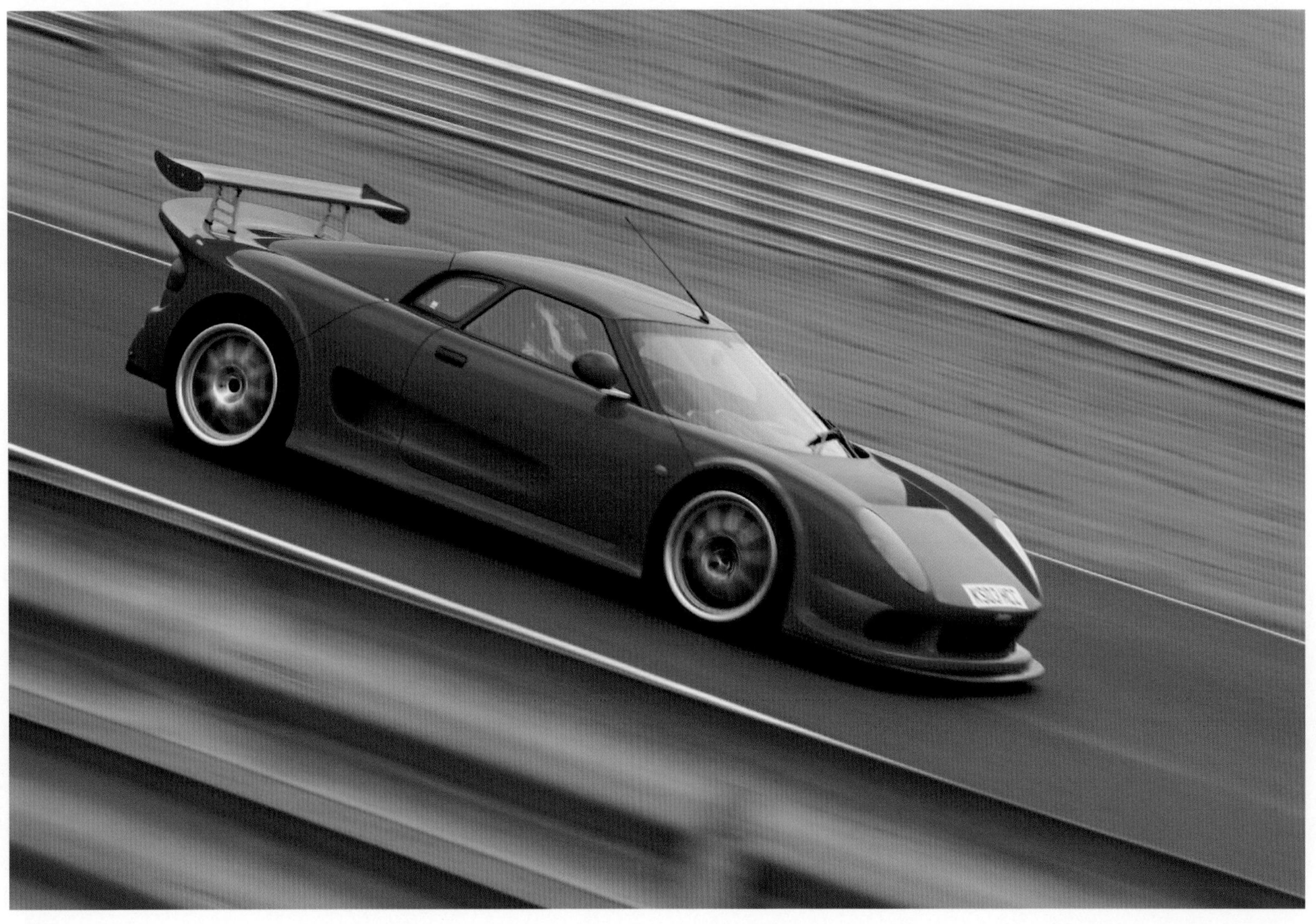

Camera	Pentax *ist D
Focal length	18mm (35mm equivalent: 28mm)
Exposure	1/125sec at f/19
ISO setting	200

Motor sports are dangerous, and not only for the competitors – if you are unaware of what is going on around you it is all too easy to put yourself at risk while you are looking through the viewfinder. If you understand what is happening you can take precautions. For this shot I waited until the driver stopped at his pit, and before stepping in front of the car I made sure that he was getting out to swap with his co-driver. Had he not got out of the car, the pit-stop would have been much quicker and it would not have been safe for me to move into this position.

Safety

There are many racing disciplines that I have not even mentioned in this chapter, and all offer great opportunities for any photographer who is willing to take an interest in them. Whatever type of motor sport event you decide to attend, you must remember that your own safety and that of others is the most important consideration. Take note of the safety recommendations already given in this chapter, and always make sure you pay attention to any safety information provided at the venue. Observe any instructions given by event organizers or marshals, and – most of all – use your common sense.

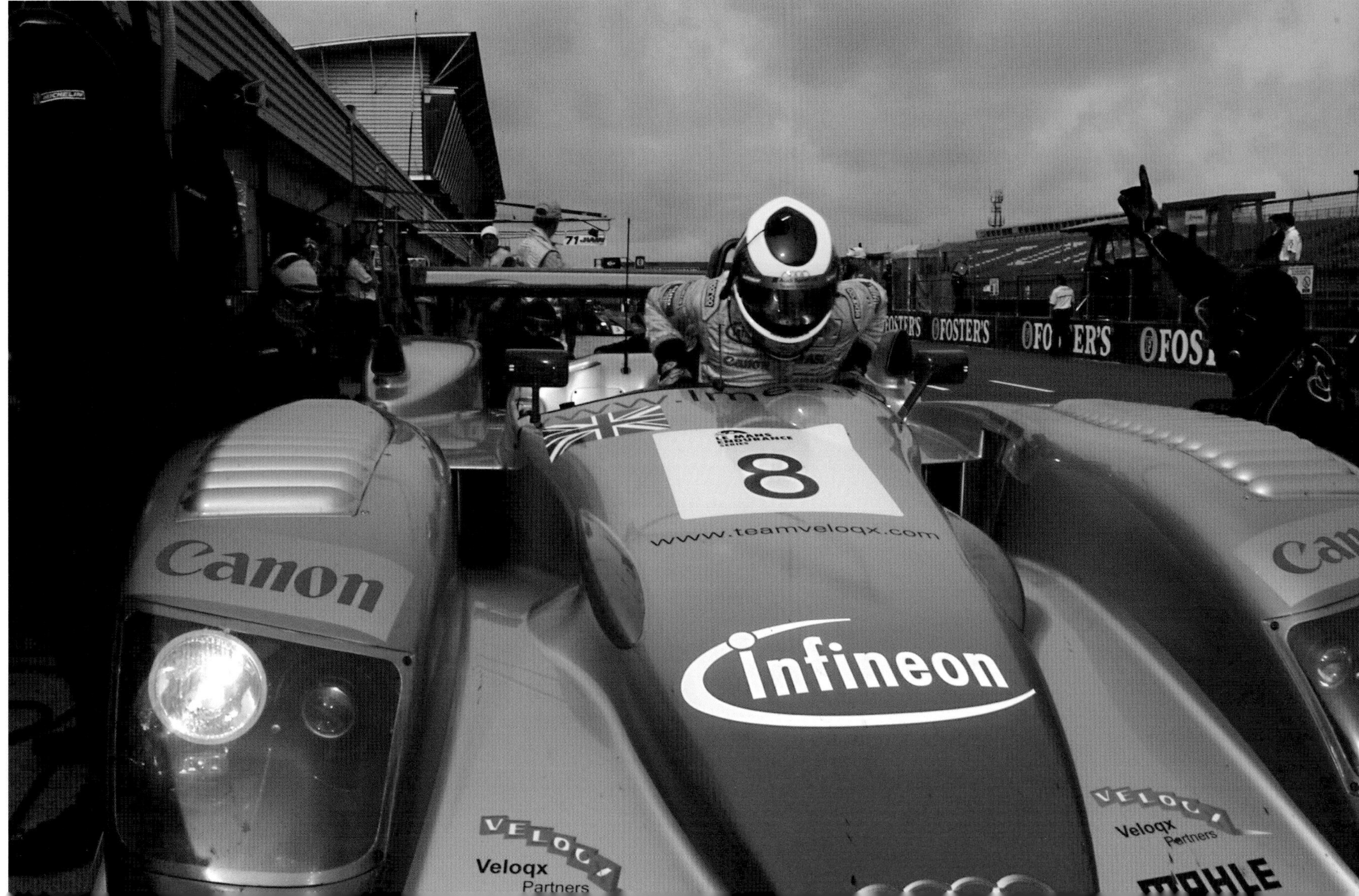

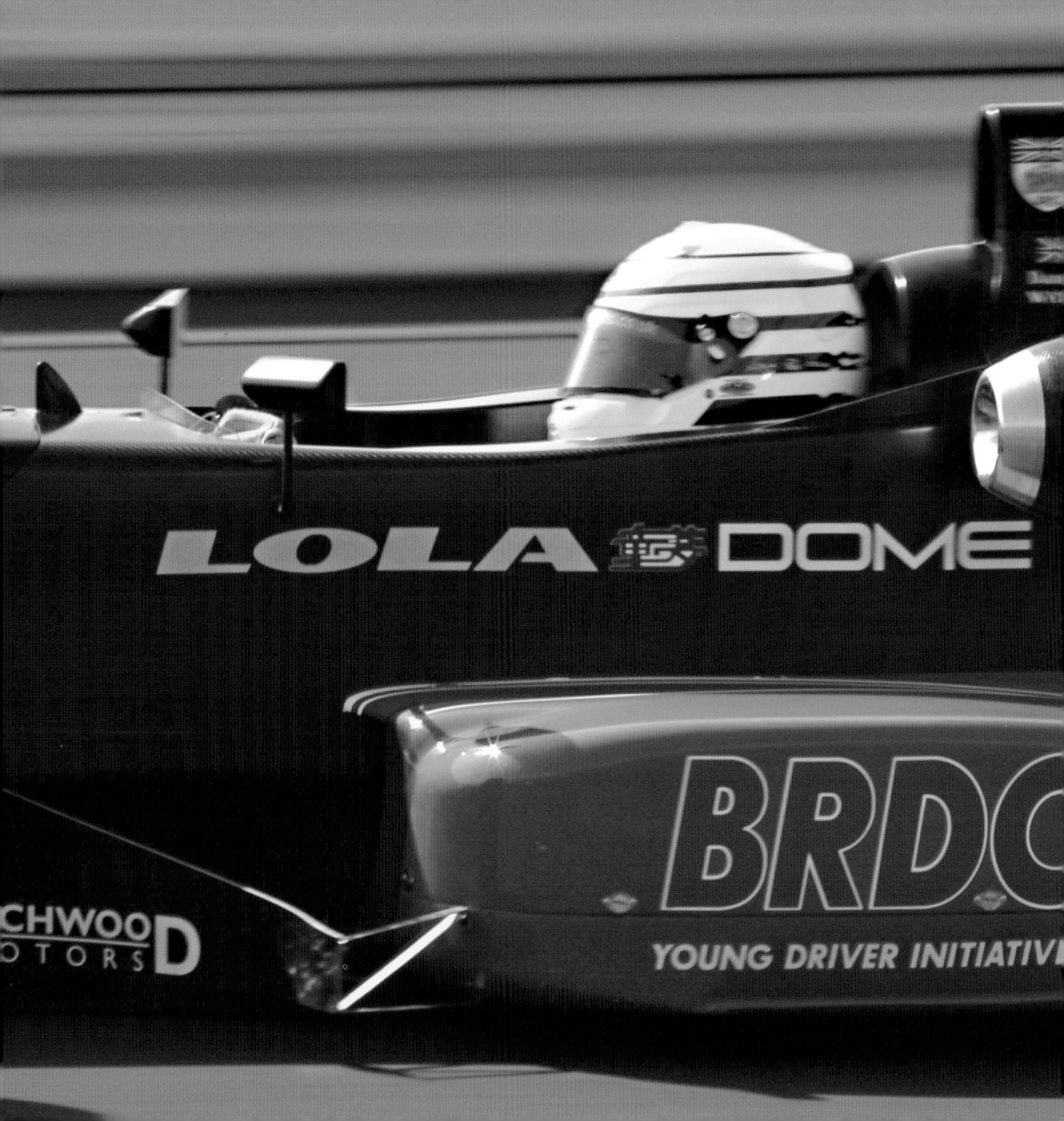

LOLA DOME
BRD
YOUNG DRIVER INITIATIV
CHWOOD
OTORS D

CHAPTER 3

Planning

Planning is a major factor in shooting successful motor sport photographs – not only deciding what events to visit or what shots you are going to take, but also what equipment you'll need, and your travel and accommodation requirements. Before the start of the motor sport season I sit down and spend a fair amount of time planning the coming 12 months. The primary consideration for me is to think about the type of images I want to take; with this in mind I can then look at the events calendar and plan how I am going to achieve my goal.

Rallying and off-road events often carry on throughout the year, usually with a month off around Christmas, whereas the circuit racing season gets under way in the spring and runs through until late autumn. I generally choose to cover national championship events, together with any UK-based rounds of international series. National events involve many professional teams and widely recognized competitors; these championships receive television coverage and generally provide plenty of spectacle from a photographic point of view.

When planning your season, do not confine yourself to your local racing circuit: this would drastically reduce the type and number of shots available to you. You can only do so much with one circuit – visiting a variety of circuits provides far wider opportunities for images, but this does mean that other factors, such as accommodation, have to be considered well in advance.

Camera	***Pentax Program A***
Focal length	***200mm***
Exposure	***1/250sec at f/8***
Film	***Kodak Elitechrome 100***

Motor sport events take place throughout the year and you should be prepared for all weather conditions. Although snow like this is a rarity in the UK it is more common in other parts of the world, so plan carefully for such eventualities and make sure you have the right equipment to protect both your camera and yourself.

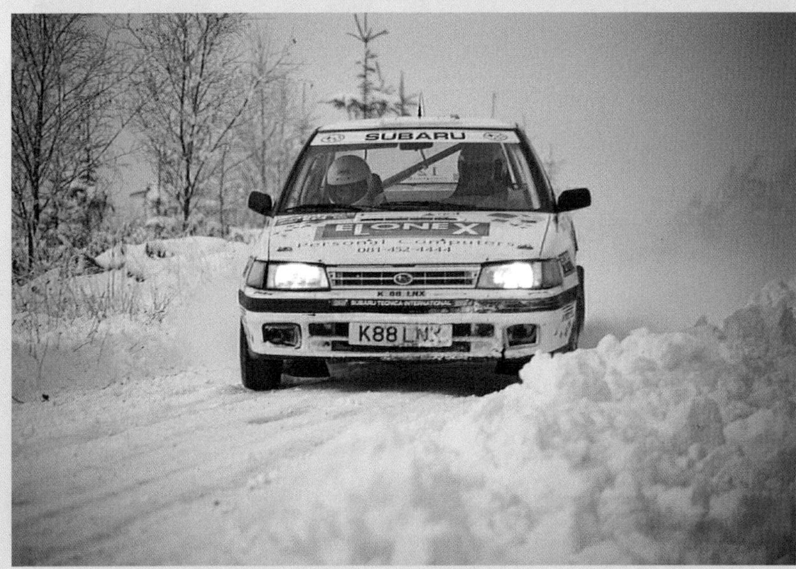

Sources of information

Online resources

The Internet is my main resource for planning a season's race photography. Before beginning my research I will already have a good idea of some of the main meetings I want to cover, but I don't make my final selection until I have had a look at the overall calendar of activities for the coming season. During the busy summer months events in differing disciplines often clash, so it is important to look at all the main dates and work back from these to ensure you can cover as much variety as possible.

While there are many websites that provide information about racing events – such as www.motorsport.com, www.crash.net and www.racer.com – the one I use most for my race planning is www.racedates.net. Here you will find international listings for a broad range of racing disciplines, with the racing calendar broken down into individual months to help you plan well in advance. In addition to this, all the major national championships have their own websites – often linked to the racedates.net site – so you can find information about the events, competitors and venues. Any of the major Internet search engines will direct you to a wealth of information about all sorts of motor sports.

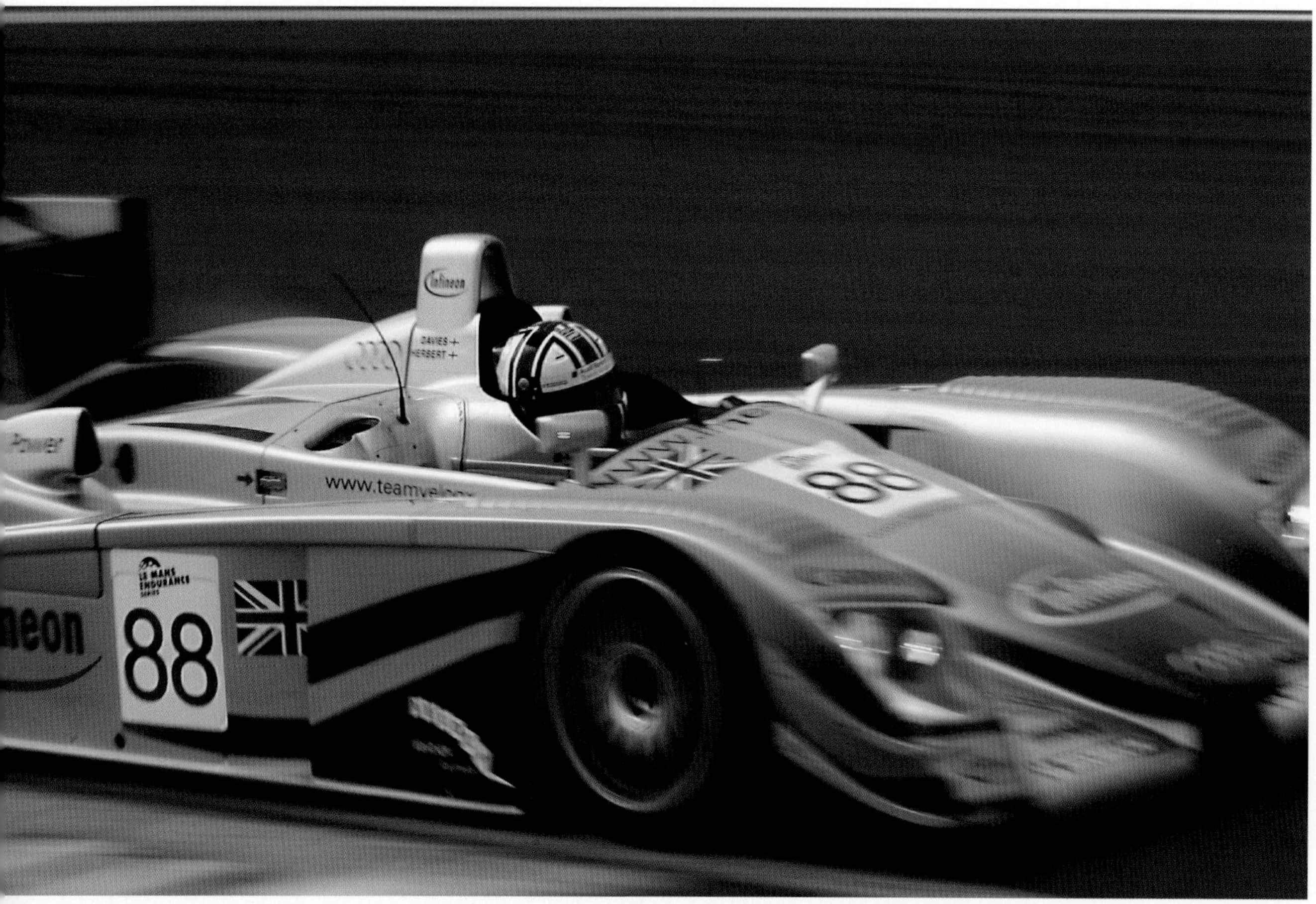

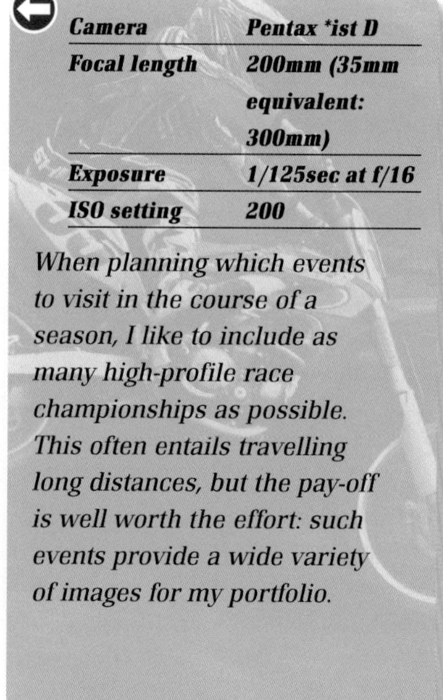

Camera	Pentax *ist D
Focal length	200mm (35mm equivalent: 300mm)
Exposure	1/125sec at f/16
ISO setting	200

When planning which events to visit in the course of a season, I like to include as many high-profile race championships as possible. This often entails travelling long distances, but the pay-off is well worth the effort: such events provide a wide variety of images for my portfolio.

Printed sources

You only have to look at the news-stands to see that there is a wide variety of weekly and monthly motor racing magazines covering all sorts of disciplines and championships. For car racing, for example, magazines such as *Autosport* and the US publication *Racer* contain news of all kinds of racing from Formula 1 to local clubman events. Similar publications for motorcycle racing are available; notable examples are *Motorcycle Racer* (UK), *Motorcycle News* and *MX Racing*.

Camera	***Pentax *ist D***
Focal length	***200mm (35mm equivalent: 300mm)***
Exposure	***1/125sec at f/11***
ISO setting	***200***

Race championship organizers often have websites which are a valuable source of information relating to their series, including details on teams and drivers as well as full race calendars. You can often find image galleries which may give you inspiration for your own work.

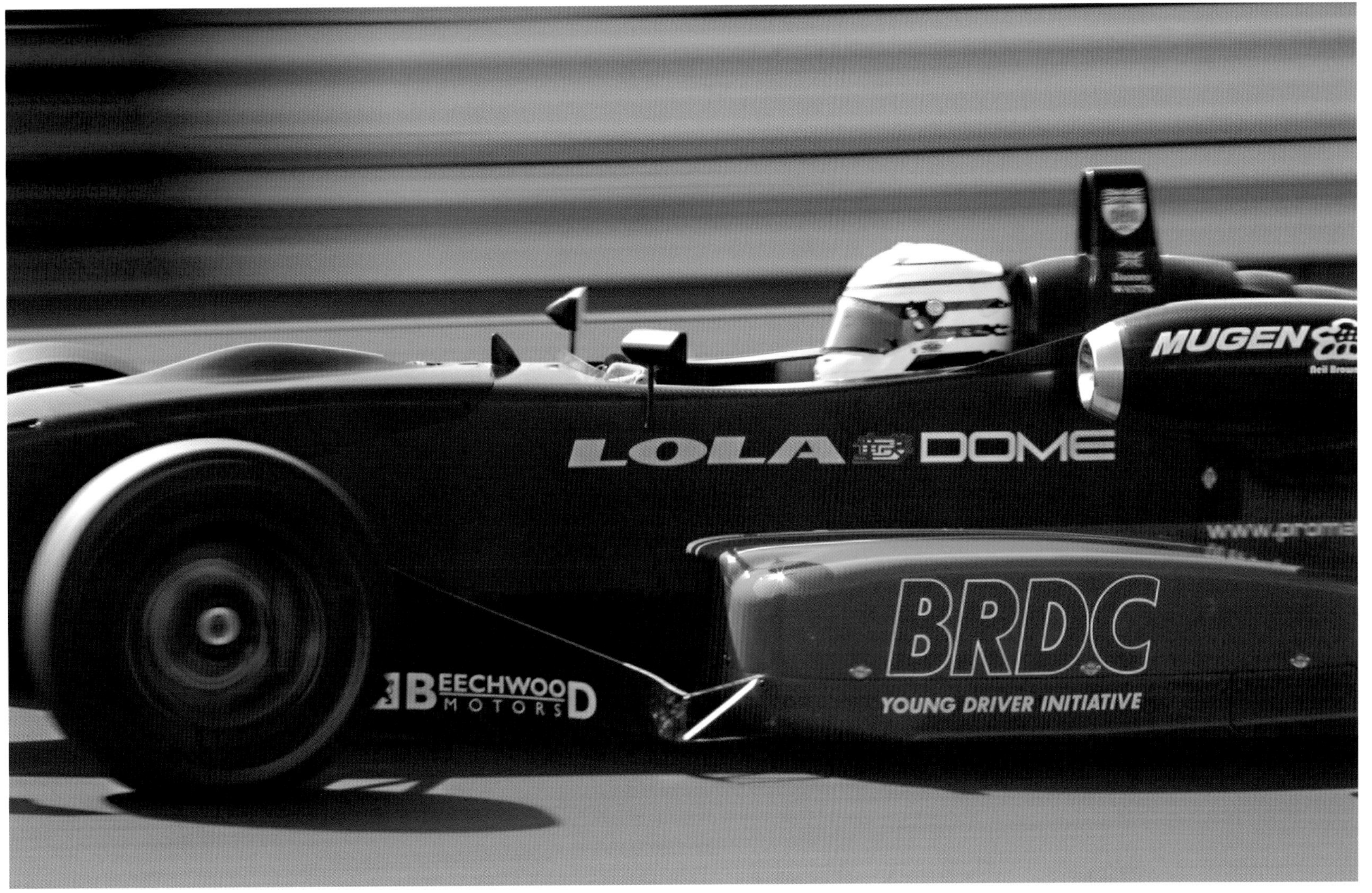

Choosing your events

If you don't have a press pass for an event (see pages 158–61), you will be shooting from the public areas, in which case planning which events to cover becomes doubly important.

There are certain racing circuits that provide the photographer with better access to the track than others, so if, for example, you want to cover a round of a particular championship, you should pencil in the events that are to be held at the more photographer-friendly circuits. On those weekends where the races take place at less accessible circuits, you could take the opportunity to go and shoot a different discipline which offers better photographer access, such as a forest rally or a motocross race.

Once you have a broad list of the race meetings you will be covering, it is important to book any accommodation you may need in plenty of time; hotels close to events soon get booked up, and if you don't get in early you will find you have to take accommodation further away from the venue. If you need help finding accommodation close to an event it's well worth contacting the local tourist information board, who will be able to point you in the right direction. Alternatively, many national hotel chains will have sites near to circuits, but these can prove more expensive.

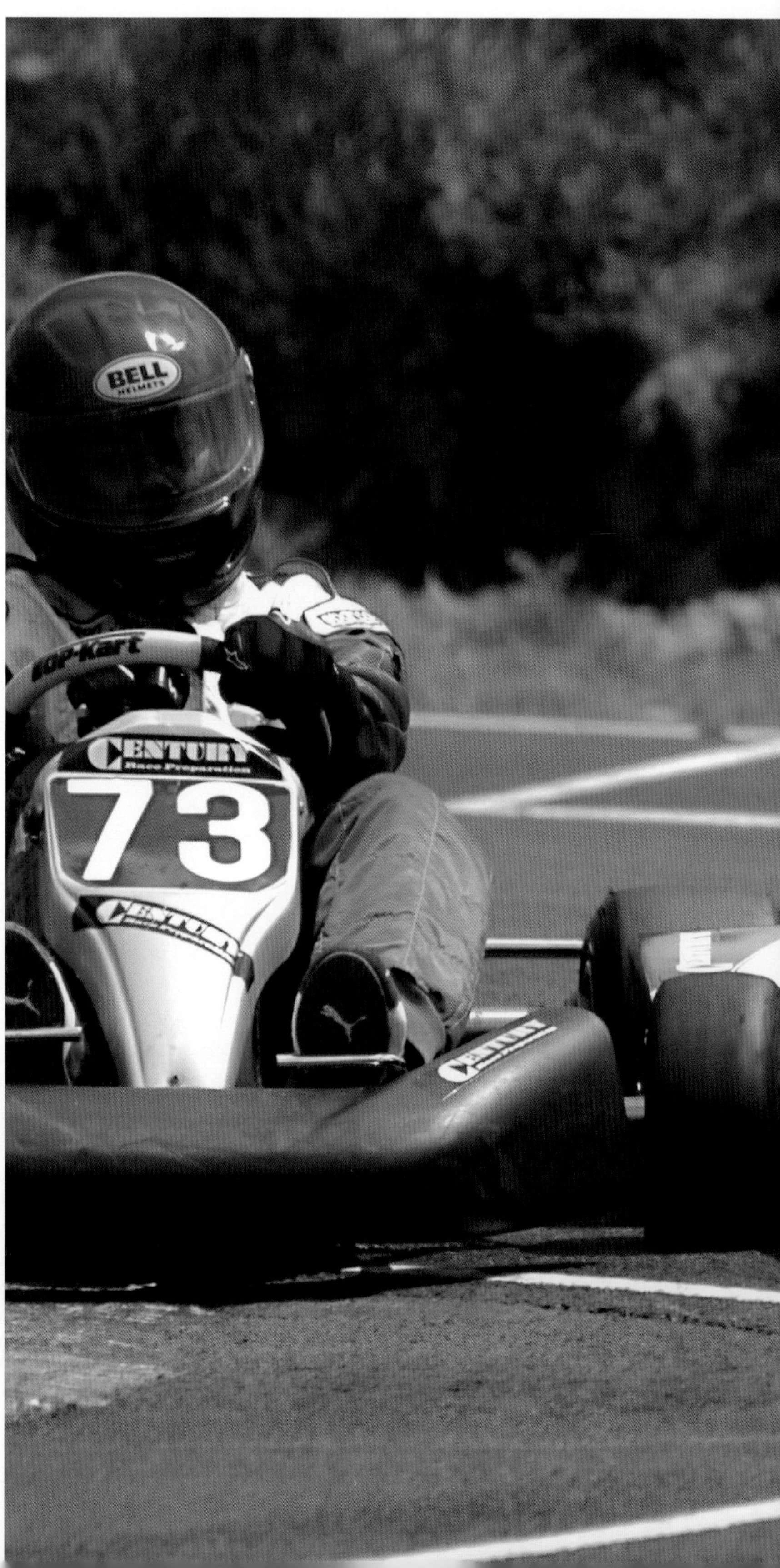

Camera	***Pentax *ist D***
Focal length	***170mm (35mm equivalent: 250mm)***
Exposure	***1/500sec at f/4.5***
ISO setting	***200***

Smaller events such as kart racing can provide good trackside access without the need for a press pass. There is plenty of high-octane action to photograph, as demonstrated by these two racers who came close to colliding as they vied for position in this corner.

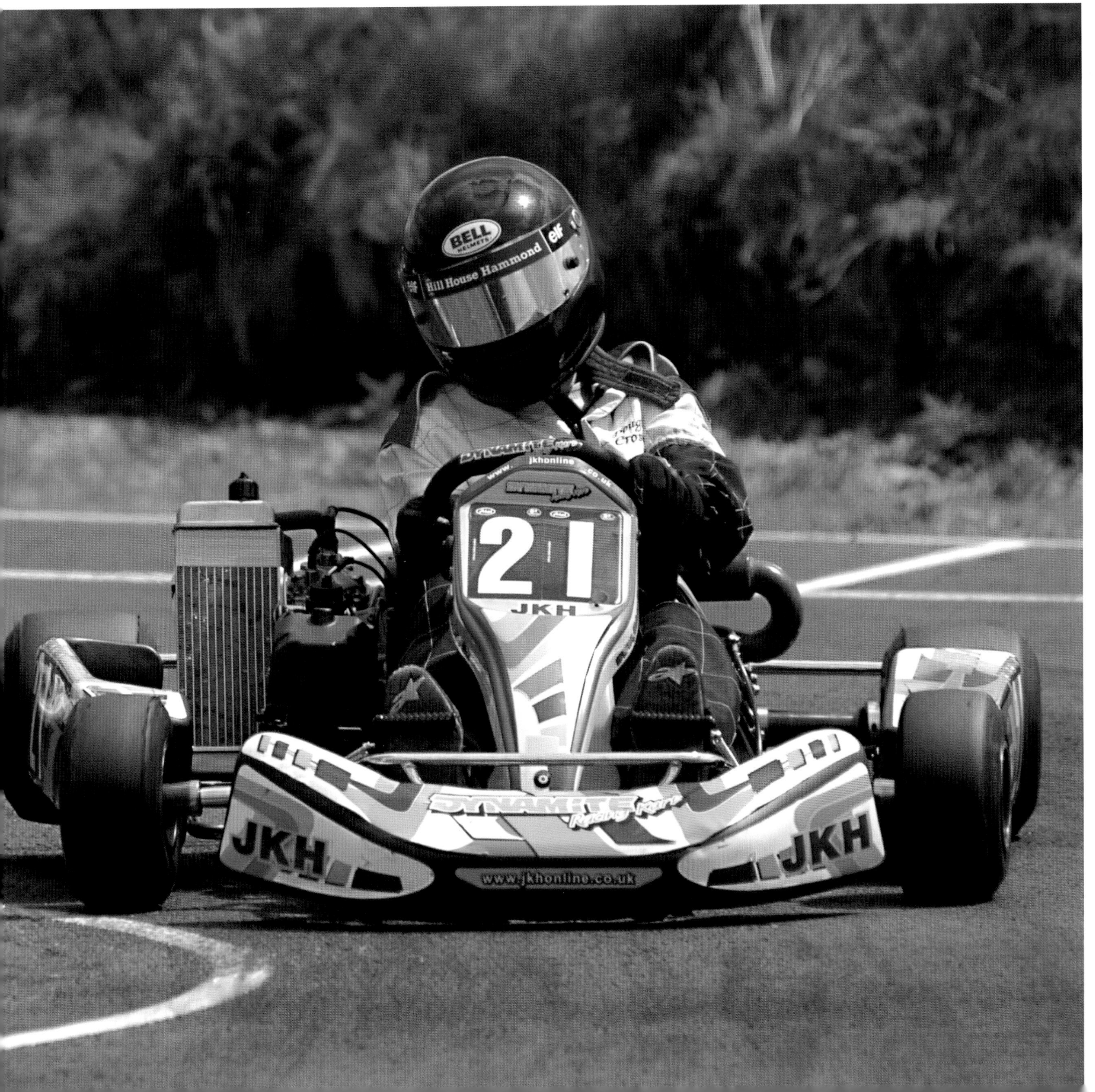
BELL
Hill House Hammond
elf
21
JKH
DYNAMITE
JKH
JKH
www.jkhonline.co.uk

Planning your shots

Planning the images you want to take is an important part of getting good motor racing photographs. This is especially necessary if you haven't visited the circuit before, as you may not be aware of the best places to take photographs from. For this reason it is always worth arriving early at a venue to give yourself plenty of time to look around and choose your viewpoints. However, I prefer to prepare further in advance by finding out more about the venue in the planning stages.

A good way of researching this is to use the Internet to view images that have been taken at the circuit at previous races. My favourite sites for this are generally those of the professional motor sport photo agencies, such as LAT (www.latphoto.co.uk), Sutton Images (www.sutton-images.com), Jakob Ebrey (www.jakobebrey.com) or Double Red (www.doublered.co.uk); but there are a number of other equally useful sites which can be found by using Internet search engines. This allows you to get an idea of the types of image you can expect to take at a particular venue – but bear in mind that it is important you develop your own style rather than simply replicating other people's images.

When planning the photographs I want to take, I try not to be influenced by pictures taken previously at that venue by others – I like to produce images that are unique to me and are representative of how I interpret a particular scene. However, it is always useful to take a critical look at another photographer's work; the comparison can be helpful when evaluating your own.

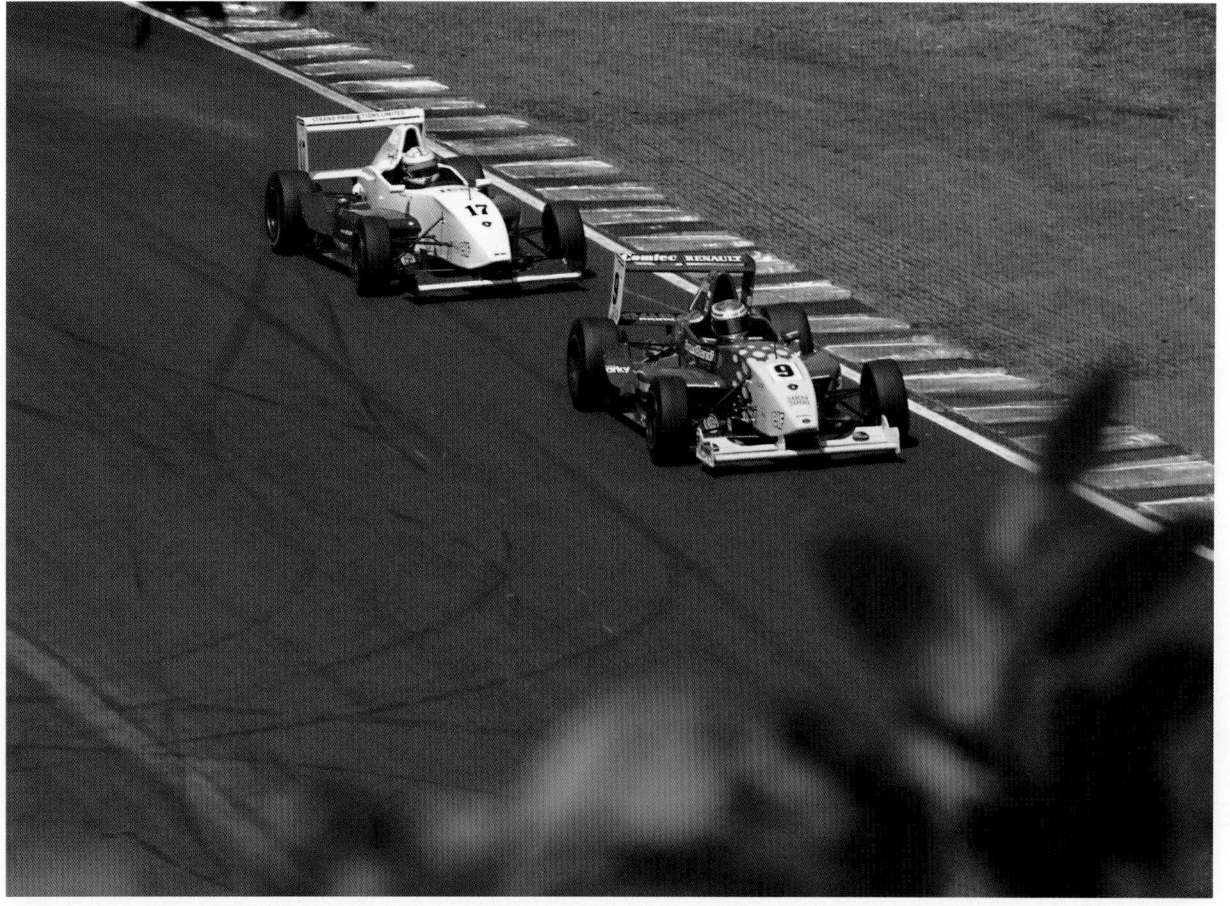

Camera	Pentax *ist D
Focal length	200mm (35mm equivalent: 300mm)
Exposure	1/350sec at f/9.5
ISO setting	200

Arriving at a venue in plenty of time allows you to have a good look around and search out photographic viewpoints. In this case, by standing on a small set of steps I was able to include the leaves of a tree in the foreground, adding a sense of depth to what would otherwise have been a fairly plain photograph.

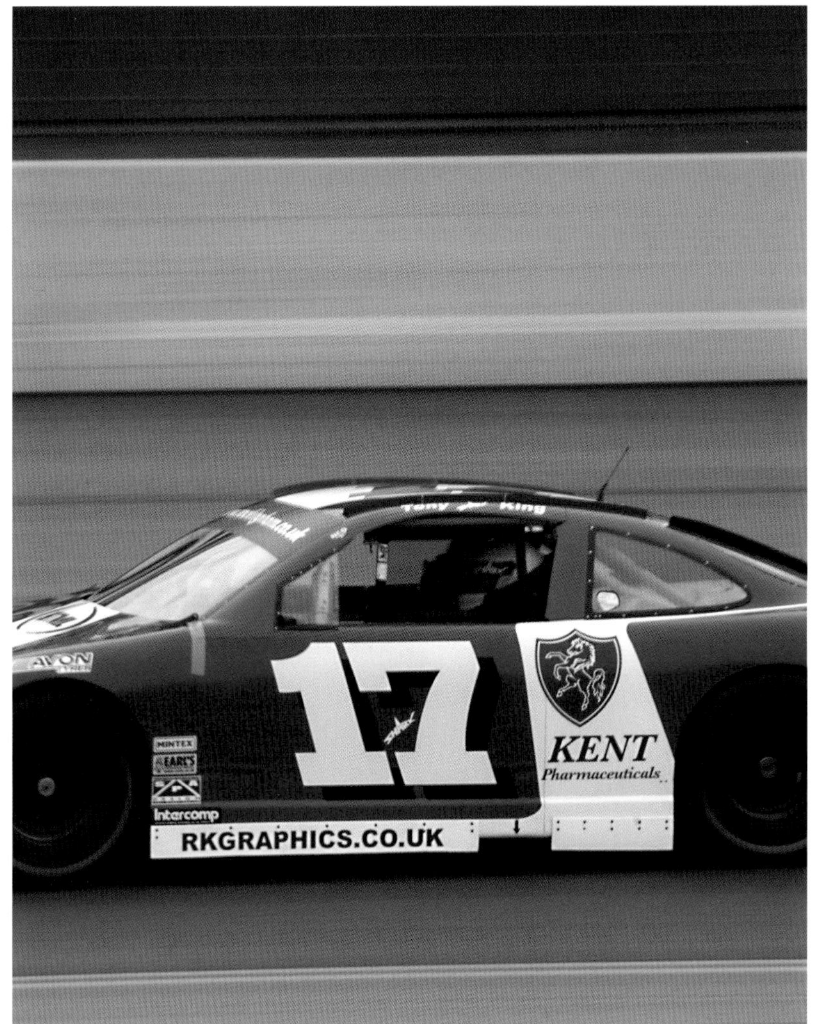

Camera	***Pentax *ist D***
Focal length	***190mm (35mm equivalent: 285mm)***
Exposure	***1/60sec at f/11***
ISO setting	***200***

Before arriving at the venue I had already planned to produce an image that would include the concrete wall and high barrier fencing that are so characteristic of oval racing. Holding the camera in the portrait position and carefully framing the car to include both front and rear wheels, I panned the shot at a slow shutter speed (see pages 88-9); the blurred fencing adds to the impact of the image.

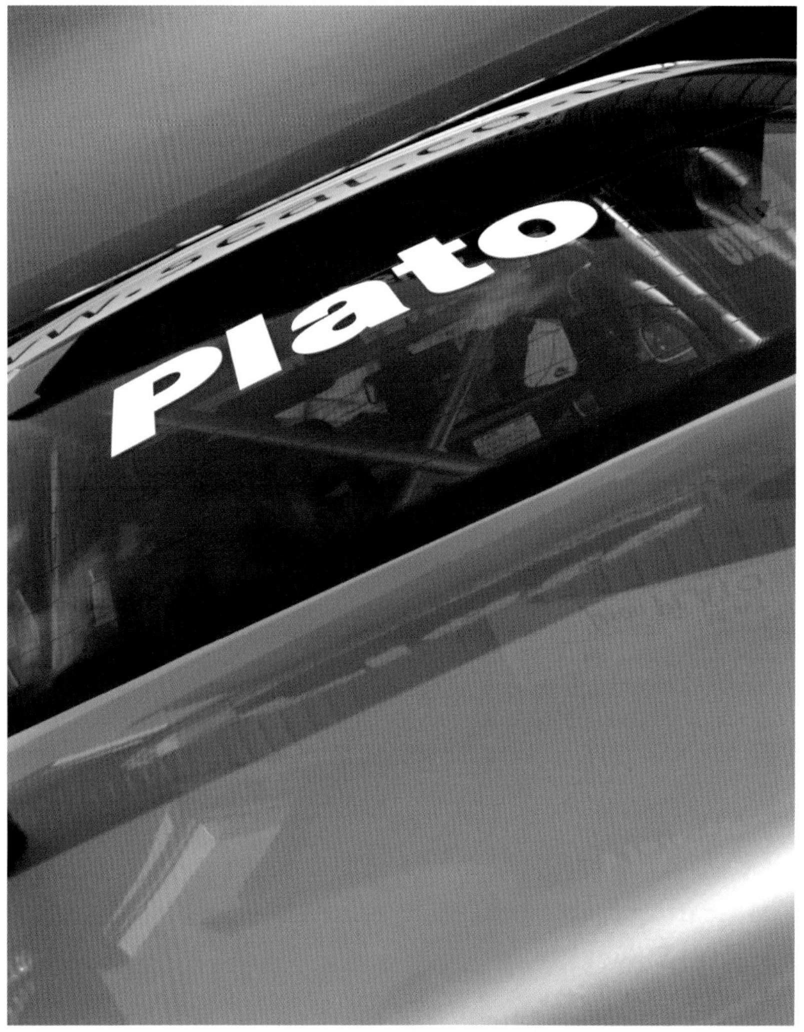

Camera	***Pentax *ist D***
Focal length	***18mm (35mm equivalent: 28mm)***
Exposure	***1/90sec at f/16***
ISO setting	***200***

Though it's always useful to look at other photographers' images, try not to be influenced too much by these – look for images that represent the subject as you see it. This will help you to develop your own style that will differentiate you from other photographers, and will sometimes lead to quirky shots like this one.

The wish list

I find it useful to make a list in advance of the type of images I want to take at a particular event – a wish list of shots, bearing in mind the type of racing involved. This list will not be definitive – I can't be sure at this stage of the exact shot I want to take – but it gives me a basis on which I can start to build ideas. This means that once I am at the event I already have a structure to work from; I find this helps me to develop images and keeps me thinking creatively about what I want to achieve.

I generally split images down into categories along these lines:

- **action full frame**
- **action whole subject**
- **action wide**
- **pits and paddock**
- **detail studies**
- **slow shutter speeds**
- **driver portraits**
- **experiments.**

Giving consideration to the type of event I'm attending, I will jot down a few ideas for each category and spend a little time thinking about how I'll go about getting the shot I want. By preparing like this I get my mind into 'image mode', and even if I don't adhere to my wish list it does get me thinking about the compositions I want to capture.

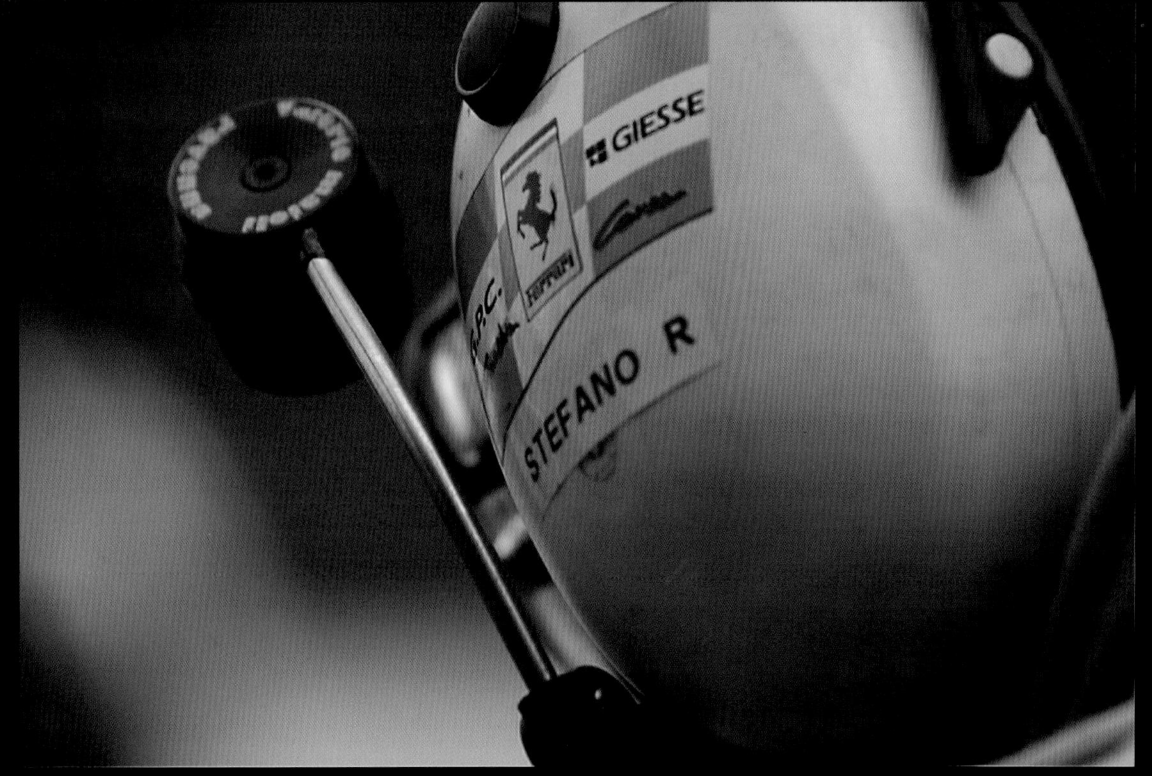

Camera	***Pentax *ist D***
Focal length	***200mm (35mm equivalent: 300mm)***
Exposure	***1/500sec at f/5.6***
ISO setting	***200***

Before attending a race I plan a number of shots that I want to take. In this case I wanted to capture some 'arty' images from the pit lane during a GT endurance race. I used a long telephoto lens to fill the frame with the mechanic's earphone, and a wide aperture to provide very shallow depth of field (see page 99) and prevent the background intruding on the image.

Preparing your equipment

Before you set off it is well worth taking the time to make sure your equipment is all clean and in good working order. As I normally use a D-SLR, I always check that the batteries are fully charged and I have a supply of spare ones in my bag. Another consideration with digital cameras is to ensure that the sensor is clean: sensors attract dust particles and can easily become dirty when you change lenses at an event, so it is very important to make sure you at least begin the weekend with a clean sensor.

When I first started using a digital camera I was very wary of cleaning the sensor myself, but having taken advice from the manufacturer I bought a pack of cleaning fluid and wipe pads which, as long as you follow the instructions, appear to do an excellent job. In view of the ease with which dust particles gather on a sensor, try to avoid changing lenses too often in the field; in an ideal world one would have a couple of digital bodies to reduce lens changing even further, and this is certainly my plan for the future. In the mean time, I make sure that when changing lenses I find a spot which is sheltered from any breeze, and keep the camera body facing downwards in order to keep dust out as much as possible.

Remember also to bring protective filters for your lenses, as discussed on page 31.

Camera	***Pentax *ist D***
Focal length	***110mm (35mm equivalent: 165mm)***
Exposure	***1/30sec at f/32***
ISO setting	***200***

I was really pleased with this shot when I first viewed it through my camera's display; only when I downloaded it onto my laptop during the lunch break did I realize that I'd allowed dirt to get onto my camera's sensor while changing lenses. You can see that the image is covered in specks of dirt; although these could be removed in an image-editing application such as PhotoShop, it is a time-consuming process and far from ideal. This was my first experience of getting dirt on a sensor, and since then I have become very careful when changing lenses.

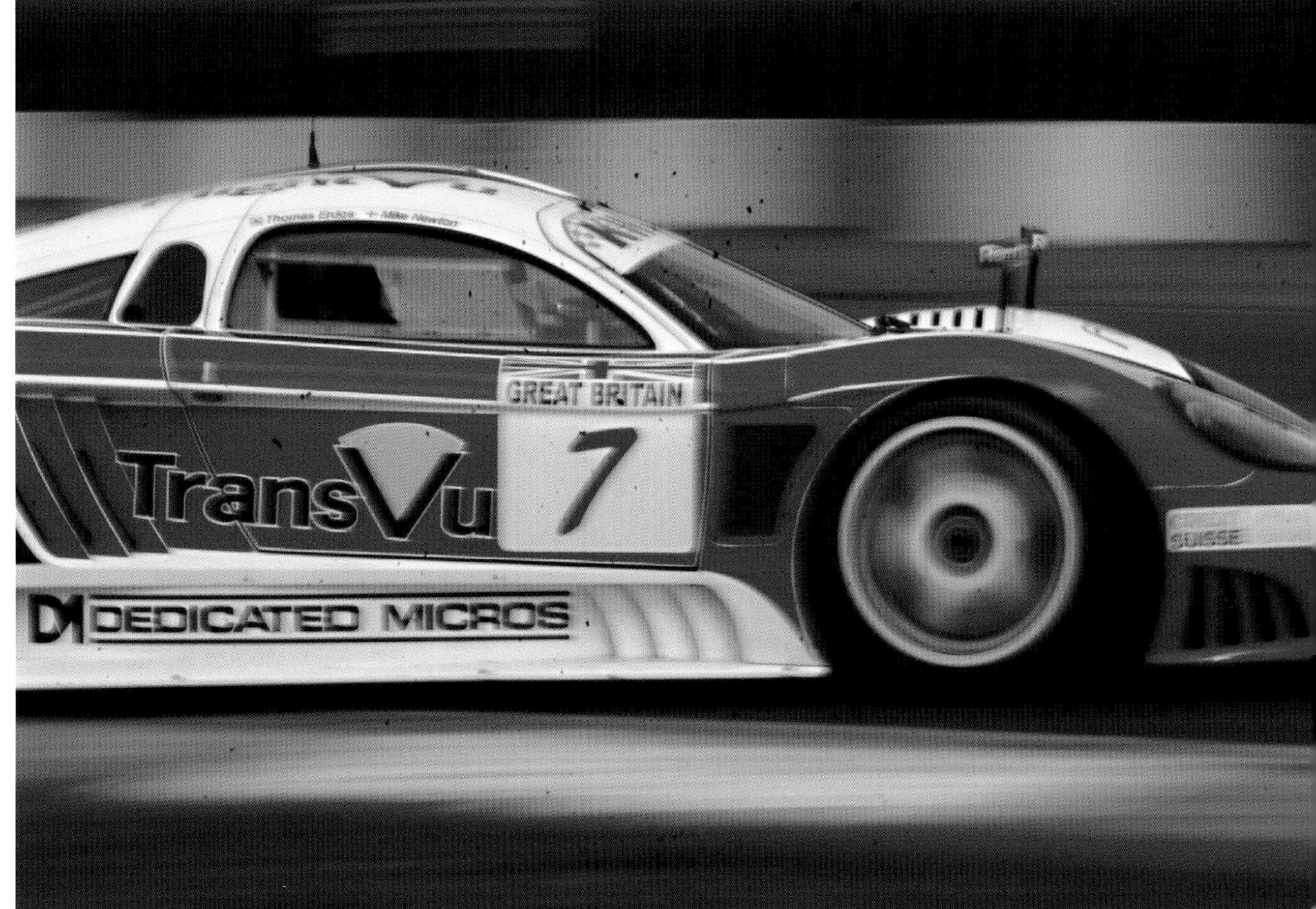

Backing up

I also carry a laptop computer to all events so that I can download my images at regular intervals. I do this during breaks in racing. This not only provides a secure back-up of my work, but also allows me to review the images I have taken. Before every event I always make sure the laptop battery is fully charged, as you can't guarantee access to a mains power source at the venue. Shooting digitally requires much more reliance on power sources than when shooting with a film camera; this can be a problem if you are not fully prepared, but if you have planned properly it should not be an issue. Nevertheless I always take 35mm cameras with me as a back-up, more for peace of mind than anything else. To date I have not encountered a situation when I have needed to use them, but you can be sure that on the first occasion that I leave my 35mm gear behind, I will need it.

Camera	***Pentax *ist D***
Focal length	***135mm (35mm equivalent: 200mm)***
Exposure	***1/1000sec at f/4***
ISO setting	***200***

Race teams and competitors spend a great deal of time prior to an event making sure their cars and equipment are in good working order. The same principles apply to the photographer. It doesn't take long to make sure your equipment is clean and fully functioning before setting off for a race meeting. Light filtering through an awning gave this picture its odd colour cast.

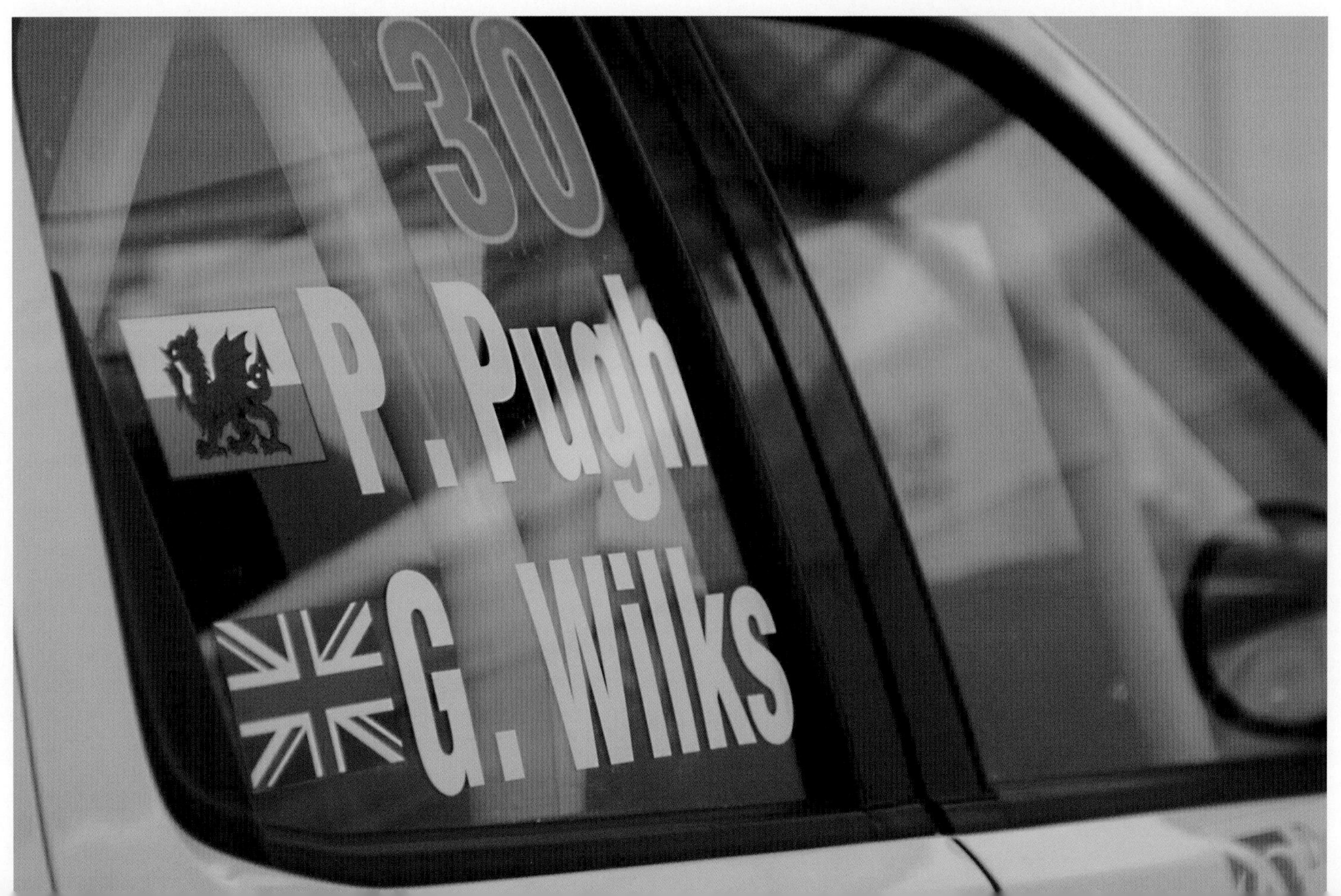

Beating the weather

Although I check the weather forecast before setting off, I always take the necessary clothing for all eventualities – having the foresight to pack wet-weather gear on a weekend when no rain was forecast has saved me a wetting on many occasions. More importantly, if you have the right clothing you can concentrate on getting the shots you want rather than having to worry about keeping your camera clean and dry.

Cameras and cold

Low temperatures can reduce battery lifetimes, so if your camera relies on batteries it is important to keep it stored in a bag or inside a jacket when you're not shooting. However, be aware that condensation can affect lenses (and films, to a lesser extent) when they are moved between warm and cold environments. Keep them well wrapped up until they have had time to acclimatize.

Camera	***Pentax *ist D***
Focal length	***160mm (35mm equivalent: 240mm)***
Exposure	***1/125sec at f/11***
ISO setting	***200***

Weather conditions can cause problems for a photographer who is not fully prepared. A poncho is good to protect you from the rain, and provides a shelter for your camera; using it like a mini-tent allows you to change films or memory cards in the dry. A quality chamois leather is also a useful accessory when shooting in the rain: draping it over the body and lens keeps your camera dry – but be careful not to let it fall in front of the lens.

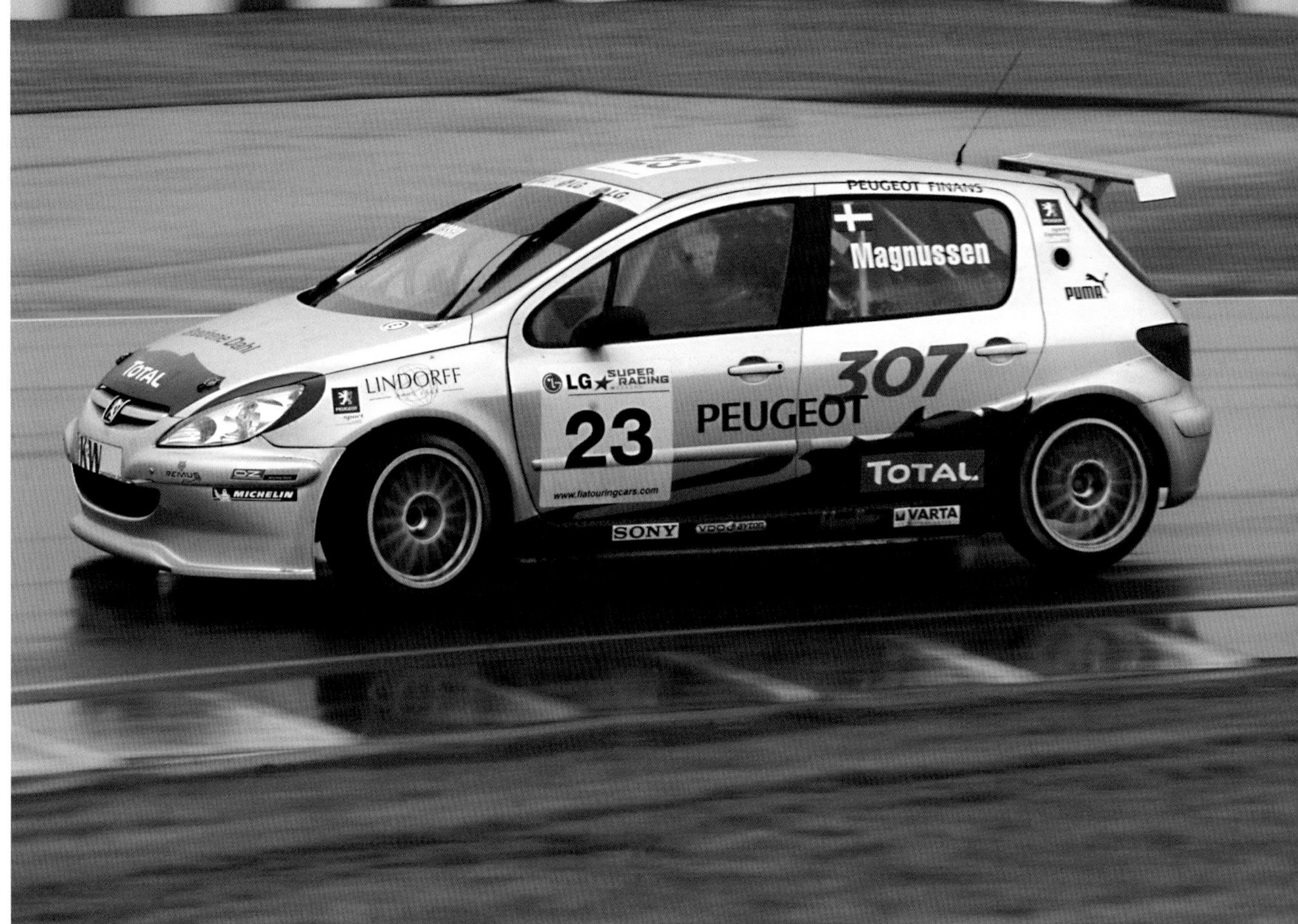

Knowing who's who

As part of the planning process you should make the effort to get to know who the key competitors are in any given discipline. There are many different magazines and websites that profile competitors, as well as television coverage for most of the major national and international racing championships. Understanding who the competitors are and where they stand in a championship can help you to plan your images. Television also helps you to learn about a discipline and builds understanding of the characteristics of the particular sport. By immersing yourself in the coverage of racing events you become much more aware of the way in which the sport works, and I find this of great benefit when attending an event.

Camera	**Pentax *ist D**
Focal length	**170mm (35mm equivalent: 250mm)**
Exposure	**1/500sec at f/4**
ISO setting	**200**

Well-known racing drivers are certainly the easiest to spot, but as a consequence of their popularity they are often mobbed by autograph hunters while in the paddock. I managed to grab this shot of Allan McNish in a quiet moment while he spoke to one of his team; my only disappointment is that I couldn't crop out the team member's arm.

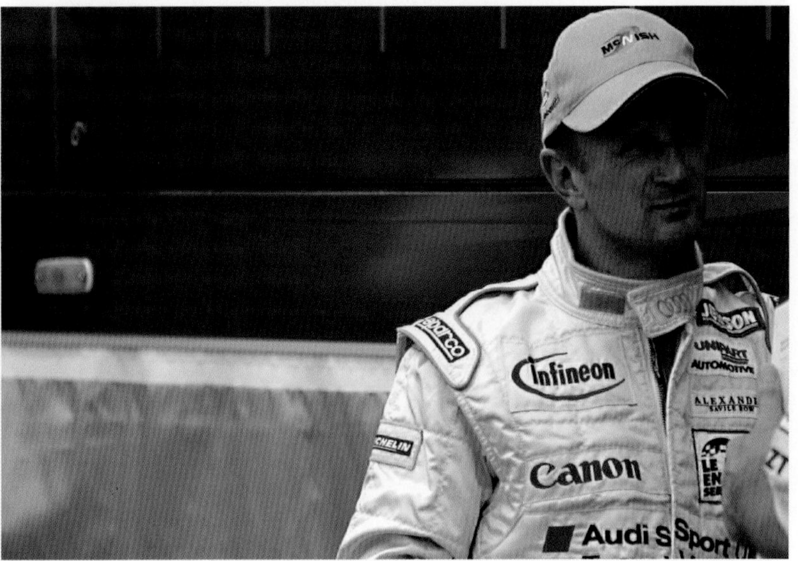

Camera	**Pentax *ist D**
Focal length	**135mm (35mm equivalent: 200mm)**
Exposure	**1/750sec at f/4.5**
ISO setting	**200**

Knowing who are the key competitors at a race is helpful when you're walking around the paddock looking for images; you will often have to 'grab' shots as drivers go about their business. I chose to include the journalist's shoulder and microphone in this image, but used a wide aperture to throw them out of focus.

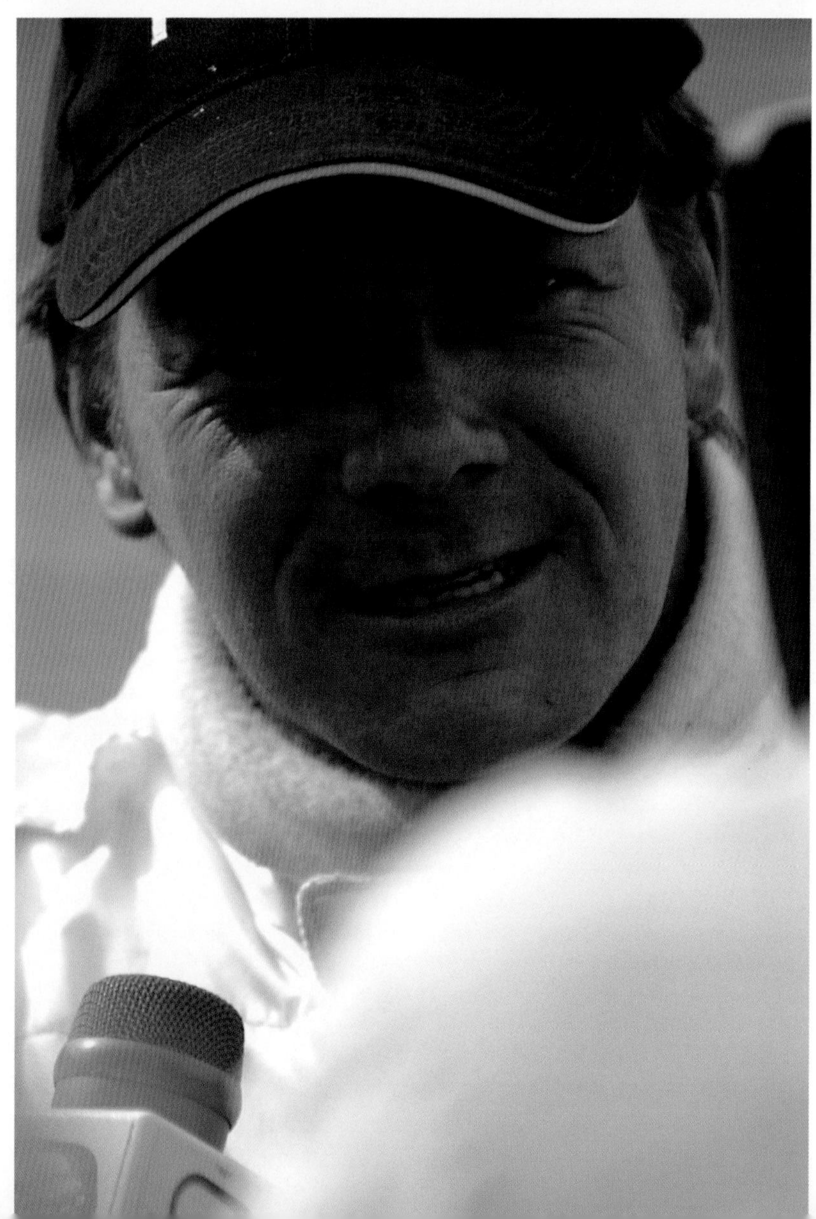

It is also worth taking a little time to get to know some of the key people who may be able to help you out with your photography needs. Though most team personnel are perfectly approachable, it is important that you choose your moment wisely – they won't have much time to stand and chat if they are busy preparing a vehicle or if they have a competitor out on the track. Wait for a lull in the activity if you want to get their full attention.

As with any branch of photography, having a genuine knowledge and understanding of the subject greatly improves your chances of producing good-quality images; it is well worth putting in the time and effort to learn how each sport works.

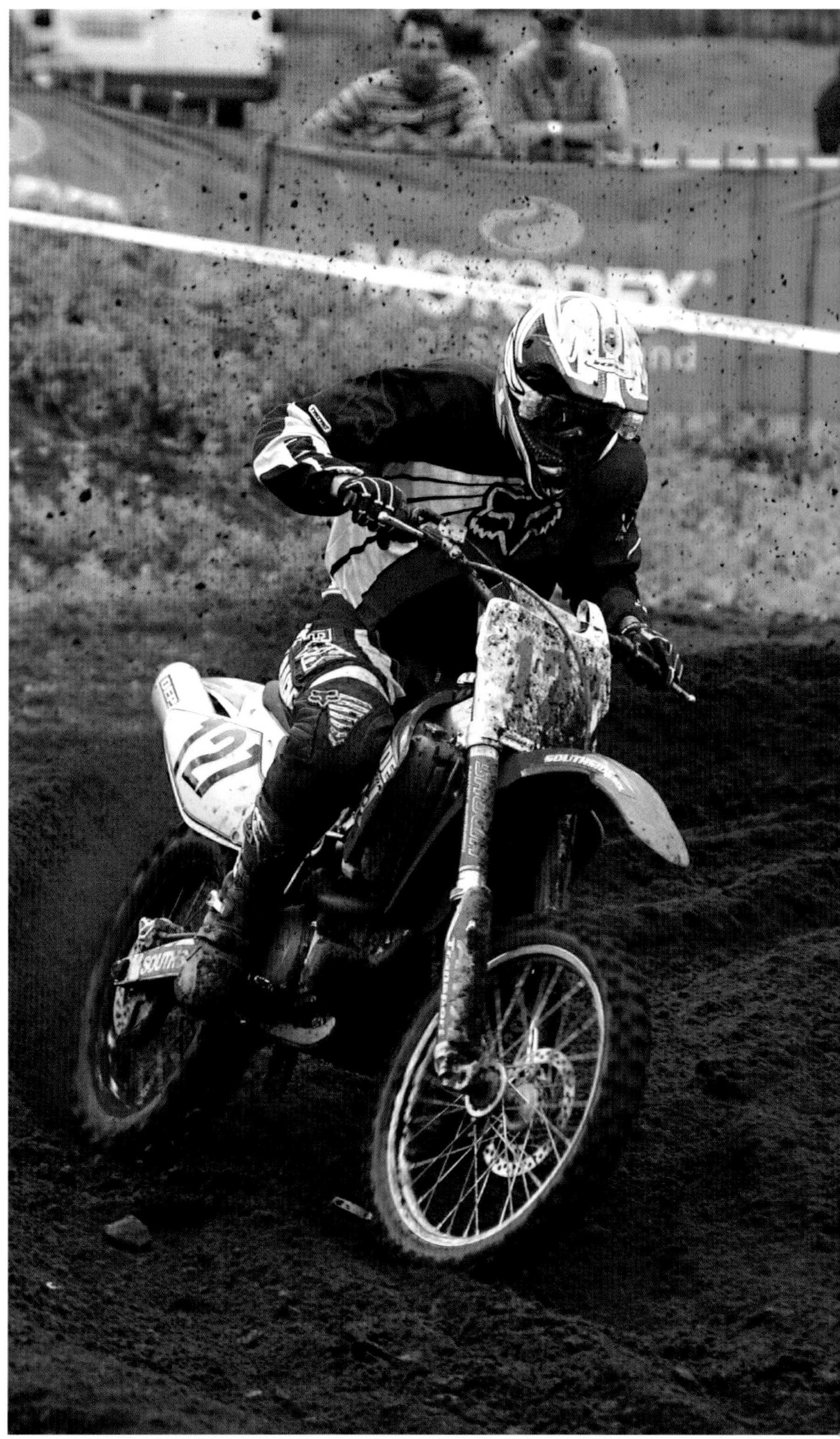

Camera	***Pentax *ist D***
Focal length	***135mm (35mm equivalent: 200mm)***
Exposure	***1/350sec at f/4.5***
ISO setting	***200***

Motocross is one of my favourite motor sport subjects, offering plenty of action combined with relatively easy access, so I always plan a few meetings into my calendar. To date I have not felt the need to apply for a media pass when attending these races, as you can generally get good access to the action without one; it therefore provides excellent opportunities for the amateur and professional alike.

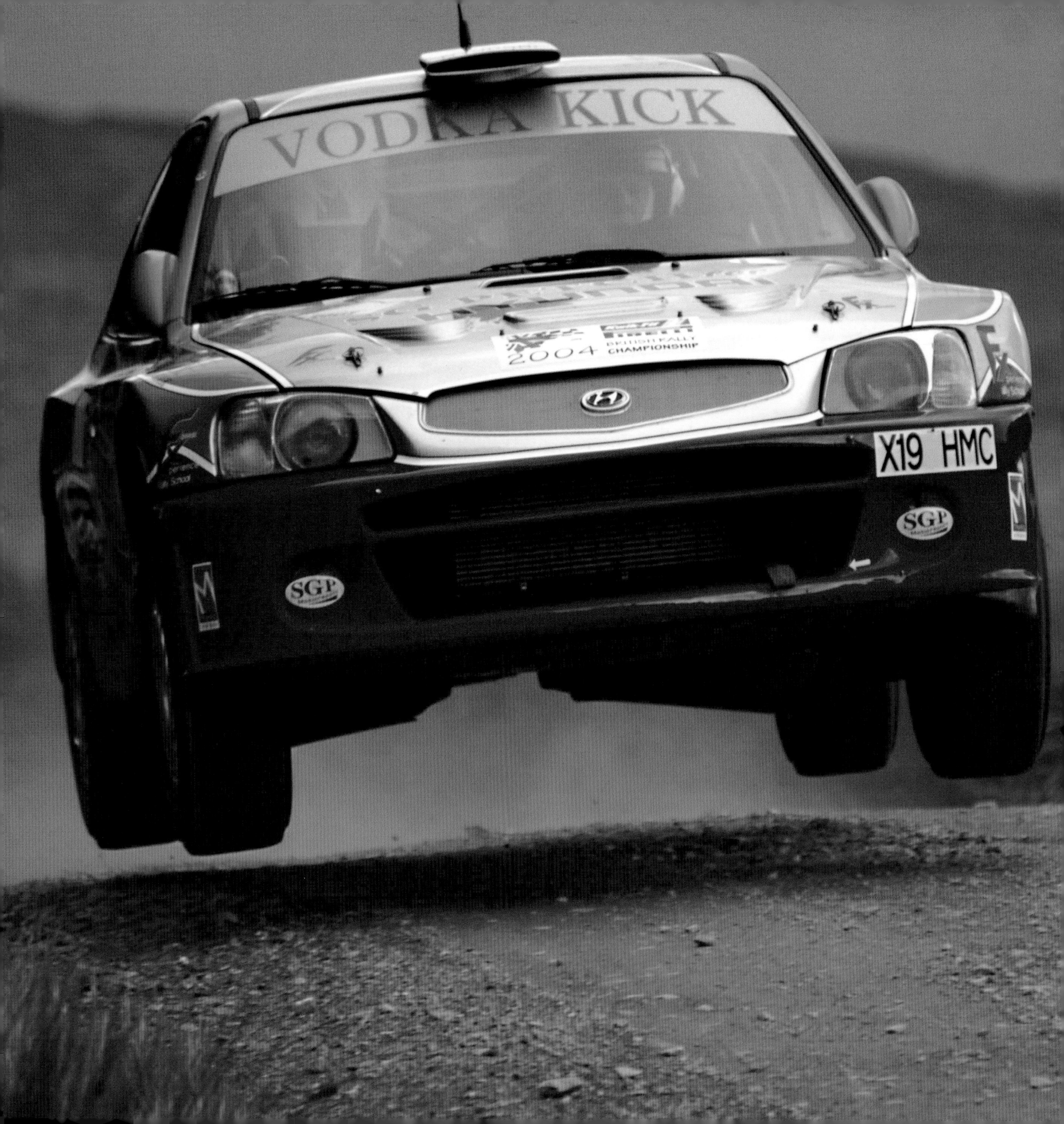
VODKA KICK
2004
CHAMPIONSHIP
X19 HMC
SGP
SGP

CHAPTER 4

Camera technique

Many factors combine to make a successful motor racing image, including lens choice, shutter speed, aperture, lighting and composition. Without knowledge and skill in each of these areas you are unlikely to produce images of a consistently high standard.

It is all too easy to look at published racing pictures and say to yourself that you could have done as well or better if you'd had the high-end equipment that professionals use – but the equipment you have is not nearly as important as the way in which you use it. Professionals rely on skills and knowledge that they have built up over time by applying themselves to their craft. There is nothing to stop anyone becoming a successful professional – it's just a matter of time and effort. Remember, most professionals were amateurs once, and they will have faced many of the challenges presented to amateurs today.

In order to produce consistently high-quality motor sport images it is essential that you fully understand your camera and its functions. The control of exposure time, aperture and light is the key to all photographic technique, whether conventional or digital, and there is no amount of technological wizardry that can do this for you without compromising your images in some way.

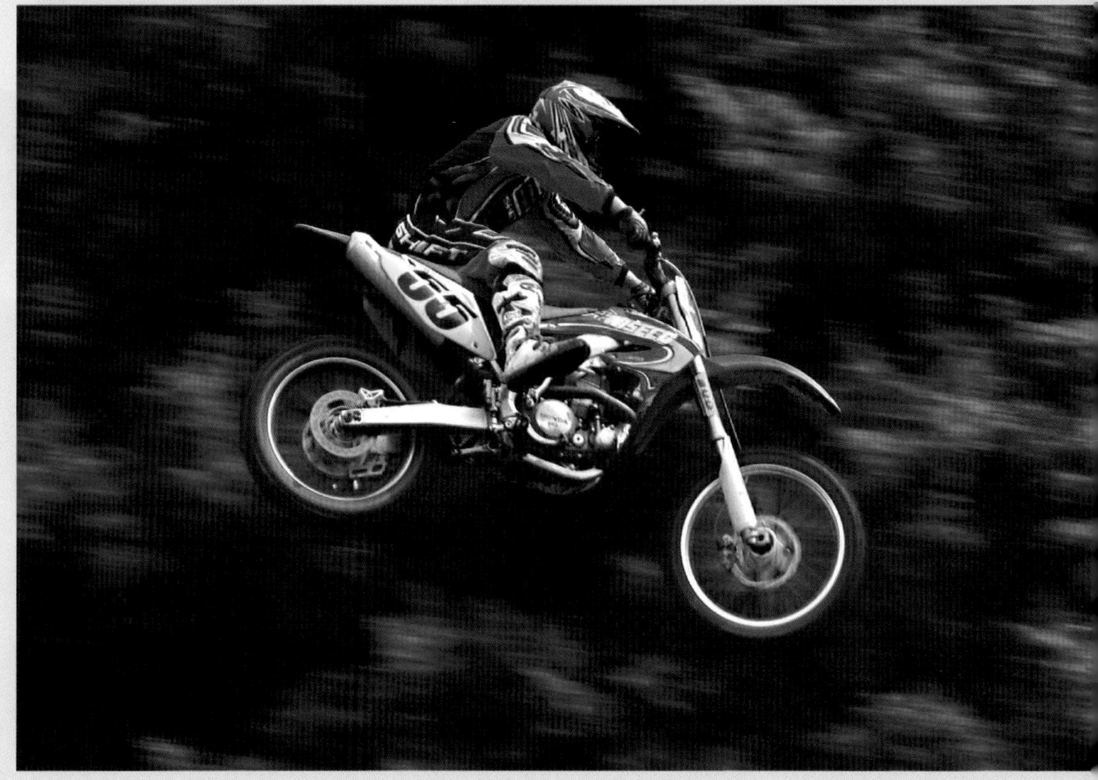

Camera	**Pentax *ist D**
Focal length	**210mm (35mm equivalent: 315mm)**
Exposure	**1/90sec at f/13**
ISO setting	**200**

Motocross events provide excellent opportunities for good action shots. For this one I pre-focused on the ground below the point where the rider would pass, and then made fine adjustments to the focusing as the bike flew through the air. Selecting a slow shutter speed and panning with the rider blurred the trees in the background, adding to the impression of speed. Firing the shutter as the rider's foot came off the foot peg adds to the excitement of the composition.

Metering and exposure

Like many people, my interest in photography blossomed when I got my hands on my first 35mm SLR camera, a low-budget East German Praktica that my father bought me for my 14th birthday. It was a manual-only camera with very basic metering and no fancy program modes, and to this day I still think it was the best camera I have ever owned because I learned so much while using it. Maybe I see the past through rose-tinted spectacles, but the experience gained by using a basic manual camera has stood me in good stead over the years, and the skills learned then are just as important today.

Modern SLRs now come with a range of exposure controls, which usually include at least manual, aperture priority, shutter priority and program modes. Of these four I generally only use two: shutter priority and manual. I will occasionally use aperture priority, but never use the fully automated program mode.

Exposure basics

The amount of light reaching the film is determined by a combination of the aperture (the size of the adjustable opening in the lens, measured in f-stops; see page 28) and the shutter speed (the length of time that the shutter remains open, measured in seconds or – more usually – fractions of a second). A doubling of the amount of light reaching the film is defined as a one-stop increase in exposure; a halving of the light is a one-stop decrease. You can increase exposure by widening the aperture or reducing the shutter speed; you decrease exposure by narrowing the aperture or increasing the shutter speed. Under most circumstances there is a reciprocal relation between aperture and shutter speed, so that, for example, a one-stop increase in aperture combined with a one-stop increase in shutter speed results in the same overall exposure as before. This useful fact allows you to select – within limits – the aperture and shutter speed that will give the effect you want. Changing the aperture chiefly affects depth of field (see page 99); the effects of different shutter speeds are considered in this section.

Exposure modes explained

Aperture priority: This mode allows you to select the aperture size (the f-stop setting), while the camera automatically selects the correct shutter speed.

Shutter priority: The opposite of aperture priority: you set the required shutter speed while the camera selects the aperture size.

Program: A fully automatic mode where the camera sets both aperture and shutter speed. Modern cameras often have a number of different **pre-set modes** such as Sport (or Action), Portrait or Landscape. Generally the camera selects a 'middle-ground' setting for both aperture and shutter speed.

Manual: You have full manual control over both aperture and shutter speed. Symbols in the viewfinder tell you when your exposure is correct according to the camera's built-in meter.

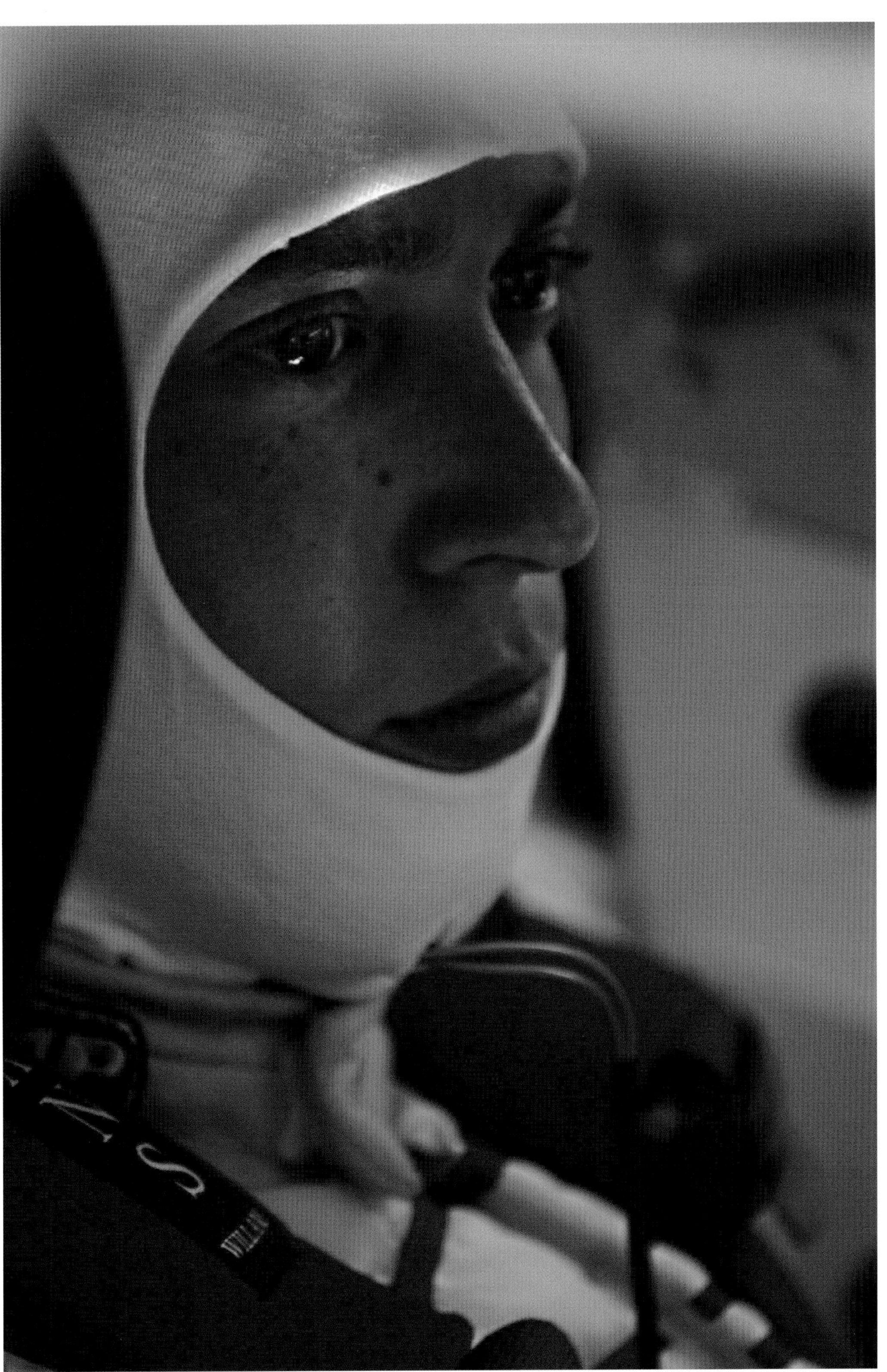

Camera	Pentax *ist D
Focal length	200mm (35mm equivalent: 300mm)
Exposure	1/500sec at f/4
ISO setting	200

Using your camera in aperture priority mode you can quickly control depth of field (see page 99) by altering the aperture while looking through the viewfinder. Selecting a wide aperture provides very shallow depth of field, blurring out the roof of the car and highlighting the concentration on the driver's face. I had very little time to grab this shot before a mechanic shut the passenger door.

Shutter priority

For the majority of action images I use the shutter priority mode – in which the shutter speed is chosen by the user and the aperture is set automatically by the camera – because shutter speeds have the most influence on how much 'motion' an image shows. For example, if you are shooting a car from the side as it passes by, and you want the car to remain sharp while the background and wheels are blurred, you can set a slowish shutter speed and pan the camera, while the camera's metering system takes care of the aperture size. Conversely, if you want to 'freeze' a motorcycle as it comes towards you, you will need a faster shutter speed, and once you have selected this you can again let the camera work out the aperture setting.

Camera	***Pentax *ist D***
Focal length	***120mm (35mm equivalent: 180mm)***
Exposure	***1/90sec at f/8***
ISO setting	***200***

Using the camera in shutter priority mode allows you to choose the exposure time that will give the creative effect you want, while the camera's meter takes care of the aperture size. Here is an example of what I would call a 'bread-and-butter' motor racing image, using a fairly slow shutter speed and panning with the car so as to make the subject pin-sharp and blur the backgound.

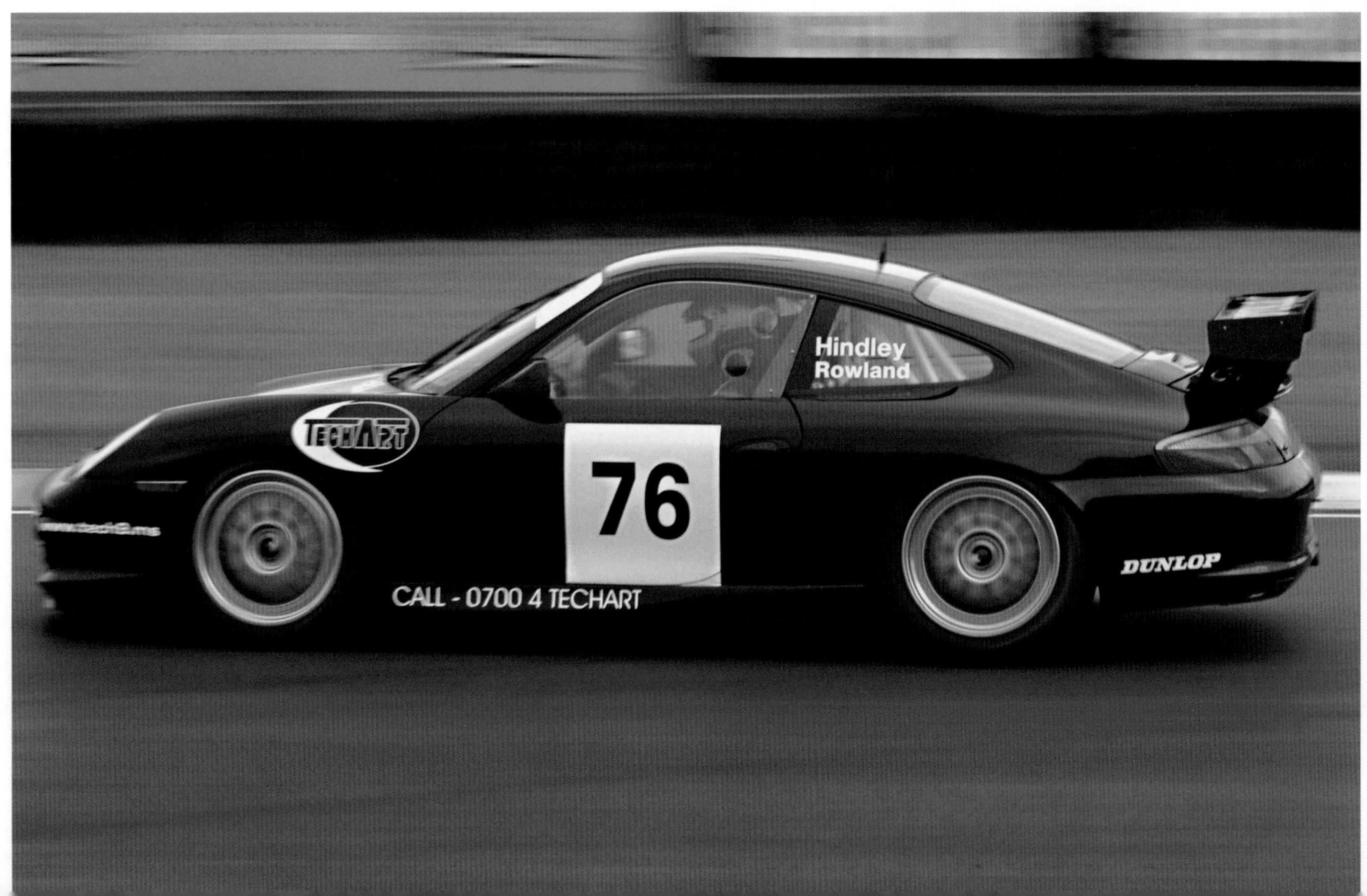

It is only recently that I have come to rely more on this exposure mode; previously I tended to use manual settings only, but this presents a problem when photographing motor sports. Because I am used to working with manual cameras (I shoot landscapes on manual medium-format cameras using a hand-held exposure meter) I used to meter a scene in manual, set the shutter speed first, and then adjust the aperture to suit. The problem with this approach, as far as motor sport is concerned, is that you have to take your meter reading *before* the subject has moved into the frame. You are therefore taking readings from a piece of tarmac and the surrounding landscape, and a few seconds later, when a white (or black) car rushes into view at 80mph (130kph), the lighting in the scene could be quite different. You then have to adjust the aperture rapidly to avoid over- or underexposing. A camera with a reliable shutter priority mode, used correctly, can make this adjustment for you in a fraction of a second.

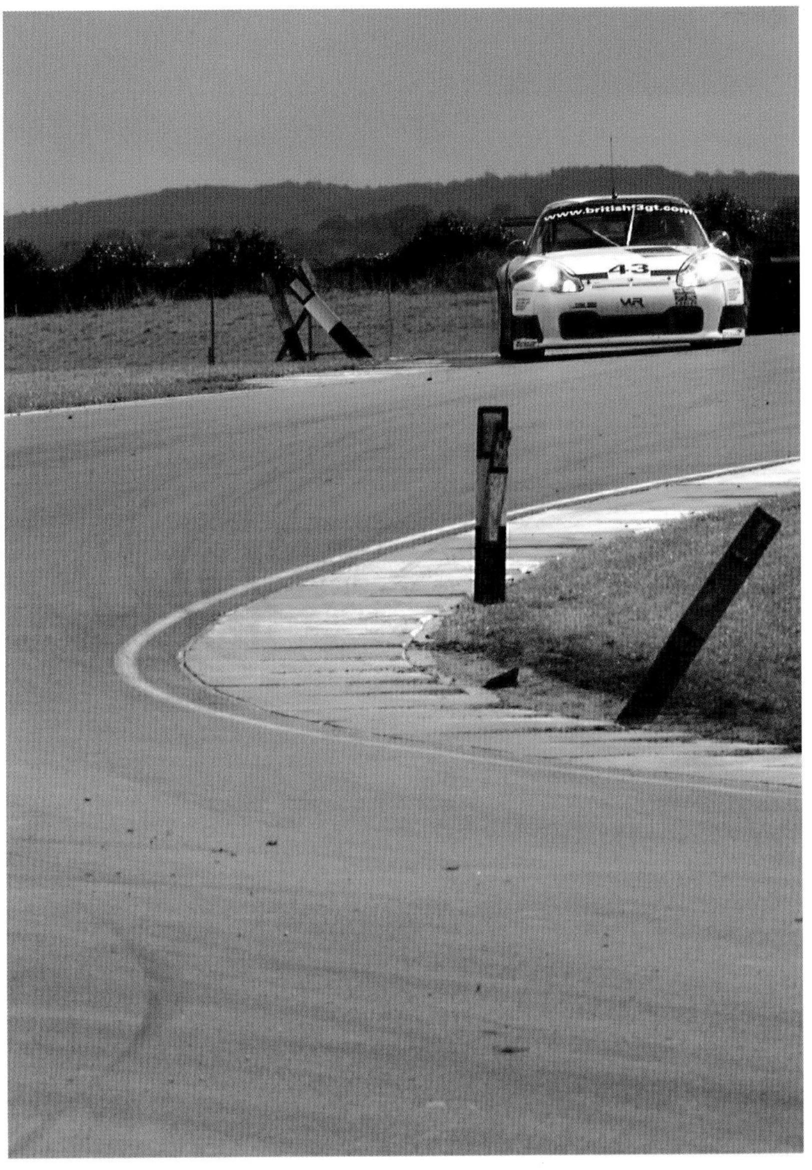

Camera	Pentax *ist D
Focal length	200mm (35mm equivalent: 300mm)
Exposure	1/350sec at f/13
ISO setting	200

Bright light from car headlights can fool your camera into underexposing. If you're using the shutter priority mode you can combat this by taking a reading before the car arrives and using the exposure lock facility to keep the correct exposure. Alternatively, you can use the manual exposure setting by taking a reading from the scene without the influence of the headlights; then, when the car comes into shot, ignore the meter when it tells you that you are overexposing.

Shutter speeds

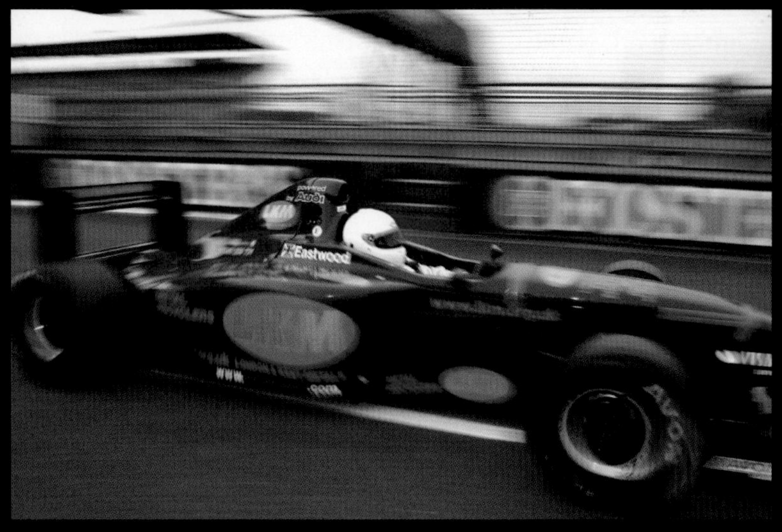

Camera	Pentax *ist D
Focal length	22mm (35mm equivalent: 33mm)
Exposure	1/20sec at f/16
ISO setting	200

By using shutter speeds slower than you normally would without a tripod you can inject a real sense of movement into your images. Combining this technique with fill-in flash can provide a very dramatic effect.

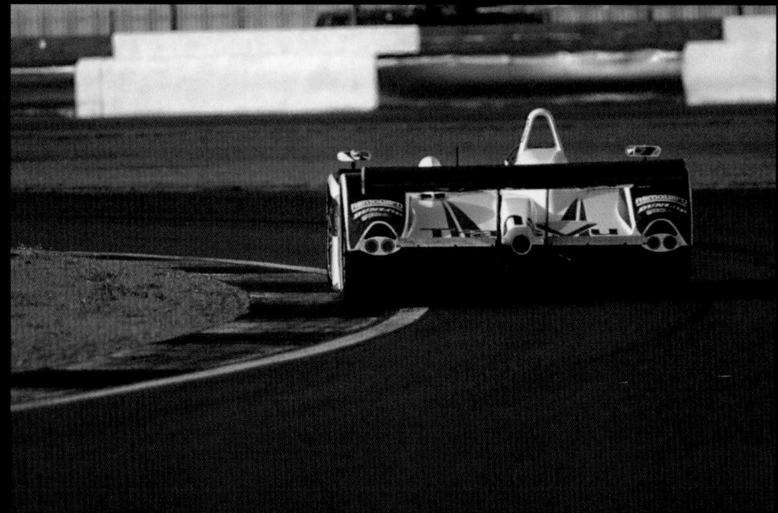

Camera	Pentax *ist D
Focal length	300mm (35mm equivalent: 450mm)
Exposure	1/1000sec at f/4.5
ISO setting	200

It is equally important to understand when to use faster shutter speeds. In this case I wanted to freeze the car and have fairly short depth of field to make the subject stand out. Using the camera in aperture priority mode, I chose an aperture of f/4.5, which gave a shutter speed of 1/1000sec in the late afternoon sun. When working in situations where there is less light, you can use speeds as low as 1/250sec to freeze objects moving towards or away from you, but it is better to use at least 1/500sec if you can.

Exploiting the effects of different shutter speeds is a key element in action photography. Slower speeds (1/125sec and below) are used to add a sense of movement to your images, whereas faster speeds will allow you to 'freeze' the subject. For general photography it is not recommended to use speeds of less than 1/60sec if you are hand-holding the camera; but for action shots I often hand-hold at speeds as low as 1/8sec to create 'motion blur' and lend the image a strong sense of movement.

Faster shutter speeds (over 1/350sec) will allow you to freeze the action, especially when a competitor is moving towards or away from you. Differing subjects travel at different speeds, so you may need to experiment to get the exact effect you require.

Aperture priority

The aperture priority mode allows you to select the aperture (or f-stop setting), while the camera selects the shutter speed. This gives you greater control over the depth of field in your images (see page 99). I tend to use this mode in the pit lane or paddock, where controlling depth of field is a key element of the image. In this environment it is important that I can select a wide aperture and use the resulting shallow depth of field to throw any unwanted background elements out of focus.

Whichever exposure mode you use, it is important to keep an eye on both aperture and shutter speed: it is all too easy to forget to check the one while you are concentrating on the other. This is especially relevant if the light levels are low and the range of exposure options is limited.

Why not use program mode?

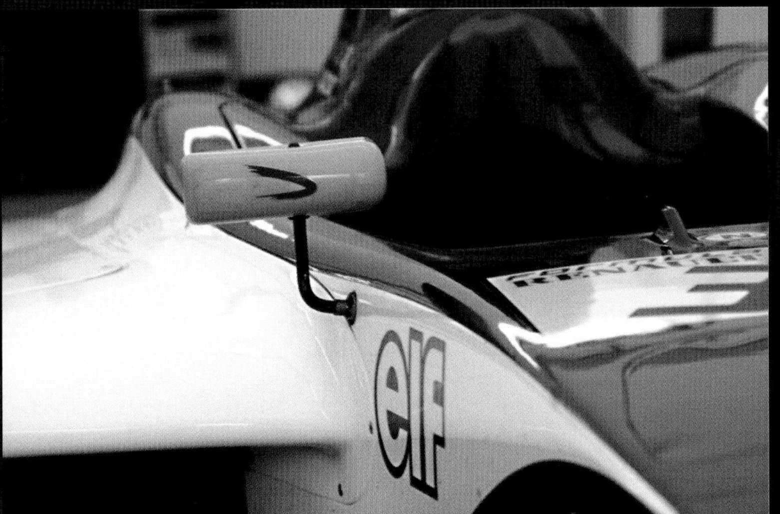

Camera	***Pentax *ist D***
Focal length	***160mm (35mm equivalent: 240mm)***
Exposure	***1/125sec at f/5.6***
ISO setting	***200***

I would recommend you avoid using any of your camera's fully automatic metering modes. Though they will often produce well-exposed results, you don't have sufficient control over aperture or shutter speeds, which have considerable impact in the overall image. Being able to control the depth of field within your images will allow you to pick out areas within a scene that you wish to highlight.

Whatever your preference for exposure modes, it has to be said that manual, shutter priority and aperture priority modes give you great control over your images – you can actively choose the best shutter speeds or apertures to gain the effects you require. The program mode lets the camera make all the exposure decisions, but the camera cannot tell what you are shooting – it just provides a general exposure for the scene based on the information it gets from its own metering system. It is fair to say that your images will usually be correctly exposed, but as the camera does not know how you wish to interpret the scene, the images will only ever be a straightforward record and will not have the dramatic impact that you can add by using the camera's controls creatively. For me, full program mode is for fun photography or taking snaps – I'm sure it will come in handy one day, but so far I have failed to find a use for it in motor racing photography.

In-camera metering

Most modern cameras have various metering options, usually including multi-segment, centre-weighted and spot metering. I tend to stick with centre-weighted metering most of the time, and make any adjustments manually when I think the camera is going to be fooled by tricky lighting conditions. Experience will help you get better at judging how effective your camera's metering system is.

Camera	**Pentax *ist D**
Focal length	**170mm (35mm equivalent: 255mm)**
Exposure	**1/350sec at f/4**
ISO setting	**200**

Bright or dark areas in an image can fool your camera's meter into under- or overexposing the part of the scene you particularly want to capture. In this case the camera, in shutter priority mode, suggested an aperture of f/5.6; manually opening the aperture one stop to f/4 ensured that the fire extinguisher was correctly exposed, while the bright, sunlit background is slightly overexposed.

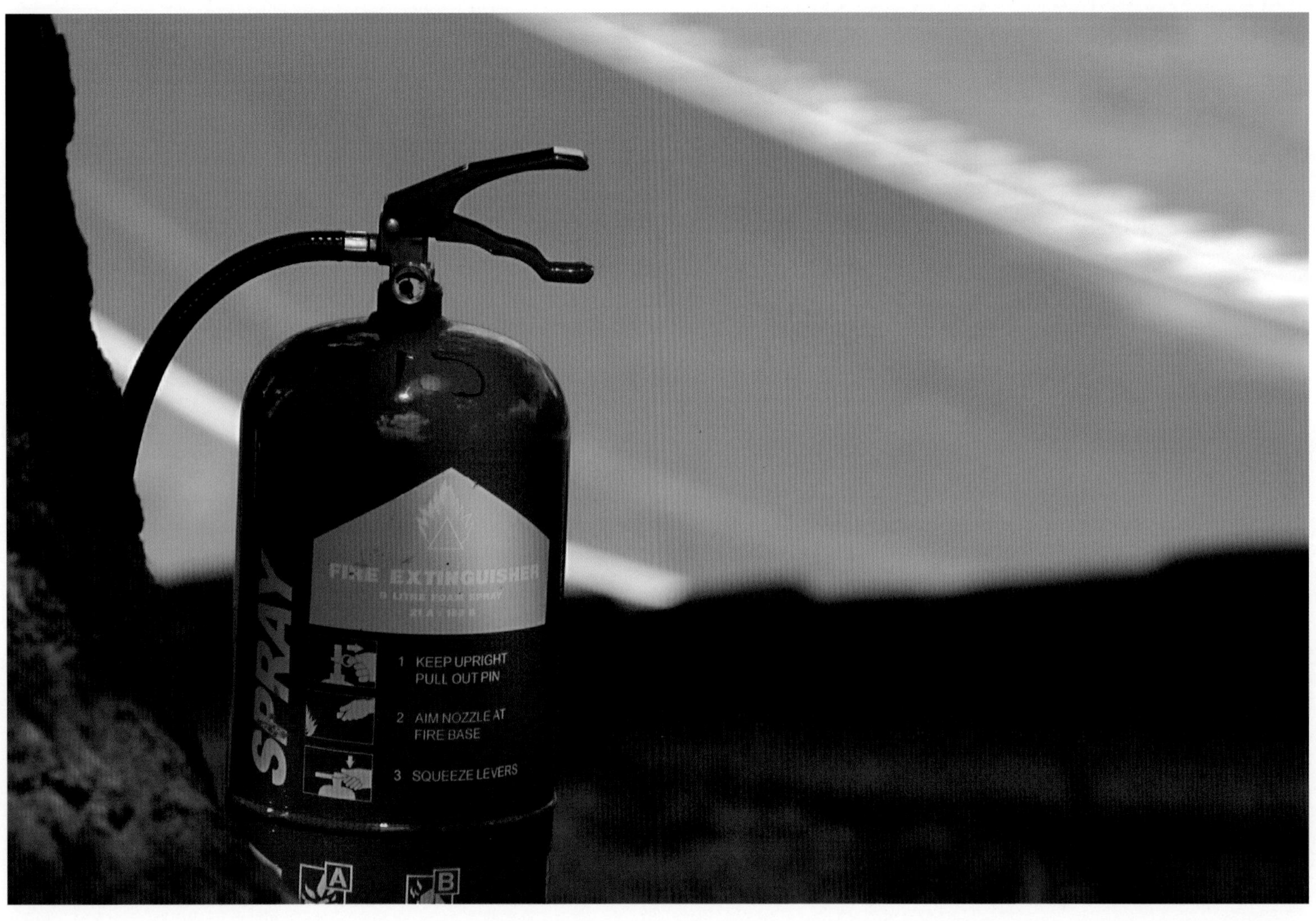

Centre-weighted metering

Centre-weighted metering reads the light levels across the whole of the scene in the viewfinder, but with a bias towards the central area of the image, on the assumption that your main subject is positioned here. This type of metering is often used by photographers who are willing to make adjustments to the given exposure by experience, rather than relying on the camera to do this for them. Generally speaking, this type of reading can usually be relied upon, but it is important to remember that the camera will provide an averaged reading for the central part of the image, and if any part of the scene is unusually light or dark this may bias the average reading and cause your main subject to be over- or underexposed. If this is the case you will need to alter the exposure setting to compensate for this; in manual mode you can easily increase or decrease the exposure by a stop or two as necessary. It is especially important to bear this in mind if the scene you are shooting is backlit (which means that the main source of light is behind the subject): the subject will appear in silhouette unless you increase the exposure by at least one stop, and the camera will not automatically make this adjustment for you.

Of course, if you are using a digital camera you can review your images immediately and make any necessary adjustments. If you're using film you just have to remember where you got caught out and try not to make the same mistake next time.

Camera	***Pentax *ist D***
Focal length	***170mm (35mm equivalent: 255mm)***
Exposure	***1/125sec at f/19***
ISO setting	***200***

Centre-weighted metering is biased towards the centre of a scene. By using it for this image in bright sunlight, I knew the area to the right of the scene would be falling off into shadow, providing the effect I wanted.

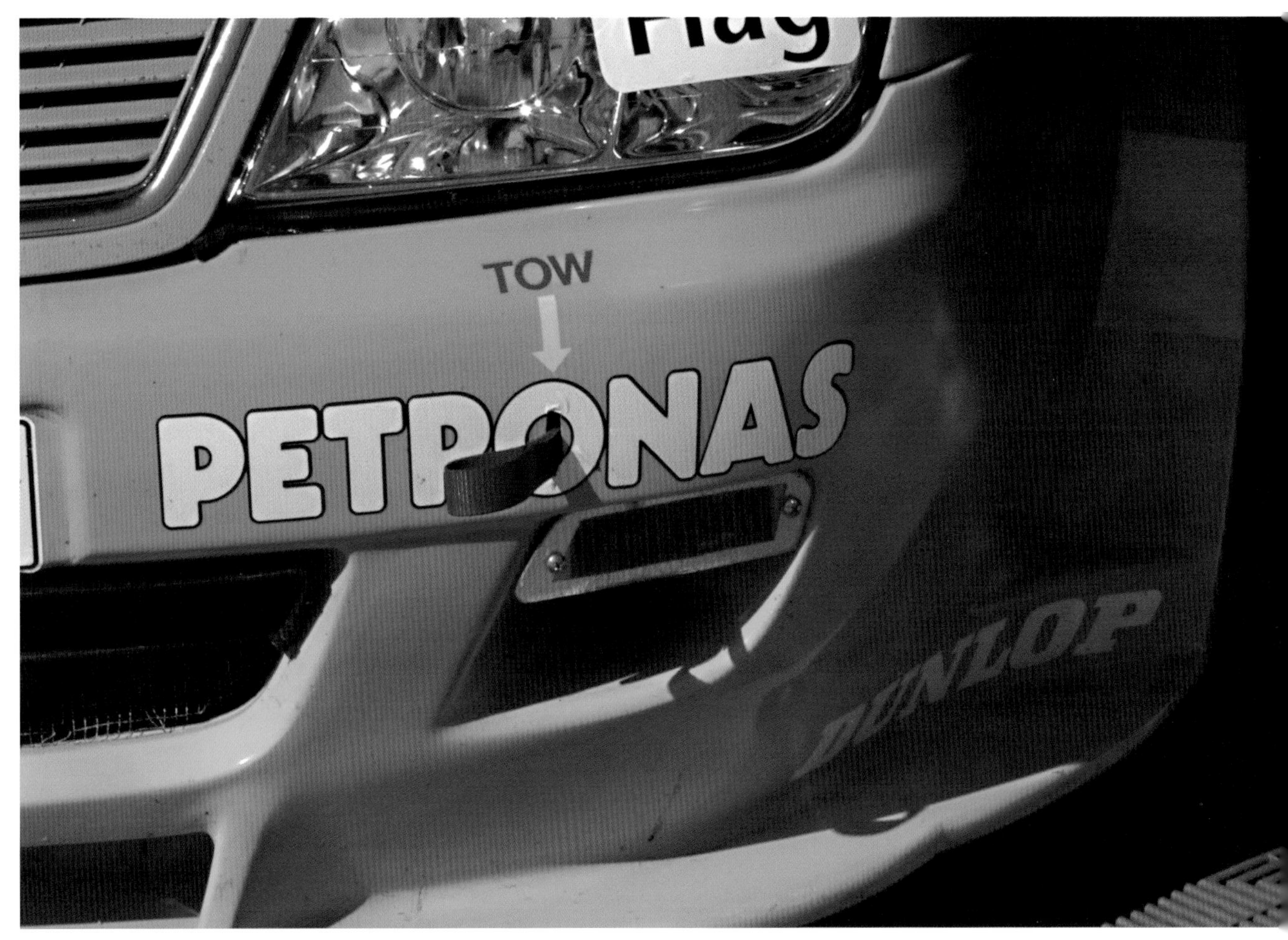

Some other metering modes

Spot metering gives a reading from a specific part of the scene you have composed – usually the centre, but most cameras will allow you to alter this to suit. This setting permits very accurate exposures, but is not always easy to use: it is important that you understand how a reading taken from one part of the scene will affect the exposure of the other parts, and it may be necessary to take and compare multiple readings from different areas. I use a hand-held spot meter when taking landscape photographs, but there is rarely time to use this method in motor sport photography.

Multi-segment metering (sometimes called **multi-zone metering**) divides the viewfinder into a number of different zones. The meter will take a reading from each zone and calculate a mean exposure from these readings. This mode is also very reliable, but it can be caught out by areas of high or low contrast, so once again it is important that you understand how areas of light and dark will be represented.

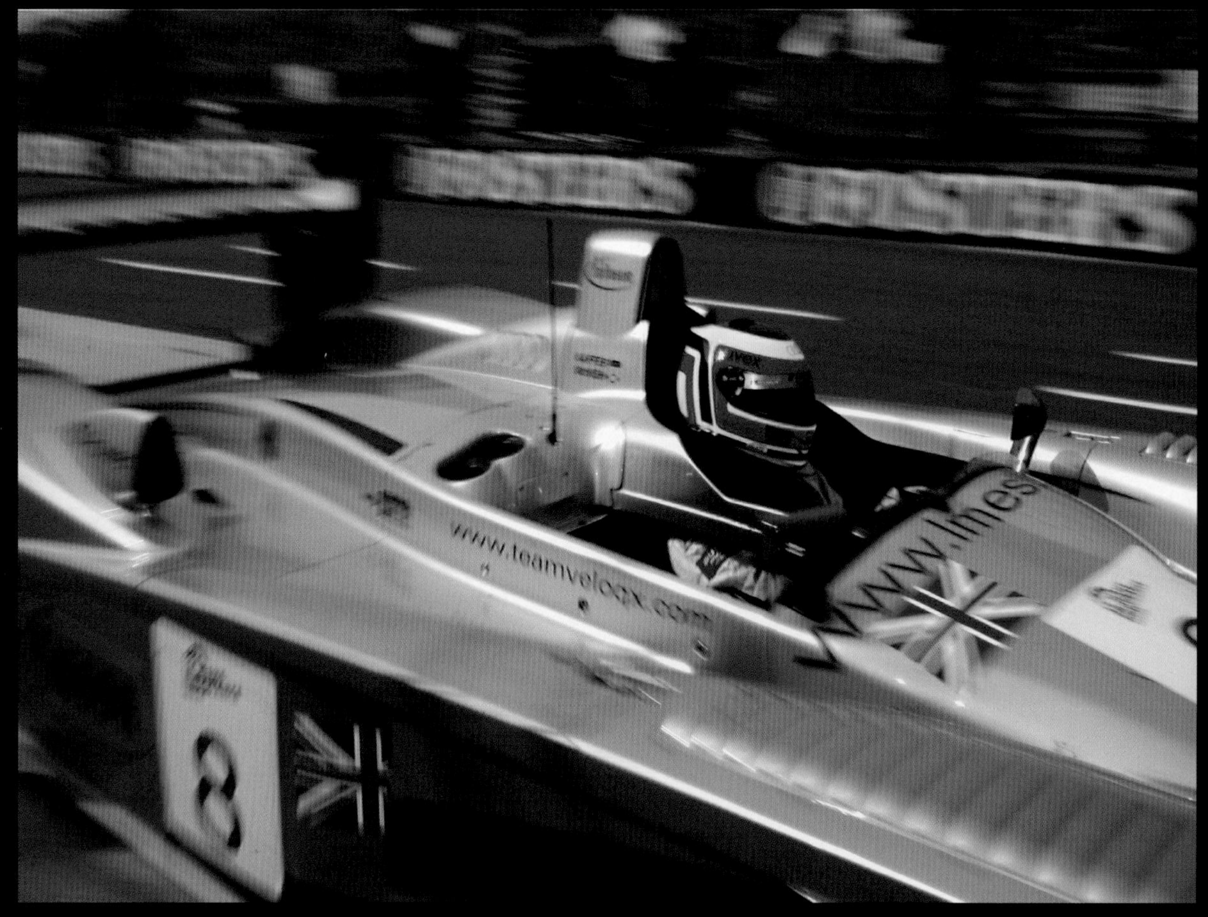

Camera	*Pentax *ist D*
Focal length	*20mm (35mm equivalent: 30mm)*
Exposure	*1/125sec at f/22*
ISO setting	*200*

Though I tend to use centre-weighted metering for most of my images, it is important to understand other metering modes. Without any input from the photographer, multi-segment metering will probably produce more evenly exposed images, but can sometimes limit the creative control you have over the light in a picture.

Shutter speed

Shutter speeds are a crucial aspect of action photography. A high speed will 'freeze' your subject and make it appear sharp, while a low speed will increase blur and give an impression of movement. Shutter speeds are crucial to the success of your images: it is important to convey the feeling of speed and action, while still maintaining a degree of clarity. If you use a shutter speed that is too slow you risk the subject appearing blurred and unsharp; use one that's too fast and the subject may appear to be stationary.

Calculating the correct speed for the effect you want depends on a number of factors, but the most important points to consider are the speed and direction in which the subject is travelling. For this reason a range of different photographic techniques is needed, of which the most important is panning.

Camera	***Pentax *ist D***
Focal length	***135mm (35mm equivalent: 200mm)***
Exposure	***1/250sec at f/5.6***
ISO setting	***200***

Though this is quite a dark scene, it is still legible thanks to the highlights on the rider's helmet, arm, leg and foot. The use of a moderate shutter speed enhances the effect of the mud thrown up from the back wheel of the bike as it accelerates away.

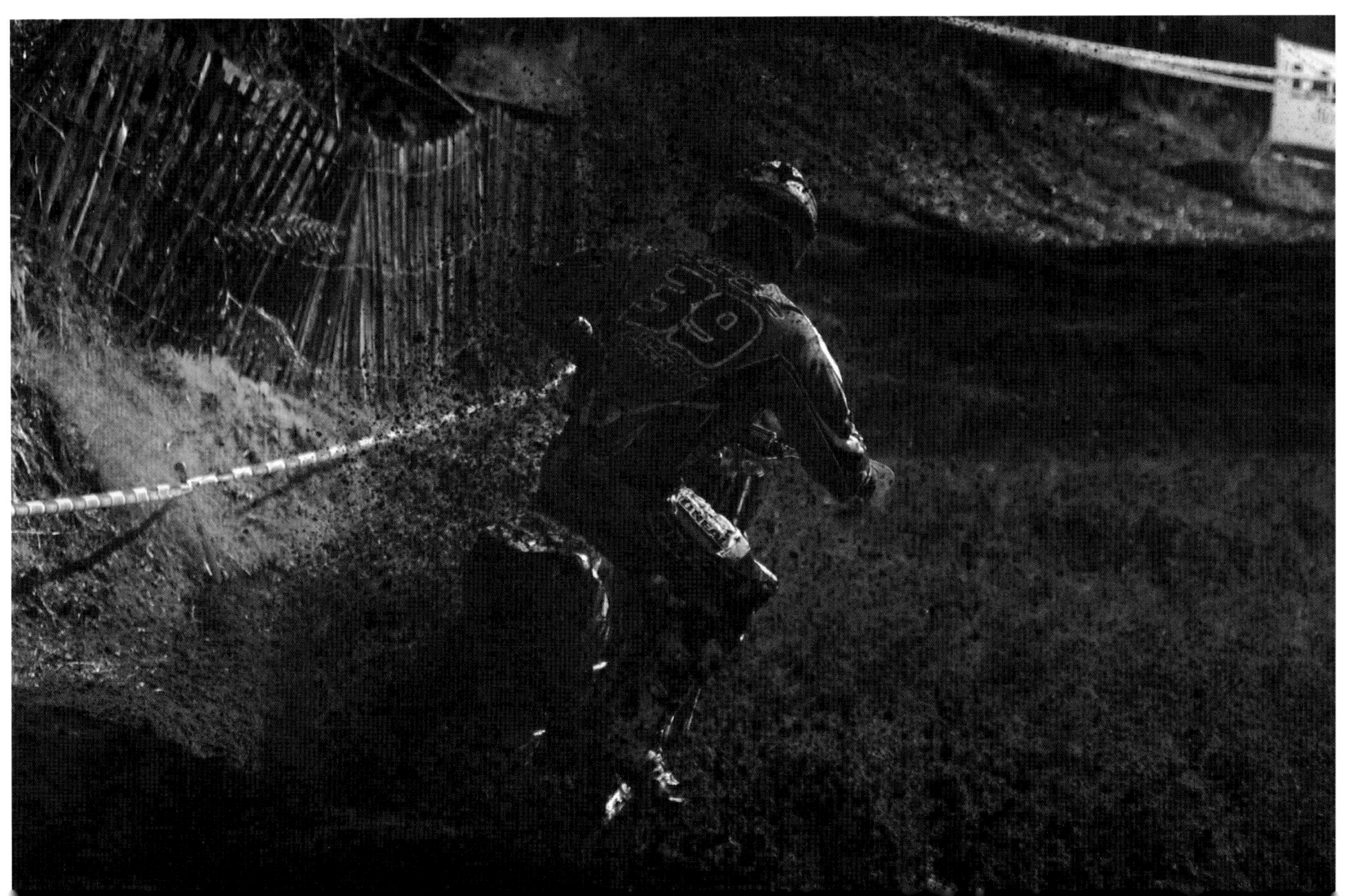

Panning

Panning – tracking the moving subject through the viewfinder and shooting as it passes by – is the cornerstone of motor racing photography. Panning is used to photograph a vehicle as it traverses from one side to the other, generally along a horizontal plane. Using the correct shutter speed will ensure that the subject appears crisp, while the blurring of the wheels and the background area gives the feeling of speed. In order to produce successful racing shots you will need to master basic panning first.

Camera	***Pentax *ist D***
Focal length	***135mm (35mm equivalent: 200mm)***
Exposure	***1/125sec at f/11***
ISO setting	***200***

Panning involves using comparatively slow shutter speeds to enhance the impression of movement as the subject passes by. Panning smoothly with the car allows the vehicle itself to remain pin-sharp, while the low shutter speed ensures that wheels, foreground and background are blurred.
I chose to include the barrier in the background because it complements the colour scheme of this American-style Legends car; the barrier in the foreground provides synergy with the one behind.

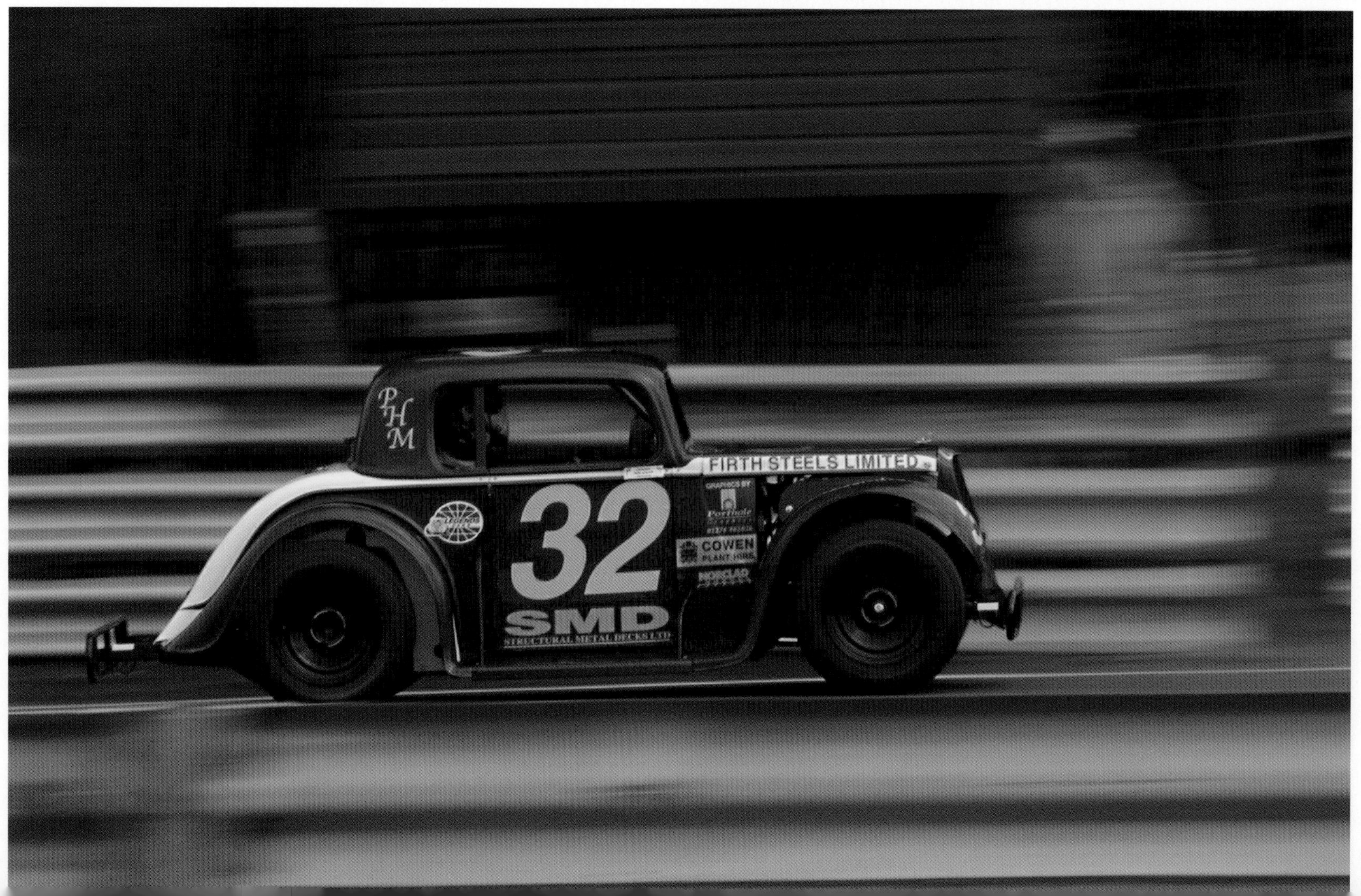

Depending on the type of racing involved and your location, the subject could be travelling at speeds between 20 and 200mph (32–320kph). This means that to create an effective panned shot you might need to use shutter speeds from 1/30 to 1/500sec.

You can use most lenses for panning, from wideangles to telephotos and zooms. The positioning of your body and the way you hold the camera are important to achieving successful results. If you're new to panning it is probably best to practice at a motor-racing circuit, where cars or bikes will be passing on a similar racing line for a number of laps; this will give you the chance to hone your technique.

Camera	***Pentax *ist D***
Focal length	***210mm (35mm equivalent: 315mm)***
Exposure	***1/125sec at f/13***
ISO setting	***200***

Panning lends a sense of movement to an image, and experimenting with composition can enhance this further. Capturing images such as this one is not difficult but needs practice – this car was probably travelling in excess of 100mph (160kph), and if you want to frame the image to include all of the car with the camera held at the diagonal, you need to be very familiar with your camera's controls.

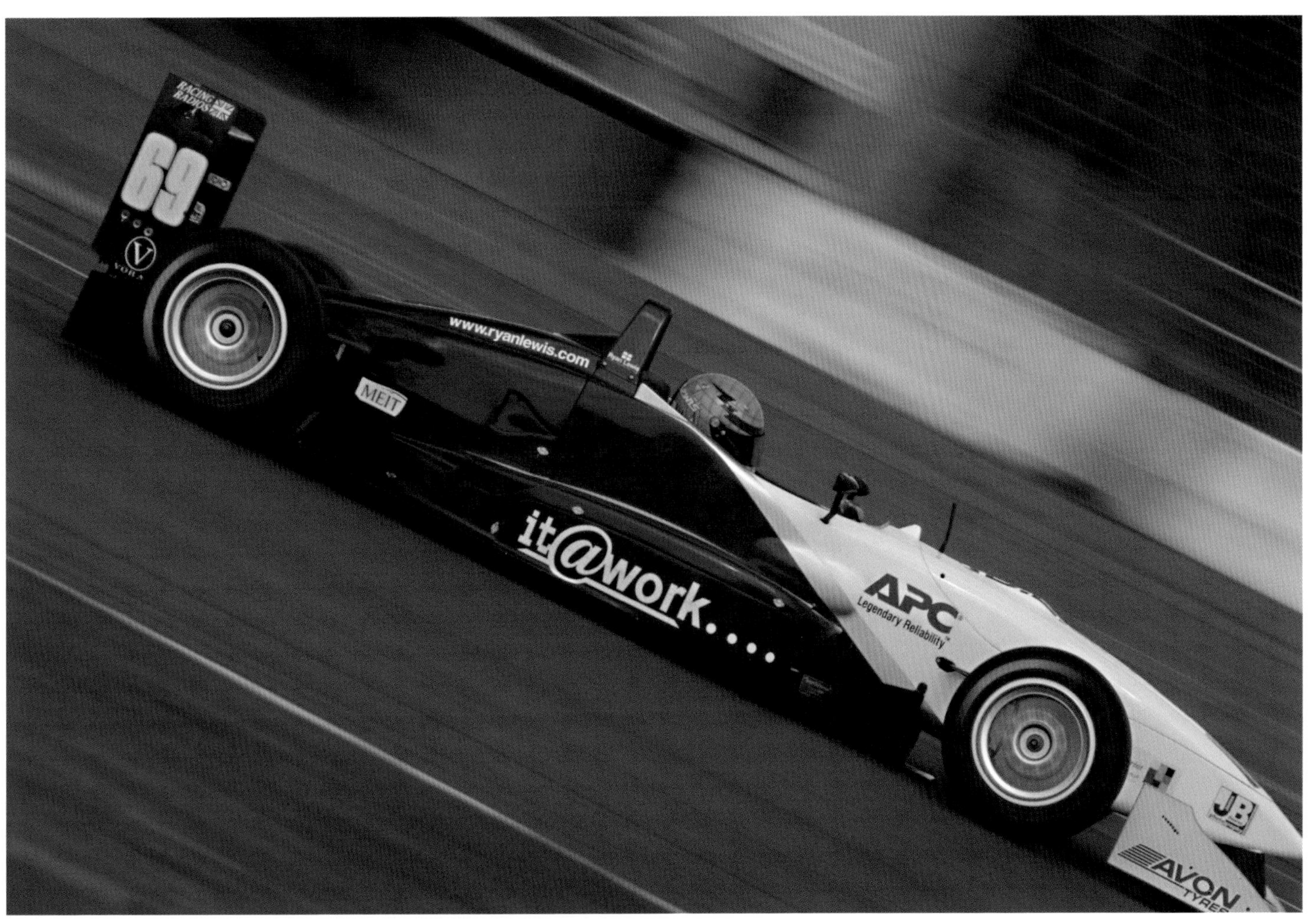

Case study: Panning at different shutter speeds

Panning is a core element of motor sport photography. By following your subject through the viewfinder and firing the shutter as you do so, you can blur the wheels and the backgound while the subject itself remains sharp – thus injecting a sense of movement. These five images demonstrate the effect of differing shutter speeds – as the shutter speed increases the blurring of the background reduces until the car in the final image looks as if it is stationary. It is very important that you continue to pan with the subject after you have fired the shutter in order to maintain a smooth swing.

Camera	*Pentax *ist D*
Focal length	*135mm (35mm equivalent: 200mm)*
Exposure	*1/125sec at f/19*
ISO setting	*200*

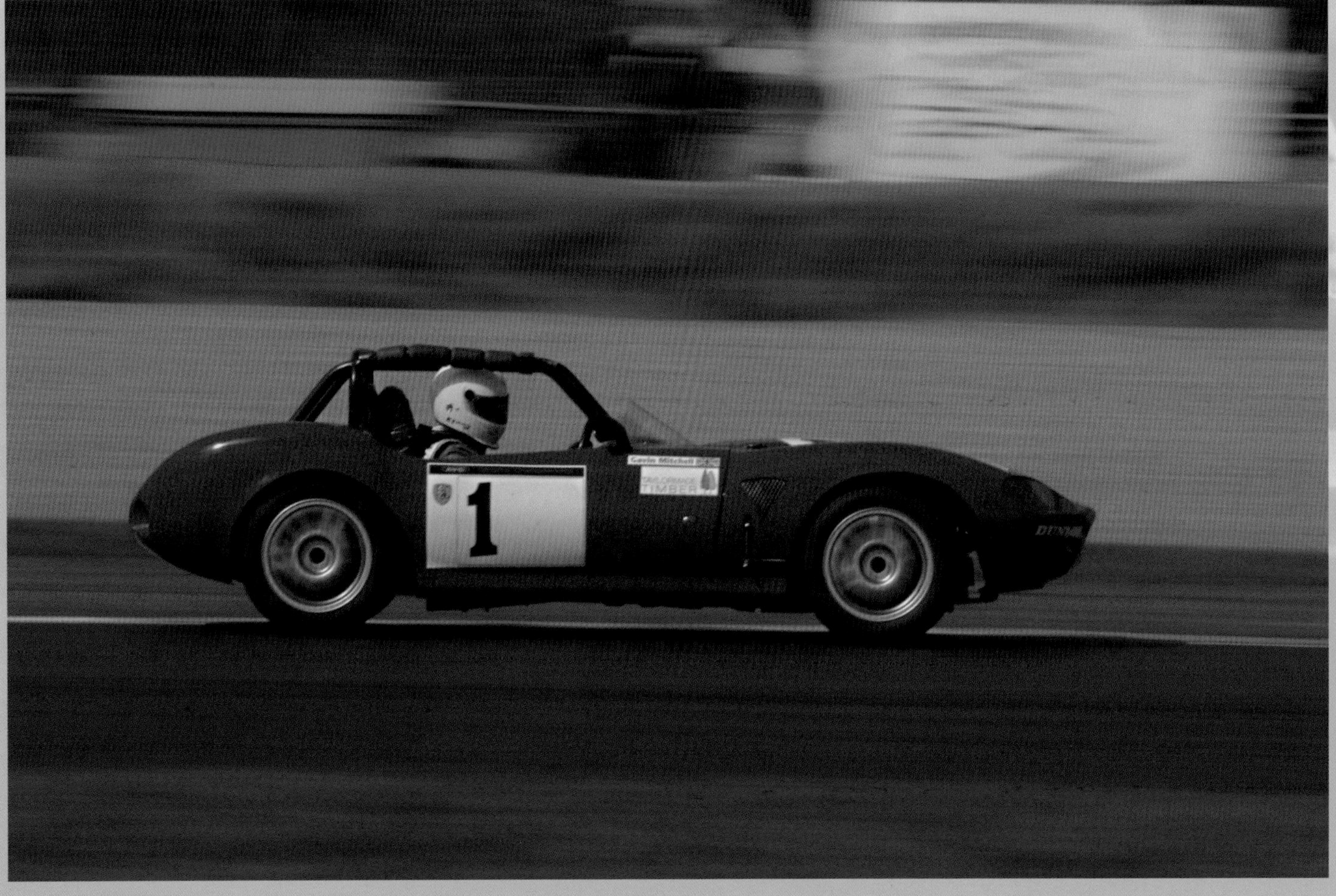

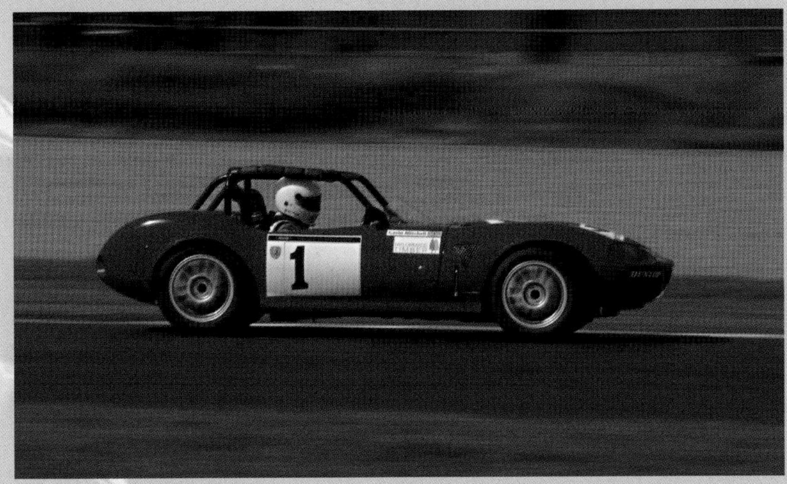

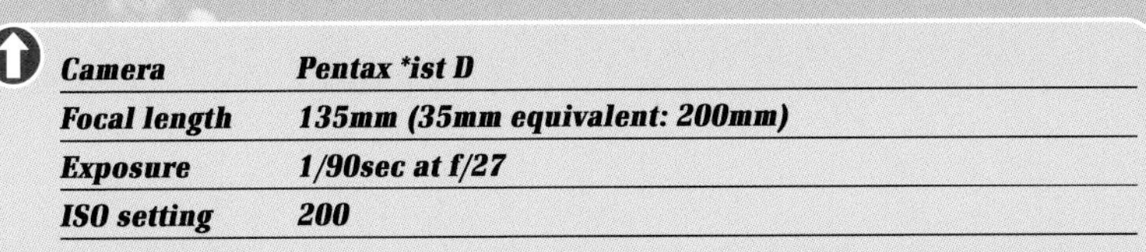

Camera	Pentax *ist D
Focal length	135mm (35mm equivalent: 200mm)
Exposure	1/90sec at f/27
ISO setting	200

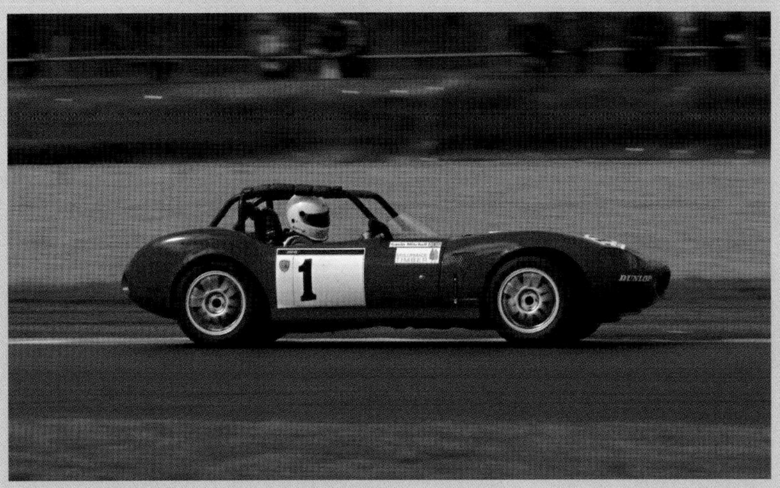

Camera	Pentax *ist D
Focal length	135mm (35mm equivalent: 200mm)
Exposure	1/250sec at f/11
ISO setting	200

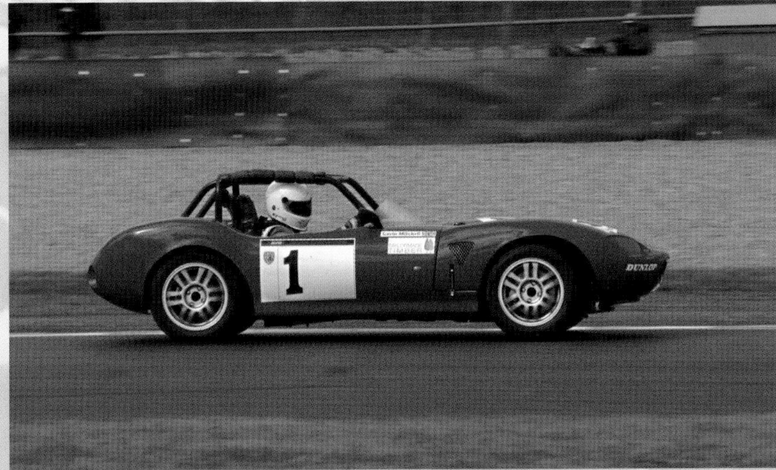

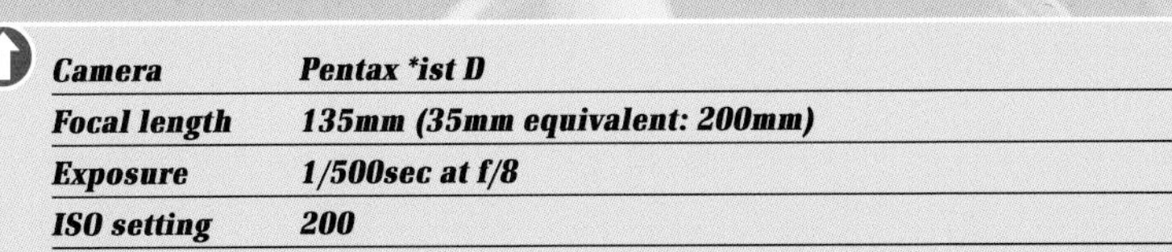

Camera	Pentax *ist D
Focal length	135mm (35mm equivalent: 200mm)
Exposure	1/500sec at f/8
ISO setting	200

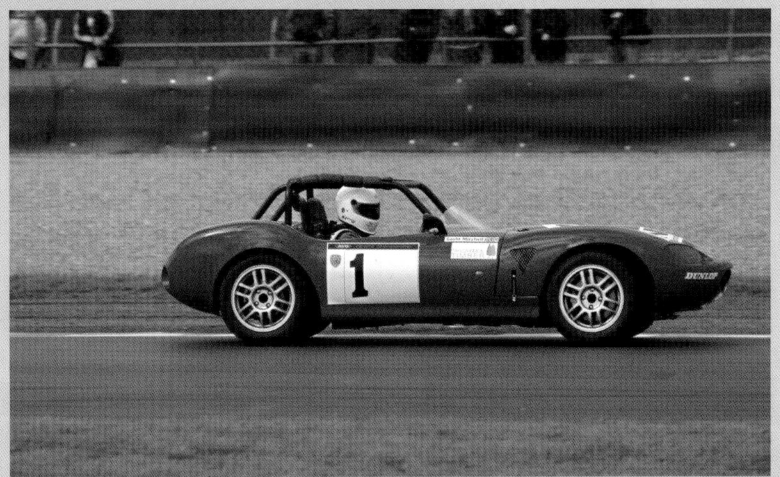

Camera	Pentax *ist D
Focal length	135mm (35mm equivalent: 200mm)
Exposure	1/1000sec at f/5.6
ISO setting	200

Predicting the action

Having selected your viewpoint you should know whether your subject will be coming from the left or the right. Let's assume that you have chosen to stand on the inside of a corner at a circuit; your subject is approaching the corner and will be braking on its approach, moving through the corner and then accelerating away. There are three kinds of action you can expect to see, and your choice of where to stand depends on the action you wish to capture:

- **At the entrance to the corner your subject might brake too late and lock a wheel, providing tyre smoke; or, depending on the type of vehicle, it could belch flames from its exhaust as excess fuel burns in the engine.**
- **In mid-corner it may lift a rear wheel, get 'out of shape' due to excessive entry speeds, or attempt to pass another competitor, all of which can add drama to your shot.**
- **On the exit from the corner the driver might apply too much throttle and the rear of the vehicle might 'step out'; or it might spin altogether, or run out of road and take to the grass.**

What I am saying here is that knowing your subject and its characteristics will determine where you choose to shoot.

Camera	***Pentax *ist D***
Focal length	***180mm (35mm equivalent: 270mm)***
Exposure	***1/180sec at f/9.5***
ISO setting	***200***

The speed of your subject will determine what shutter speed is needed to blur the background. Motorbikes invariably accelerate faster than cars, so a higher shutter speed can be used to gain the same results. Holding the camera at a slight angle accentuates the lifting of the front wheel as the bike crests the brow of a hill. Panning at an angle requires a little more care than usual.

Basic panning technique

Let's say you have chosen to take your shot in the middle of the corner. First you will need to pre-focus your lens on the piece of track where your subject will pass. I prefer to do this manually and let the subject come towards me, rather than relying on autofocus; I don't always trust autofocus to produce pin-sharp results.

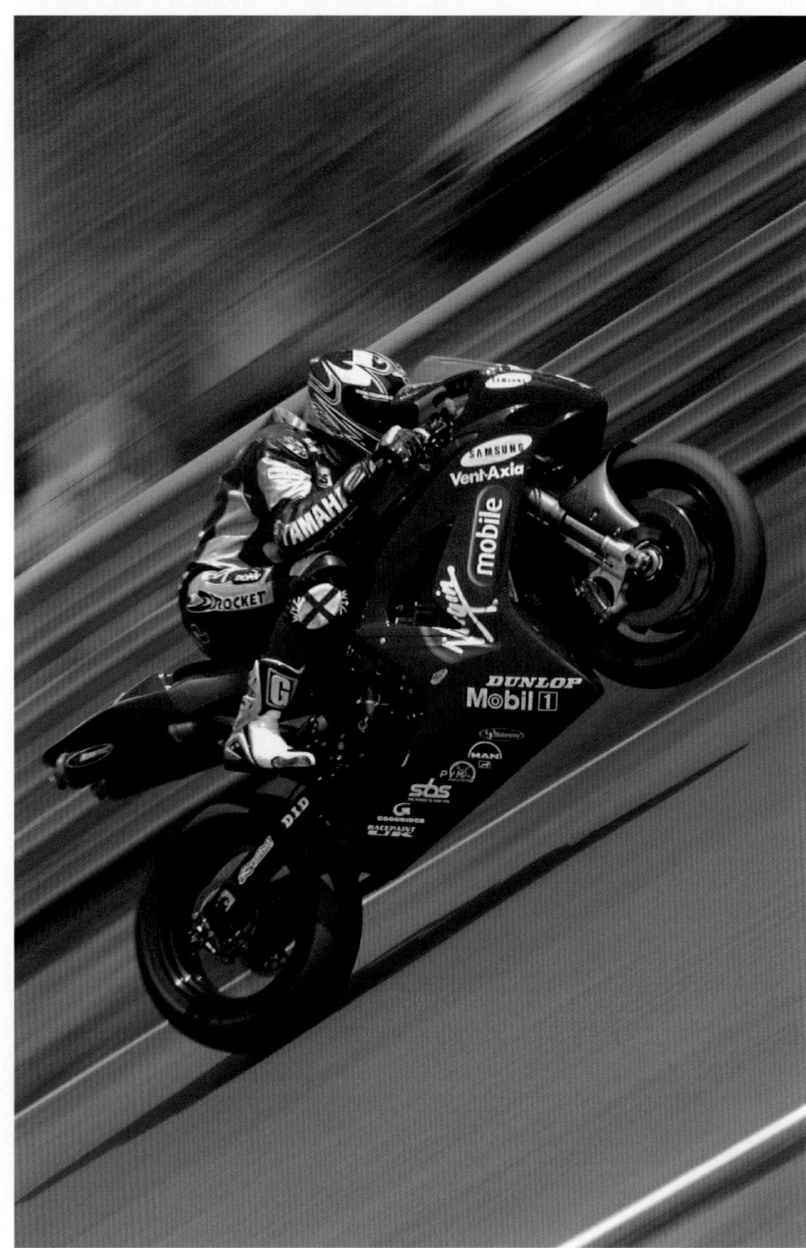

Shutter speeds for panning

If we assume that the subject is a car travelling at between 50 and 70mph (80–110kph), we have a range of shutter speeds that can be used for a successful panned shot. I would normally work between 1/60 and 1/180sec. Any faster than 1/180 and you will begin to 'freeze' the wheels and show more detail in the background, making the car appear static; any slower than 1/60 and your subject will start to become unsharp; so a setting of 1/125sec is a good starting point.

Camera	Pentax *ist D
Focal length	190mm (35mm equivalent: 285mm)
Exposure	1/125sec at f/9.5
ISO setting	200

If I can't get close enough to the subject to fill the frame, I look for other ways of making a composition. By deliberately including the barrier in the foreground and tilting the camera, I was able to make a strong image from what would otherwise have been a fairly uninteresting scene.

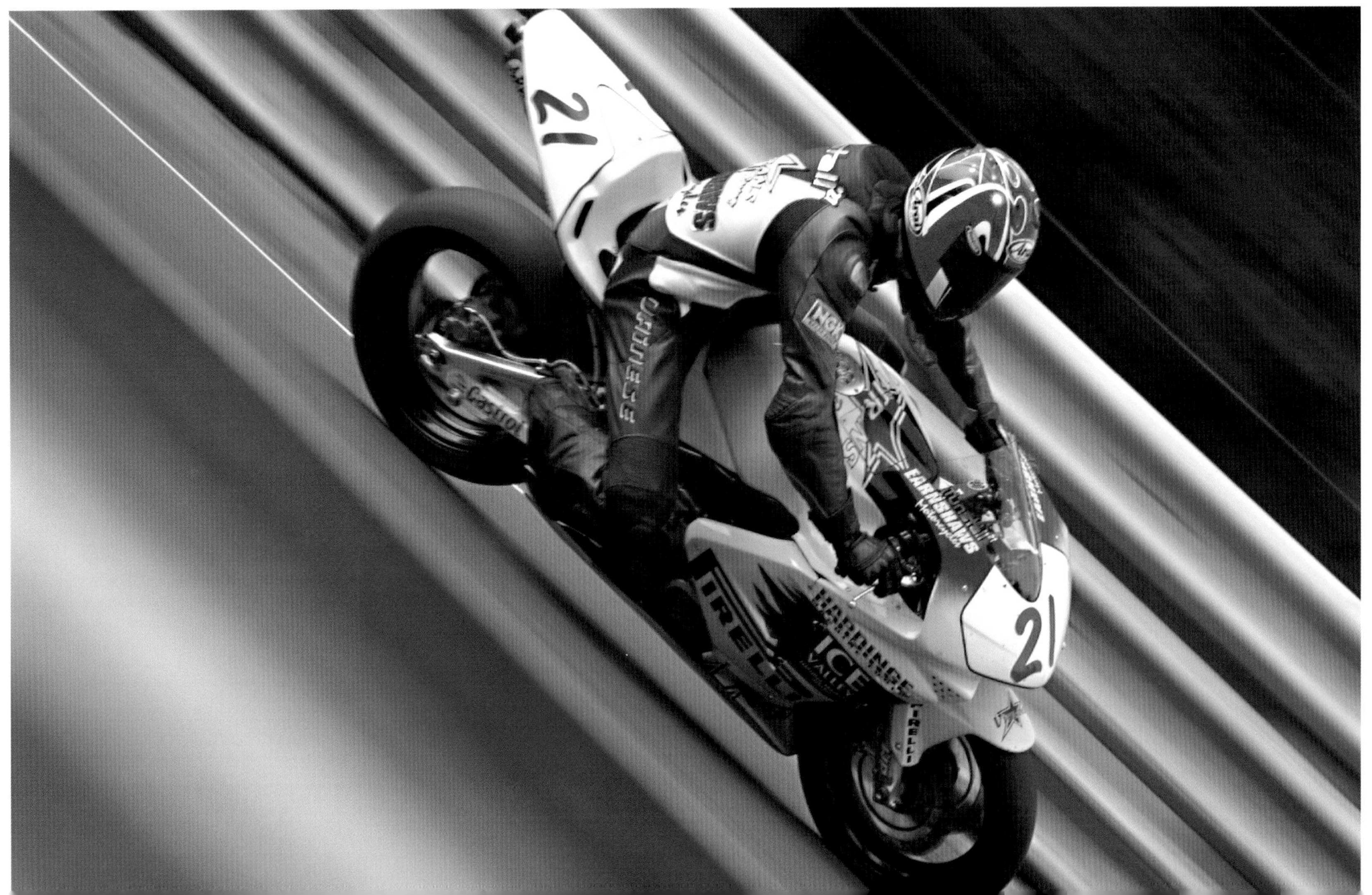

Perfecting your swing

Working in shutter priority mode, set your chosen shutter speed and pre-focus on the track where the car will pass. I like to pick up the subject through the lens as soon as I can, but remember not to adjust your pre-set focusing. Stand with your feet slightly apart for balance, with your toes pointing at the place where you will take the shot. As the car approaches the corner, rotate your hips and pick up the car in the viewfinder, supporting the lens with your left hand; you can then follow it as it enters the corner, waiting for it to come into focus at your chosen point.

If the light is bright, you can half-press the shutter release so the camera can make any necessary adjustments to the aperture setting. (Make sure you have switched off or deselected the autofocus, if you have it, or it may be activated as you half-press the release.) As the car reaches your pre-focused point you can gently squeeze the shutter release as the image becomes sharp. Try not to stab at the release, as this can cause the camera to wobble in the middle of your swing. If you have a motor drive or

Camera	***Pentax *ist D***
Focal length	***210mm (35mm equivalent: 315mm)***
Exposure	***1/125sec at f/11***
ISO setting	***200***

Having pre-focused manually on the track where the car will pass, you can pick up your subject as it approaches and wait while it comes into focus. As the subject arrives at your pre-focused spot, gently pressing the shutter release will prevent your pan from 'wobbling'; continuing to pan after you have fired the shutter will help you to keep the subject sharp.

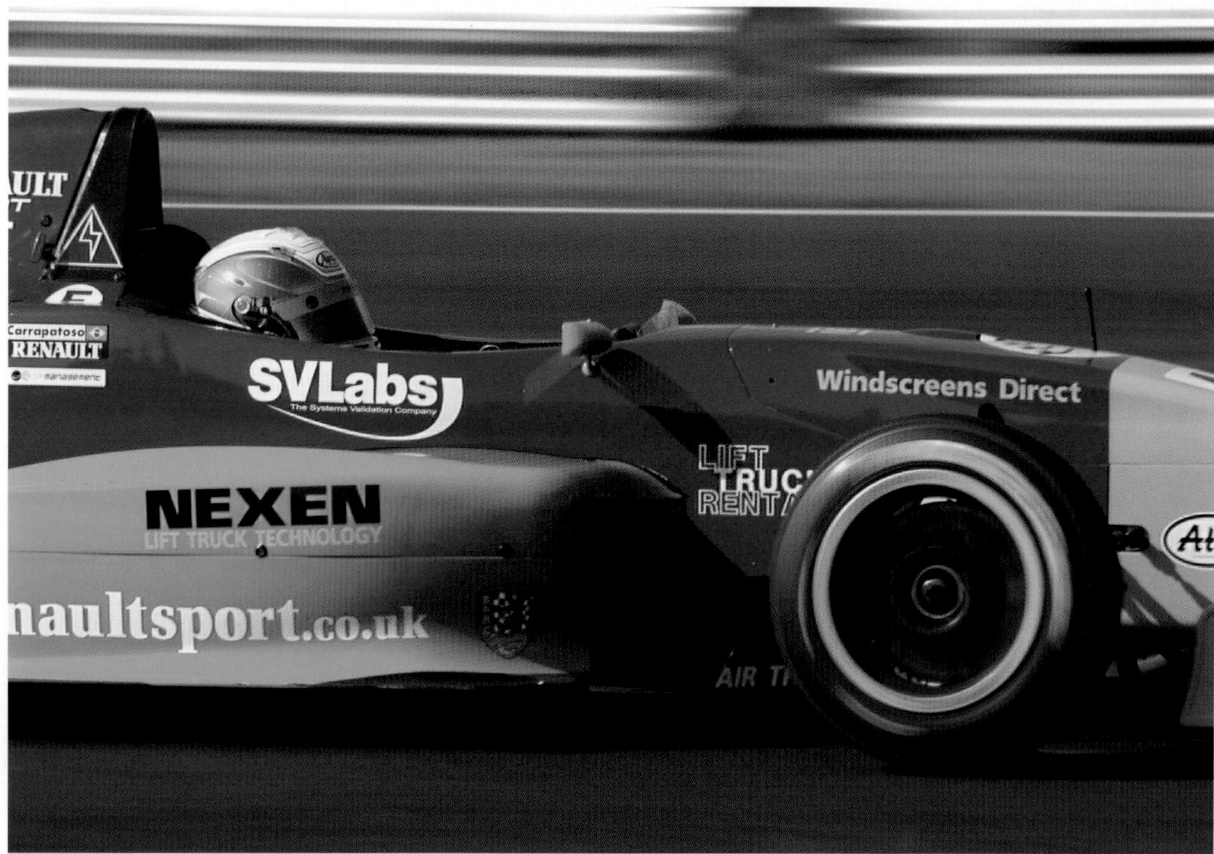

Camera	Pentax *ist D
Focal length	200mm (35mm equivalent: 300mm)
Exposure	1/45sec at f/22
ISO setting	200

The speed at which your subject is travelling will affect the outcome of your pan. Because this car was braking into a corner, it wasn't travelling particularly quickly; a shutter speed of 1/45sec was sufficient, and resulted in blurring of the entire image. If your subject is moving fast, the swing of the pan will need to be faster; this provides a smoother arc of movement, allowing the subject to be sharper. Time, experience and trial and error will help you learn what shutter speeds to use in order to get the desired effect.

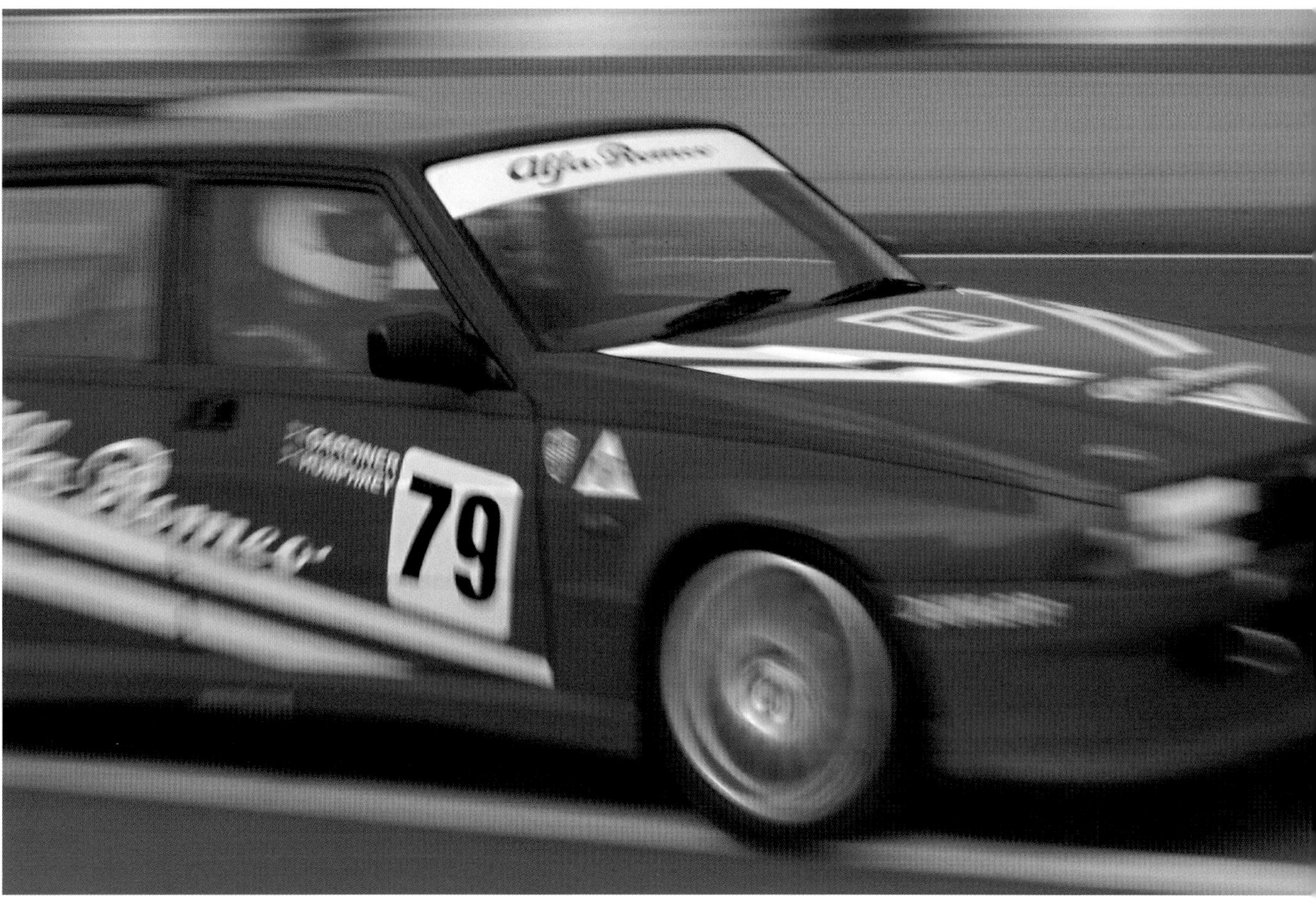

automatic frame advance you may choose to shoot several frames, but I prefer to concentrate on capturing one pin-sharp image. It is vital to continue your swing after you have fired the shutter and 'follow through' the subject in order to keep your swing as even and smooth as possible.

As the cars lap the track you can take a few shots in this way before thinking about changing the shutter speed. It may sound strange, but as a rule of thumb the faster a subject is travelling, the *slower* the shutter speed you can use. This is because the faster the panning movement, the easier it is to move smoothly; if the subject is moving slowly there is a greater chance of wobbling mid-swing.

You will need to practice your technique until you are able to pan with confidence. If you are shooting transparencies it is worth making a note of the shutter speeds you use, so that you can evaluate your success when viewing your results on the lightbox. If you shoot digitally you have the benefit of checking your results immediately, which is a real bonus when you're learning or experimenting.

Once you are able to produce consistently crisp results, with your subject pin-sharp against a blurred background, you can try experimenting with different shutter speeds. When I'm confident I've boxed off a panned shot I will usually shoot a few frames at 1/15 or even 1/8sec to try and inject a little motion blur. I said before that the faster the subject the slower the speeds you can use, but I rarely expect to achieve pin-sharp results once I drop the shutter speed below 1/60sec.

Three-quarter panning

Once you have mastered the basic technique you can start to look at other types of panning. As well as panning from the side as the vehicle passes by, you can also pan as your subject approaches or drives away from you: this is called three-quarter panning.

This time, let's move to a position where we can shoot the car as it enters the corner. Three-quarter panning shows your subject from the front and side, so it is both coming towards you and moving horizontally across your field of view. Since the subject is coming towards you, you will need to use faster shutter speeds than you would for a side-on pan, to prevent it being blurred

Camera	***Pentax *ist D***
Focal length	***180mm (35mm equivalent: 270mm)***
Exposure	***1/250sec at f/4.5***
ISO setting	***200***

Three-quarter panning involves shooting your subject as it moves in two axes simultaneously: from one side to the other, as well as towards or away from you. Using slightly faster shutter speeds than for normal side-on panning will help keep the subject sharp while maintaining the blurred background effect.

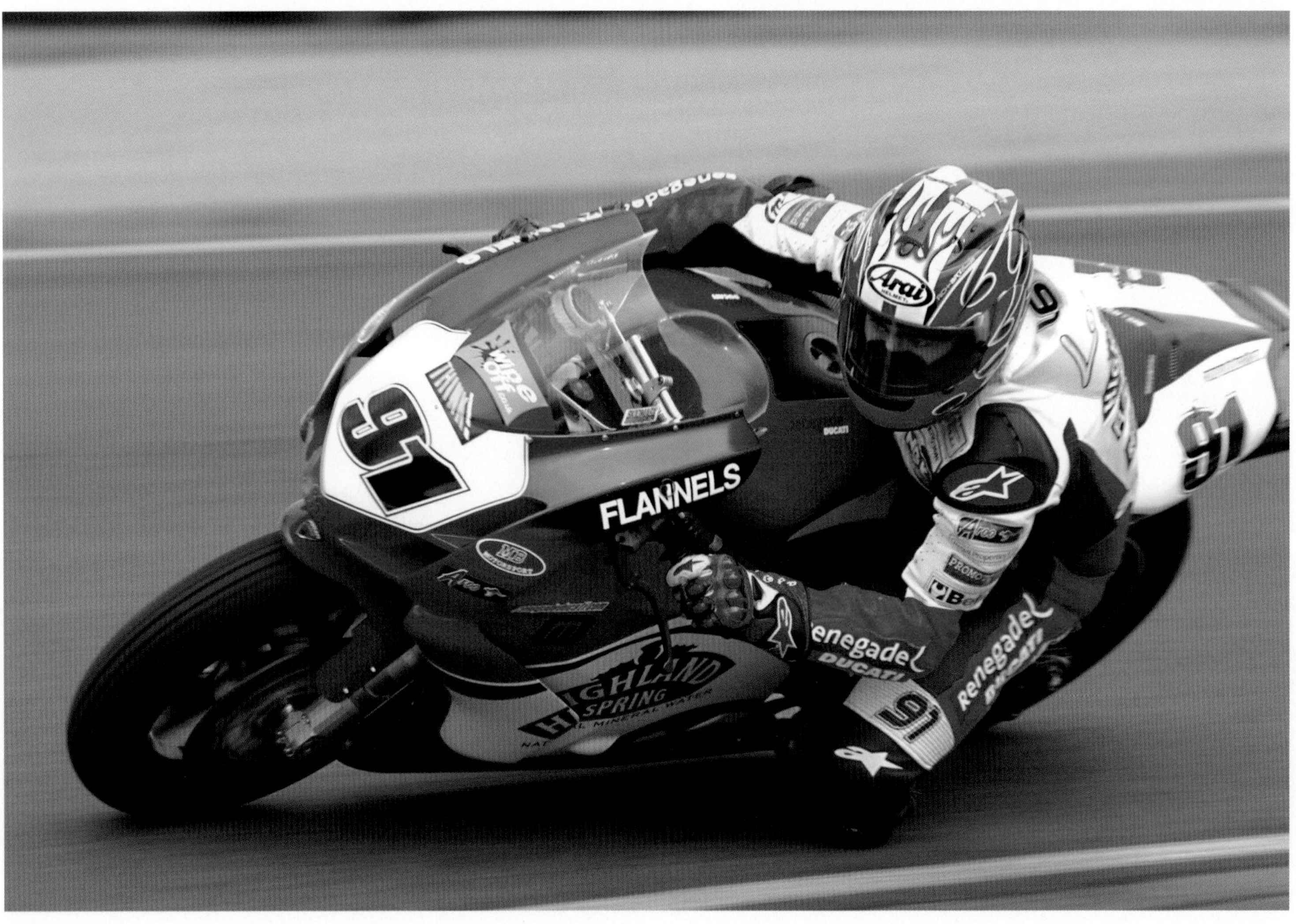

as it passes through and moves away from the point on which you have focused. As you still want the subject to retain a sense of movement you should avoid increasing shutter speeds too much. A suitable range for this type of shot is between 1/125 and 1/500sec, again depending on the speed of the subject. Using the same criteria as for the basic panned shot, I would choose a shutter speed of 1/180sec as a starting point. I am also conscious that depth of field is more of an issue with this type of shot, so check to ensure that the aperture is at least f/5.6, but preferably f/8 or smaller. (For more on depth of field, see page 99.)

Camera	***Pentax *ist D***
Focal length	***200mm (35mm equivalent: 300mm)***
Exposure	***1/180sec at f/16***
ISO setting	***200***

The comparatively slow shutter speeds used in panned shots usually allow for reasonably small apertures, thus ensuring adequate depth of field. This is especially useful when three-quarter panning with telephoto lenses – these lenses suffer from reduced depth of field and the smaller aperture helps to compensate for this, ensuring the subject remains in focus from front to back.

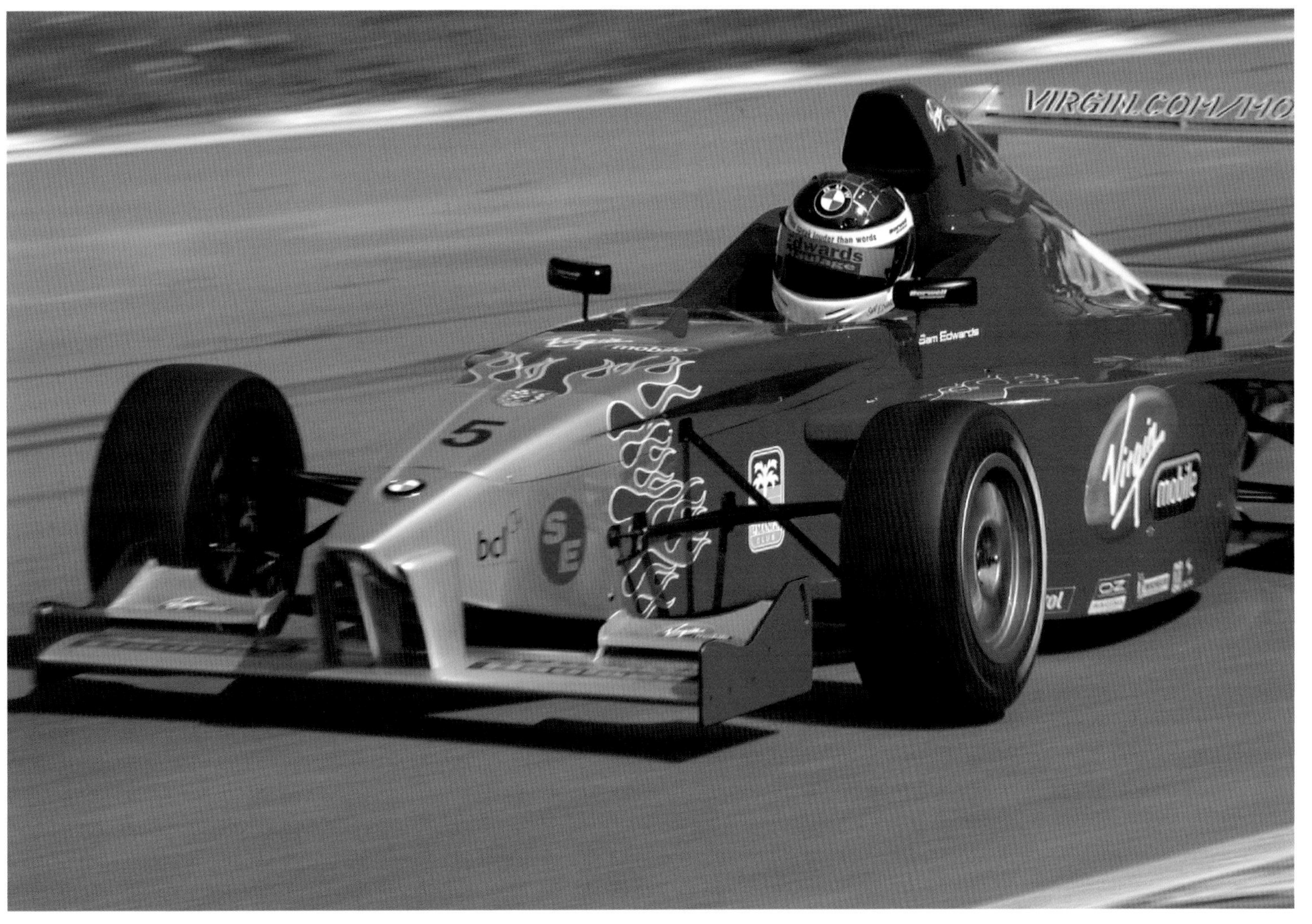

I pre-focus on a point at the corner entry and follow the car in the same way as before; the stance is similar but the swing of your pan will be shorter. By picking up the subject early you can follow it towards your pre-focused point. However, as the car is approaching you it will pass through the focal point much more quickly than in a side-on pan, so it is important to predict the moment *just before* it comes into focus – this is the point at which you should fire the shutter. Shooting just before the subject comes into focus allows for the time it takes for the message to get from your brain to the camera shutter – in that split second the car will have moved forward into your pre-focused area, ensuring a sharp result. As before, it is vital that you continue your pan by following through the subject after firing the shutter.

Camera	***Pentax *ist D***
Focal length	***200mm (35mm equivalent: 300mm)***
Exposure	***1/90sec at f/19***
ISO setting	***200***

Using slower shutter speeds than normal when three-quarter panning will blur part of the subject, adding to the sense of speed. In this shot the rear quarter of the car is pin-sharp and the movement blur increases towards the front end.

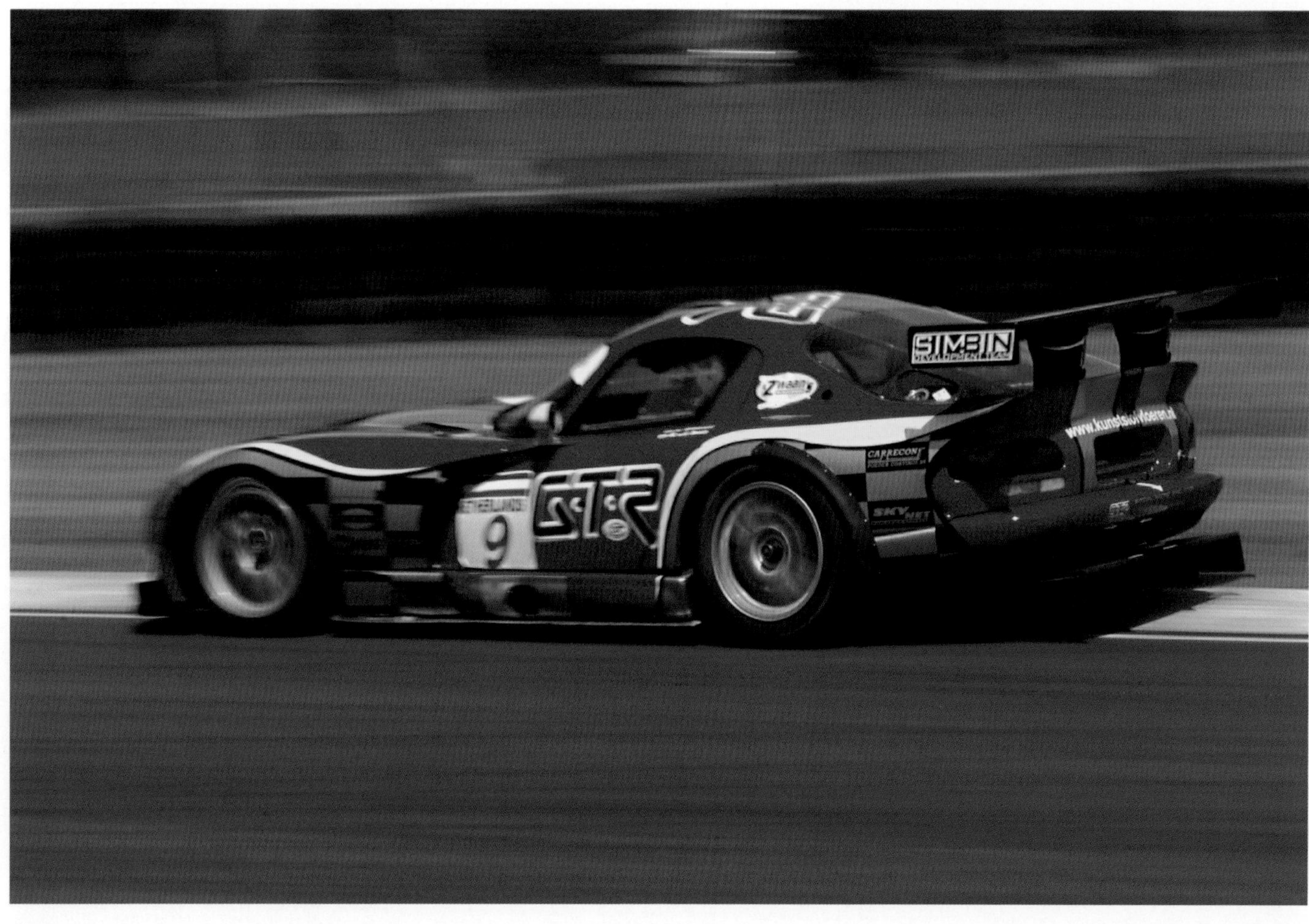

Rear three-quarter panning

The same technique can be used as the subject moves away from you to achieve a rear three-quarter pan – the only difference is that your pre-focused point is on the far side of the car. As before, you pick up the car in the viewfinder as it begins passing through the corner and pan with it until the split second before it comes into focus. Shutter speeds can be in the same range as before, although I prefer to use slower speeds to achieve greater motion blur – I find this gives a more pleasing, creative effect.

Other uses of panning

Once you've mastered these aspects of panning it's worth experimenting with the technique in other contexts. Using wideangle lenses at slow shutter speeds can produce stunning images if the composition is strong enough. You can use panning in the pit and paddock as well as on the track – as long as your subject is moving, panning can be used. If a driver is seated in his car and being pushed through the paddock by mechanics on the way to the track, you can get very close to the subject and use a slow shutter speed, possibly with a burst of fill-in flash (see page 108), to produce excellent results. As in all things, we are always learning. I am always on the look-out for ways to use the skills I have to produce fresh and dynamic pictures.

Camera	***Pentax *ist D***
Focal length	***90mm (35mm equivalent: 135mm)***
Exposure	***1/60sec at f/16***
ISO setting	***200***

As long as your subject is moving, you can add motion blur by using slow shutter speeds. This car may look as if it is travelling very quickly, but in fact it is moving at about 20mph (32kph) as the driver approaches the grid ready to line up for the start. A burst of fill-in flash has added a little light to the car in dull conditions and picked out the reflector on the bollard on the left side of the frame.

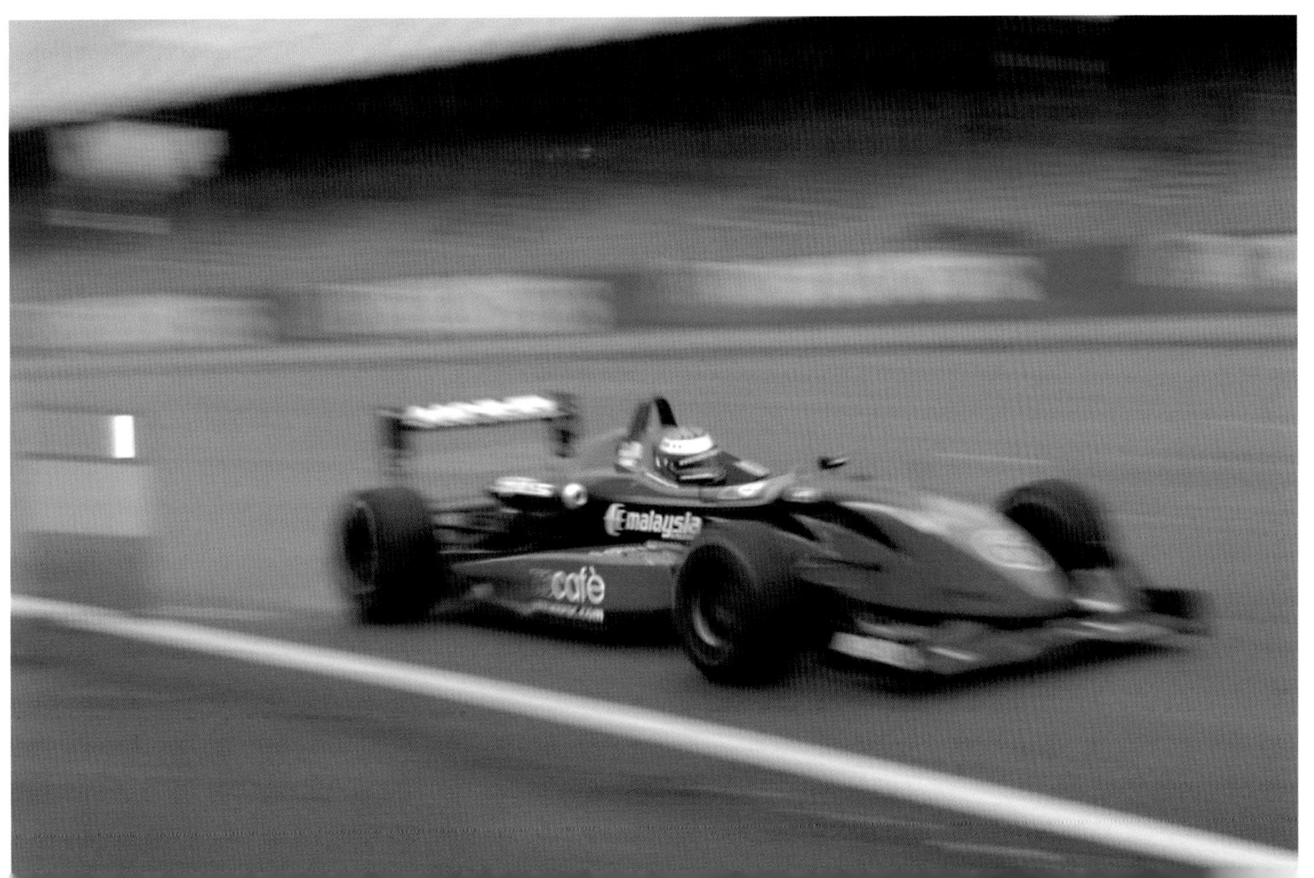

Freezing the action

Panning, as we have seen, is an effective technique for suggesting movement in a static photograph. The opposite approach is to 'freeze' the motion so that the subject appears completely sharp in the image, with little or no suggestion of movement. This is done by keeping the camera still and using a fast shutter speed.

Shooting a subject that is coming towards or moving away from you requires particularly high shutter speeds – a motorbike approaching at over 100mph (160kph) is naturally going to move in and out of focus very quickly. Note also that from this angle the wheels will be less visible, so there is little to be gained by using slower shutter speeds to capture their movement. The background of such an image is not going to be blurred as with a panned shot, so you have to be more careful about how you compose your image in order to keep out unwanted distractions.

This type of shot usually calls for a long telephoto lens, typically at least 300mm, which allows you to 'get closer' to the subject and crop out any unwanted foreground objects. An added benefit of using such a lens is that it gives the appearance of compressing perspective, compared to a standard or wideangle lens. Long lenses also have less depth of field, so by using a wide aperture you can easily throw unwanted foregrounds or backgrounds out of focus.

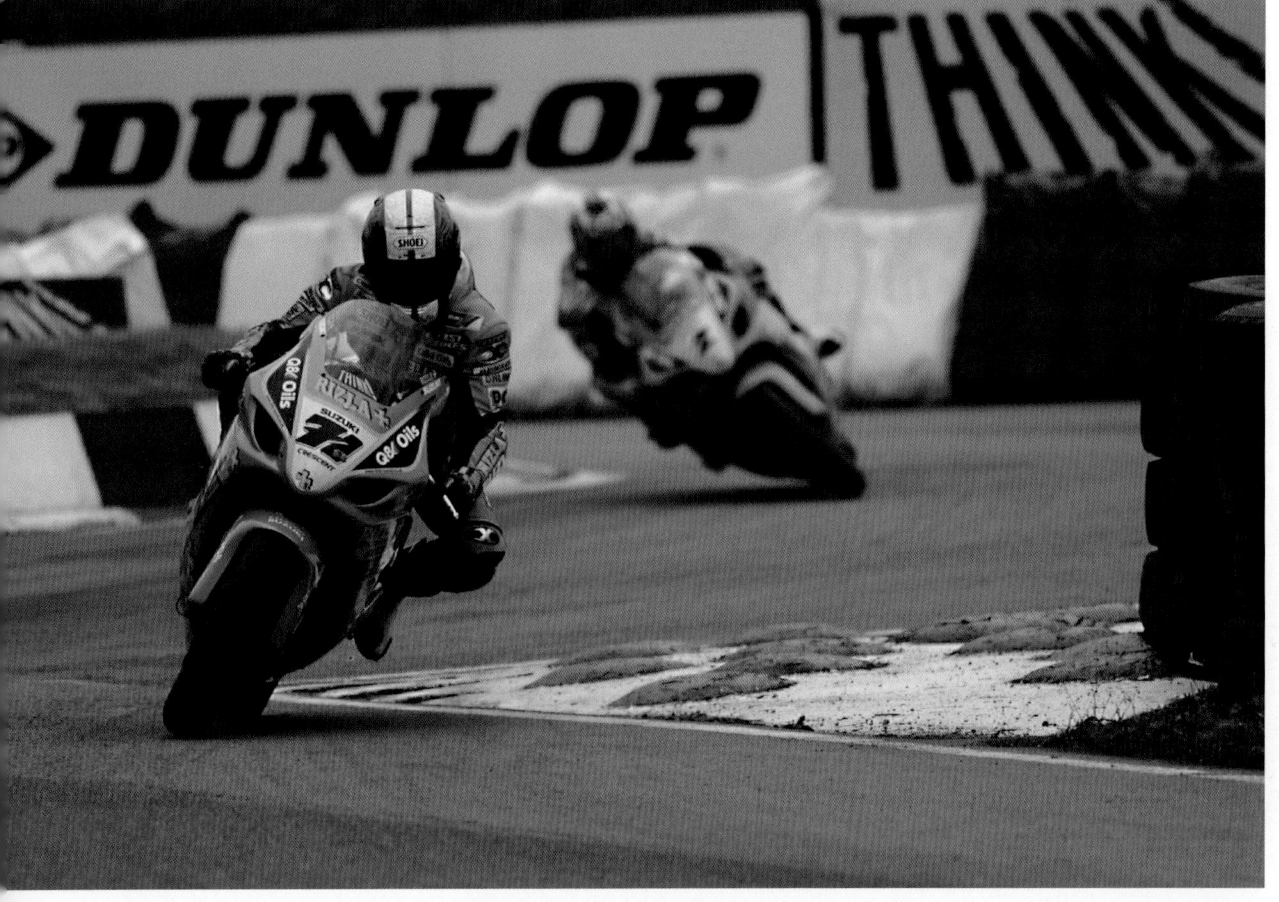

Camera	**Pentax *ist D**
Focal length	**300mm (35mm equivalent: 450mm)**
Exposure	**1/1000sec at f/5.6**
ISO setting	**200**

Fast shutter speeds will freeze the subject; they also require a wider aperture which will reduce the depth of field in the image, thus giving more prominence to the main subject. Focusing becomes more critical in this type of shot because of the reduced depth of field.

Depth of field

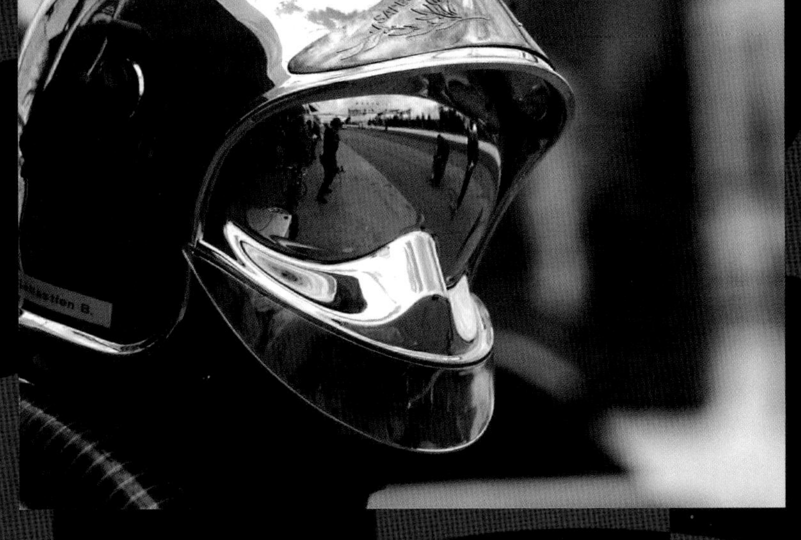

Camera	Pentax *ist D
Focal length	200mm (35mm equivalent: 300mm)
Exposure	1/750sec at f/5.6
ISO setting	200

By limiting the depth of field you can throw distracting backgrounds out of focus and give prominence to the main subject of your image. This technique is especially useful in the pit lane or paddock, where uncluttered backgrounds are hard to come by.

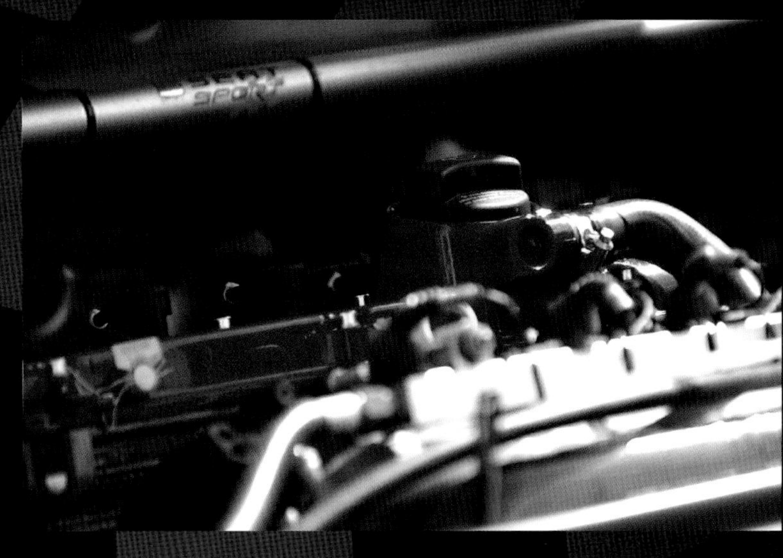

Camera	Pentax *ist D
Focal length	200mm (35mm equivalent: 300mm)
Exposure	1/500sec at f/4
ISO setting	200

Long telephoto lenses used at wide apertures provide very shallow depth of field. By using centre-weighted metering I knew that the highlights in the foreground of this image would be overexposed; this combines with the long lens and wide aperture to draw attention to the filler cap as the focal point of the image.

Depth of field refers to the distance between the nearest and furthest parts of a scene which appear acceptably sharp to the viewer. An image with maximum depth of field may be pin-sharp from the foreground to the horizon, whereas in one with minimal depth of field only the spot on which the camera is focused will appear sharp, and everything else will be more or less blurred.

The longer the focal length of a lens, the less depth of field it is capable of; with this proviso, depth of field can be controlled by using the aperture setting on the lens. For a lens with an aperture range from f/1.4 to f/22, f/22 will provide the maximum depth of field and f/1.4 the minimum. If you look into a lens as you move the aperture ring, you will see that at f/22 the opening is very small, while at f/1.4 the lens is unobstructed. Naturally, the bigger the hole, the more light can get through, and therefore the less time the shutter has to be open in order to admit the required amount of light for an exposure. Because landscape photographers need to use small apertures to maximize depth of field, they have to use a tripod to keep the camera still during exposures lasting a second or more. Tripods are a non-starter for the motor racing photographer, who needs to be mobile, so you will have to stick to relatively high shutter speeds and learn to work with limited depth of field.

Focusing

When using a fast shutter speed to freeze the action, you will probably have a fairly large aperture setting; consequently the depth of field will be fairly short, and it is therefore crucial that you get your focusing right. I always focus manually, as I'm not confident that autofocus is reliable enough to guarantee pin-sharp results all the time. To be fair, in most circumstances modern autofocus systems work very well and can produce excellent results, but I've always used manual-focus lenses and am used to working with them. Maybe I'm stuck in the past, but I prefer the control that I feel this gives me.

Camera	**Pentax *ist D**
Focal length	**190mm (35mm equivalent: 285mm)**
Exposure	**1/500sec at f/4**
ISO setting	**200**

When using manual focus to shoot subjects coming towards you at speed, it is important that you learn to fire the shutter a split second before the subject comes into focus. This allows for the time it takes for your brain to react and send the message to your finger to press the shutter. Learning this technique takes time, but it is a key ingredient in this type of shot.

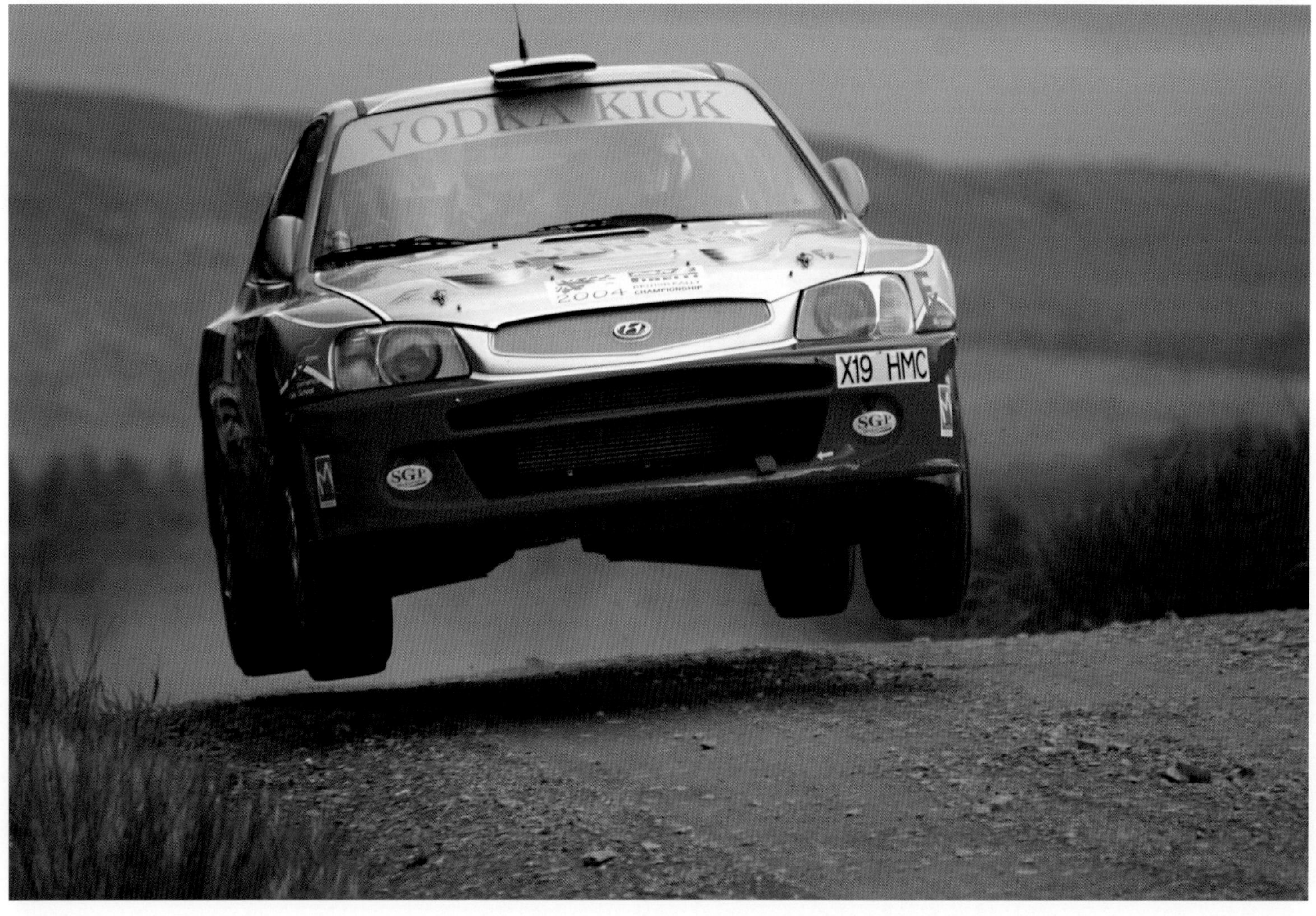

Once I have worked out the composition I want, it's a case of pre-focusing on the track at the relevant position, selecting the correct shutter speed and then shooting the subject as it comes into the pre-focused area. As the vehicle is likely to be moving pretty quickly, it is important to fire the shutter at the right time – generally a split second before the subject becomes pin-sharp. However, the speed of the vehicle has to be taken into account, and this technique can only be acquired through practice. As you are using faster shutter speeds, camera shake is less of a problem than when panning, but if using a heavy telephoto lens it is worth investing in a monopod to help support the weight.

Camera	***Pentax *ist D***
Focal length	***210mm (35mm equivalent: 315mm)***
Exposure	***1/500sec at f/6.7***
ISO setting	***200***

Touring cars provide very competitive racing, with regular contact between vehicles throughout the field. Since I prefer to focus manually for action shots, it is important to pre-focus on a part of the track where I want to make an exposure. Good-quality, fast lenses make this much easier than slower lenses, which darken the viewfinder and make fine focusing quite difficult.

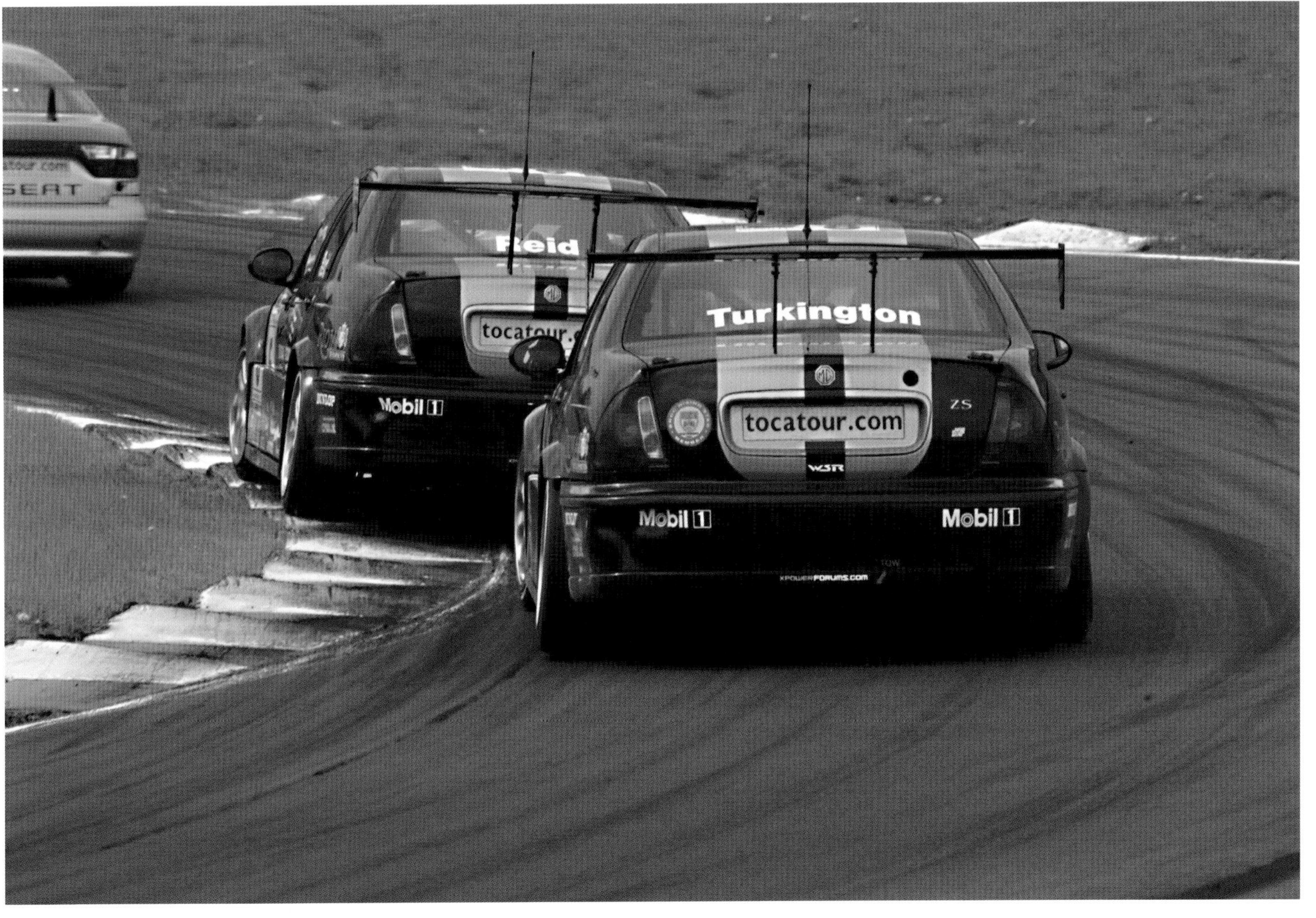

Shutter speeds

Once more, the choice of shutter speed depends on the speed of the subject. When I want to freeze the action I generally work with speeds between 1/350 and 1/1000sec. If there is enough light to support faster exposures, I can then consider how much depth of field I want in the image, and make adjustments accordingly. Just because you *can* use a shutter speed of 1/1000sec at f/4 doesn't mean you should – it may be beneficial to use 1/500sec at f/5.6 and have a little more depth of field.

Camera	***Pentax *ist D***
Focal length	***300mm (35mm equivalent: 450mm)***
Exposure	***1/2000sec at f/4***
ISO setting	***200***

Telephoto lenses as long as this are pretty heavy. Attaching a monopod to the lens for stability will prevent camera shake as well as saving your arms from becoming tired.

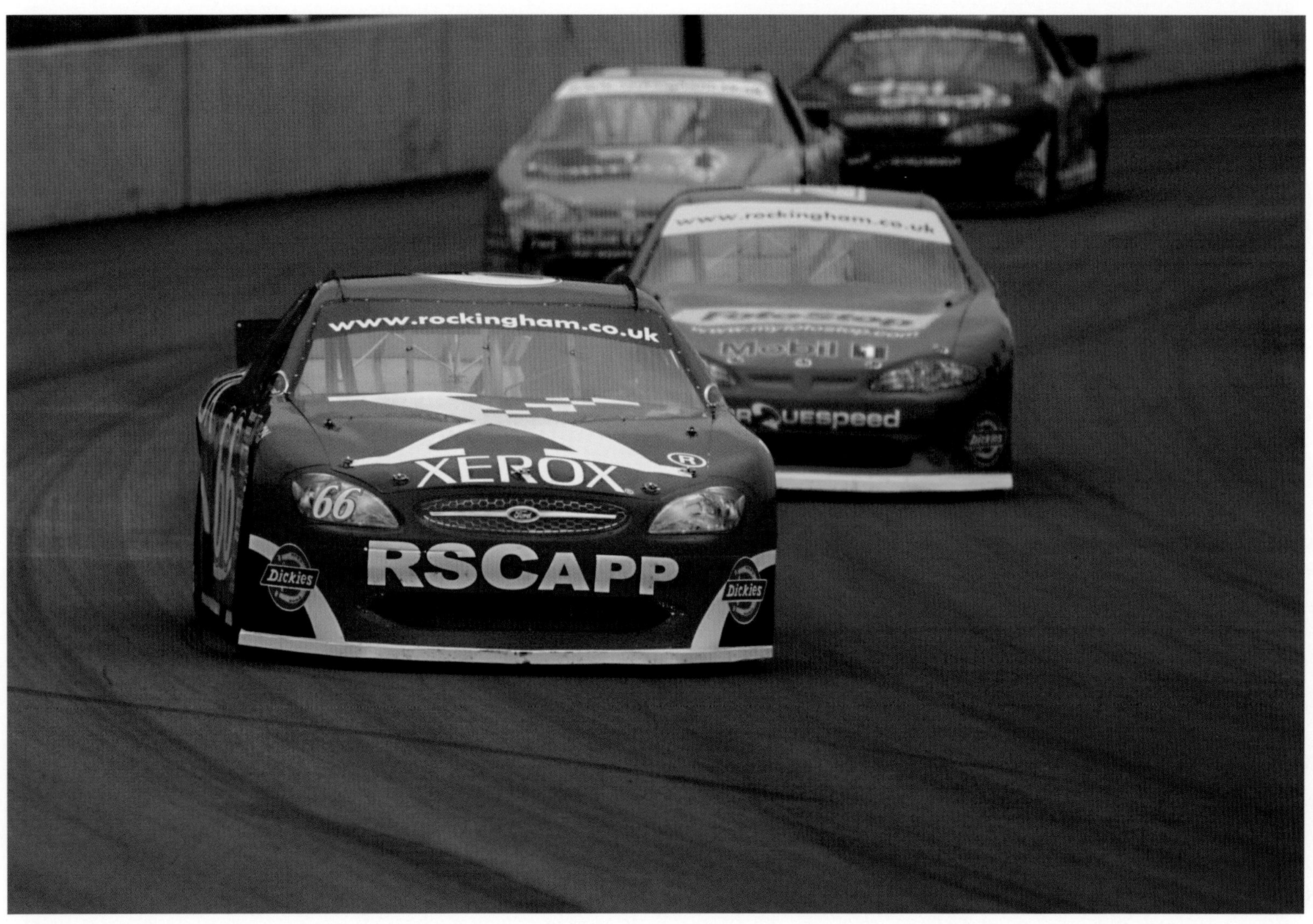

If you're shooting an off-road event such as a gravel rally or motocross race, you will have the added bonus of being able to utilize mud and stones as they are thrown up from the vehicles' wheels. You can create different effects from this, according to the shutter speed you choose. A fast shutter speed of 1/500sec or quicker will usually freeze mud or stones flying into the air. This can produce pleasing results, but I prefer to use a slower speed to emphasize the movement of the flying debris – speeds of between 1/125 and 1/350sec are usually fine for this. Remember that flying mud and stones have to land somewhere, so ensure you're either well out of the way or are ready to turn your back to protect your face and camera once you are certain the vehicle has passed by safely. **It bears repeating: never turn your back on a speeding vehicle – it might be the last thing you never see.**

Camera	***Pentax *ist D***
Focal length	***200mm (35mm equivalent: 300mm)***
Exposure	***1/180sec at f/11***
ISO setting	***200***

Flying mud and stones will be frozen by very high shutter speeds, and this can often look a little unrealistic. I prefer to use moderate shutter speeds that will keep some appearance of movement in these circumstances but still prevent the car from being blurred.

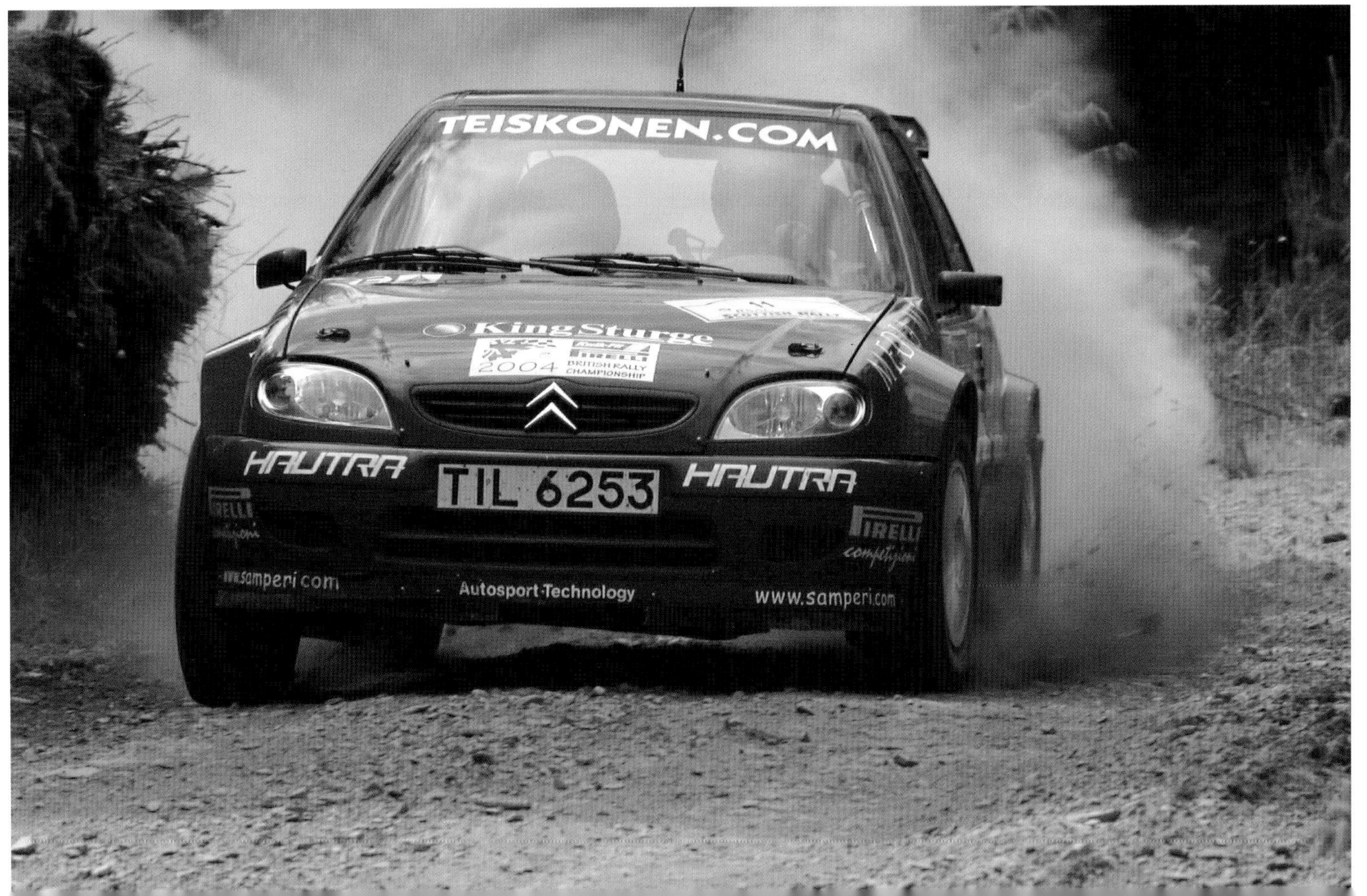

Action sequences

Capturing action sequences such as crashes or overtaking manoeuvres is usually done in one of two ways: you can predict it and be ready for it, or react to it and have to move quickly to capture it. If you know your racing disciplines well it is easier to predict a bit of argy-bargy than you might think – knowledge of the drivers and the type of vehicle will help. Open-wheeled cars such as Formula Fords will only make contact with each other as the result of driver error, whereas those with more bodywork, such as touring cars, will deliberately give each other a little 'rub' or 'love touch' as part of their normal racing technique. Understanding these differences will help you to increase your chances of capturing a moment of contact.

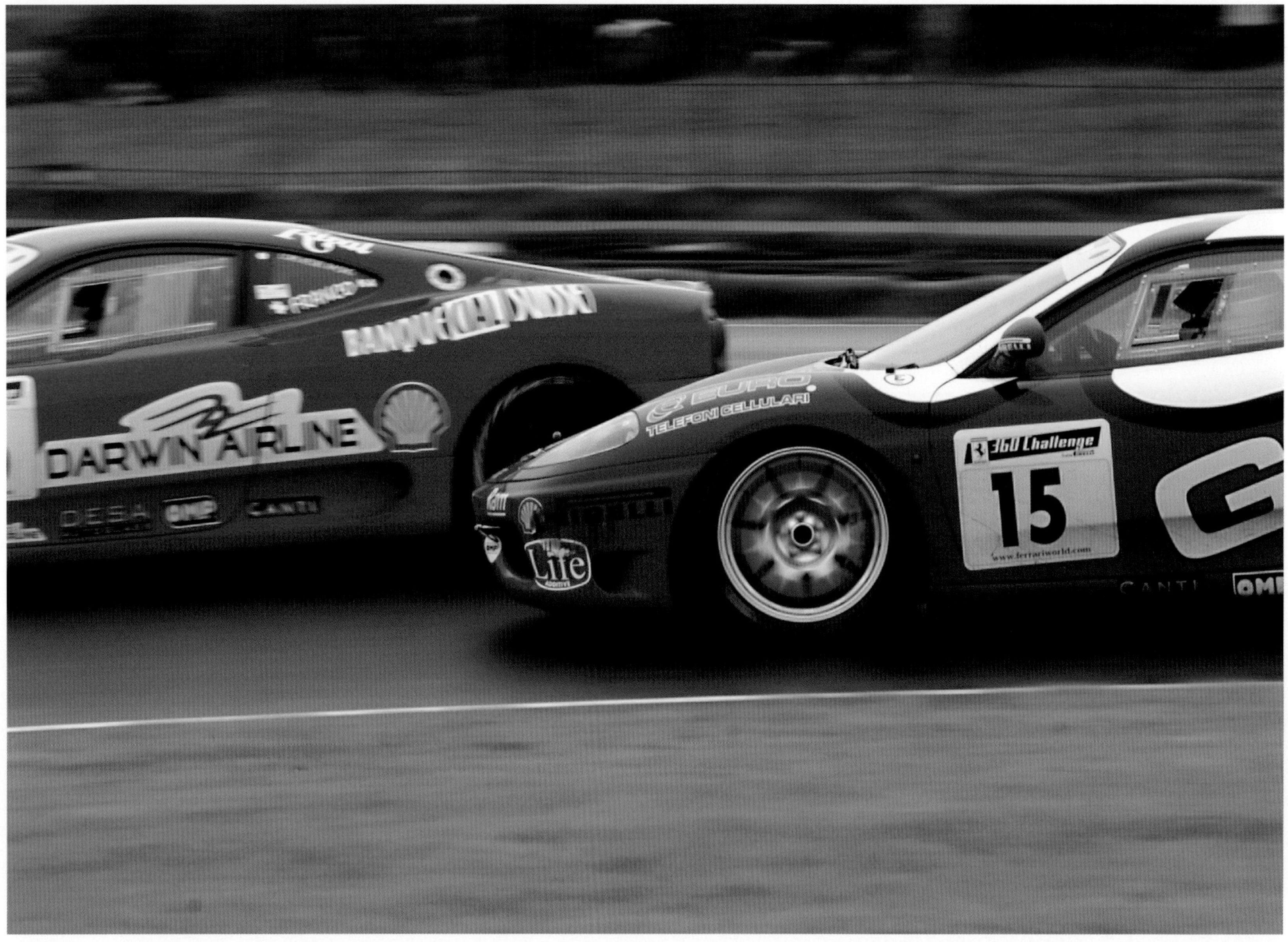

I don't spend a lot of time specifically trying to capture collisions, but I do bear it in mind if I'm at a race where there is normally a fair degree of contact. When I think there may be an opportunity to capture a 'racing incident' I will use a zoom lens so that I can zoom out to a shorter focal length if need be – cars may not follow the normal line as they collide, so I like to have a little more area in the viewfinder to allow for this unpredictability.

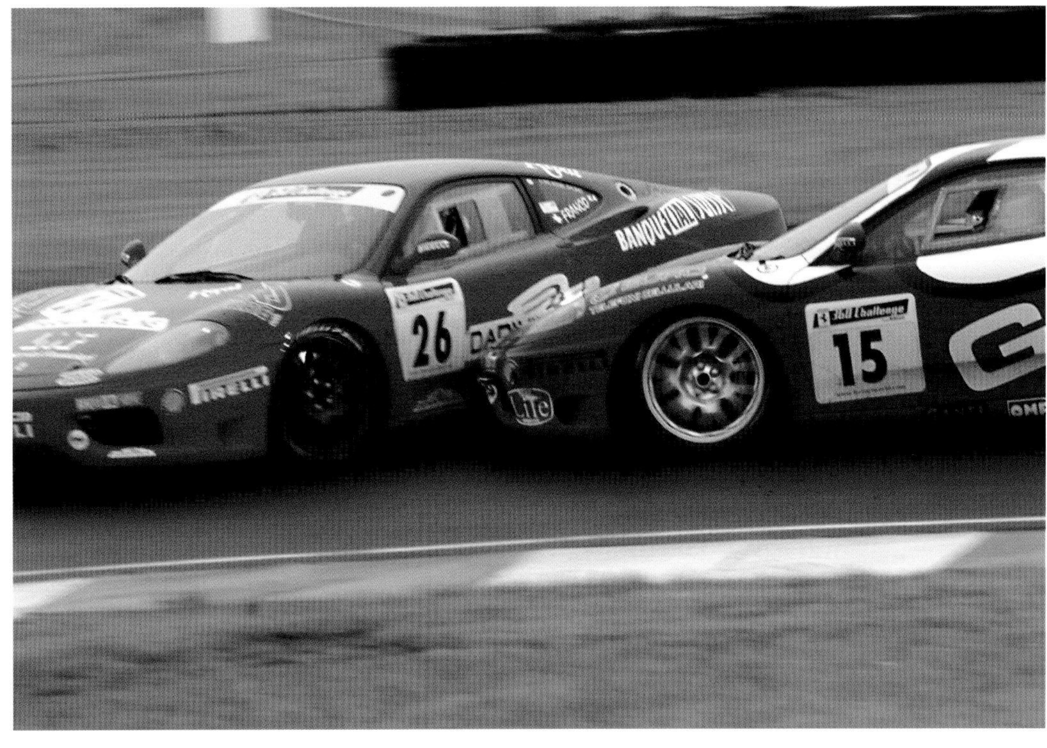

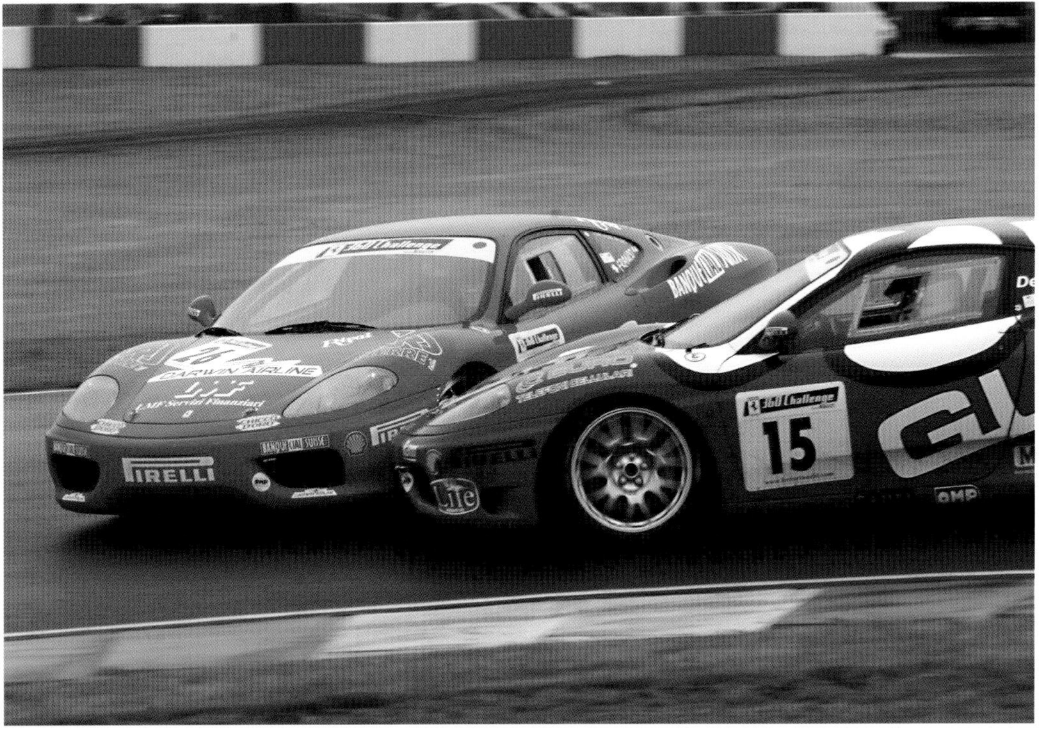

Camera	***Pentax *ist D***
Focal length	***180mm (35mm equivalent: 270mm)***
Exposure	***1/125sec at f/9.5***
ISO setting	***200***

Capturing action sequences often involves as much luck as judgement. In this case I shot a total of six exposures, three of which were not good enough to print because the shutter speed was too slow (I had the camera set up for a panned cornering shot). In these situations you just have to shoot the scene and hope for the best - there is no time to amend your camera settings.

Seizing the moment

There is a certain degree of luck involved in capturing such incidents. Not only do you have to be in the right place at the right time – you also have to be aware that an accident is happening, and have your camera set to capture it. In my experience you may get a couple of these factors once in a while, but it is rare to get all three. For example, if you are at a corner looking for panned shots you will be picking up your subject in the viewfinder as early as you can; you will have a relatively slow shutter speed and will be panning with the vehicle. Looking through the viewfinder, you will not see that the car behind the one you are following has locked its brakes and is beginning to spin; you may also have difficulty hearing the tyres squeal over the noise of the other cars. Even if you are lucky enough to spot this, you still have your lens pre-focused at a different point for the panned shot you intended, and the camera is set to a fairly slow shutter speed, so you have to make the best of a bad job. There's nothing you can do about changing the shutter speed – the action will be over before you've moved – so the best thing to do is concentrate on the action and amend your focus as quickly as you can. Sometimes you'll get it right, sometimes you won't.

Dramatic situations like this are the only times when I question my choice of manual focus over autofocus. I'm not convinced that autofocus would be accurate all the time, but I bet it's quicker than my reactions when I need to re-focus on a spinning car. Still, it's better to capture the moment with less than ideal camera settings than miss it altogether as you try to adjust them.

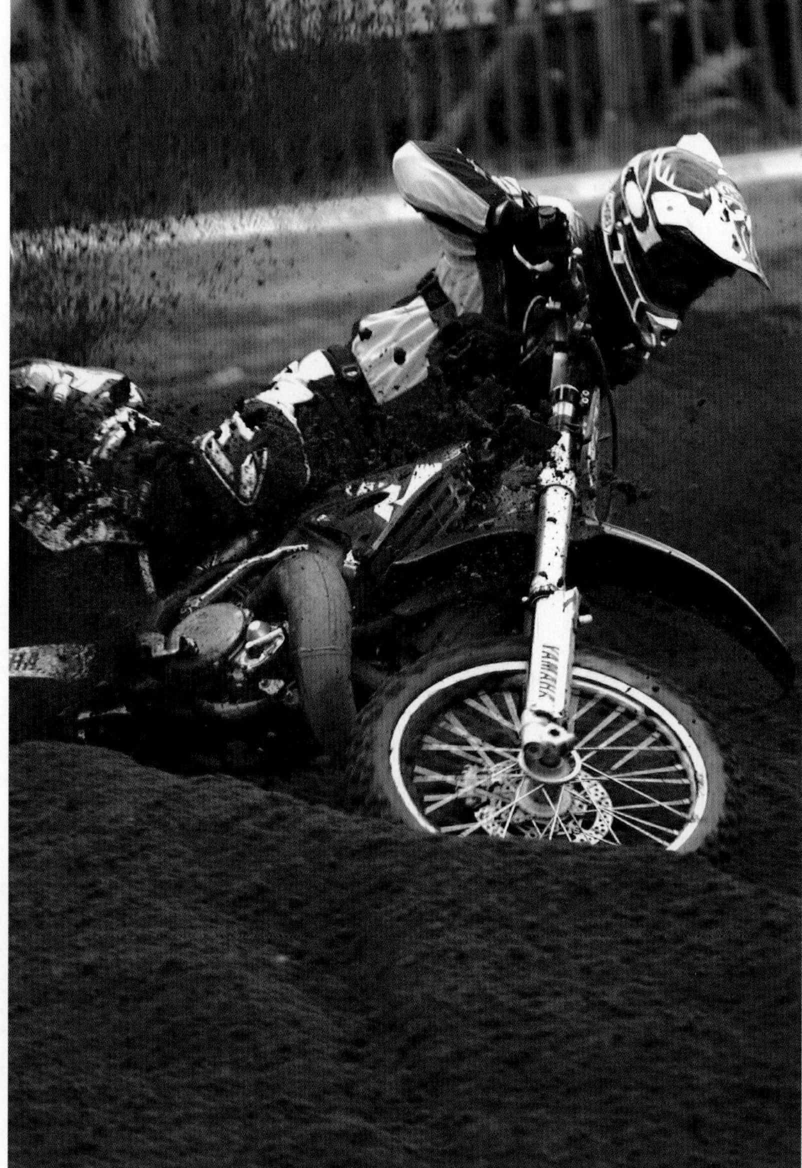

Camera	***Pentax *ist D***
Focal length	***190mm (35mm equivalent: 285mm)***
Exposure	***1/350sec at f/4***
ISO setting	***200***

Crashes and spills often unfold in front of you – but you can't plan for them to happen, and neither can you afford to wait around on the off chance of someone coming off. You often have to react quickly when the opportunity arises – and knowing your equipment inside out will help you cope with these situations.

Autofocus

I prefer to use manual focusing when shooting motor sports, because I'm not wholly confident that autofocus (AF) will do the job reliably every time. I should stress that this is only my opinion, but it is born of experience.

If you do want to use AF it is important that you fully understand how the focusing system on your camera works – AF systems vary in type and functionality. Some older systems have multiple focusing points, allowing you to select which portion of the composition you want to be pin-sharp – but if you're shooting action there is often insufficient time to make this selection. On the other hand, if your AF system relies on the main subject being placed in a specific area of the viewfinder (often the centre), you could easily 'fool' it when using an off-centre composition. However, modern AF systems have become so sophisticated that some have the capacity to recognize which part of the viewfinder your eye is looking at and automatically adjust the focus to that point. This is the type I would choose if I were unable to use manual focusing.

With all this said, the majority of AF systems struggle when lighting conditions are low, or when there is little contrast in the subject. You can overcome this by using autofocus lock (AFL), but again this may need more time than you have available when taking action shots.

Camera	*Pentax *ist D*
Focal length	*300mm (35mm equivalent: 450mm)*
Exposure	*1/250sec at f/5.6*
ISO setting	*200*

I used follow-focusing for this shot: I needed to fill the frame with the rider and bike, so had to choose the exact moment of exposure carefully. Follow-focusing involves picking up the subject early on and then continually adjusting the focus as it moves towards (or away from) you. It's not an easy technique to master and it's not one that I use often, but it's a handy skill to have.

I find AF unhelpful when I am taking more creative shots, because the camera doesn't 'know' what effect I'm trying to achieve – so, reverting to my brain's 'default' setting, I switch off the AF and use manual focus.

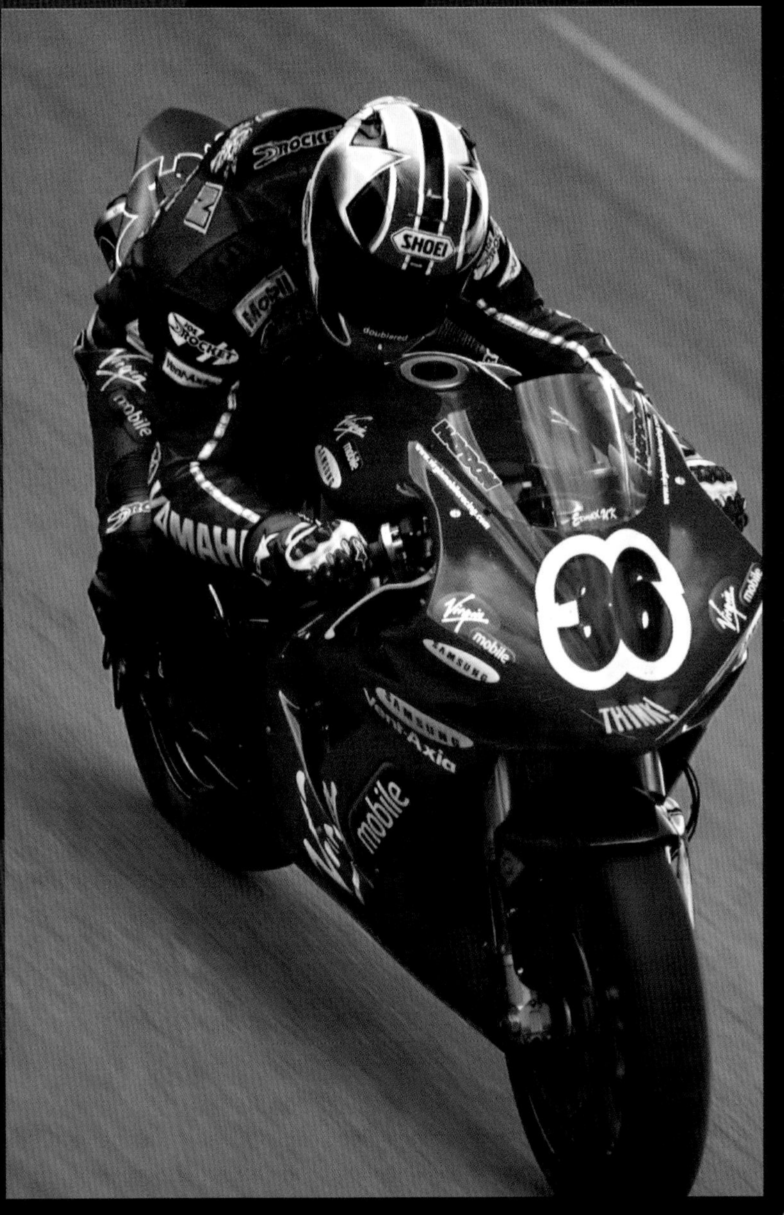

Flash photography

Using flash to improve a scene's lighting is an integral part of successful motor sport photography. Don't think that your flash is only necessary in conditions where natural light is poor – when shooting motor sports, often the opposite is the case. Bright, sunny conditions create strong shadows, and flash is often needed to help balance the light and shade. This technique, known as fill-in flash, is best used when you are fairly close to your subject; you won't use it for action shots at a racing circuit, but you might use it in the paddock for shooting people or detail shots.

There was a time when I shied away from using fill-in flash, because I'd had some bad results when using it and didn't fully understand how to control the settings to get the effect I needed. However, I persevered, and after much hair-pulling and many wasted frames my flashgun now goes everywhere with me.

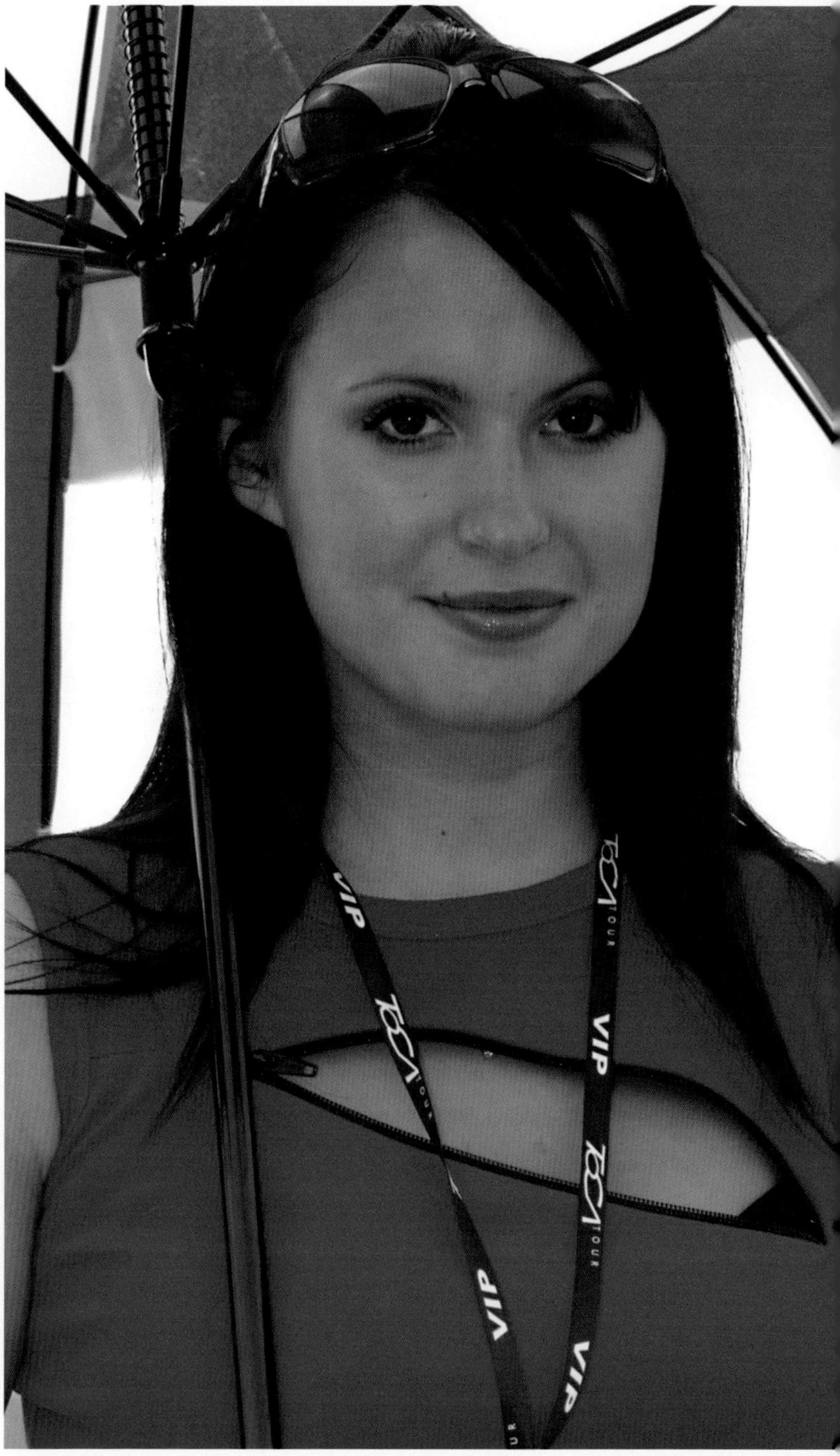

Camera	***Pentax *ist D***
Focal length	***180mm (35mm equivalent: 270mm)***
Exposure	***1/350sec at f/8***
ISO setting	***200***

Fill-in flash helps to bring out detail in shaded subjects. In this shot I 'fooled' the flash unit by setting it to underexpose by a couple of stops, so that the flash does not dominate the image. The flash has taken away the shadows from the girl's face and added highlights to her eyes.

Making your own light

Landscape photographers usually prefer to shoot at dawn or dusk; this ensures good-quality 'soft' light, as the sun is low in the sky and does not produce the harsh shadows which we see during the middle hours of the day. As a motor sport photographer you cannot afford to be so choosy: you will often be shooting in harsh lighting conditions and, though flash is not needed for capturing the majority of action shots, it can be very useful if you're shooting in the paddock. A portfolio of action shots can be much improved by the addition of one or two images of racing personalities or paddock 'grab shots' taken with a bit of fill-in. A very small percentage of my shots are taken using flash, but there are occasions when it is absolutely vital – so it is well worth the time it takes to learn how to use it effectively.

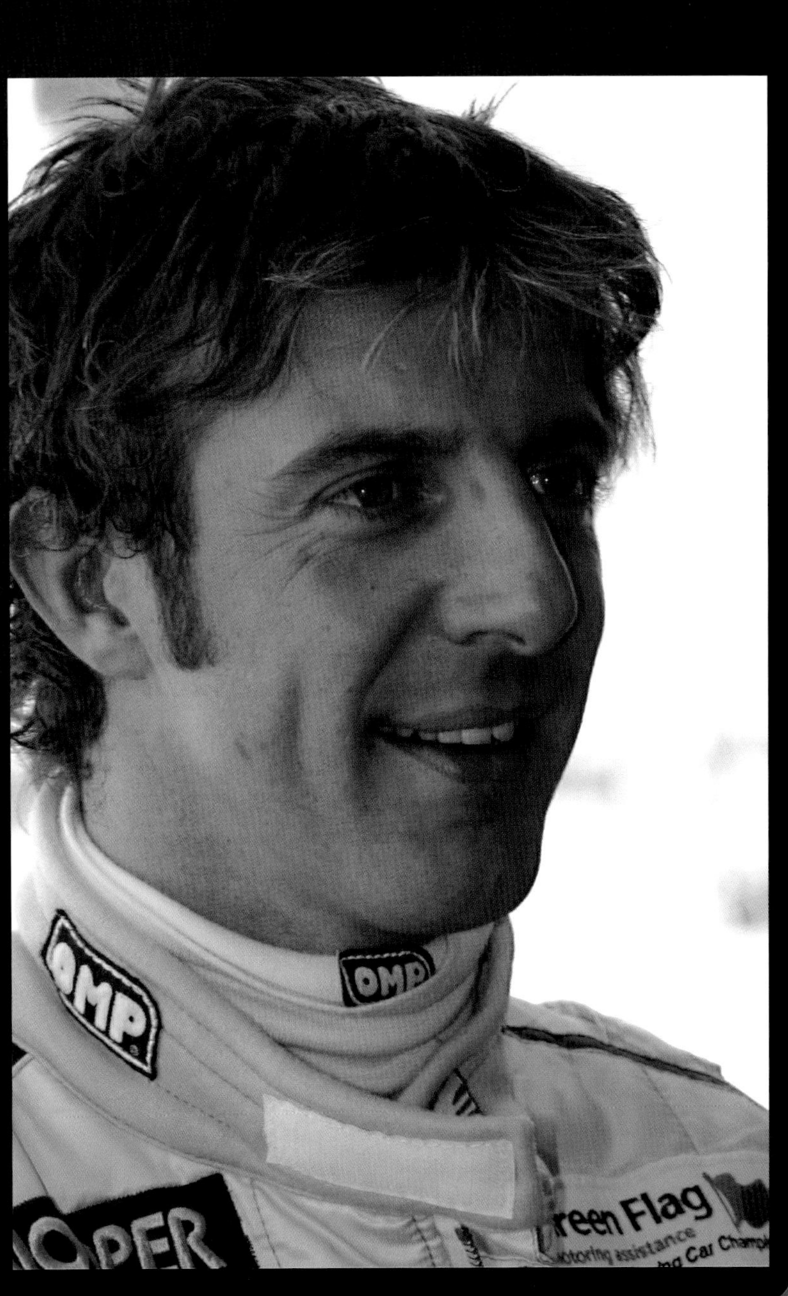

Camera	**Pentax *ist D**
Focal length	**135mm (35mm equivalent: 200mm)**
Exposure	**1/90sec at f/8**
ISO setting	**200**

Many photographers find flash a bit daunting, but learning how to use it effectively is a crucial part of motor sport photography.

Understanding fill-in flash

In order to get the results you want it is important to be aware of how your flashgun works. Though most modern cameras now come with a built-in pop-up flash, I would recommend that you use a portable flashgun fitted to your camera's hot shoe. Built-in flash units can produce good results, but they generally have neither the power nor the control to provide the flexibility you need. You may have either an automatic flashgun or one that is fully dedicated to your camera; both are perfectly adequate, but I prefer to use an automatic one as it is easier to control.

It is important to know the maximum shutter speed that can be used with flash on your particular camera. Flash sync speeds vary between 1/60 and 1/300sec, depending on the camera; if you're not sure what yours is, check in your owner's handbook or contact the manufacturer. You can use your flash at shutter speeds slower than your camera's sync speed, but if you use a speed that is faster than this the burst of flash will not be synchronized with the shutter, and your image will either have no fill-in flash or have flash exposure on only part of the frame. Some digital cameras have no limit to sync speed, because they use an electronic shutter which turns the sensor on and off.

In general, I don't like flash to be obvious in my images. I find it can often be too harsh and unflattering, and the main reason I use an automatic flashgun is so that I can override it in order to get the lighting I need. As a general rule I will take a meter reading with the camera and then reduce the setting on the flash by a couple of stops; this causes the flash to effectively underexpose the flash part of the image, and prevents the light from the flash being too dominant. For example, if I get a meter reading of 1/125sec at f/8 I will set the flash for an exposure of f/4, but leave the camera at f/8. By using this technique in daylight I am making sure that the light delivered by the flash is merely complementing the natural light, brightening any areas that would otherwise be underexposed or need highlighting. In this way the light from the flash adds to the scene rather than dominating it.

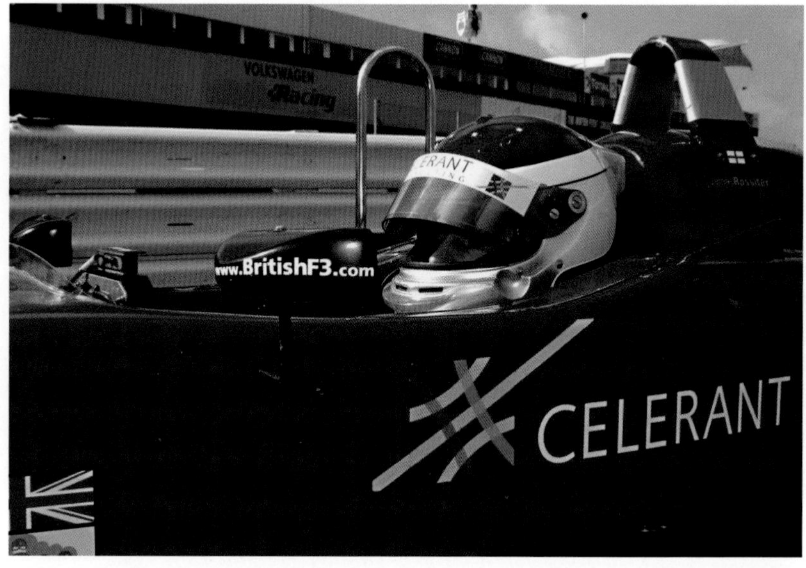

Camera	***Pentax *ist D***
Focal length	***50mm (35mm equivalent: 75mm)***
Exposure	***1/125sec at f/16***
ISO setting	***200***

This is a very simple shot of a driver on the grid as he waits for the start of a race. I used fill-in flash to even out the harsh shadows caused by the midday sun.

Warning!

If you're photographing an evening or night event, be aware of the effect that the flash might have on your subject. Try not to shoot directly in the driver's line of sight, as this could momentarily impair their vision and could prove dangerous.

What type of flashgun?

Automatic flash units contain a sensor that measures the light from the flash as it reflects off the subject, and sets the duration of the flash burst accordingly to achieve the correct exposure. You can control the output by using a calculator on the rear of the flash unit.

Dedicated units are designed for use with a specific camera or range of cameras, and automatically set the correct lens aperture and shutter sync speed. They are then able to control the exposure by regulating the amount of light they emit. These units either have a built-in light sensor or work via the camera's own metering system to produce the correct exposure.

Camera	***Pentax *ist D***
Focal length	***200mm (35mm equivalent: 300mm)***
Exposure	***1/125sec at f/4.5***
ISO setting	***200***

This shot was taken through the gap between the car door and the bodywork as the driver sat on the grid waiting for the race to start. I used a large aperture on the 300mm lens to focus on the driver's eyes and throw the door and side netting out of focus. A small amount of fill-in flash was used to highlight the driver's face, which would otherwise have been in shadow.

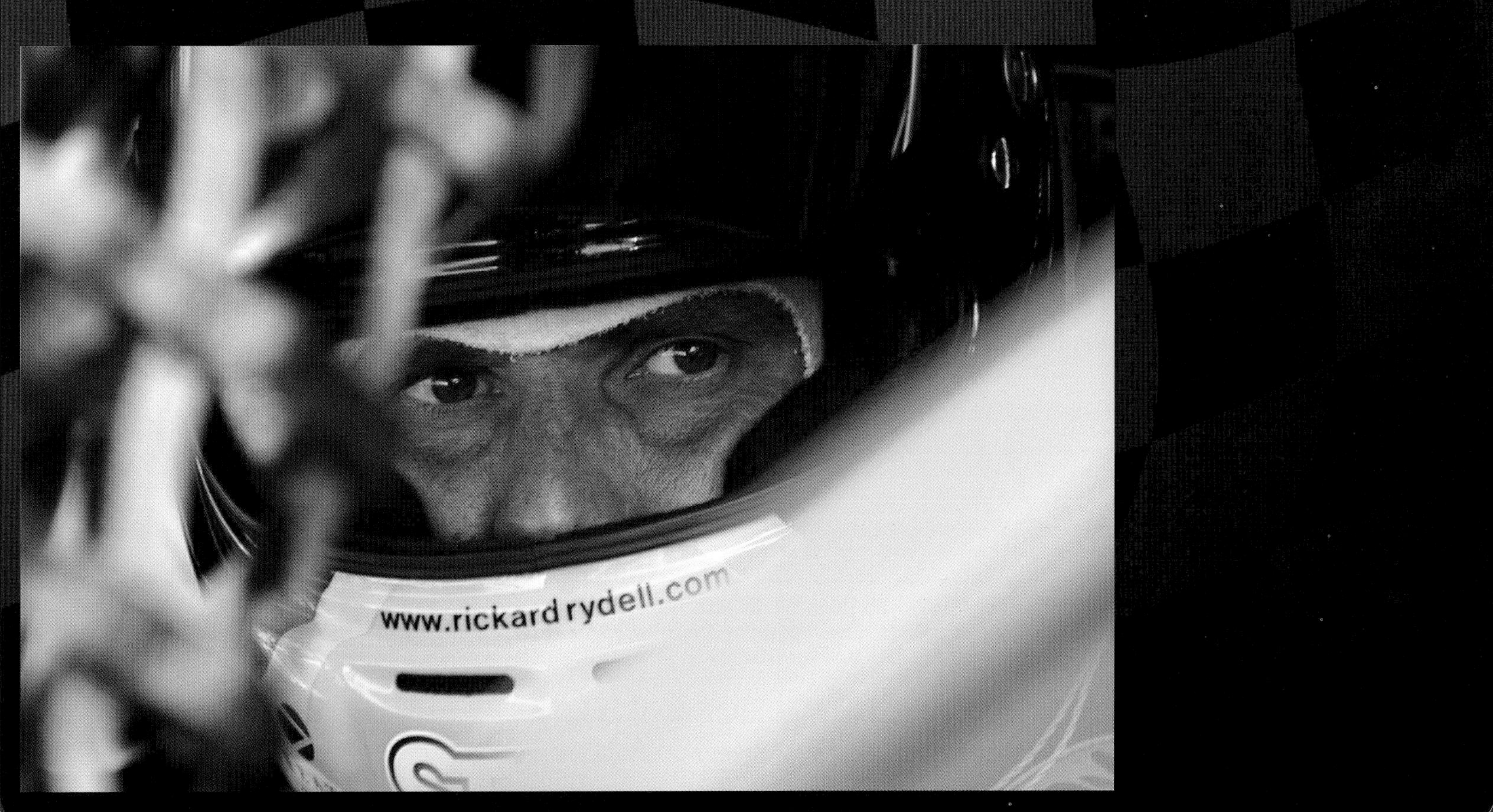

Slow-sync flash

Another very effective method is to use flash in conjunction with slow shutter speeds; this is called slow-sync flash. The basic principle is to use a slow shutter speed to blur your subject, coupled with a burst of flash which appears to freeze any movement. As a way of portraying action this works very well, provided you can get close to your subject – at longer distances the power of the flash will drop off and have less impact on the final image. Motocross is an ideal subject for slow-sync flash: you can usually get very close to the action, and when the bikes are not airborne they're churning up spectacular amounts of dirt.

A shutter speed of between 1/15 and 1/90sec (depending on the speed of the subject) will make for a pleasing result. I normally start off by shooting a few frames at 1/60sec, then drop down to 1/30 and then 1/15. I find that using shutter speeds below 1/15sec is a very hit-and-miss affair, but will often take a couple of shots at 1/8sec just as an experiment.

Having set the flash at one stop under the meter reading (if the meter reads f/11, I set the flash to f/8), you can pretty much forget about it and concentrate on capturing the image. As slow shutter speeds are being used, you will have to pan, and because you need to be close to your subject in order for the flash to have the desired effect, you will need to pan very quickly. I like to fill the frame with the subject, as this adds to the impact created by the slow shutter speeds and burst of flash. This can mean that there is only a split second to compose the image as your subject flies by a few metres away. Getting your composition right in that time is pretty tricky, but once again, practice makes perfect.

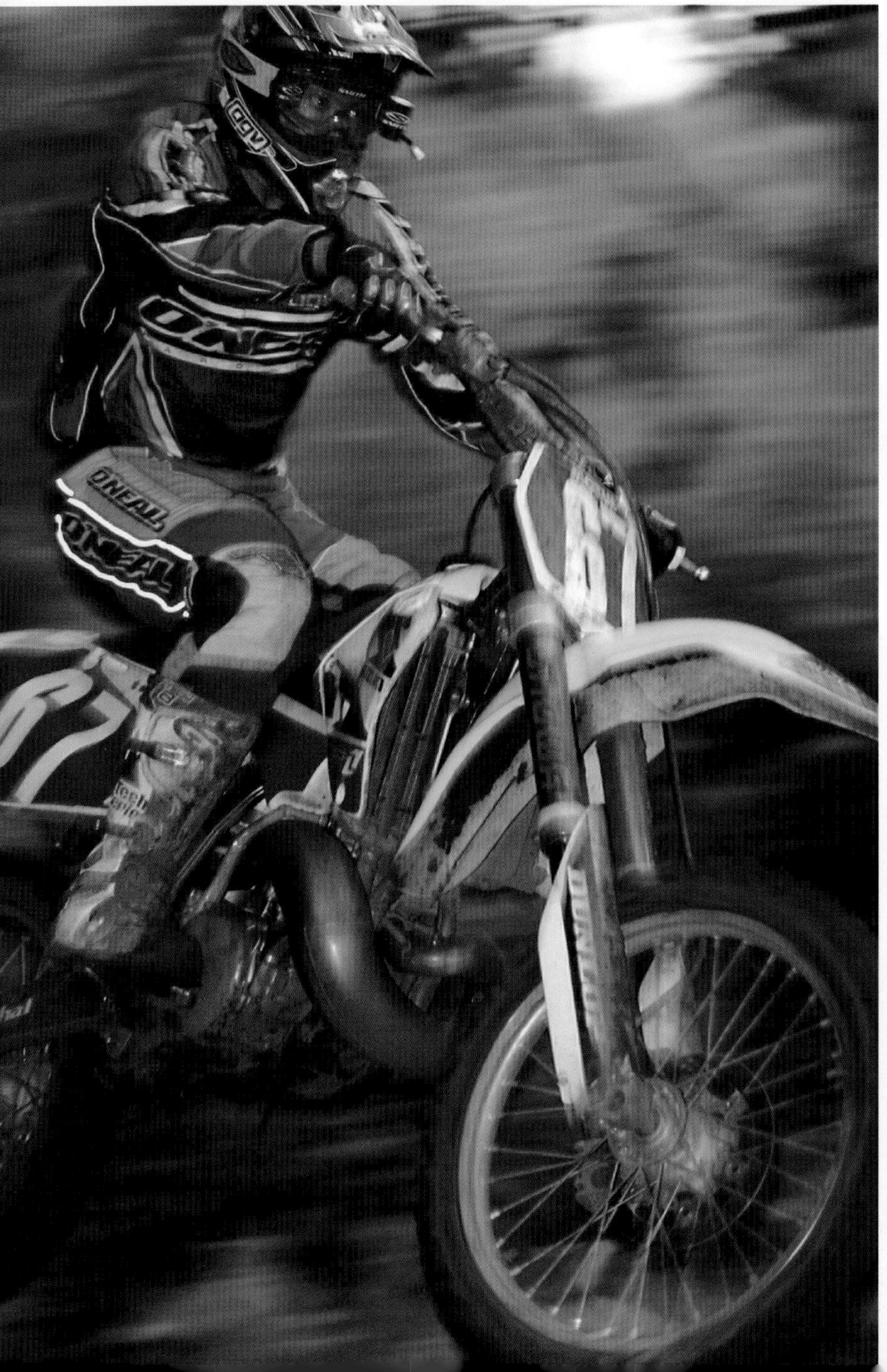

Camera	**Pentax *ist D**
Focal length	**100mm (35mm equivalent: 150mm)**
Exposure	**1/60sec at f/4**
ISO setting	**200**

In low light conditions such as those found in this wooded scene, slow-sync flash can provide pleasing results. The burst of flash serves to freeze the bike and rider, while the slow shutter speed adds movement to the image.

As before, I pre-focus on a piece of track. If the subject is in the air – as is often the case in motocross – I focus on the track beneath where the bikes will pass and then check the focusing through the lens just to make sure before I start shooting. It is very important that you continue to pan with the subject as you fire the shutter; your pan will be faster than in normal conditions but the shutter speed will be slower, so it's essential to keep your panning action as smooth as possible.

As with many areas of photography, mastering slow-sync takes time and effort. I began using this technique well before the introduction of digital photography, and found it invaluable to record the shutter speed and aperture settings so that I could evaluate what worked best when I was reviewing my shots on the lightbox. Carrying a small dictating machine is probably the easiest and most practical way of doing this. However, as I now shoot digitally I can review the image straight away – another tick in the box for digital!

Camera	**Pentax *ist D**
Focal length	**18mm (35mm equivalent: 28mm)**
Exposure	**1/15sec at f/16**
ISO setting	**200**

Combining flash with slow shutter speeds can produce very effective results. While panning this wideangle shot I was careful not to get my toes run over as the driver pulled into his pit garage after a qualifying session.

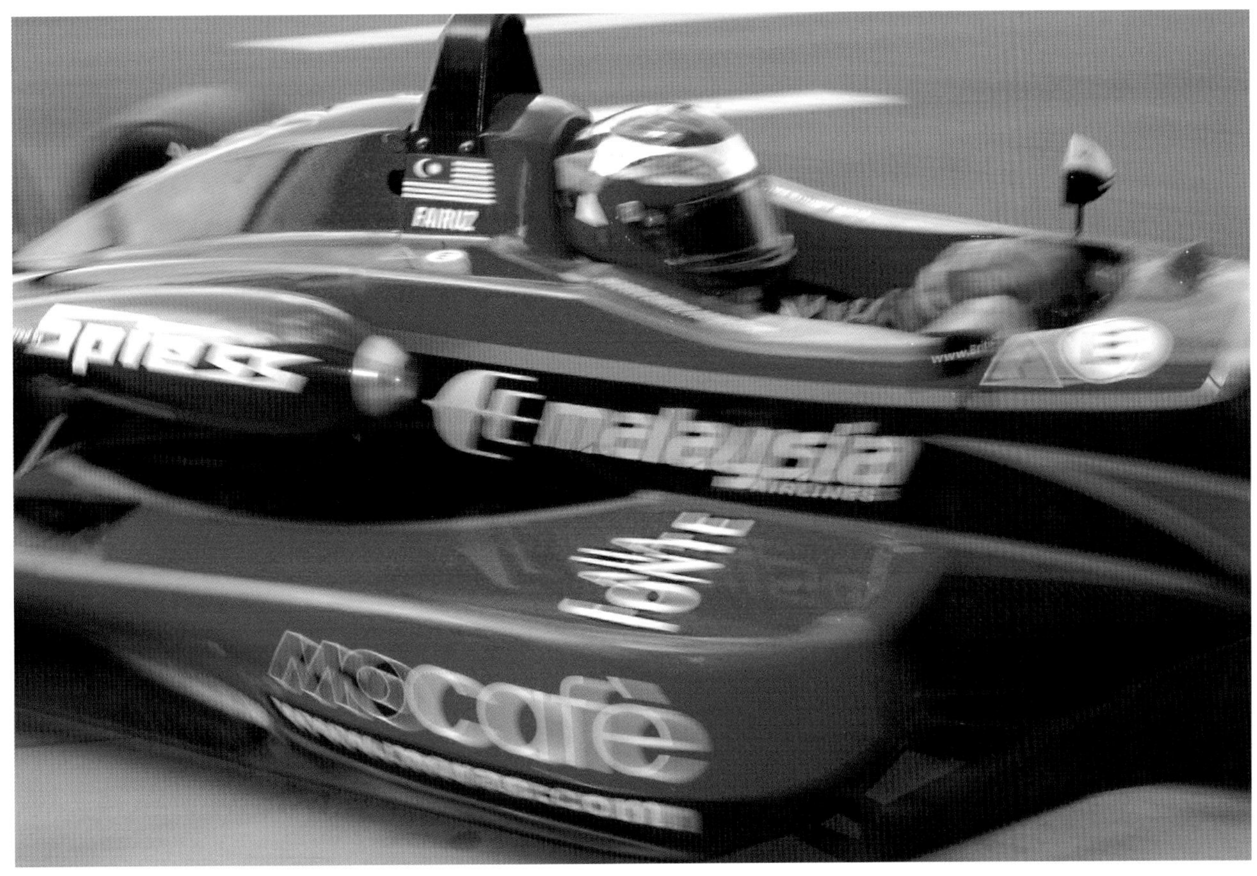

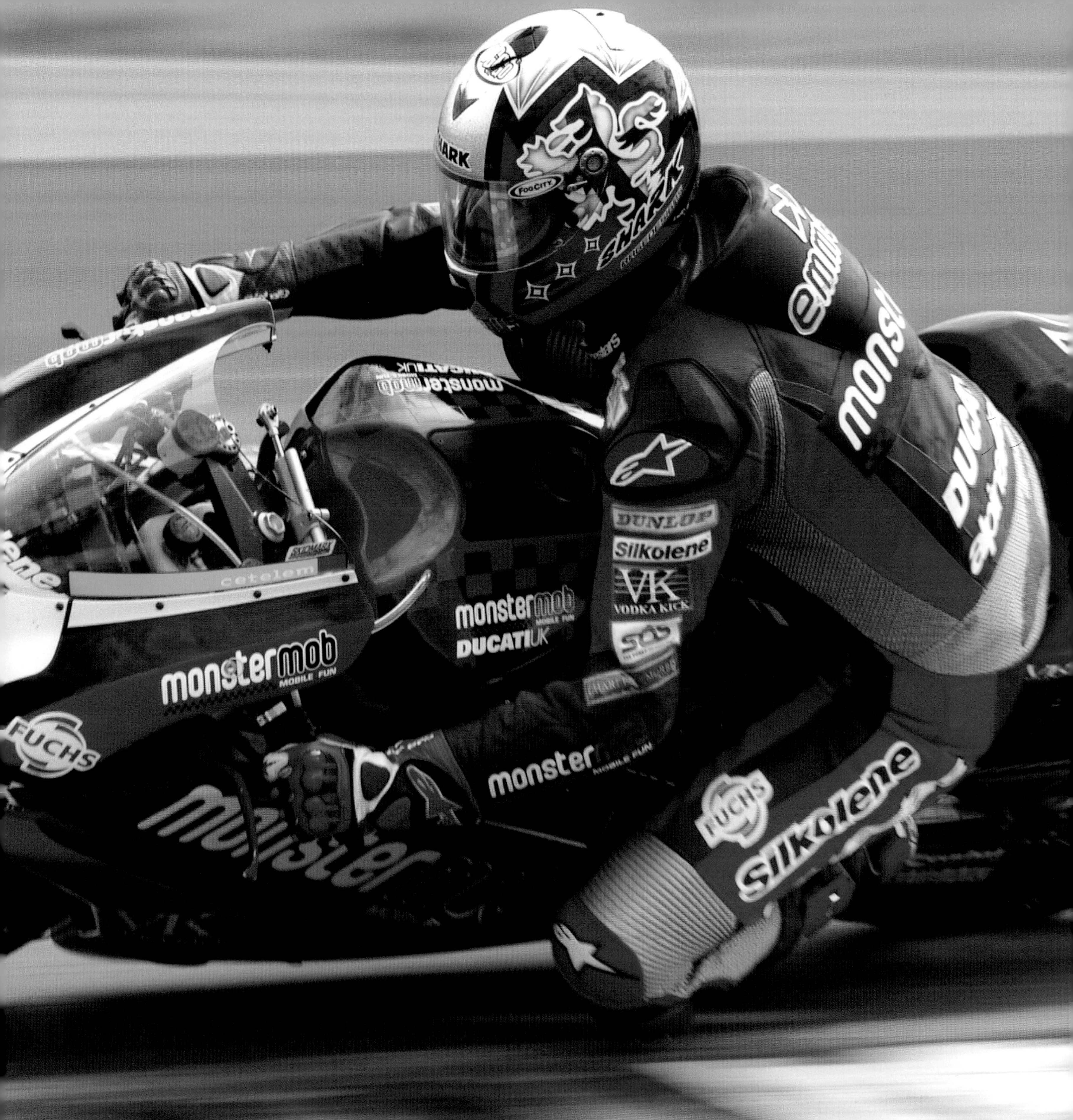
SHARK
FOG CITY
monstermob
DUCATI UK
DUNLOP
Silkolene
VK
VODKA KICK
monstermob
MOBILE FUN
DUCATI UK
cetelem
monstermob
MOBILE FUN
FUCHS
MOBILE FUN
FUCHS
Silkolene
Silkolene

CHAPTER 5

Composition

Composition is crucial to the success of a photograph. Before putting your eye to the viewfinder you should have a vision of the shot you are looking for, and all the technical decisions you make should be informed by the image you have visualized in your mind. This is the key to taking successful motor racing images, and because it is a creative process there is no textbook that can tell you how to do this. The easiest way to develop this skill is to think constantly about image composition, whether you're attending an event, planning your next shoot, or sitting in the dentist's chair.

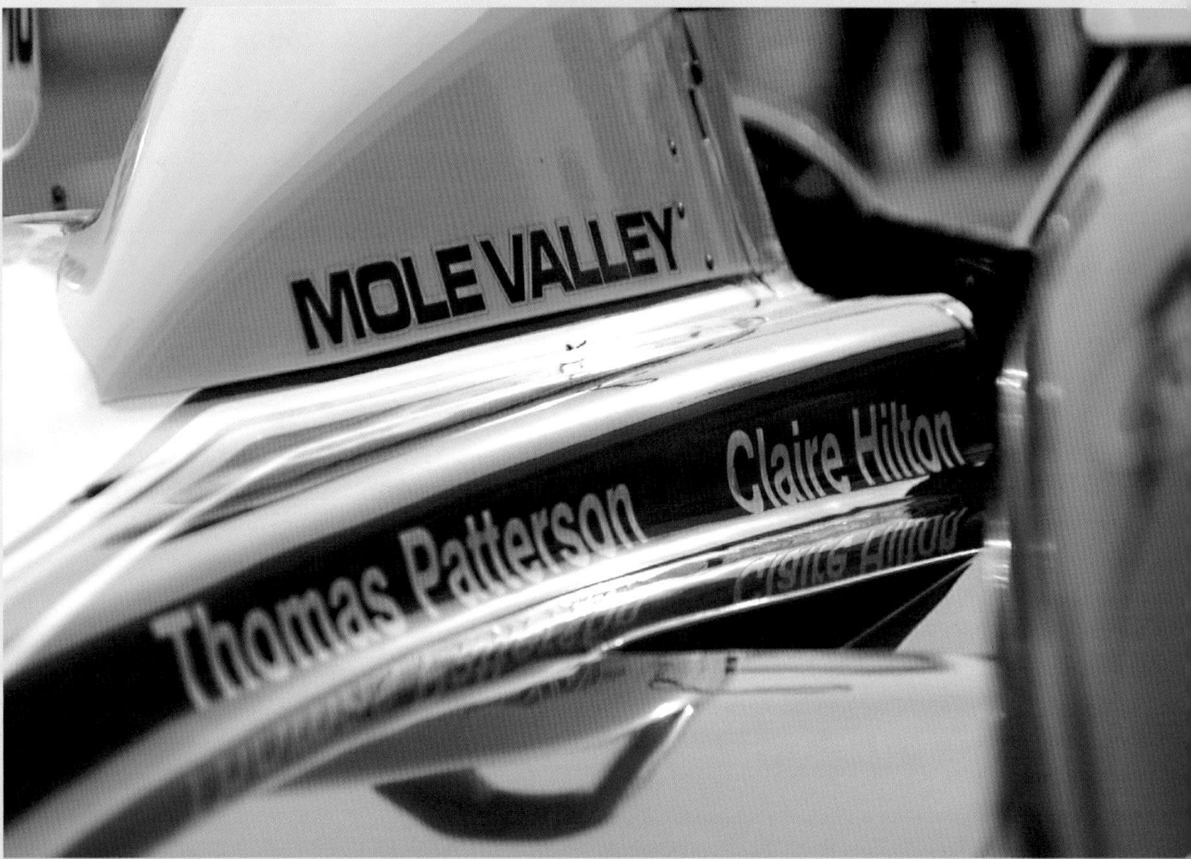

Camera	Pentax *ist D
Focal length	190mm (35mm equivalent: 280mm)
Exposure	1/1000sec at f/4.5
ISO setting	200

Applying the basic rules of composition to your own creative interpretation will help you to create strong motor sport images. Being creative in the way you compose photographs is essential if you want to do more than simply record a scene literally.

Choosing the right viewpoint

When I visit an event I aim to come away with as great a variety of images as I can; this invariably means moving to different points around a track or rally stage. Having done my research prior to an event, I will already have a good idea where the best viewpoints are; in order to complete my preparation I always arrive with plenty of time to reconnoitre. I like to check out where the sun is positioned, allowing plenty of time to alter my plans if the light is poor. On rally events it is important to give yourself time to walk through some of the stage and identify a number of potential viewpoints, making mental notes as you go. Then, once the action has started, you can walk back to each of the positions you have noted, so that as the stage progresses you get nearer to your car and are ready to move on to the next stage. Crowds usually gather at points of interest, so it is important to arrive in enough time to grab your spot – even though you won't be standing there too long, it is well worth the effort.

Camera	**Pentax *ist D**
Focal length	**175mm (35mm equivalent: 260mm)**
Exposure	**1/500sec at f/9.5**
ISO setting	**200**

With no safety fences or barriers between you and the action, rallying provides far greater flexibility in your choice of viewpoint.

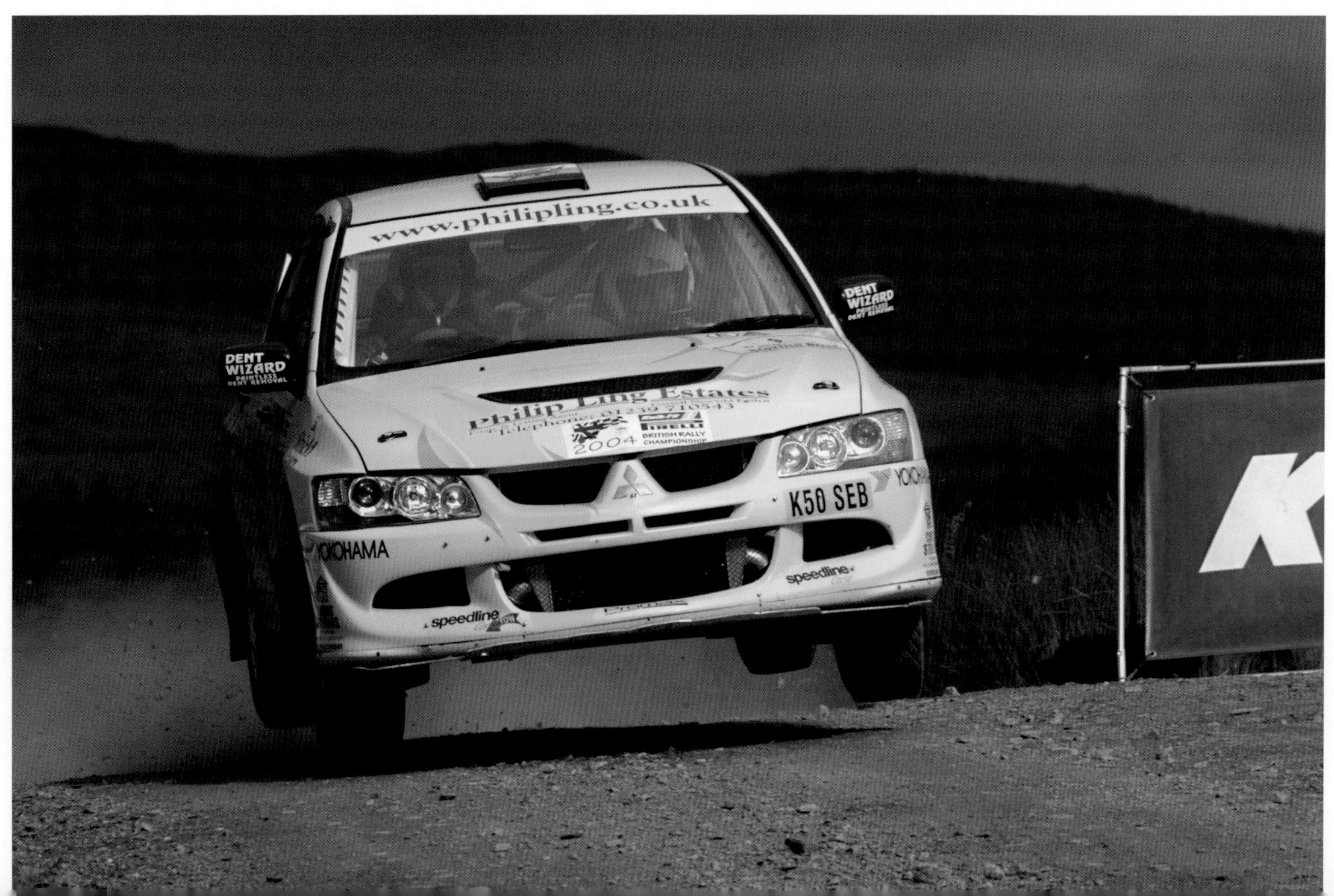

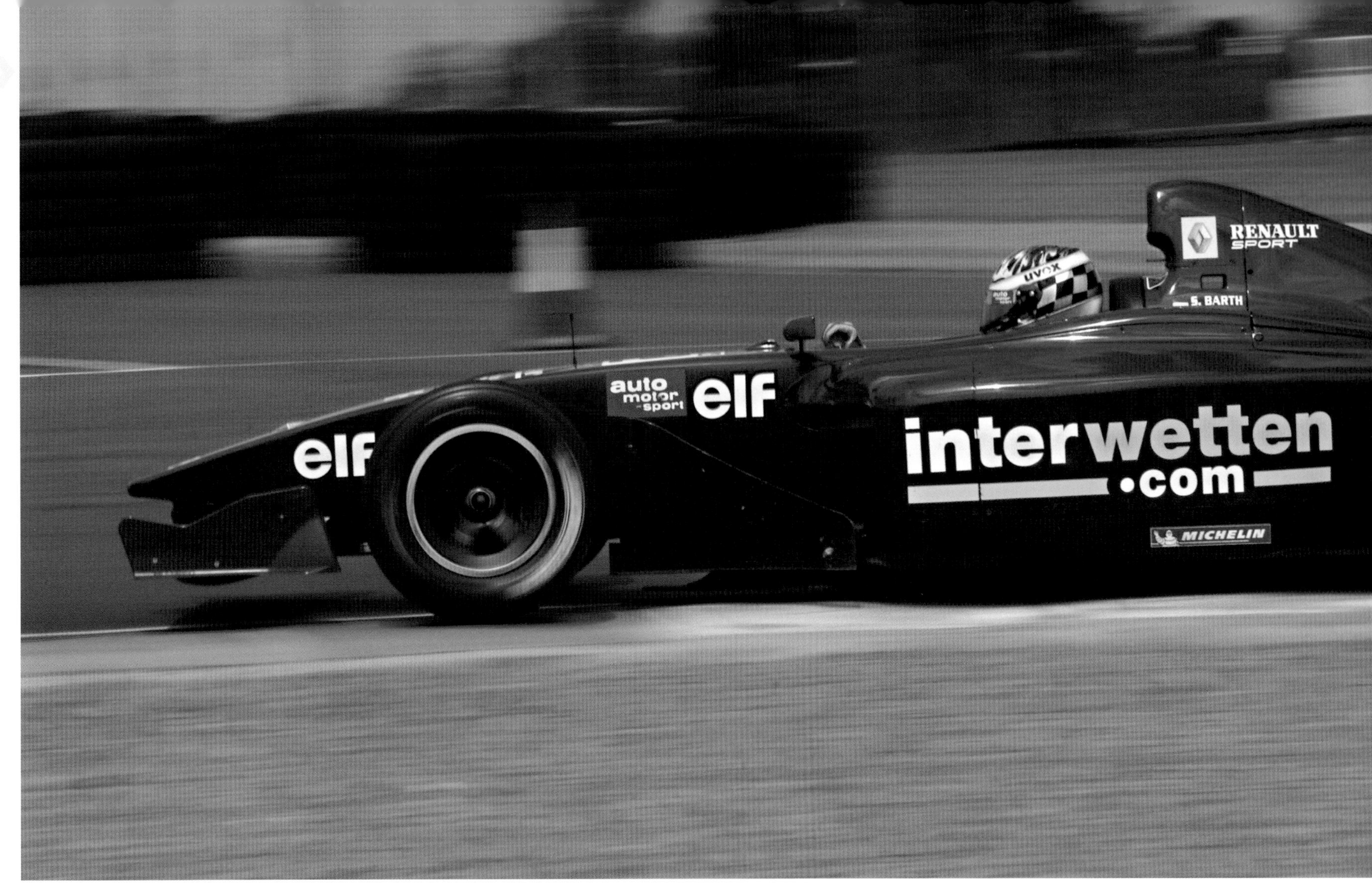

How you choose your viewpoint depends on the type of shot you want to achieve, and knowledge of the subject you are covering will help immeasurably. The best action shots are generally found where the subject is changing speed or direction: cornering, braking, cresting a brow, and so on. Most overtaking manoeuvres on race circuits take place either under braking into a corner or when accelerating away from one; but this may differ depending on the discipline you are covering, and you will need to bear this in mind when deciding where to stand. I always try to choose a position that will give me a clear view of where I expect the action to take place; I can't stress enough how important it is that you learn to predict the action as best you can.

Camera	***Pentax *ist D***
Focal length	***200mm (35mm equivalent: 300mm)***
Exposure	***1/125sec at f/16***
ISO setting	***200***

Choice of viewpoint is crucial to the composition of an image. For this shot I sat on the ground to get the low viewpoint I wanted in order to arrange the image as I saw it in my mind's eye. At racing circuits this option is not always available unless you have press access, so you will have to look around for the best opportunities.

Setting up

Once in position, you're ready to set up. Have a good look at the scene and try to visualize the images you want to capture, mentally identifying the points where you will take your shots. Check that the light is satisfactory and look at the scene through the viewfinder, making sure there are no obstructions such as cones or bollards that you don't want to include. Also check where any safety marshals are positioned – they have a very important job to do, but it's frustrating to get to your chosen viewpoint well before the action starts, only to have a couple of marshals come and stand in front of you. This doesn't happen very often, but it's worth asking them if it's OK to stand at a particular spot, just to make sure.

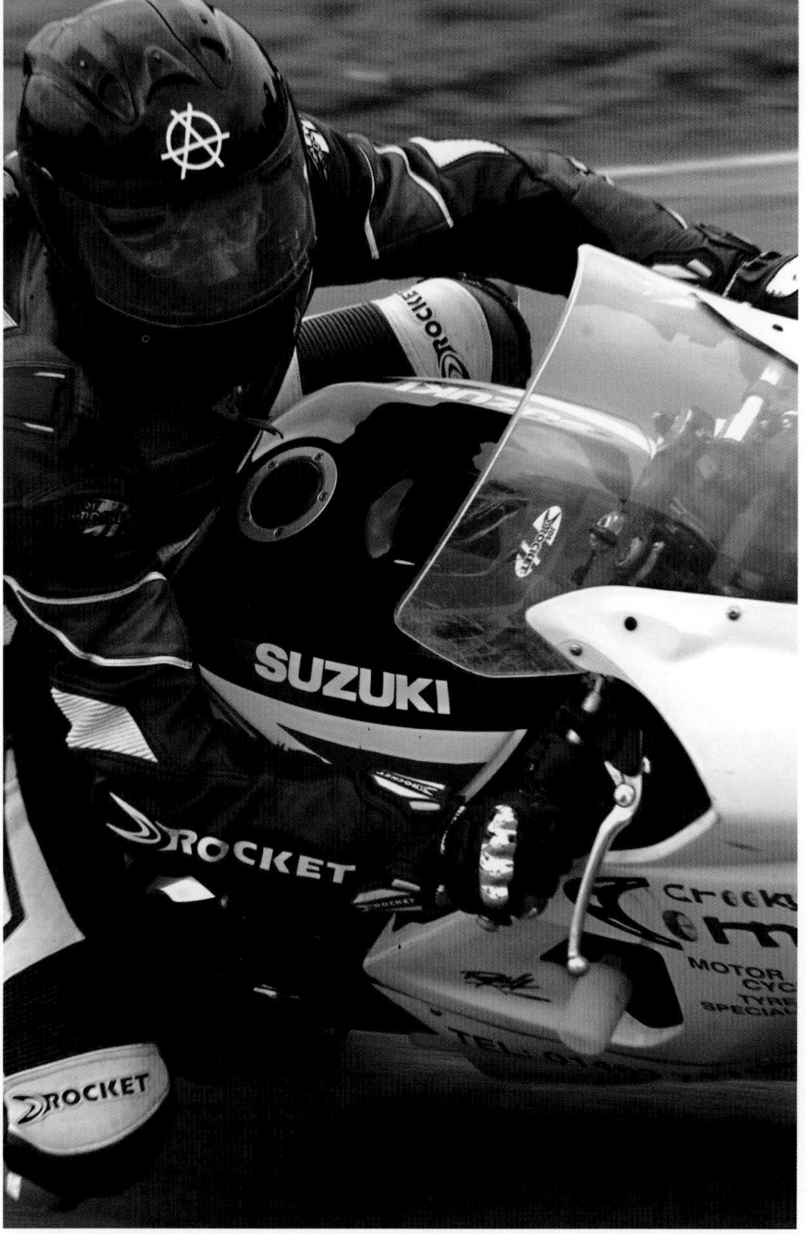

Camera	***Pentax *ist D***
Focal length	***200mm (35mm equivalent: 300mm)***
Exposure	***1/180sec at f/8***
ISO setting	***200***

When filling the frame with part of your subject, composition becomes even more crucial – moving a fraction of a centimetre can alter the composition drastically. Try to pick up the subject in the viewfinder as soon as possible and follow it smoothly until the composition looks 'right'. It takes time to learn to predict the best moment to fire the shutter, but experience makes it much easier.

Wet-weather action

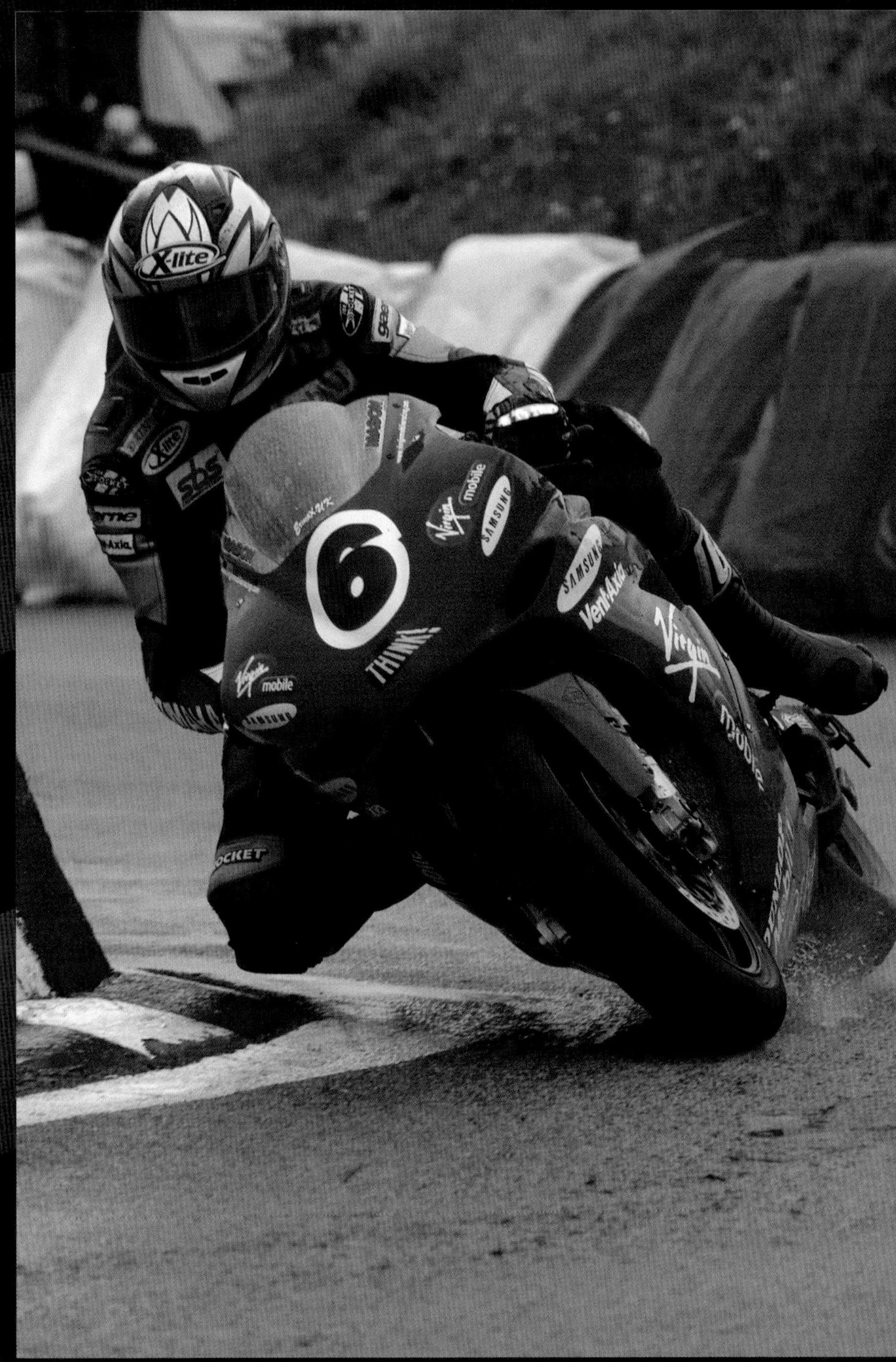

Weather conditions should always be taken into consideration when choosing where to stand. If it's wet, you can be sure that you will see vehicles out of control in places where you normally wouldn't expect to. Also bear in mind that on tarmac circuits the racing line that drivers take is often different in wet conditions: quite often drivers find better grip on parts of the circuit that are not on the normal racing line.

Camera	*Pentax *ist D*
Focal length	*200mm (35mm equivalent: 300mm)*
Exposure	*1/750sec at f/5.6*
ISO setting	*200*

Racing in the rain provides an extra dimension, with cars and bikes throwing water from their tyres and bodywork. Use faster shutter speeds than you would normally, in order to 'freeze' the water.

Overcoming barriers

Over recent years motor racing circuits have taken significant steps to improve both driver and spectator safety. The upshot of this is that public areas have been moved further away from the action, and the addition of wire fences means that many of the better vantage points are not as accessible as they used to be. Don't be put off by this: there are still many opportunities for good photographs, but you will have to think carefully and creatively about where to position yourself before you begin shooting.

If a barrier or fence blocks your view, why not include it in your picture? This may sound strange, but fences and barriers are part of the motor racing experience after all, and there are many ways you can use these to add interest to your images.

Camera	***Pentax Super A***
Focal length	***300mm***
Exposure	***1/125sec at f/11***
Film	***Fuji Velvia 50***

Barriers and fences shouldn't prevent you from taking good motor sport images. As I didn't have a press pass allowing me closer access to this event, I composed this shot by kneeling down to include the barrier, making it a strong part of the composition.

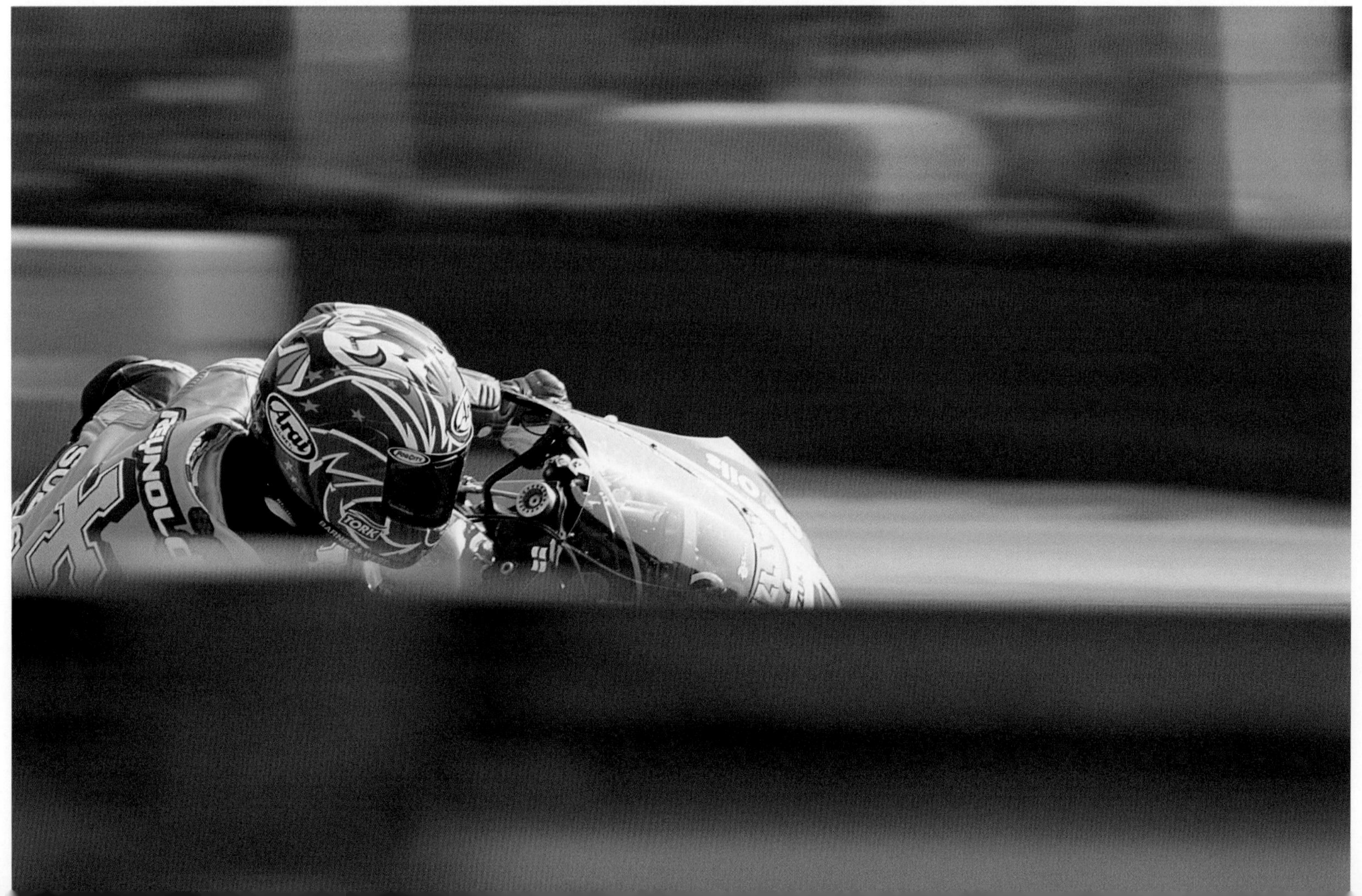

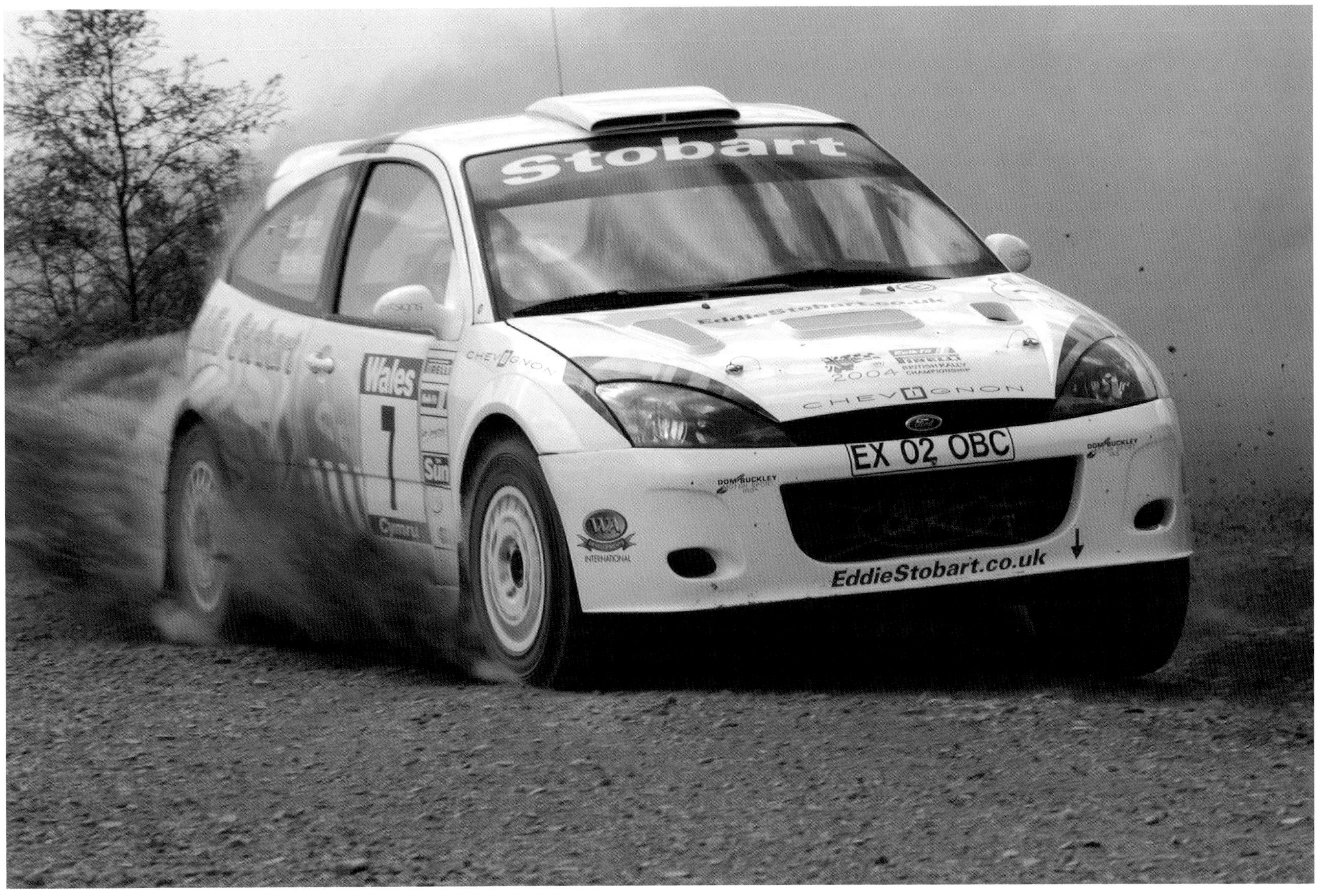

Having said that, there are still many disciplines of motor sport where you can get close to the action without having to contend with barriers and fencing. Rallying in particular allows you to get as close as you like to the action, especially on forest stages (though at 'spectator special' stages access may be limited). This provides you with an excellent opportunity to capture great action images – but do remember to think about safety, listen to the event marshals, and use common sense when choosing your position.

Camera	***Pentax *ist D***
Focal length	***170mm (35mm equivalent: 250mm)***
Exposure	***1/180sec at f/8***
ISO setting	***200***

Racing disciplines such as rallying enable you to get very close to the action without the need for a press pass, but you must make sure you stand in a safe position. Always observe any instructions given by race marshals, and be prepared to move out of the way quickly if you need to.

Case study: Selecting your viewpoint

To illustrate my principle of maximizing the number of pictures I take from any given viewpoint, here is a series of images all shot from the same corner on the same day.

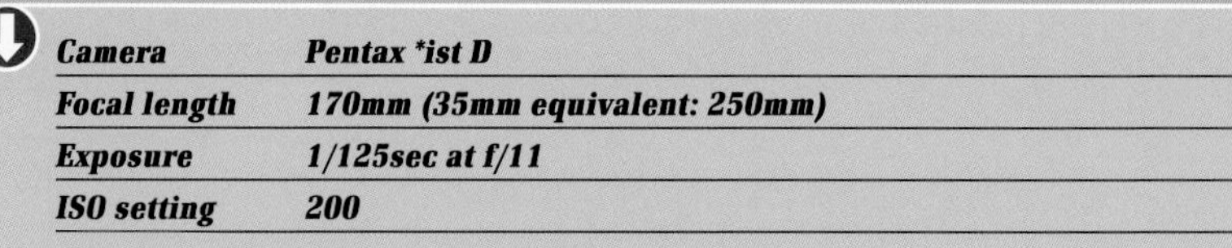

Camera	Pentax *ist D
Focal length	170mm (35mm equivalent: 250mm)
Exposure	1/125sec at f/11
ISO setting	200

For this second shot I altered the composition by using the same lens but holding the camera in the 'landscape' format.

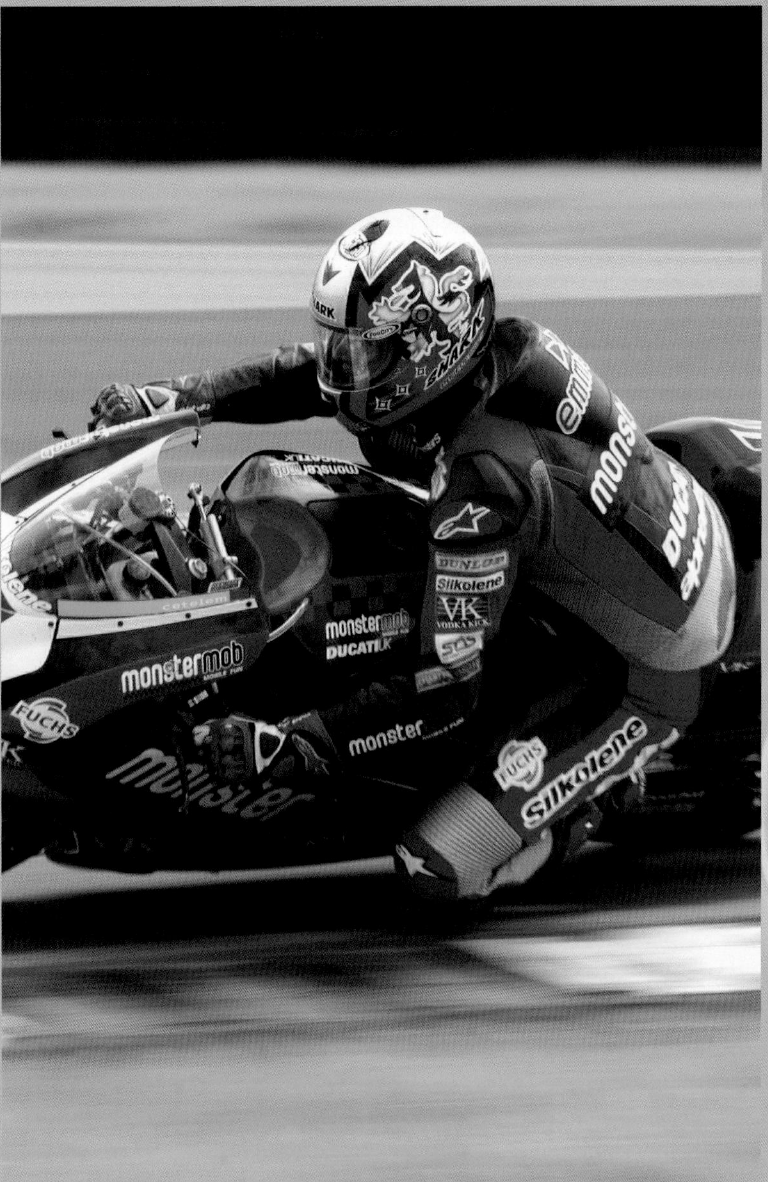

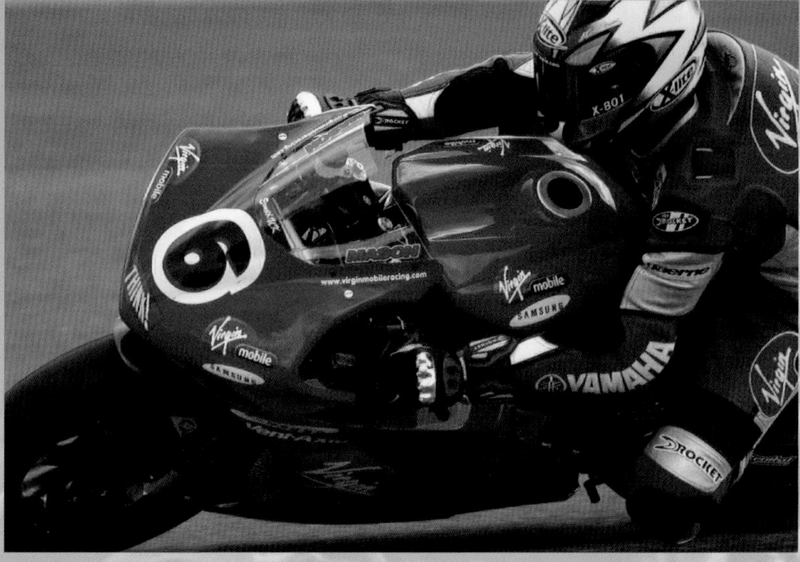

Camera	Pentax *ist D
Focal length	170mm (35mm equivalent: 250mm)
Exposure	1/125sec at f/9.5
ISO setting	200

This was my first composition at this chicane, with the rider just approaching the corner. I chose to hold the camera in the 'portrait' position in order to include all of the rider's body.

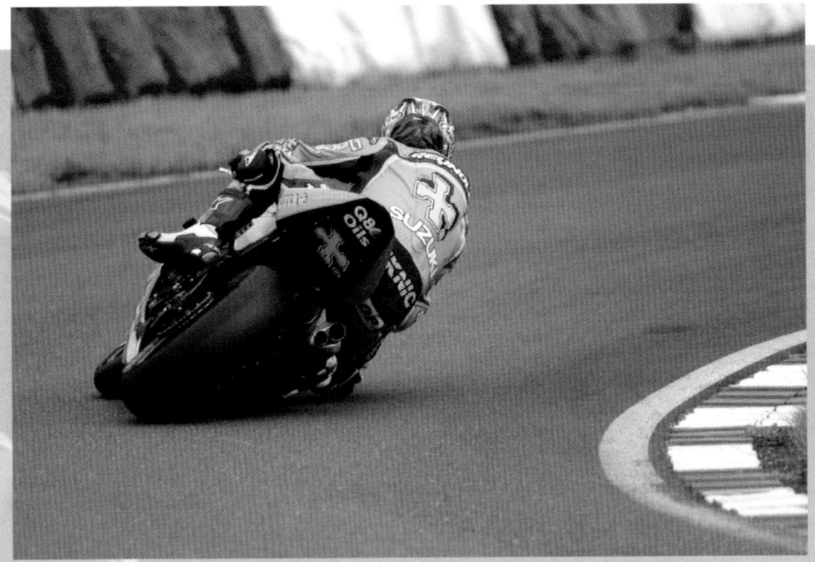

Camera	**Pentax *ist D**
Focal length	**300mm (35mm equivalent: 450mm)**
Exposure	**1/1000sec at f/4**
ISO setting	**200**

Shifting my position by a few paces to the right, I used a longer lens to capture this rider as his knee brushed the tarmac. I positioned the subject in the left-hand side of the frame in order to include the kerb, whose pattern complements the rider's leathers and the protective barrier at the top of the shot. Placing the rider in this part of the frame also means that the composition adheres to the 'rule of thirds' (see page 125).

Camera	**Pentax *ist D**
Focal length	**300mm (35mm equivalent: 450mm)**
Exposure	**1/1500sec at f/4**
ISO setting	**200**

Moving to a position at the exit from the corner allowed me to produce a shot which is almost the opposite of the previous one. The composition is very similar: once again, including the kerb rather than filling the frame with the rider provides perspective for the viewer.

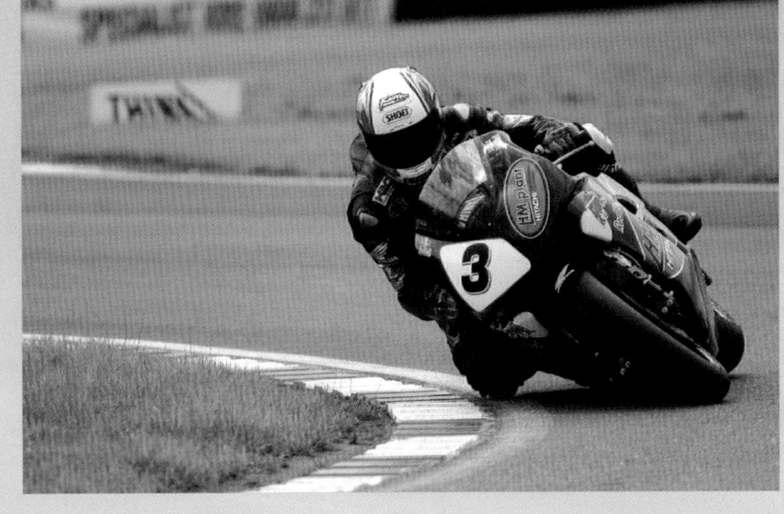

Camera	**Pentax *ist D**
Focal length	**300mm (35mm equivalent: 450mm)**
Exposure	**1/2000sec at f/4**
ISO setting	**200**

By altering my viewpoint a few more paces I took my favourite image of this sequence. The subject may be smaller this time, yet it maintains just as much impact. I composed this shot so the track would meander through the scene, but used a wide aperture on a long lens to ensure it was sufficiently out of focus not to distract from the rider.

Framing your subject

Always give careful thought to the composition of the shots you want to take. Technicalities such as choosing lenses, shutter speeds, etc. will be much easier once you have the intended image clear in your mind's eye and all you need to do is replicate it through the viewfinder.

The basics of photographic composition apply as much to this type of photography as any other. The 'rule of thirds' (see opposite) is the cornerstone of composition, and gives the image a sense of proportion and arrangement that is most pleasing to the eye. Having said this, rules are there to be broken, and you don't have

Camera	**Pentax *ist D**
Focal length	**90mm (35mm equivalent: 135mm)**
Exposure	**1/180sec at f/16**
ISO setting	**200**

You don't always have to follow the rules of composition to take strong images: in this shot the driver is almost central in the frame. Changing your viewpoint can greatly affect the composition of a shot: for this image I climbed up to the winners' rostrum overlooking the pit lane, which allowed me to shoot down on this driver.

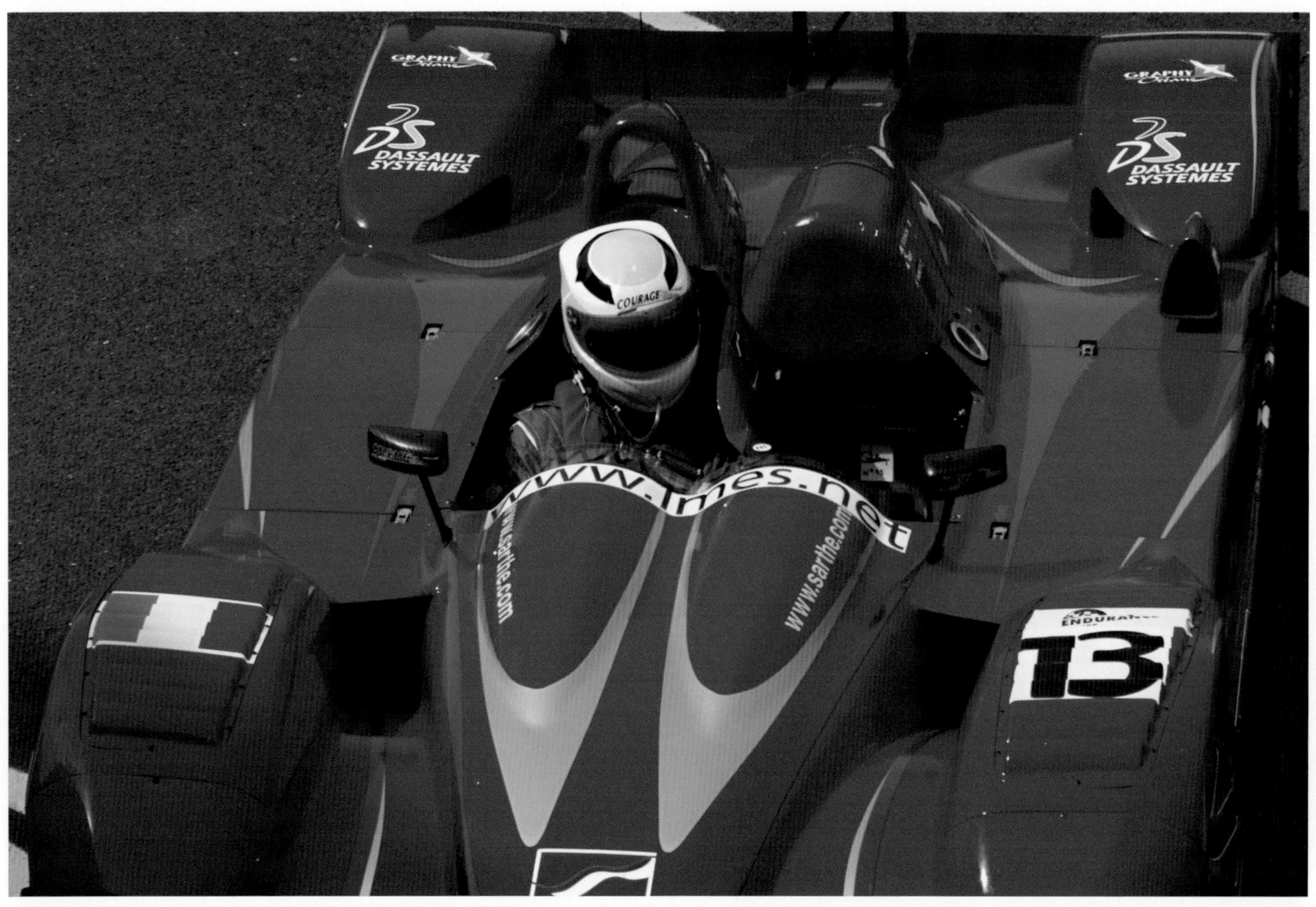

to follow this one all the time – it is perfectly possible to compose an image without using the rule of thirds. However, it is important that you understand its benefits and bear them in mind when you are out in the field. It is rare that I consciously think about the rule of thirds when I'm at an event, but when I'm reviewing my images afterwards I find the rule can be applied to many of them. Once you've worked with it for a while you will find it becomes second nature too, but don't become dogmatic: overusing it may make your style a little predictable, and prevent you from thinking creatively about the dynamics of your composition.

The rule of thirds

Using this rule is simple: all you have to do is imagine that your camera's viewfinder is divided into nine equal sections by four lines – two horizontal and two vertical. This provides you with a grid that can be used to position the subject in your image. By placing your subject or focal point at one of the four intersections of the horizontal and vertical lines you will give your image a more pleasing composition. I often place a wheel or driver's helmet at one of the four intersections, making this the main focal point of my image.

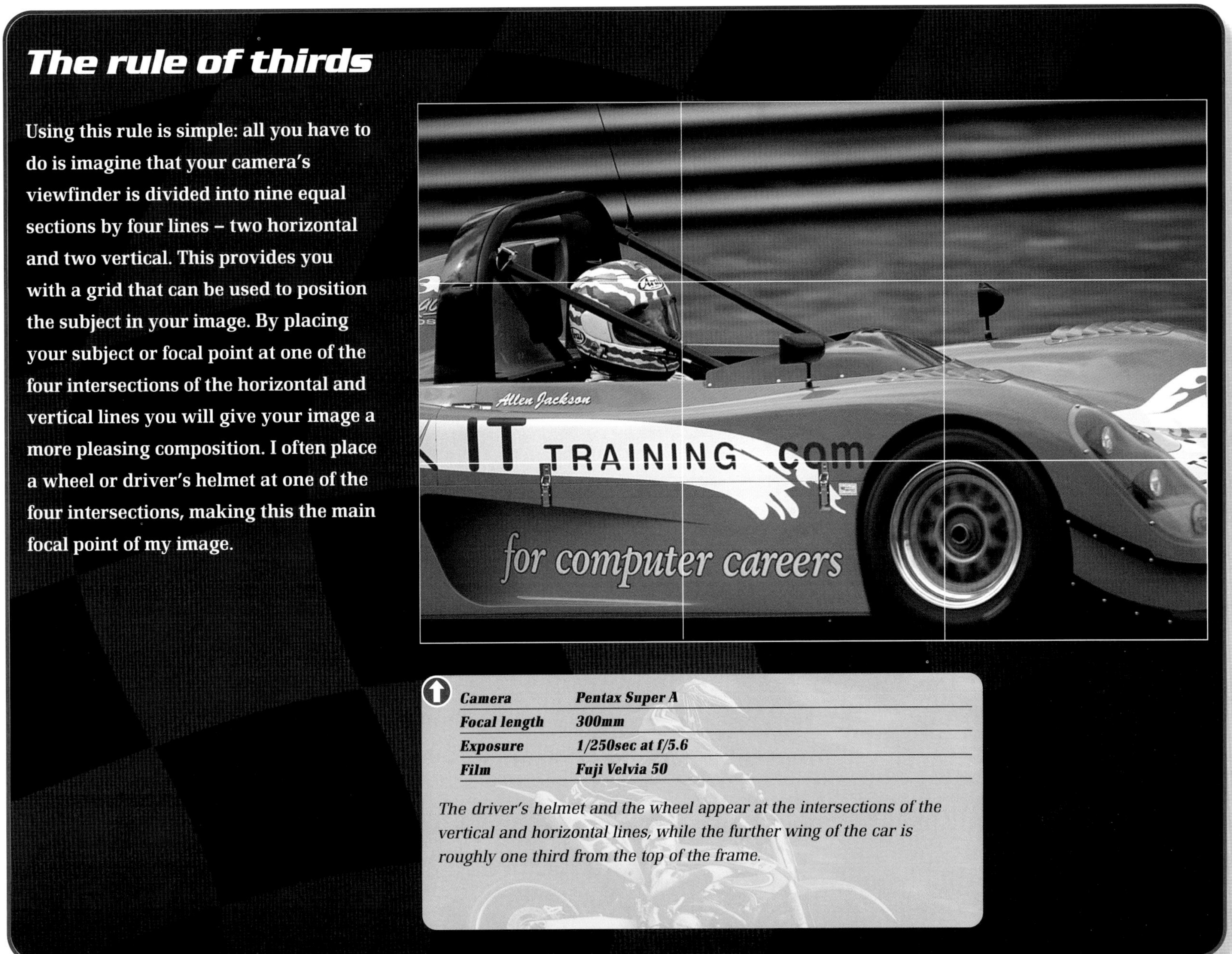

Camera	***Pentax Super A***
Focal length	***300mm***
Exposure	***1/250sec at f/5.6***
Film	***Fuji Velvia 50***

The driver's helmet and the wheel appear at the intersections of the vertical and horizontal lines, while the further wing of the car is roughly one third from the top of the frame.

Visualizing the result

I try to maximize the opportunities from each event I visit, so that I come away with a wide variety of shots rather than a lot of images that are very similar. In the planning stages I draw up a mental list of the shots I really want from a day; these do not always turn out to be my best shots, but they provide a cornerstone for my day's activity upon which I build my other images. For the shots on my mental wish list I may already have planned how the subject is going to appear in the frame; this composition will then dictate what lens I will use, so that before getting to the track I know pretty much how I'm going to get the image I'm after.

Camera	**Pentax *ist D**
Focal length	**170mm (35mm equivalent: 250mm)**
Exposure	**1/125sec at f/8**
ISO setting	**200**

I always have a mental list of basic shots that I want to take at an event – I think of pictures like this one as 'standard' images. Once I'm happy I've got these shots 'in the bag', I begin to think about more creative compositions. Working this way provides a structure to my photography that helps me explore more image opportunities and prevents me coming away with a lot of pictures that are very similar.

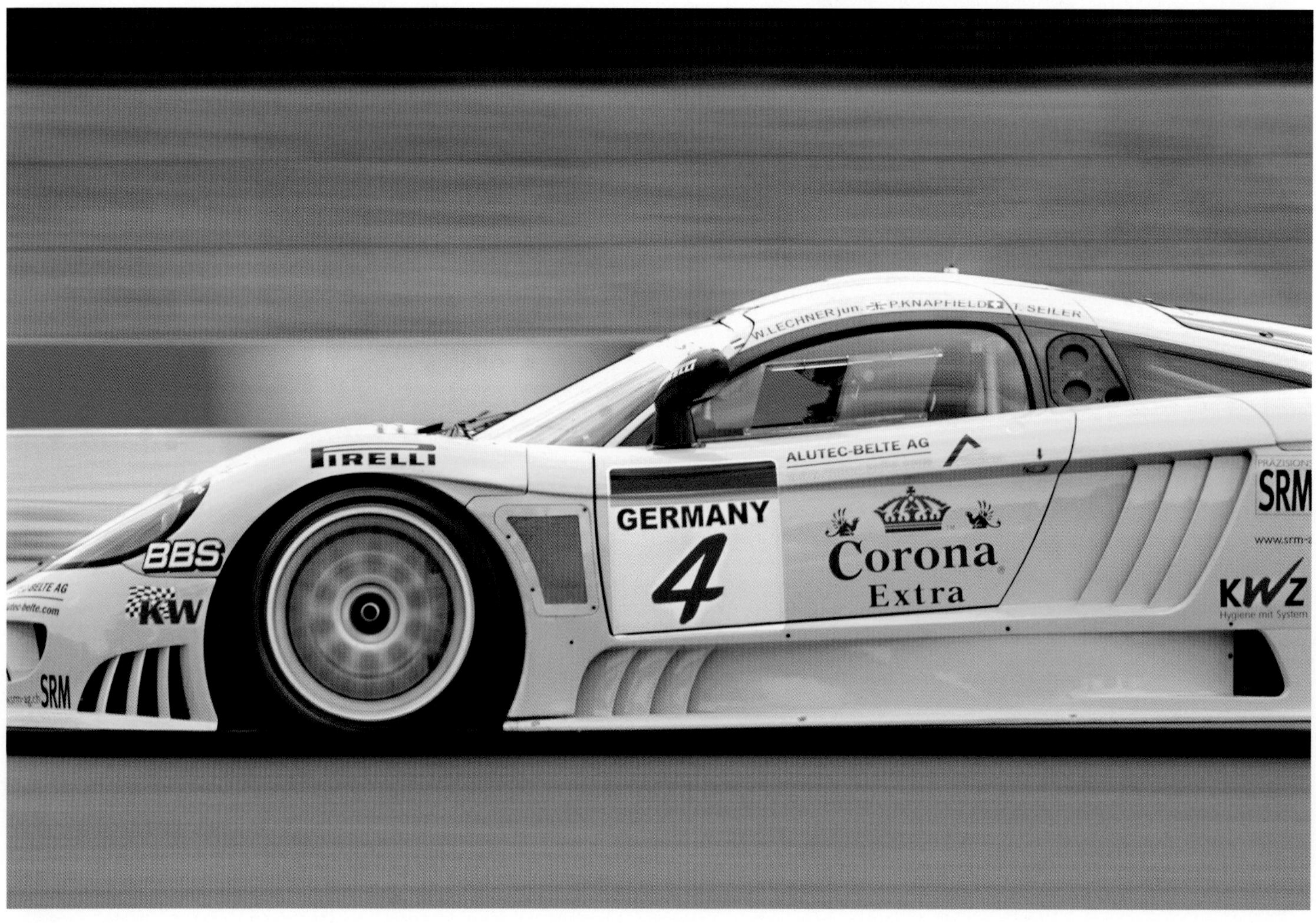

Getting in close

Filling the frame with your subject by using a long telephoto lens can produce excellent results. I often use a 300mm lens to pick out details in the action. You shouldn't be afraid to cut a car or bike in half – there is no need to have all of the subject in the image – but if you do this it is important that you balance the composition. As a rule of thumb for this type of shot, I will try to include a front wheel and the driver's (or rider's) helmet. This means the composition often falls into line with the rule of thirds, both wheel and helmet appearing roughly at the one-third intersections.

Camera	***Pentax *ist D***
Focal length	***200mm (35mm equivalent: 300mm)***
Exposure	***1/180sec at f/8***
ISO setting	***200***

Using a long telephoto lens can help you to pick out details of your subject. When using a long lens to frame your composition, it is always advisable to include the driver's helmet or hands to act as a focal point.

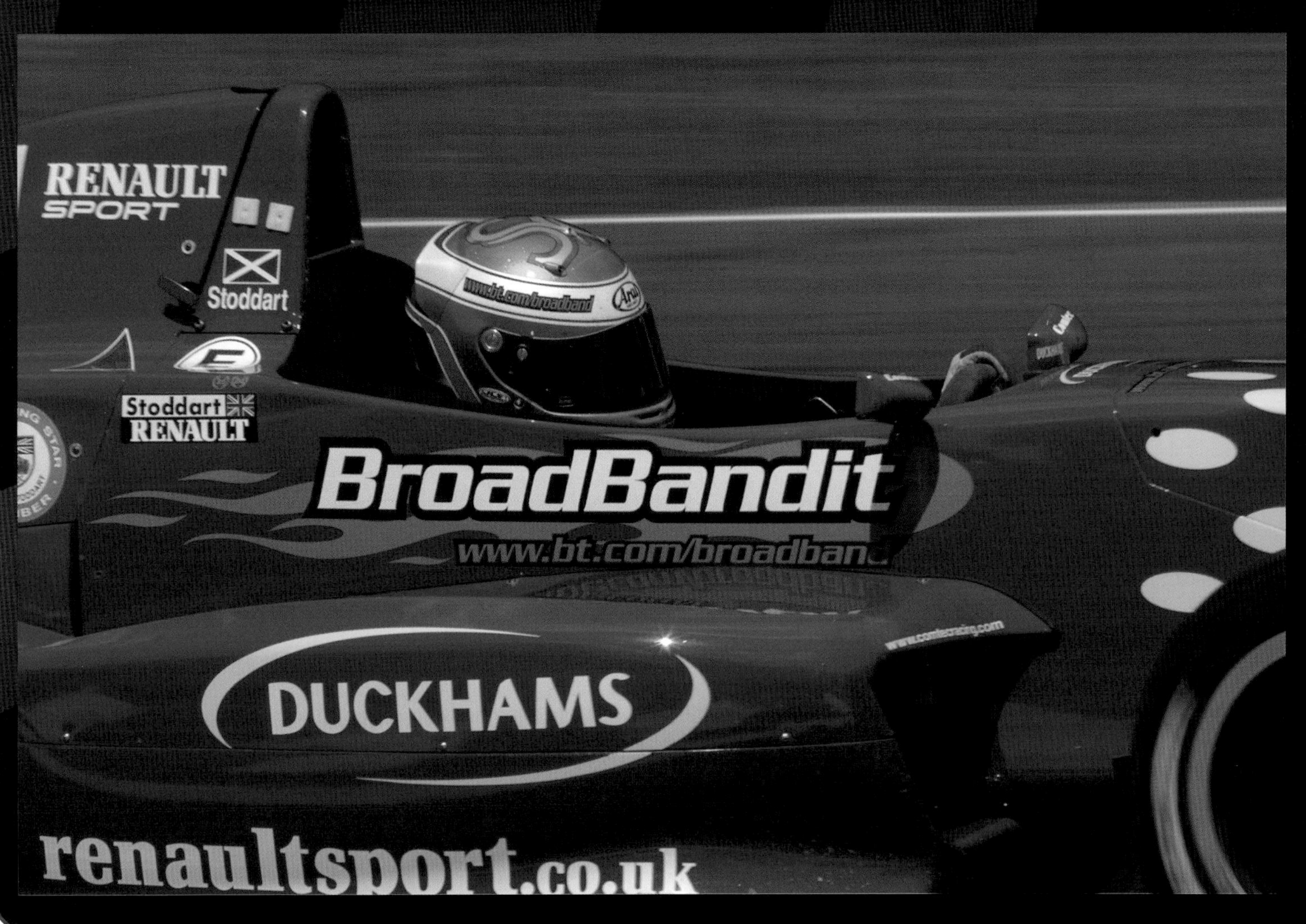

Making the most of your viewpoint

The framing of the subject is a key element in the overall success of your image. It is often dictated by a number of factors, of which your choice of lens is one of the most critical. The nature of the subject, the location and the weather all help to determine what lens I choose on any given occasion, but generally I will use a range of focal lengths at each viewpoint in order to get a variety of different shots. I find that shots in which the entire subject fills 90% of the frame are rarely successful. The SLR format dictates the frame available, and if you place a racing car or bike in that frame side on, with the subject filling most of the frame, the result is often dull. As with all things, there are exceptions to the rule. Generally, however, I much prefer to focus on a section of the subject or, conversely, zoom out to include some of the surrounding scene. By doing this I can produce much more dynamic images that provide a sense of the action rather than simply recording the scene.

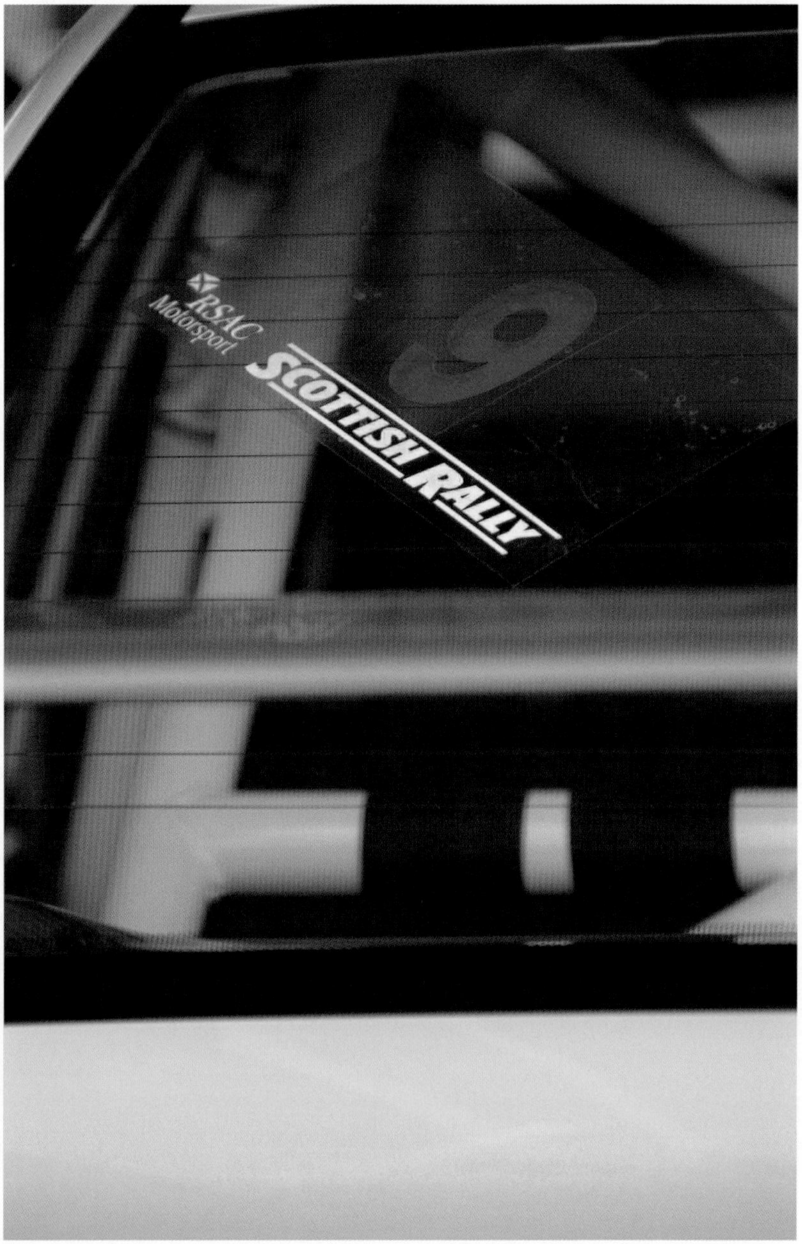

Camera	***Pentax *ist D***
Focal length	***170mm (35mm equivalent: 250mm)***
Exposure	***1/350sec at f/4***
ISO setting	***200***

Picking out sections of a car and using a long lens to crop in closely can provide strong compositions. When walking around the paddock looking for shots, take time to pick out images that you normally wouldn't take. Time spent experimenting like this is rarely wasted.

Having already visualized my 'ideal' shot at any given location, I first shoot eight or ten frames until I am happy that I have got the image I was looking for – perhaps a detailed action shot, focusing on the driver and the front section of the car. Then I consider what other images I can take from the same viewpoint, looking through the viewfinder to try out the possibilities. I may try changing to a slower shutter speed for a more dramatic effect. I will also try altering my stance, either crouching down or using my steps to gain a higher vantage point. One of the best ways to vary the composition is to change the angle of the camera from the standard 'landscape' format to the upright 'portrait' position. A further variation is to tilt the camera to an angle of between 30 and 45 degrees, so the subject is moving through the viewfinder on a diagonal path.

Camera	***Pentax *ist D***
Focal length	***135mm (35mm equivalent: 200mm)***
Exposure	***1/125sec at f/11***
ISO setting	***200***

Standing in the same position as for the image on page 127, I changed to a shorter focal length in order to capture the same driver as she exits the corner. Don't feel that you have to include all of the subject in an image – framing tightly to crop out the front and rear of the car adds to the impact of this composition.

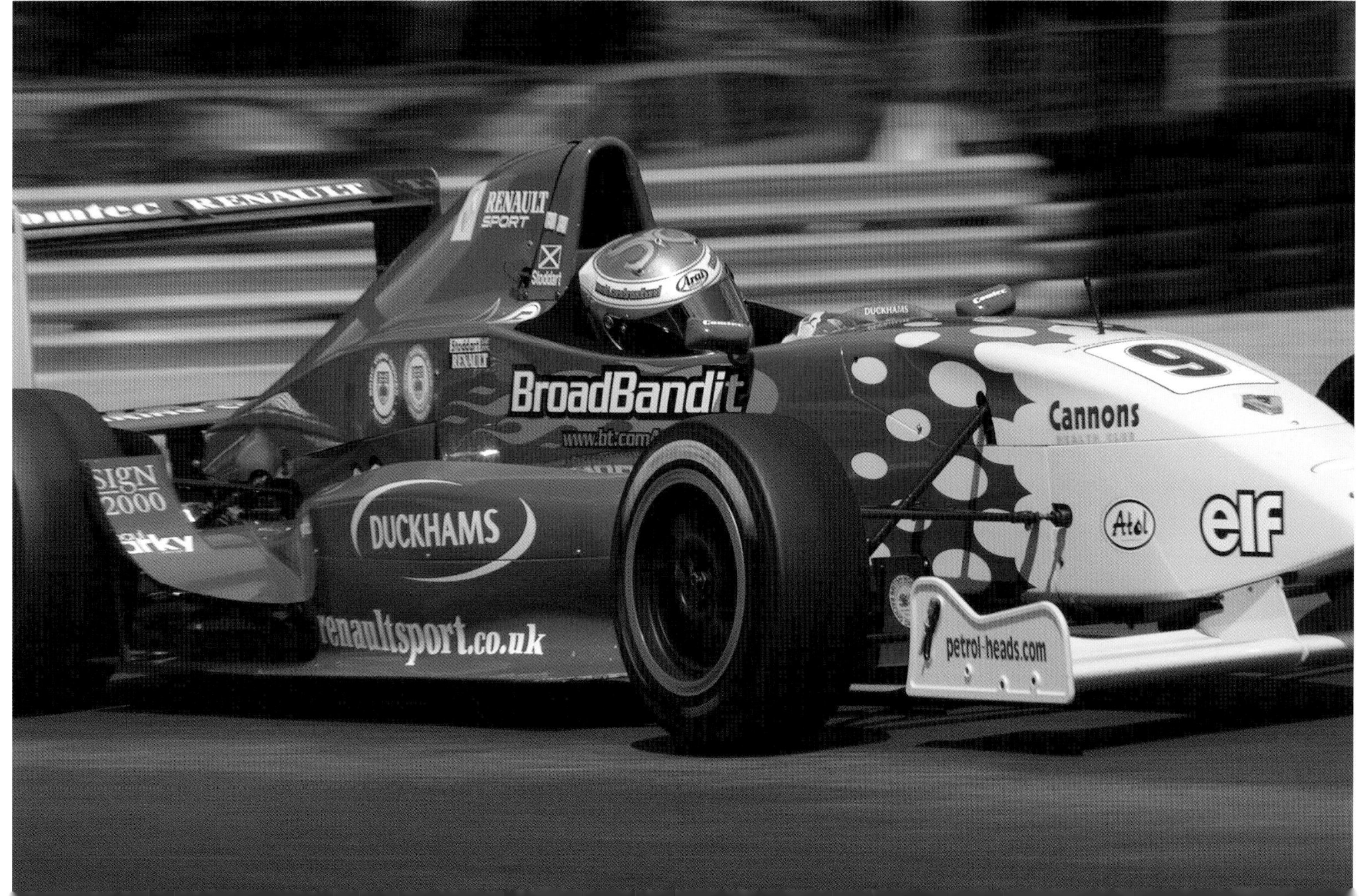

Changing lenses

By this stage I have probably shot 20 or so exposures and will have up to five different compositions, all taken from the same viewpoint with the same lens. I now look at what I can do by changing lenses or zooming. I generally start off at each location with a long focal length and then work down towards a wideangle view, or vice versa. I find this gives a structure to my shooting, and while going through this process I am always on the lookout for other promising options that I may not have considered.

Having changed to a smaller focal length I will go through the same process as before, the obvious difference being that I now see more of the subject in the viewfinder. I will probably be able to fit the entire subject into my shot; this means that more background will be visible, so I must take care to consider how this will affect the finished image. The background must not detract from the shot – it is important that the subject itself remains the main point of interest – but it may be possible to make parts of the background (and foreground) contribute to the overall effect. It may be that the colours of an advertising hoarding complement the colour scheme of a particular car or bike, in which case I pre-focus on the part of track that will allow me to capture the subject as it passes in front of the banner (see page 86).

Camera	***Pentax Super A***
Focal length	***28mm***
Exposure	***1/90sec at f/22***
Film	***Fuji Velvia 50***

Wideangle lenses can produce very dramatic results. In order to give atmosphere to this shot I moved back from the barrier so that I could include it in the foreground, thus providing a parallel with the barrier on the other side of the track. The result is a balanced composition with the car in the centre of the frame.

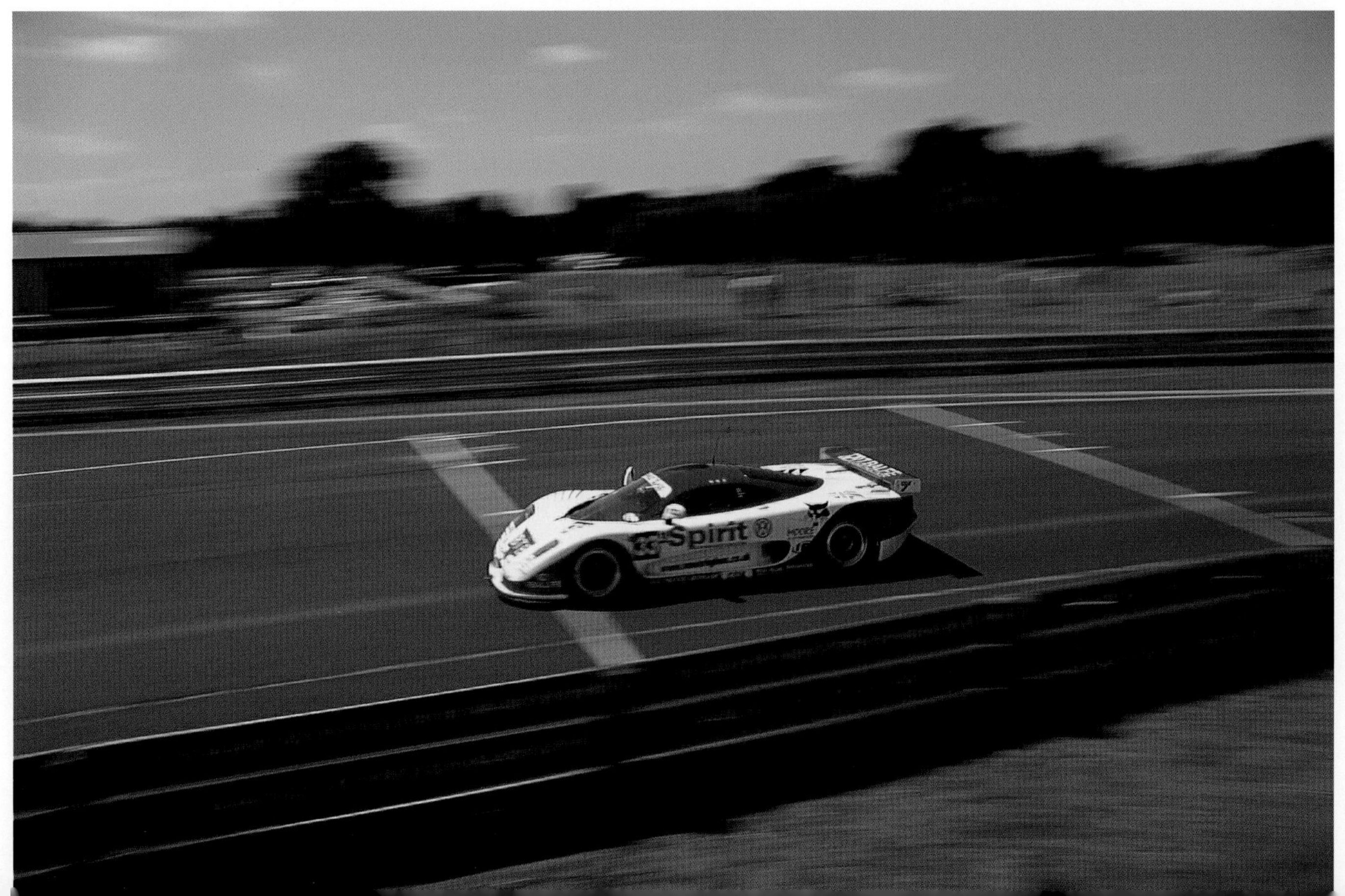

Another change of focal length may offer further possibilities. A short telephoto lens of between 70 and 135mm can give a different feel to images from the same viewpoint. I look at shots where the subject takes up maybe as little as 10 or 20% of the total image; here composition is vital, since the subject, though a relatively small part of the picture, still needs to remain as the focal point. To achieve this I try to keep the surrounding area as clean as possible, and look for features that will make a positive contribution to the finished image. Parts of the foreground and background might be used to provide lead-in lines, or to form symmetrical images that can be blurred by using slower shutter speeds. You can use the lines and flow of a piece of track to complement your composition, controlling the way in which the surrounding area is viewed so as to draw the eye to the subject. This can be achieved either by using slower shutter speeds and panning so that only the subject is sharp, or by using a large aperture to throw any distracting background out of focus.

Camera	***Pentax *ist D***
Focal length	***135mm (35mm equivalent: 200mm)***
Exposure	***1/1500sec at f/5.6***
ISO setting	***200***

Taking good action images doesn't mean you have to fill the frame with the subject – making the most of the surrounding scene can add elements to a composition that would have been lost if a longer lens were used. In this image the sinuous 'flow' of the track through the frame provides a strong, dynamic composition.

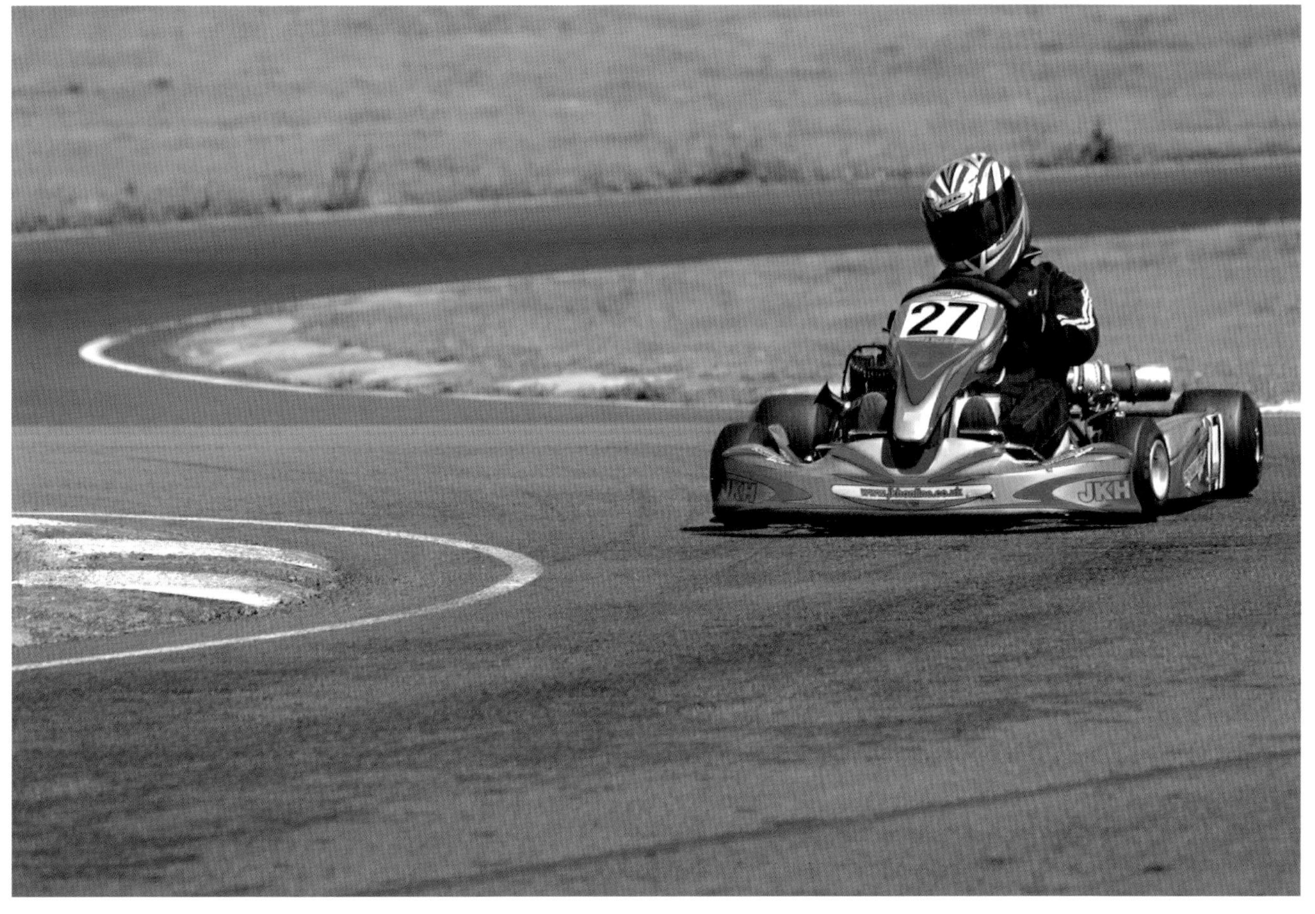

Keep your eyes open!

While you are at your chosen vantage point you should always be looking out for predictable racing situations. Keep an eye on any battles that are emerging between competitors. If a driver attempts an overtaking manoeuvre at a corner, or just 'has a look' at the car in front, be sure to be ready for him on the next lap – he may well try again.

Camera	***Pentax *ist D***
Focal length	***135mm (35mm equivalent: 200mm)***
Exposure	***1/125sec at f/13***
ISO setting	***200***

Being able to predict where action will take place is an important part of securing action shots. The car seen on the left here had 'had a look' at the other car coming into this corner on the previous lap. I pre-focused on the entrance to the corner in anticipation, and on the next lap captured this image as the two cars touched.

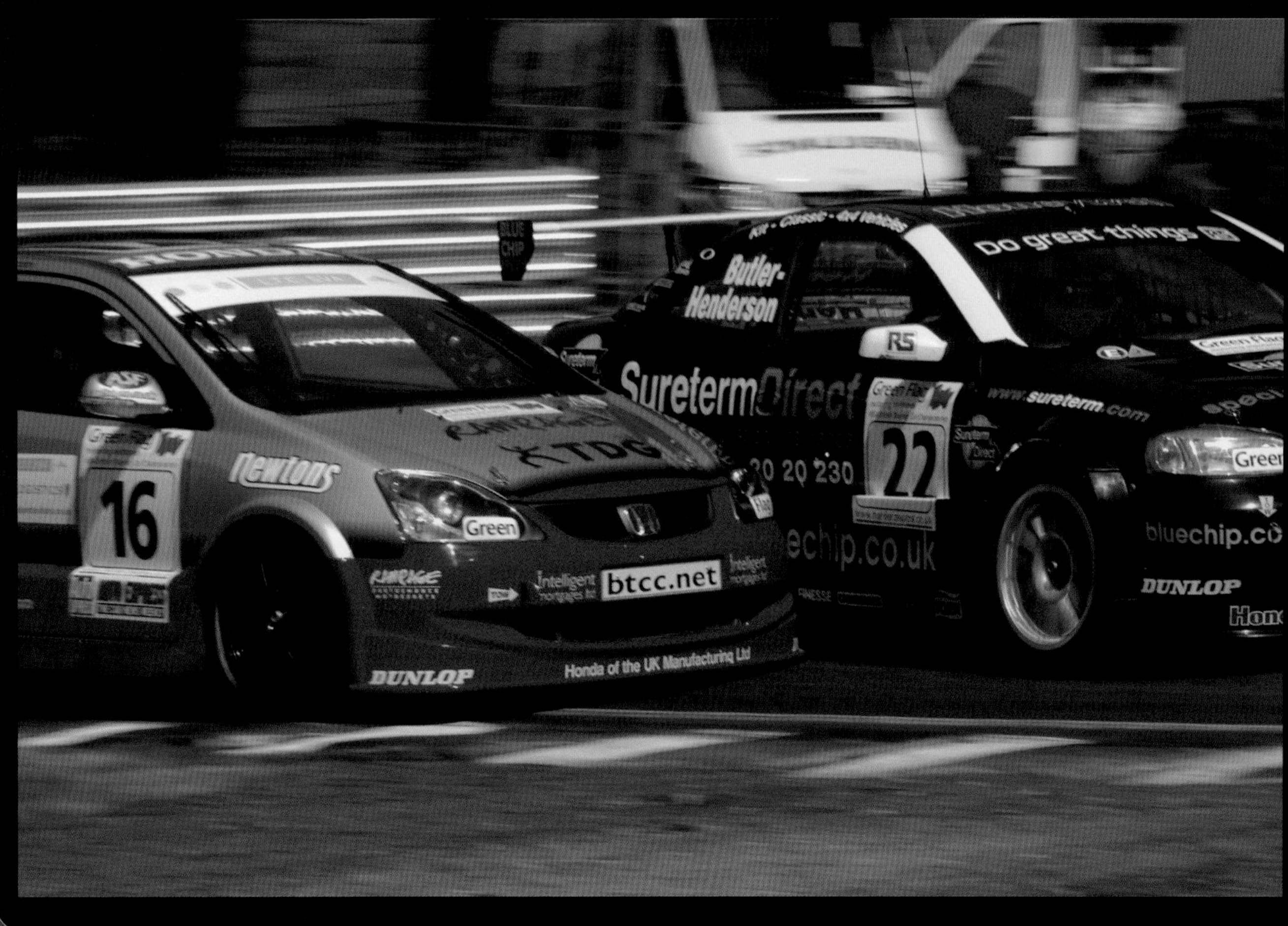

Shutter speed

Choice of shutter speed is one of the key factors in achieving successful results. The basic principles have been explained in the previous chapter, but it is worth reiterating the main points here. The rules you can read in photographic books and magazines provide a good, solid base for taking motor racing photographs, but once you have grasped the basics these rules may become an unnecessary constraint. For example, you can be pretty sure that when panning, an exposure of 1/90, 1/125 or 1/250sec will give your images a pleasingly blurred background while your subject appears clear. But once you're satisfied that you can achieve this type of shot with relative ease, don't leave it there – why not try thinking outside these parameters, and experiment with shutter speeds that you would normally shy away from? I often use speeds below the recommended norm in order to bring a greater sense of movement to my images. By using speeds between 1/8 and 1/60sec you can add a real sense of movement and drama to your images. It is true that your subject may not be as well defined as at higher speeds – but only by experimenting will you begin to widen the boundaries of what you can achieve.

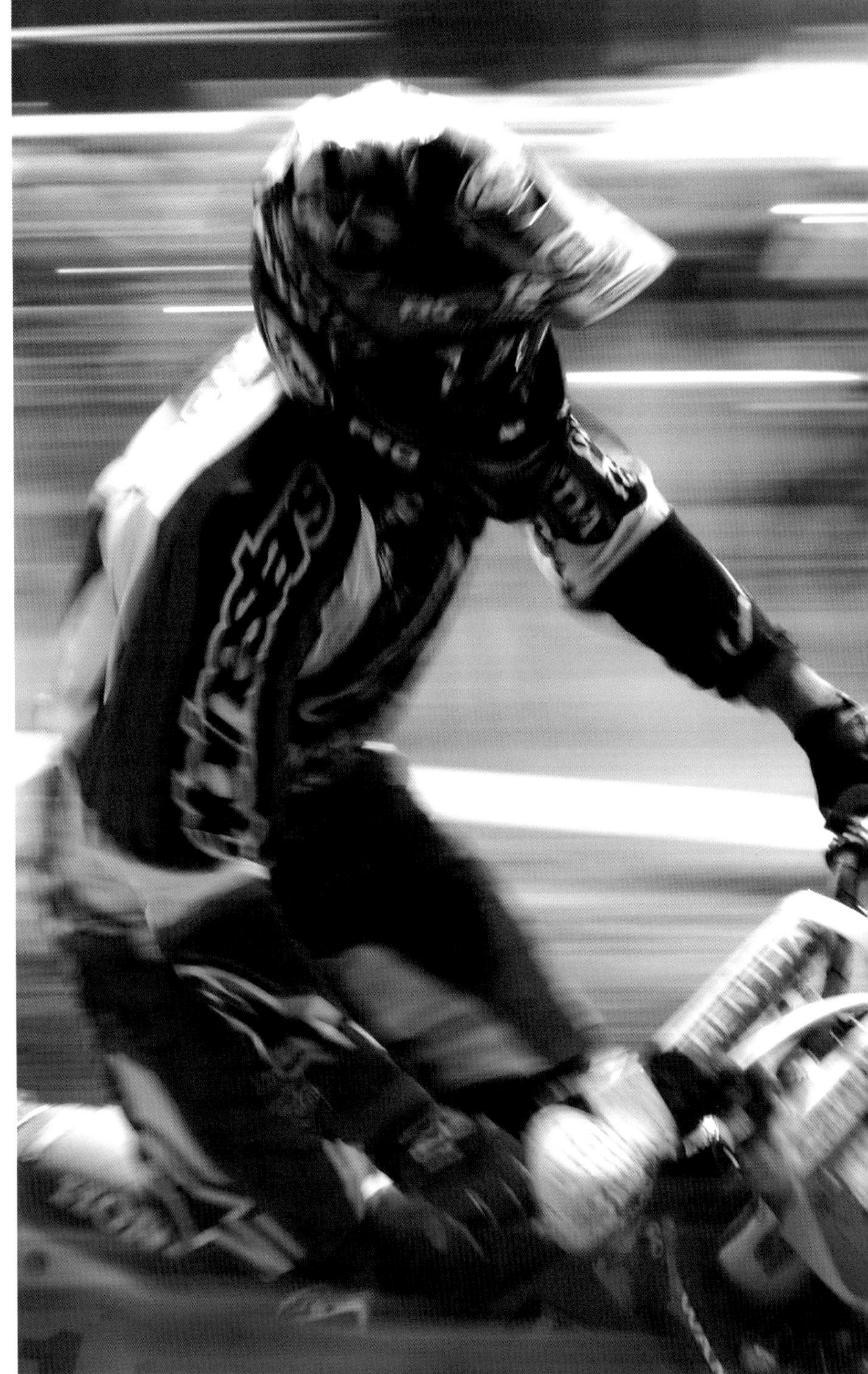

Camera	***Pentax *ist D***
Focal length	***70mm (35mm equivalent: 105mm)***
Exposure	***1/30sec at f/16***
ISO setting	***200***

Using slow shutter speeds to blur your subject can add to the sense of movement in an image. For this shot I was relatively close to the rider so had to pan very quickly. A shutter speed of 1/30sec was long enough to provide the dynamic result I was looking for. Experimenting with slower shutter speeds than you would normally use can produce very pleasing results.

Thinking creatively

Human beings never stop learning. This applies across all walks of life and is just as relevant to photography as any other field. You may have learned the basic techniques required to take good motor sport photographs, but this does not mean that you have finished learning.

Getting the technical bits right only means that you have become proficient at producing crisp, well exposed and visually pleasing images. No longer will you have to throw away 80% of your work because it is incorrectly exposed, out of focus or badly composed. At this point you can give yourself a pat on the back for achieving your initial goal, but this is not by any means the end of the journey. Once you stop challenging

Camera	***Pentax *ist D***
Focal length	***70mm (35mm equivalent: 105mm)***
Exposure	***1/180sec at f/11***
ISO setting	***200***

I wanted to include the pit lane exit in this shot to provide a diagonal symmetry between the grass, pit lane exit, track and car. With the camera held at an angle the car fits perfectly into the frame. When I first arrived at this corner I was looking for a totally different shot, but I was struck by the alternation of grass and track in the foreground and was keen to look for a composition that would highlight this.

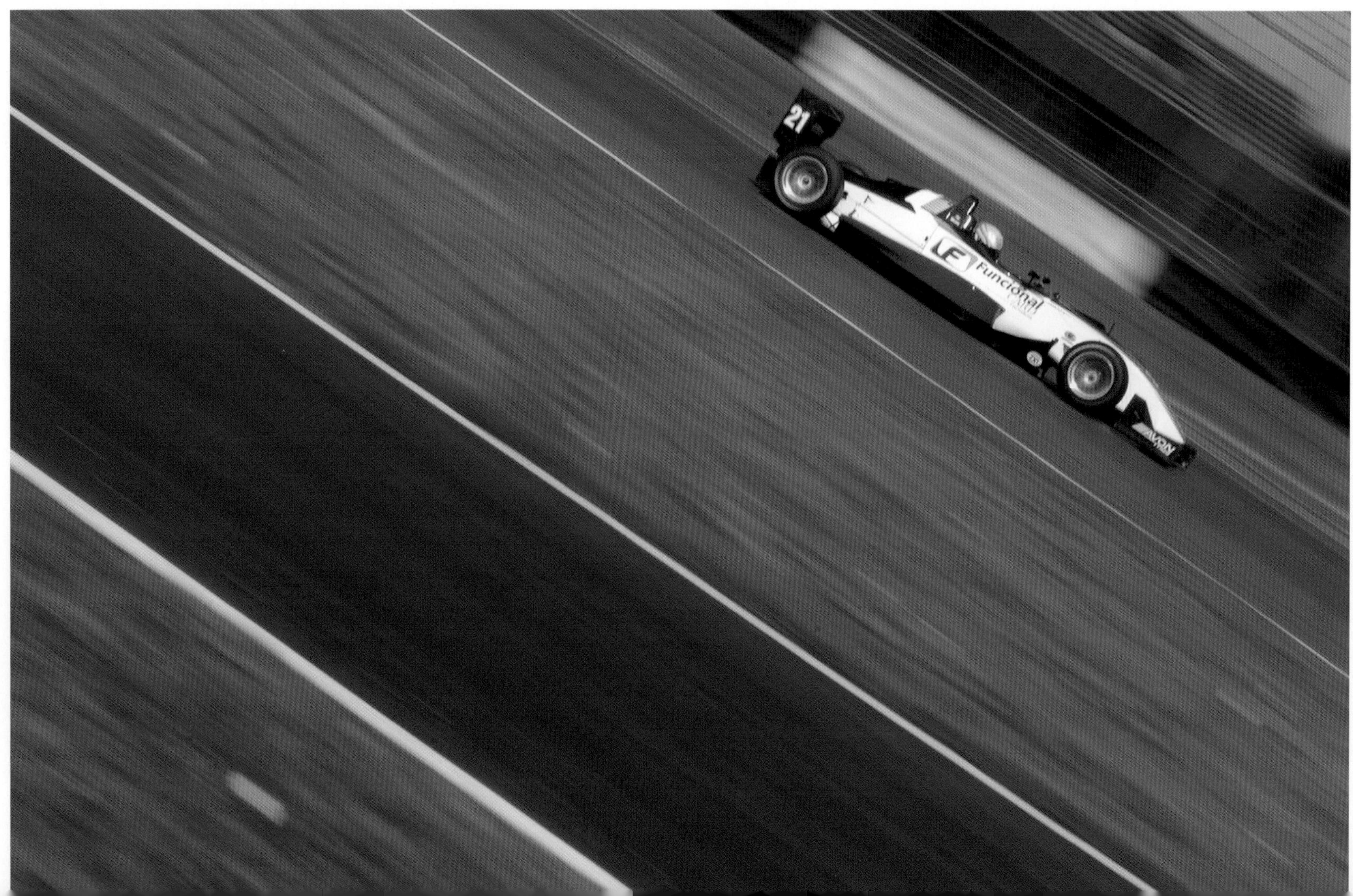

yourself, the images you make will become stale and you will come away from an event with a set of pictures very similar to the last ones you produced. You have to be your own worst critic at times: when you review your images, try to see how you could improve on them, then make sure that the next time you go to a race meeting you act on your critique. I'm not suggesting you should be negative about what you have achieved – simply that you should keep challenging yourself to get better.

The photographs you take are a direct result of using a camera to interpret a vision you have in your mind's eye. Once you have the technical skills, the real improvement in your photographs comes from the way you see images in your head. For me, this is all about developing a style.

Camera	***Pentax *ist D***
Focal length	***200mm (35mm equivalent: 300mm)***
Exposure	***1/500sec at f/4***
ISO setting	***200***

Standing in the pit lane during an endurance event, I saw this driver holding his seat insert while waiting for his team mate to return to the pits so he could take his turn in the car. Rather than shoot the whole scene, I chose to focus in on his hands. Using a wide aperture on a telephoto lens provided very little depth of field, giving exactly the effect I wanted to achieve. This subject could have been represented in many different ways – how you choose to interpret a scene and photograph it is a key part of developing your own style.

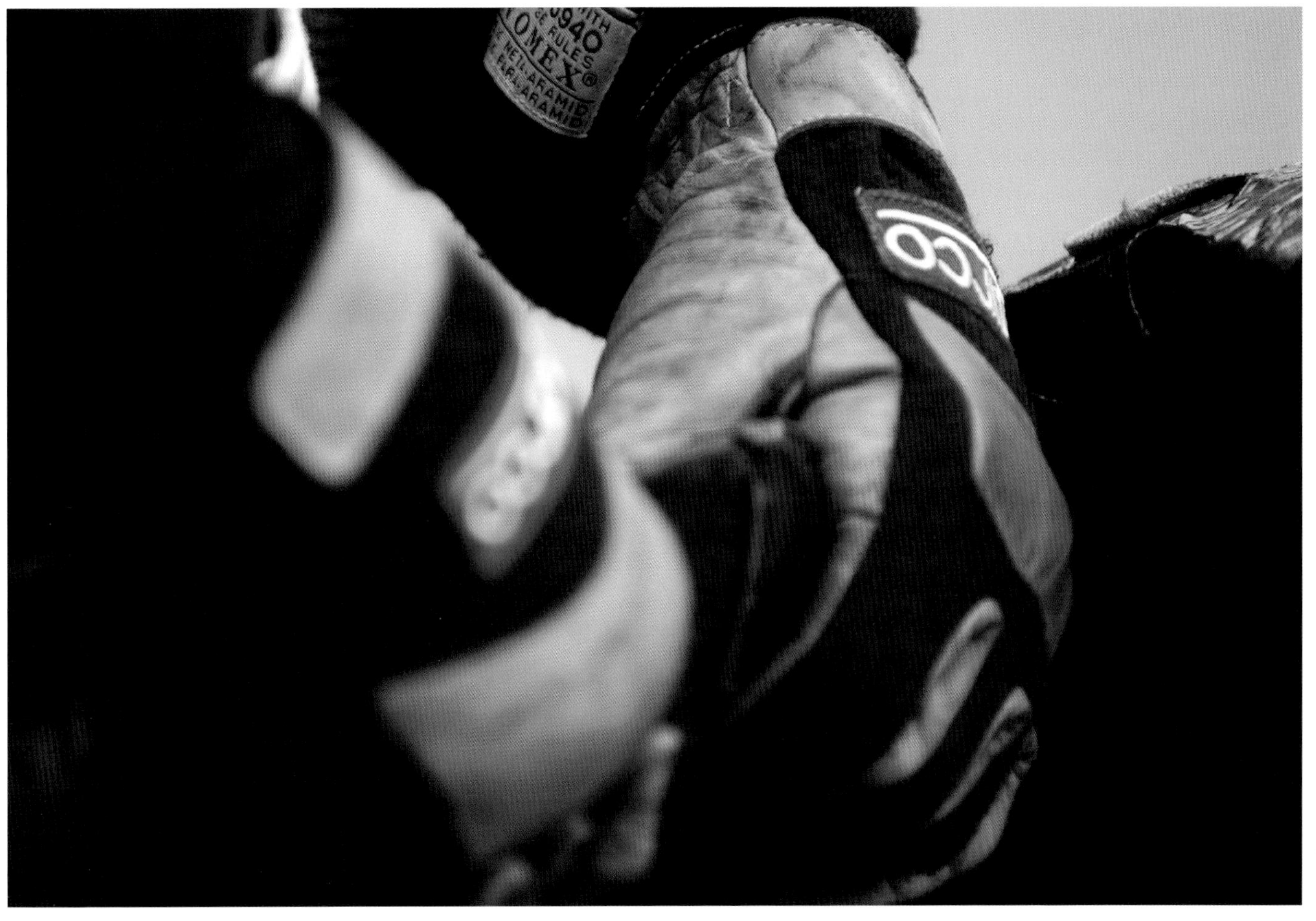

Lifelong learning

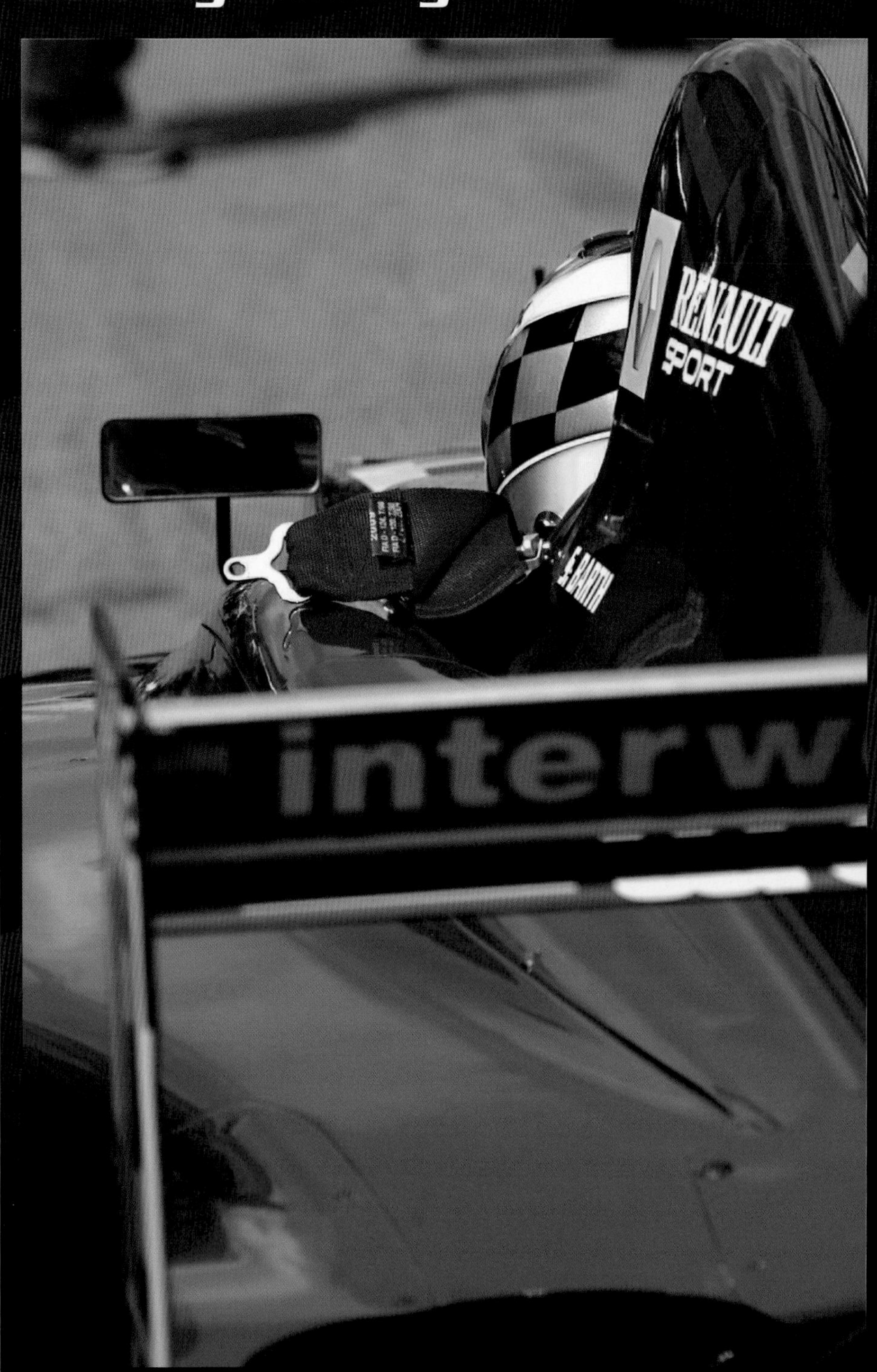

When I look back at the photographs I have taken in the past, I sometimes cringe. The image that I put first in my portfolio a couple of years ago would not make it past the first editing stage now. It wasn't a bad image, but my standards have become higher because I have kept learning and thinking about how to improve.

I'm no longer really learning about how to use a camera or take technically better pictures, but I am learning about how best to use my technical skills in order to produce more striking images. Once you've got the basics down pat and they have become second nature, can you really start to concentrate on using those skills to make your photographs better.

Camera	**Pentax *ist D**
Focal length	**145mm (35mm equivalent: 220mm)**
Exposure	**1/750sec at f/6.7**
ISO setting	**200**

Your photographs will only improve in proportion to the amount of effort you put into taking them. Once you have honed your technical skills it is important that you keep challenging yourself to look for different compositions or viewpoints in order to keep stimulating the creative thought process.

Developing a personal style

Developing your own style means using your imagination to apply the skills that you have; the culmination of this process is the images you produce. By using creativity in composition you add your own 'signature' to an image. This does not mean that your images all need to be similar – a style is your own interpretation of a split second in time.

Why do you need to develop a style, if you already have good technical skills and can take perfectly good photographs? My answer would be that good technical skills will allow you to record a scene, but pretty much anyone can learn how to do this. It is the creative application of those skills that will make your images stand out from the crowd. We all see the same things, but it is the way we interpret them that makes us different. There is no need to get arty and philosophical about it – the point is that in order to improve you need to keep challenging the way you do things and looking for different ways of doing what you've done before. Much of the time we look but don't see.

Don't be the guy standing with the other ranks of photographers all taking the same shot – stand back, look for yourself and think about how you can do something differently.

Camera	***Pentax *ist D***
Focal length	***200mm (35mm equivalent: 300mm)***
Exposure	***1/125sec at f/13***
ISO setting	***200***

The way you choose to interpret a scene is personal to you. Technical photographic skills are important, but it is up to you to use those skills to give others a glimpse into the way you see things. The slightly raised vantage point in this shot allowed me to use the blue and white kerb and the grass to frame the top and bottom of the image. Tilting the camera adds to the sense of speed and, in my view, provides a more pleasing composition.

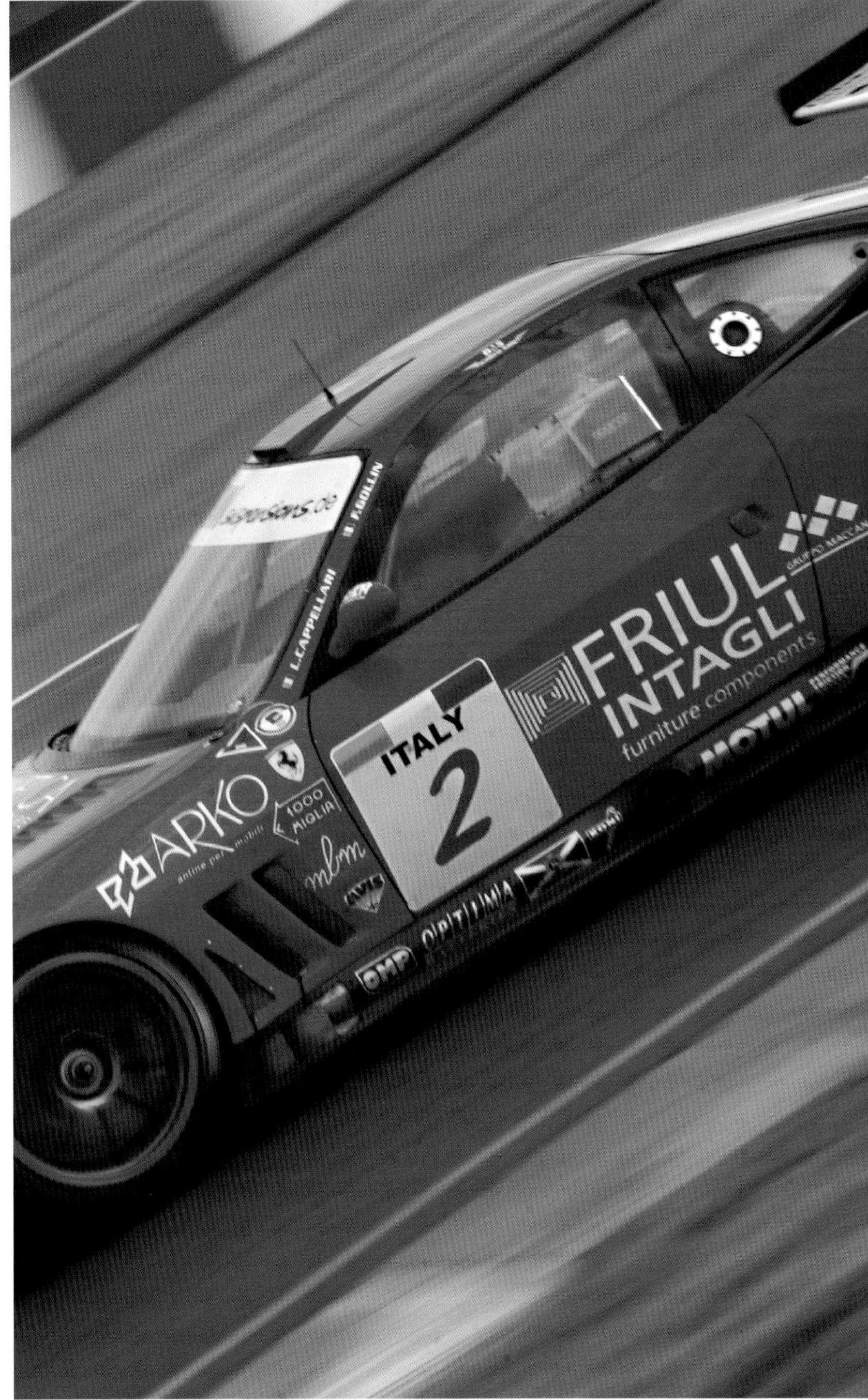

Using colour

The nature of motor sport inevitably means that you will be bombarded by colour from all directions. It's everywhere, from brightly painted liveries on cars and bikes, to competitors' helmets, sponsorship banners, team clothing, flags, crowds, and so on. Whether you're picking out detail from your subject or taking in colour from your surroundings, intelligent and imaginative use of colour will always bring that added extra to your pictures.

The use of colour in images is very subjective. I always look for strong colours that can be used to complement each other within a composition. Often trackside barriers are painted red and white at corners; using slow shutter speeds to blur these bright colours can be very effective. I am careful not to overcomplicate my pictures by including too many colours – for example, when framing a shot I will try to ensure that there are not so many background colours that they might detract attention from the main focal point. If you are not able to change the position from which you are taking a shot in order to remove a 'busy' background, you can always throw it out of focus by using a wide aperture to reduce the depth of field. Identifying when and where to do this hinges strongly on your ability to visualize the finished image in your mind's eye; once you understand how to use you camera's controls to realize a desired effect, you will be in a position to determine which aspects of a scene you want to include and which to leave out.

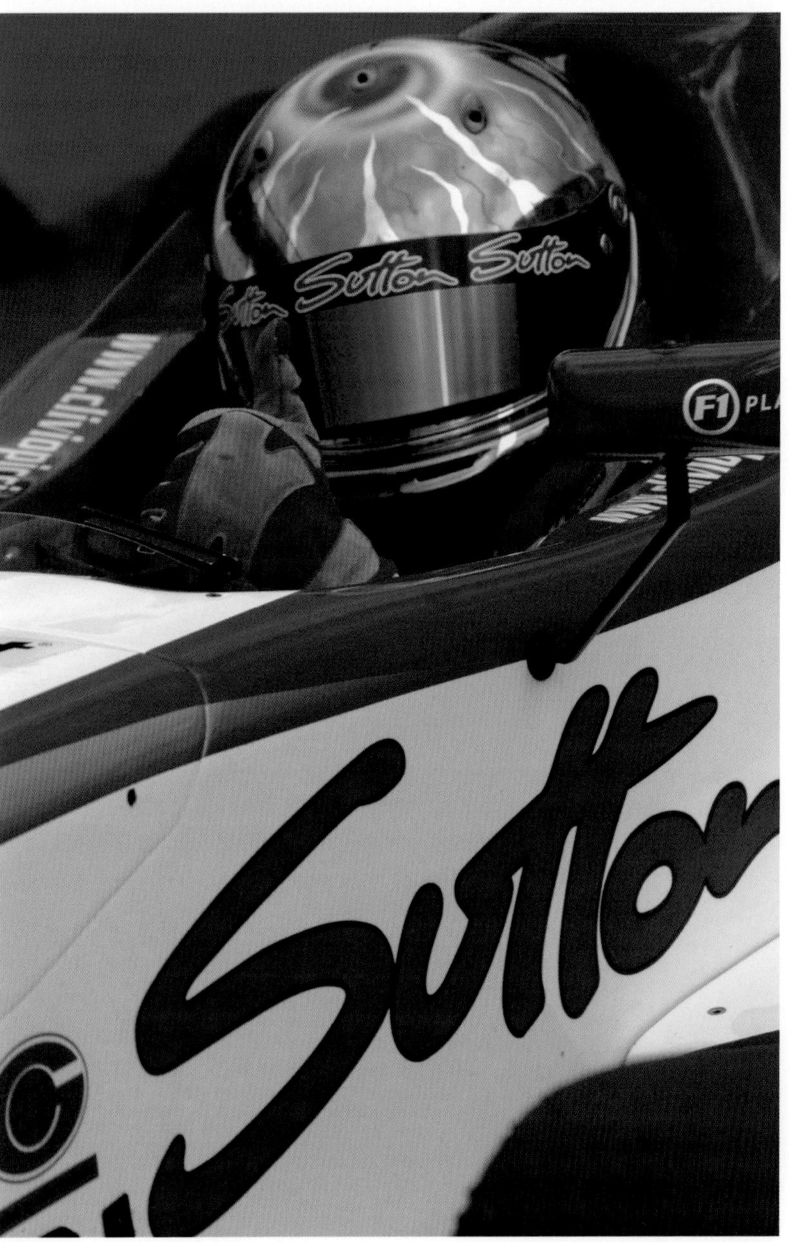

Camera	*Pentax *ist D*
Focal length	*100mm (35mm equivalent: 150mm)*
Exposure	*1/350sec at f/5.6*
ISO setting	*200*

This image shows full colour overload: the strong contrast between the driver's helmet and the car's colour scheme made me choose him for this shot. As I composed the scene I raised my thumb, and the driver kindly responded in the same way.

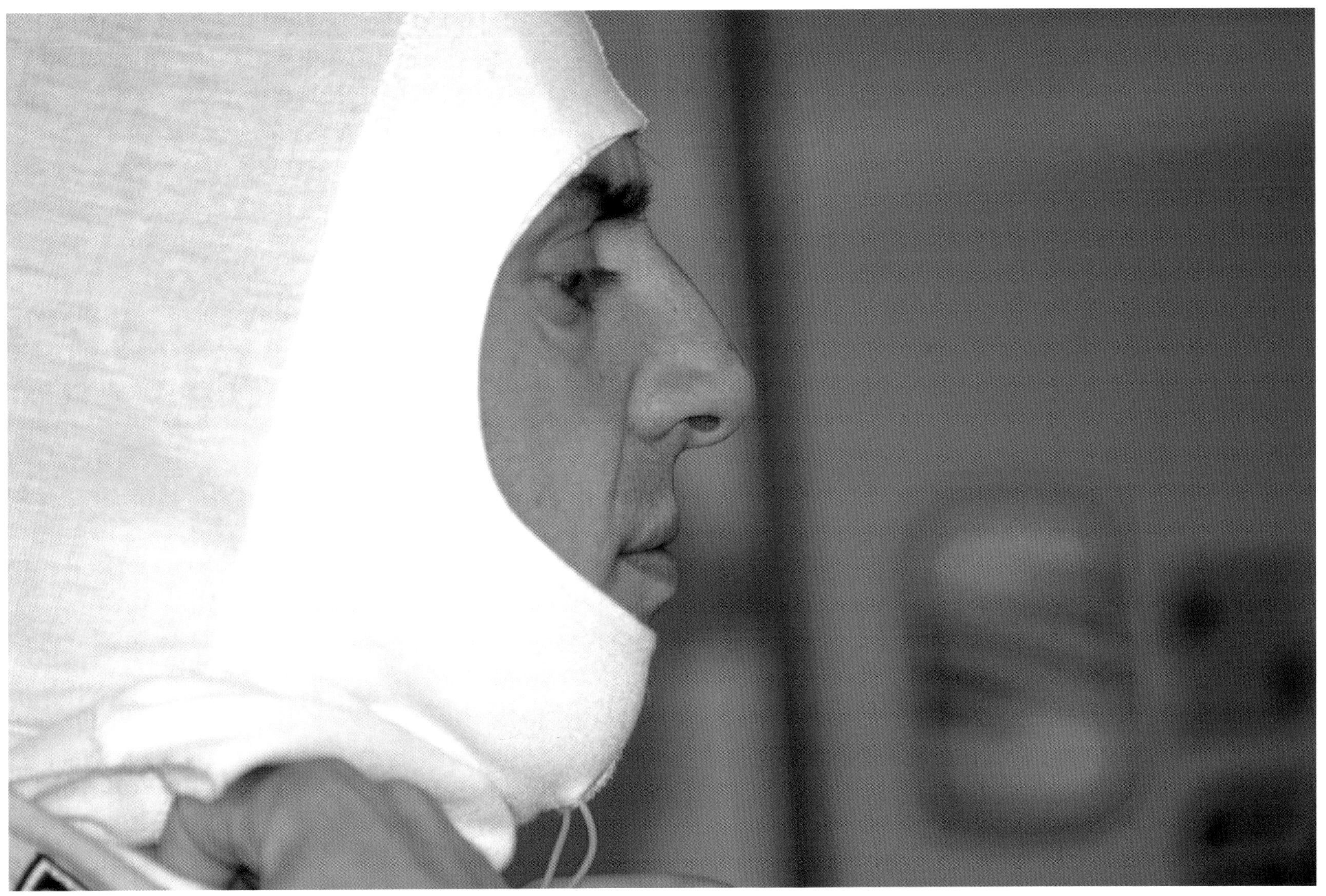

Camera	Pentax *ist D
Focal length	200mm (35mm equivalent: 300mm)
Exposure	1/250sec at f/4.5
ISO setting	200

Choose backgrounds carefully: you don't want them to be so busy that they distract attention from your subject. Here I chose a strong colour but threw it out of focus by using a wide aperture so that it complements the simple composition of this shot.

Camera	Pentax *ist D
Focal length	90mm (35mm equivalent: 135mm)
Exposure	1/1000sec at f/5.6
ISO setting	200

Strong colours are everywhere in motor sport and should be used to your advantage. The contrasting colours of this nose cone make a very simple, yet pleasing image.

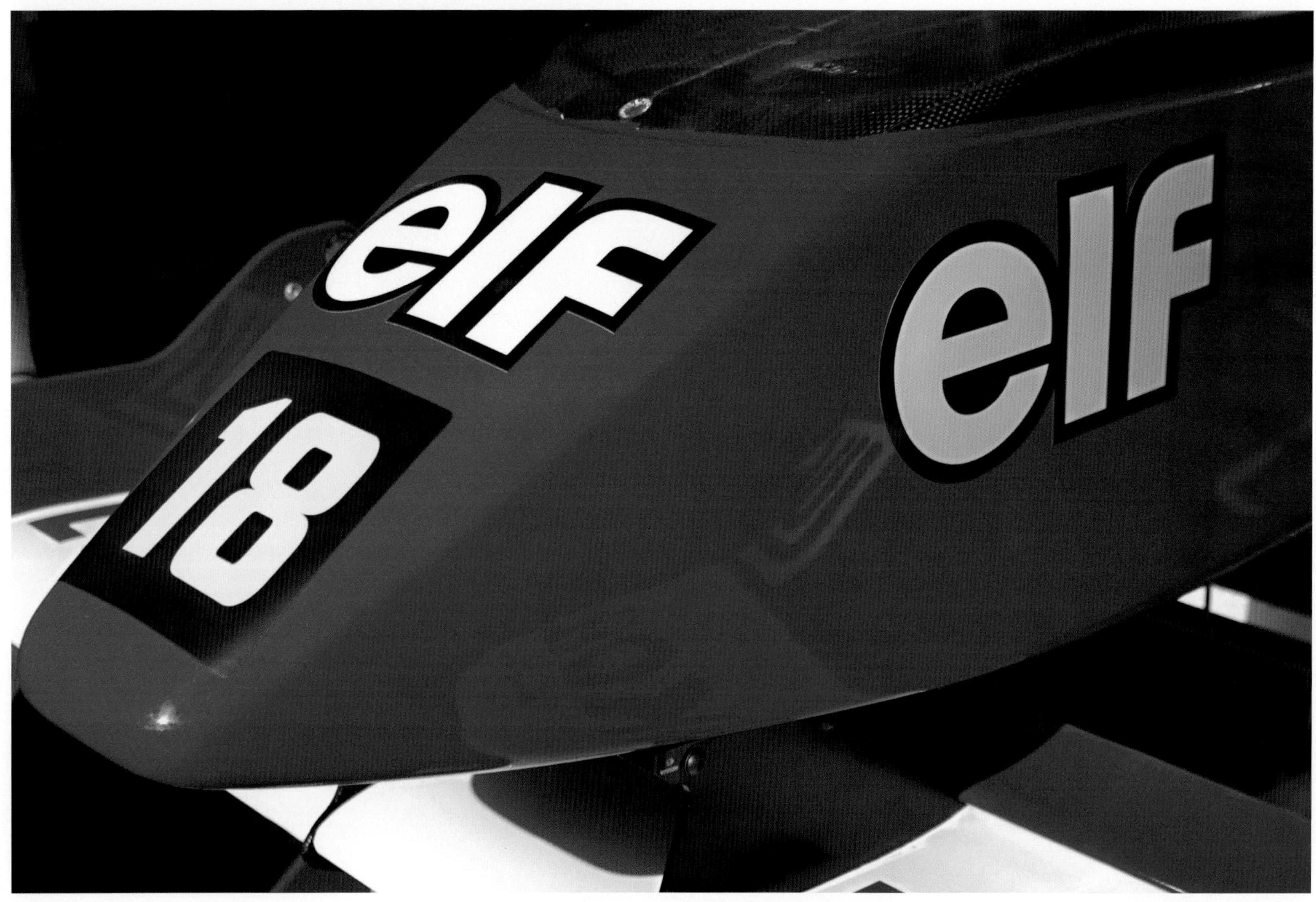

Case Study: Colour vs. monochrome

Black and white images of motor racing are rarely seen these days, and I must confess that I have not used this medium myself for a long time. The main reason for this is probably that the nature of the genre lends itself to colour so well. I'm not convinced that black and white is as effective a medium as colour for action shots, but I do feel that there is a strong argument for using it if you want to adopt a more photojournalistic approach to your images. The monochrome images on this page can be seen in colour elsewhere in this book – they were shot in colour and converted to black and white in PhotoShop – nevertheless I feel they stand up very well in this form.

If you haven't used black and white film to photograph motor sports, I would recommend giving it a try. It is quite refreshing to have to think in monotones rather than in colour, and this can produce some excellent results. I would use a fairly fast film, as this provides strong grain which I feel contributes to the mood.

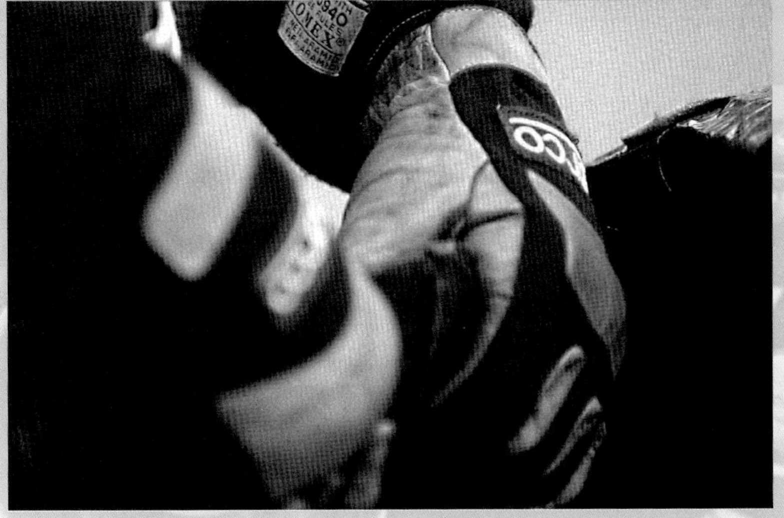

Camera	***Pentax *ist D***
Focal length	***200mm (35mm equivalent: 300mm)***
Exposure	***1/500sec at f/4***
ISO setting	***200***

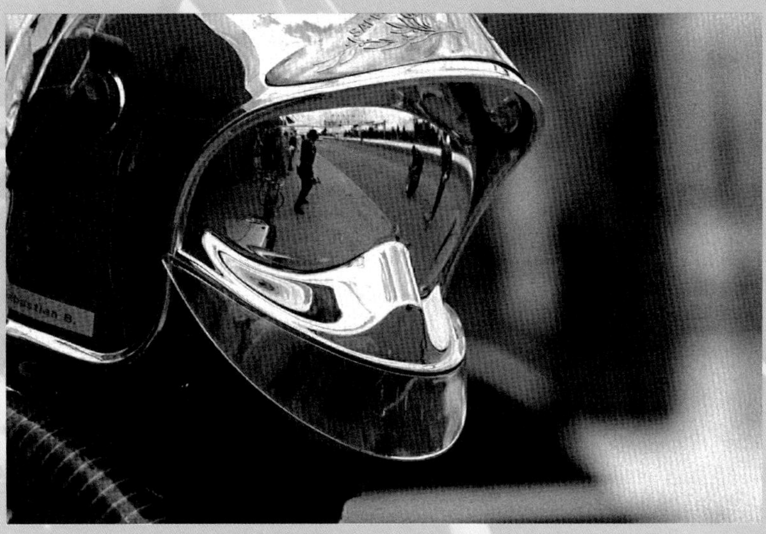

Camera	***Pentax *ist D***
Focal length	***200mm (35mm equivalent: 300mm)***
Exposure	***1/750sec at f/5.6***
ISO setting	***200***

Cropping

Cropping has been an integral part of photography for a long time. It is not something I often do, but sometimes by cropping out part of an image you can improve its composition. The downside of cropping is that you are reducing the size of the original image, which means that print quality will be reduced because more enlargement is required; this is why I try to do my cropping in the viewfinder if at all possible.

Camera	***Pentax *ist D***
Focal length	***120mm (35mm equivalent: 180mm)***
Exposure	***1/250sec at f/8***
ISO setting	***200***

I try to avoid cropping if at all possible, but the unpredictable nature of motor racing means that sometimes you will need to crop an image in order to remove unwanted distractions. As this shot unfolded in front of me I knew there was no time to change lenses, so concentrated on refocusing to get the shot in the knowledge that I could crop it later.

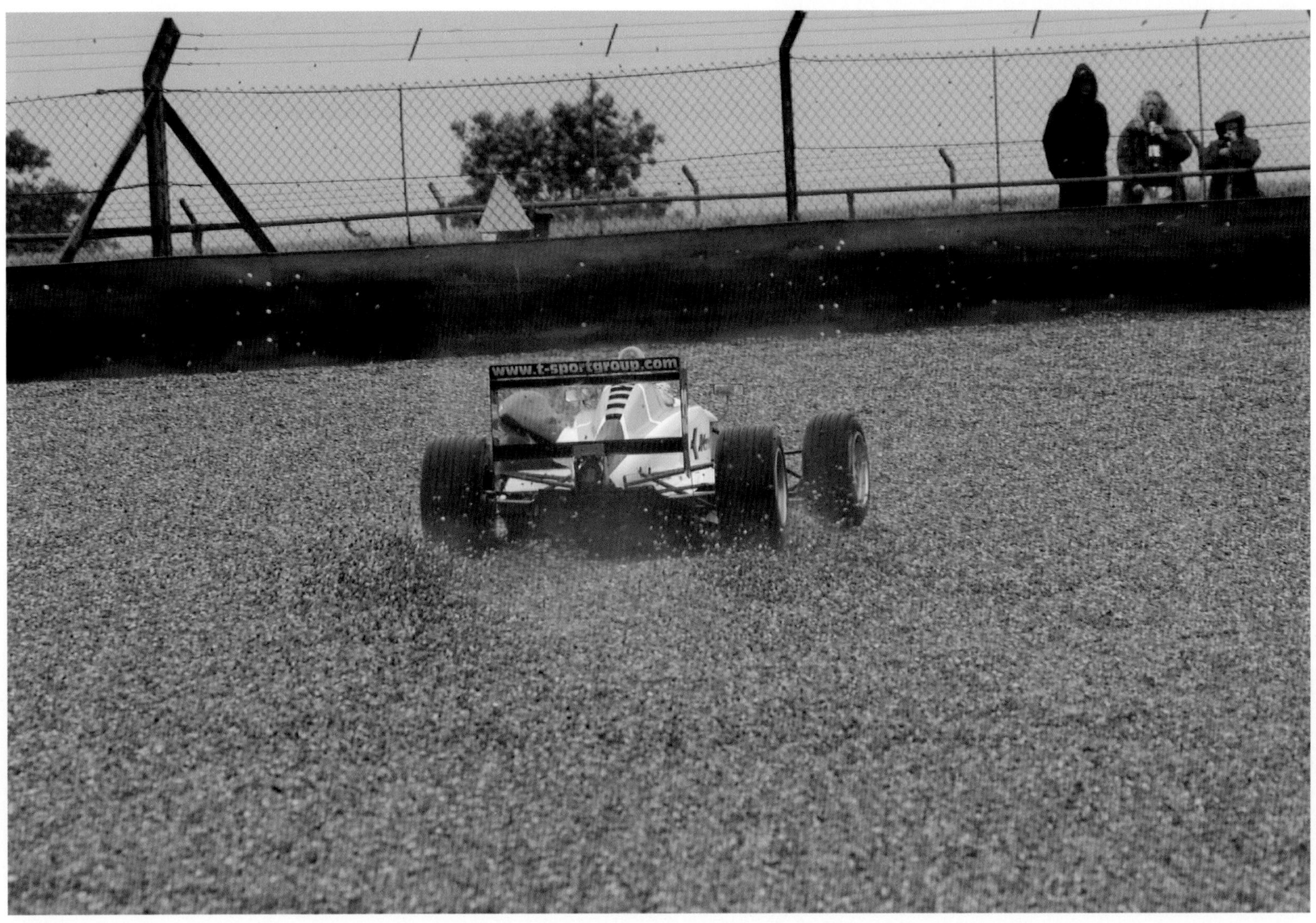

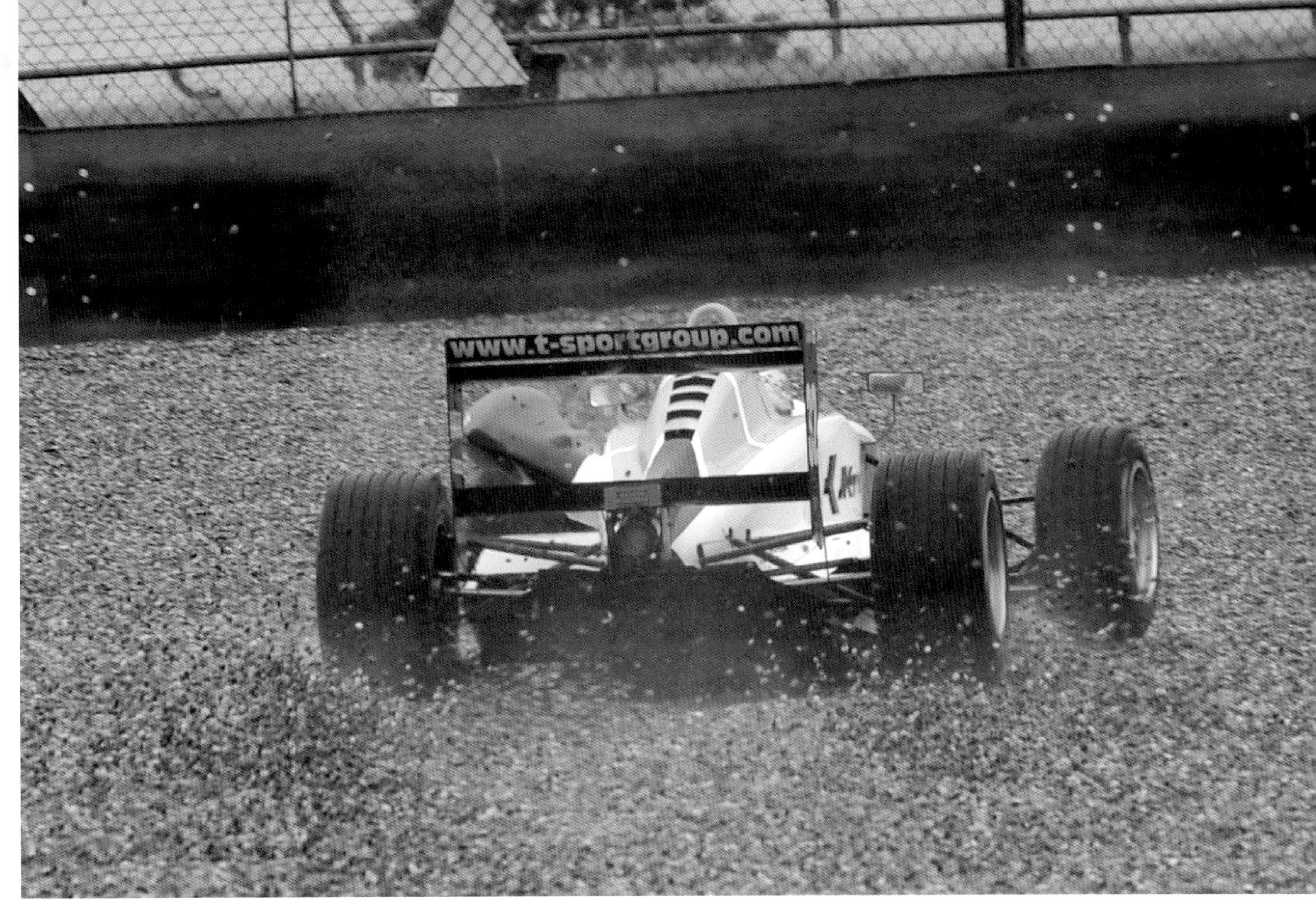

However, there are certain situations when it is necessary to crop an image. If you simply can't get close enough to your subject to create the composition you want, cropping it afterwards does help you to get around this. Due to the nature of motor sport it is often difficult to predict exactly where the action is going to occur, and this is especially true in the case of racing accidents. You may be set up at a particular corner waiting to capture your subject as it passes by, with your camera pre-focused on the appropriate section of track and the lens and exposure already selected to give you the composition you want. Then, as your subject approaches, you realize that it's not going to make the turn – and with a screech of brakes the driver loses control and is heading for the gravel trap. There is no time to change lenses or worry too much about composition – you have to quickly re-focus and capture the incident as it unfolds. The prime concern is that you get the shot; if the composition is not ideal you can always crop out unwanted distractions later on. Situations like this probably account for 90% of the cropping I do; in an ideal world I would avoid it, but the nature of this type of photography means that a little cropping may be needed now and again.

In the paddock

When photographing motor sports, try to remember that cars or bikes in action are not the only subject available to you. Pit and paddock enclosures where the teams prepare for racing provide great opportunities for images. As I invariably arrive well before racing starts, I will usually have a good walk around the paddock areas on the lookout for images, and there are always plenty to be found. I tend to look for close-up shots that depict part of the motor racing scene: it could be a stack of tyres, a detail of a car or bike, one of the liveried team trucks – the list of possibilities is huge, so it's well worth spending time looking around.

Camera	**Pentax *ist D**
Focal length	**200mm (35mm equivalent: 300mm)**
Exposure	**1/2000sec at f/4**
ISO setting	**200**

Racing paddocks provide a wealth of photographic subjects that can be used to complement your on-track action shots.

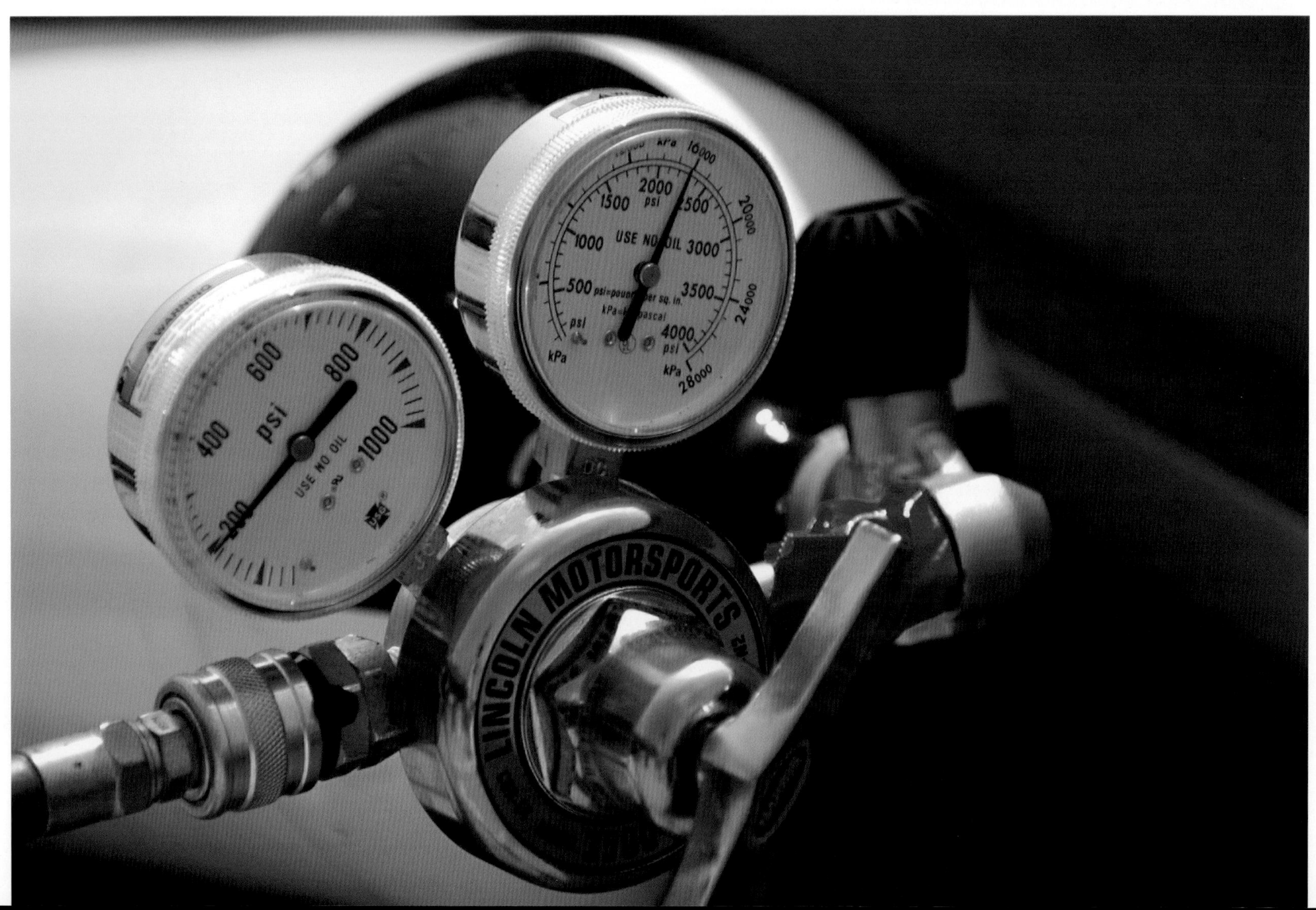

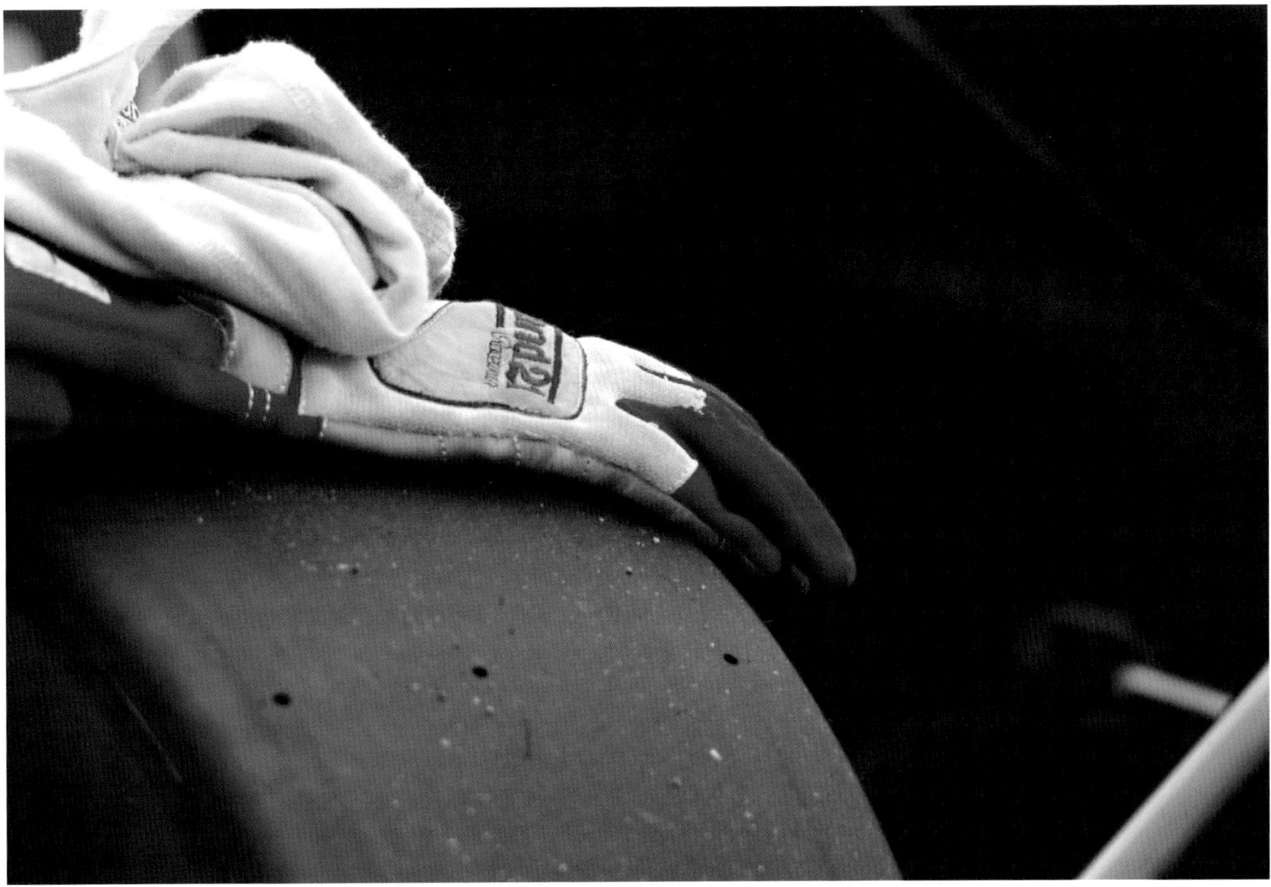

It is a rare treat in motor sport photography to be faced with a stationary subject, so if you're taking shots in the paddock ensure you make the most of it. You will generally have time to play around with composition and exposures, and this is definitely a time when you should make the most of your camera's functions in order to be in full control of the image. At racing circuits pit lane access is usually restricted to press pass holders, but in many other racing disciplines you can get close up to the areas where the teams and drivers prepare. I like to look for candid studies of drivers and mechanics prior to a race – there is often intense concentration or hurried activity to get ready. In this environment you will need to be quick to get good images – these people haven't got time to stand around and be photographed.

Camera	***Pentax *ist D***
Focal length	***200mm (35mm equivalent: 300mm)***
Exposure	***1/250sec at f/4.5***
ISO setting	***200***

As you may have noticed, I like to pick out small details from a scene: I feel that details allow viewers to interpret the mood in their own way, whereas a wider view acts more as a straightforward record of events. This was never a conscious decision of mine, but is part of the evolution of a personal style that was evident in my earliest photographs.

Be prepared

Be aware how many exposures you have left before you need to change film or memory card – there's nothing more frustrating than seeing a great shot, quickly focusing, getting your exposure right and finding when you press the shutter release that you've run out of frames. You'll also miss the shot if you have to change your lens, so it is vital that you are prepared. For this type of scenario I will usually fit a medium-sized zoom of around 80–200mm, but sometimes a wider shot presents itself, so rather than stopping to change lenses I carry a second camera with a 28–80mm lens attached. I always have a flashgun fitted to the camera so that I can quickly switch it on if the need arises.

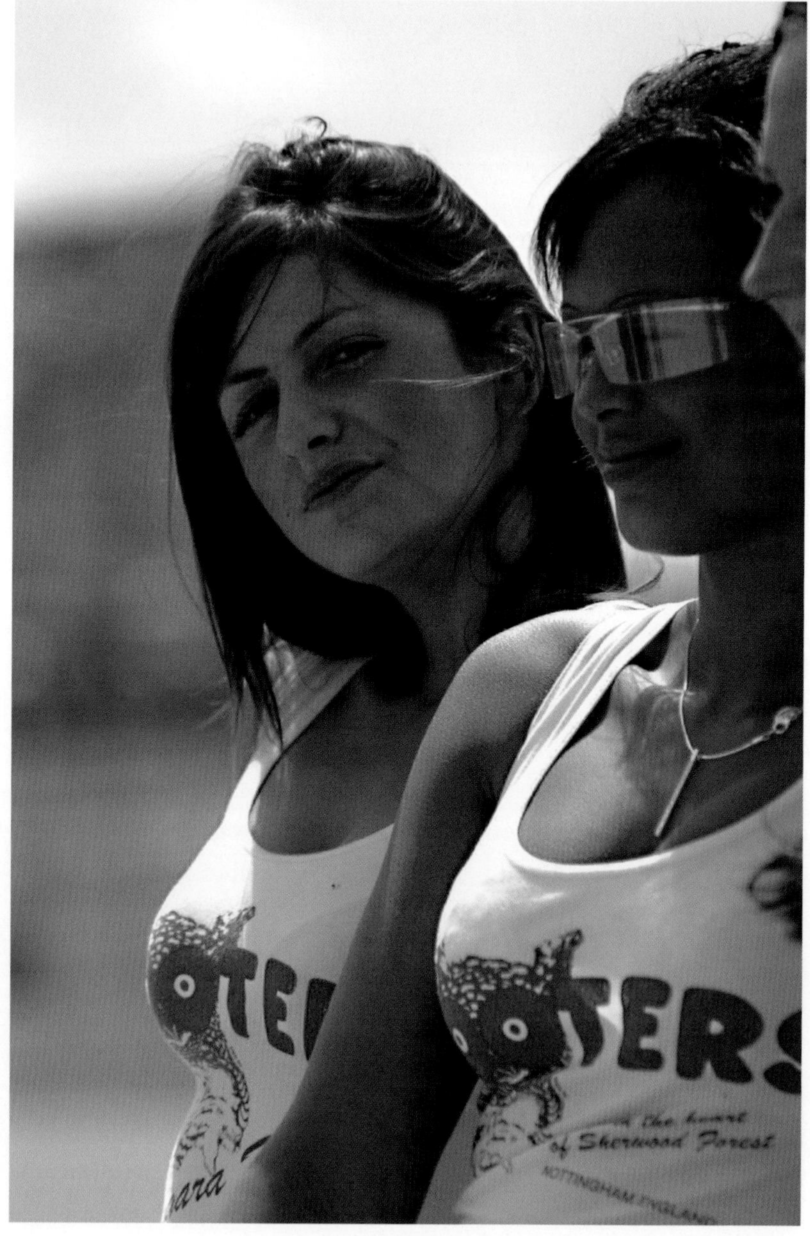

Camera	***Pentax *ist D***
Focal length	***200mm (35mm equivalent: 300mm)***
Exposure	***1/1000sec at f/4***
ISO setting	***200***

Promotions girls add a touch of glamour to a motor racing event. If you are polite and courteous they are usually happy to pose.

Camera	Pentax *ist D
Focal length	135mm (35mm equivalent: 200mm)
Exposure	1/250sec at f/5.6
ISO setting	200

The way the light was falling on the car through corrugated perspex attracted me to this shot. Amidst all the speed and action there are still plenty of opportunities for capturing still-life studies such as this.

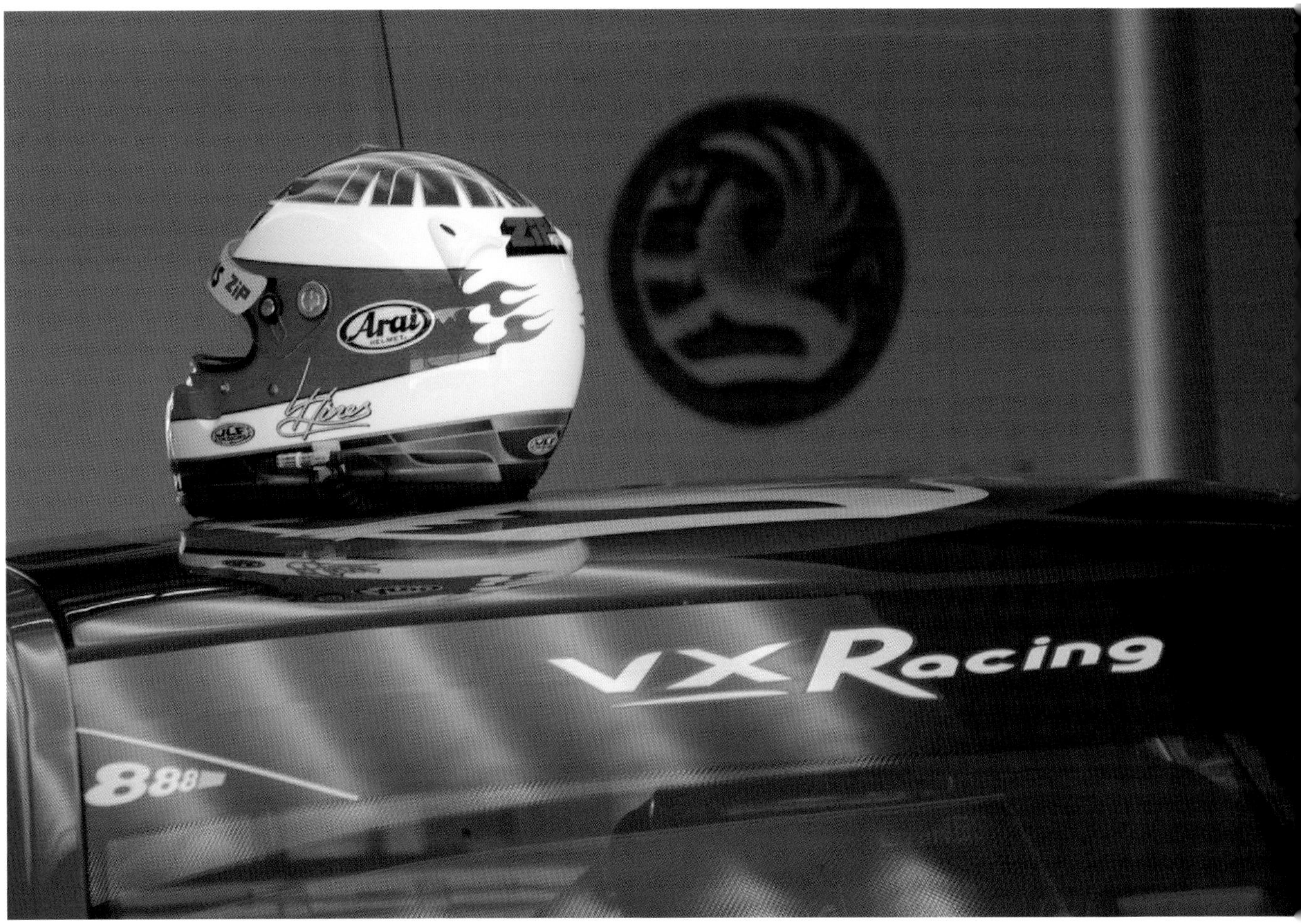

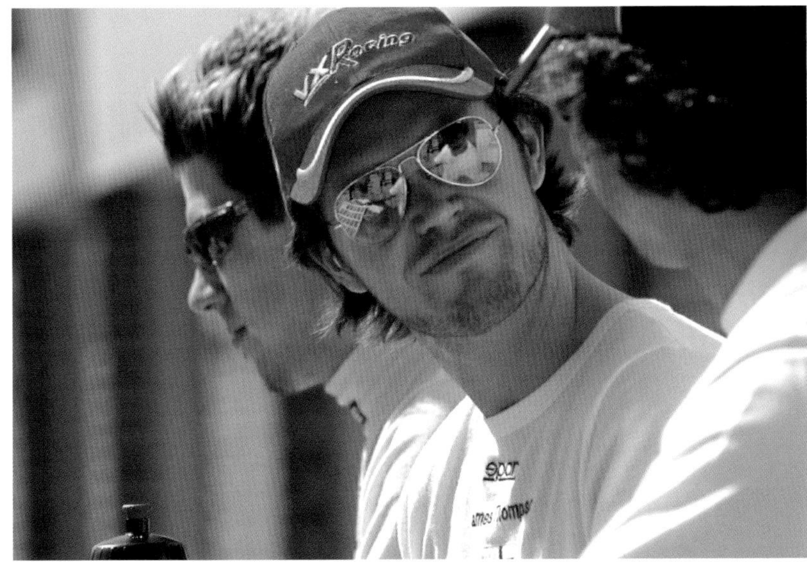

Camera	Pentax *ist D
Focal length	210mm (35mm equivalent: 315mm)
Exposure	1/750sec at f/4.5
ISO setting	200

While waiting for this driver to turn and talk to his team mate at an autograph session, I had time to focus carefully and select a wide enough aperture to make him stand out from the others.

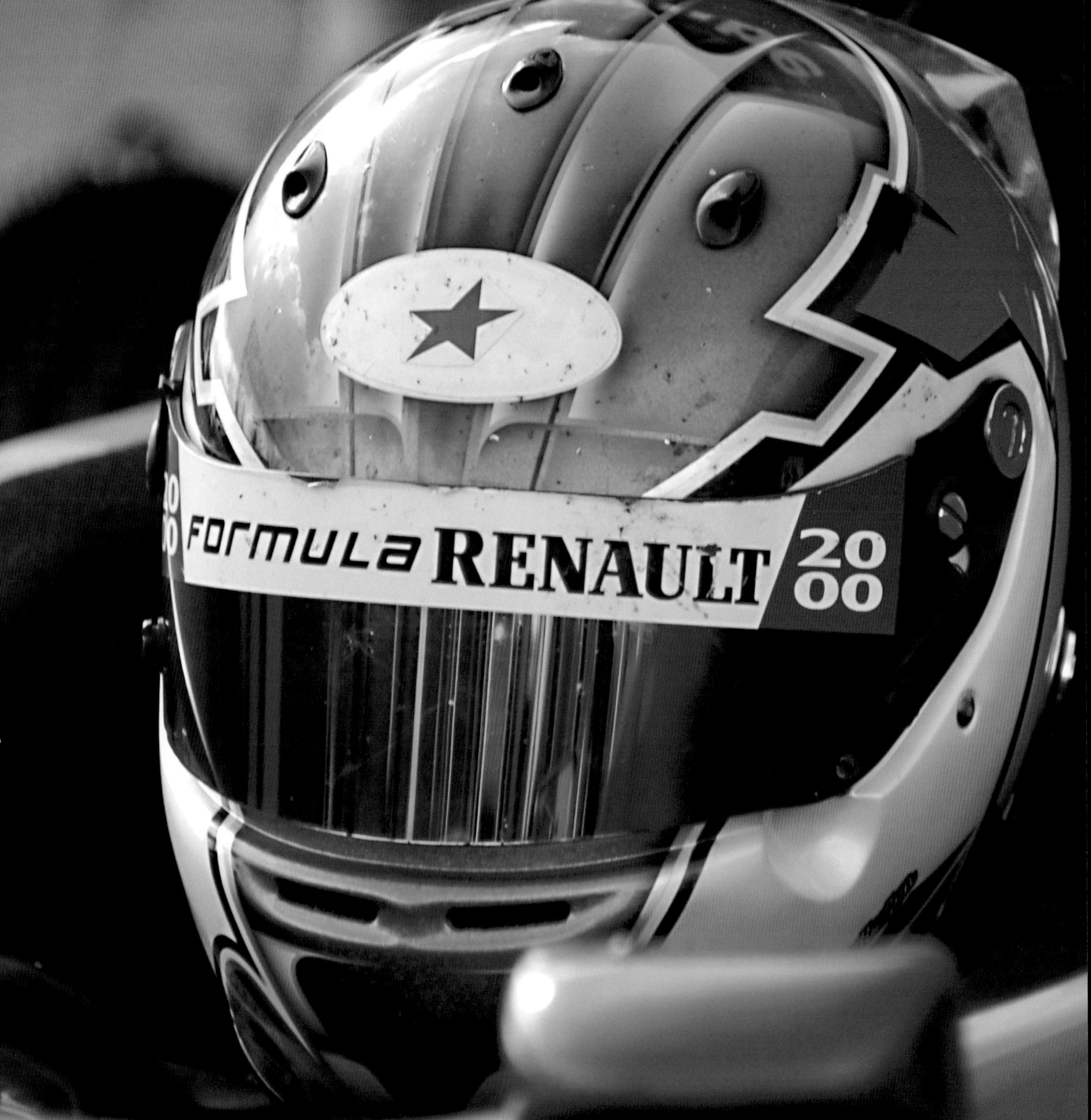
FORMULA RENAULT 2000

CHAPTER 6

Steps to selling

Many keen photographers dream of a time when they will be able to give up their day job and make a living from taking photographs. It's a great dream to have – wouldn't we all love to earn our living doing something that we really enjoy? Inevitably, reality often falls far short of the dream: outside pressures such as family or other commitments prevent many people from taking the plunge. Even if you do have the chance to make this lifestyle change, there are tough challenges ahead: motor sport photography is very competitive, and you will find yourself contending with many established names who have years of experience and a long-standing reputation.

That is not to say that it is impossible to break into this market – there are many advantages to specializing in motor sport photography, not least that the majority of events take place at weekends, so in the early days it is possible to attend events and sell your work without having to give up your weekday job.

However, there is a big difference between attending a racing event every now and then to take some photographs for your own pleasure, and making the leap to becoming a pro. During the season you will be attending a race every week, so you'll be away from home almost every weekend from spring through to autumn – that alone requires an understanding partner, before you even consider any other issues.

Camera	**Pentax *ist D**
Focal length	**18mm (35mm equivalent: 28mm)**
Exposure	**1/125sec at f/5.6**
ISO setting	**200**

Professional motor sport photography is as competitive as any other area of photography, and breaking into this market needs more than just the ability to take good pictures. Winning new clients requires careful planning, well prepared and targeted marketing, and a dogged determination to succeed.

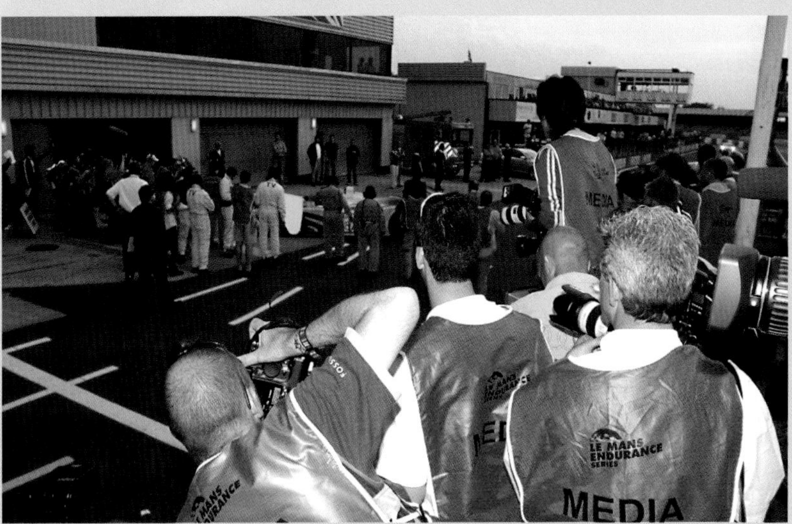

Selling yourself

As with any new player coming into an established marketplace, how you present yourself is crucial to success. Before you even think about approaching potential clients, it is vital that you carry out comprehensive market research to give yourself the best possible chance of selling your work. There are many issues unrelated to photography that will influence your chances of success – you cannot rely on the quality of your images alone to sell your pictures. You have to treat yourself as a 'brand' and work out a plan for approaching the market. The first requirement is to be very critical of your own work.

When submitting images or ideas to publishers, it is vital that you present yourself in a professional way. This picture shows some of the artwork I submitted when I first approached the publishers of this book. By setting out your ideas in a clear, practical and concise manner you will allow the viewer to grasp your proposal quickly.

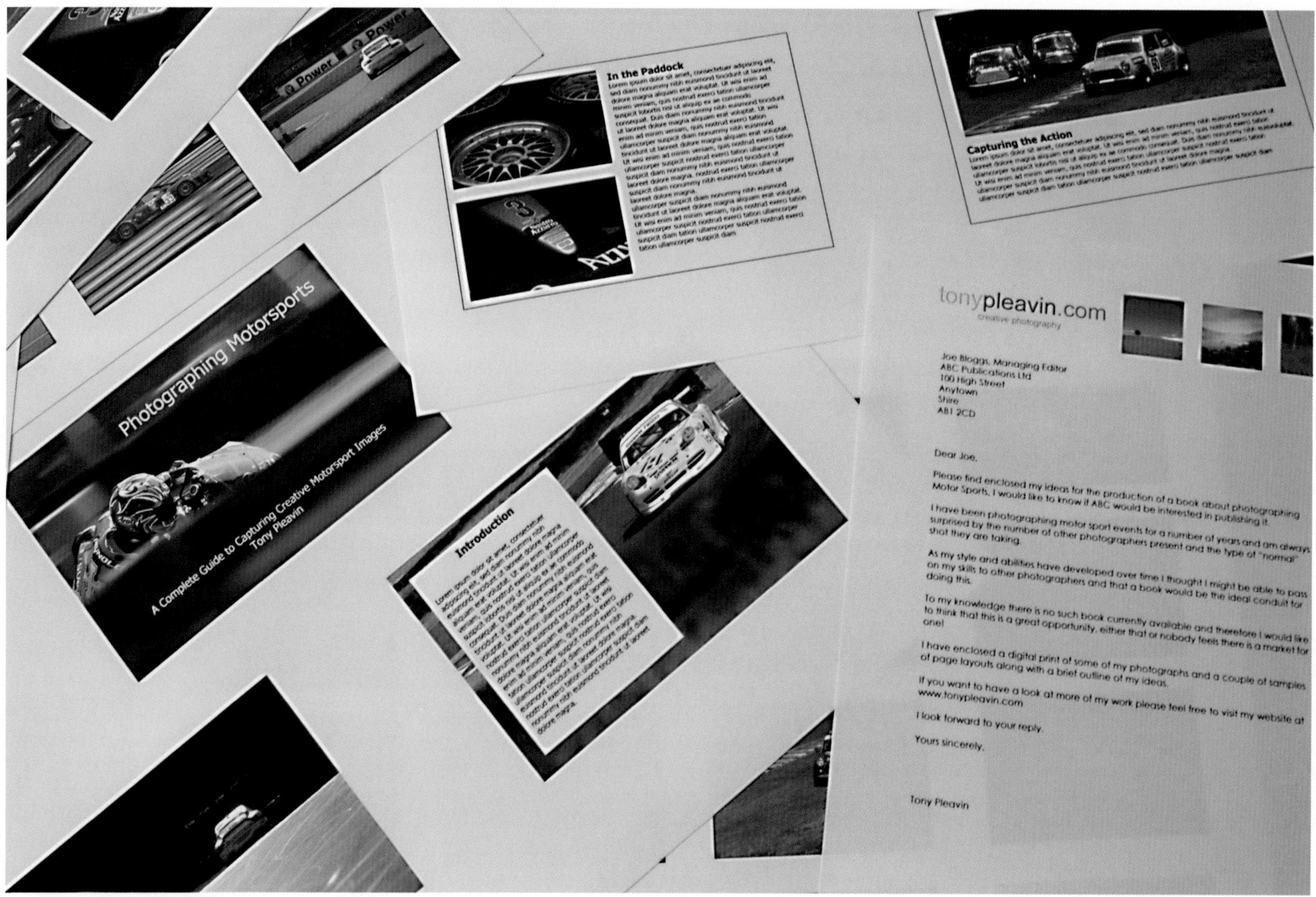

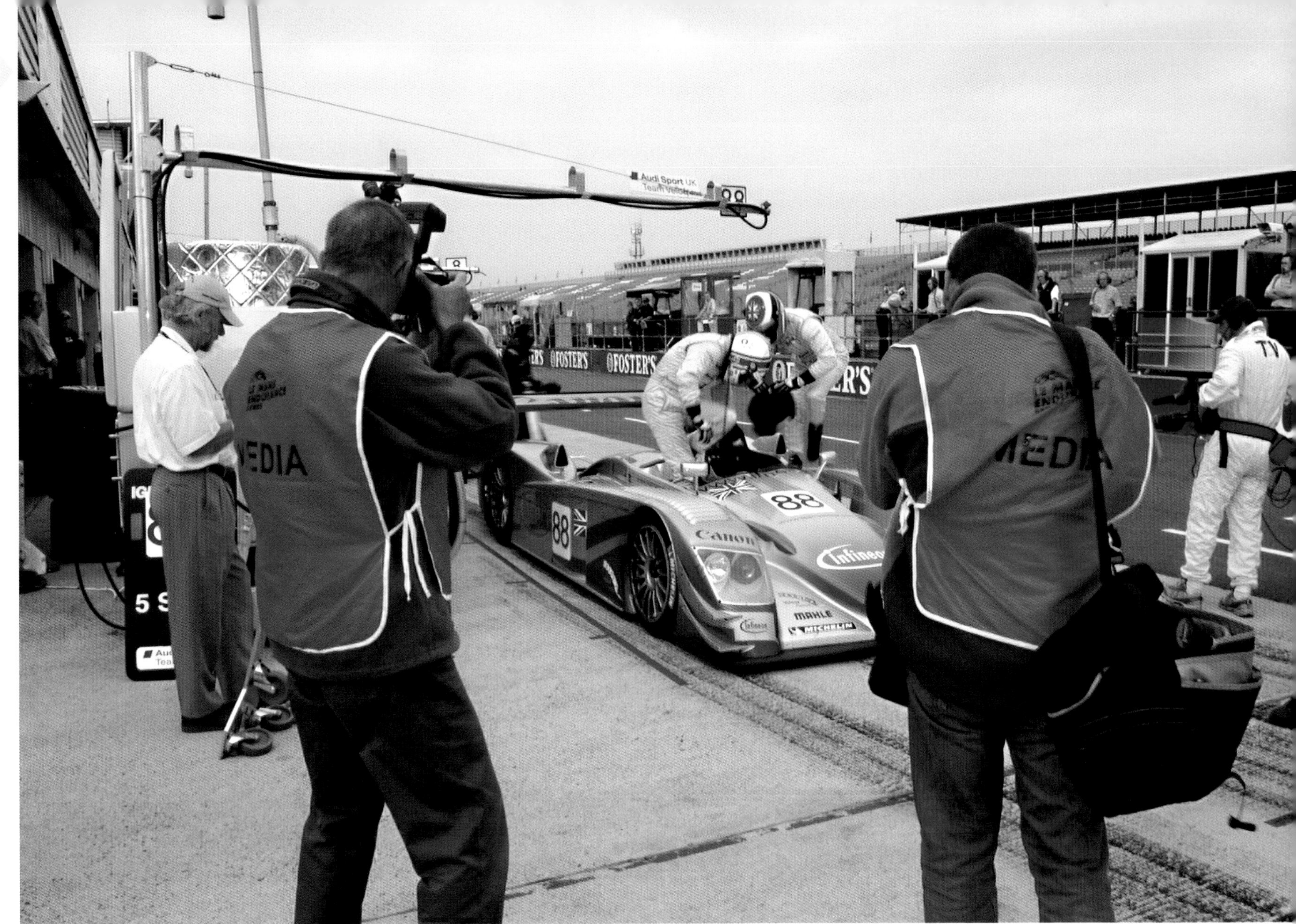

Camera	Pentax *ist D
Focal length	25mm (35mm equivalent: 38mm)
Exposure	1/30sec at f/22
ISO setting	200

If you want to get your racing images published you will have to provide potential clients with a reason to use your pictures in preference to those of better-known or more experienced photographers. Being able to differentiate yourself from established photographers is an important part of this - not only will your images have to be as good as theirs (if not better), but you will also need to find an 'edge' which sets you apart.

Questions to ask yourself

Do you consistently produce images that are as good as, if not better than, those of established photographers?
If you can't honestly answer 'yes' to this question, concentrate on improving your technique until you can. Approaching potential clients with a substandard portfolio will do you no favours at all.

What differentiates you from other photographers?
Is it the style of your images, your marketing, the services you provide? You have to try and gain an edge over your competitors – a client who already has a good relationship with an existing supplier will need a good reason to change.

What is your market?
It is important that you know who your target market is: the racing press, teams, sponsors, manufacturers? Once you're clear on this, it is useful to develop a list of target clients so that you know who you are aiming at and can start planning how best to approach them.

What does the market want?
You may think the photographs you take are the bee's knees, but if they don't represent what the market wants you'll find it very hard to make any serious headway.

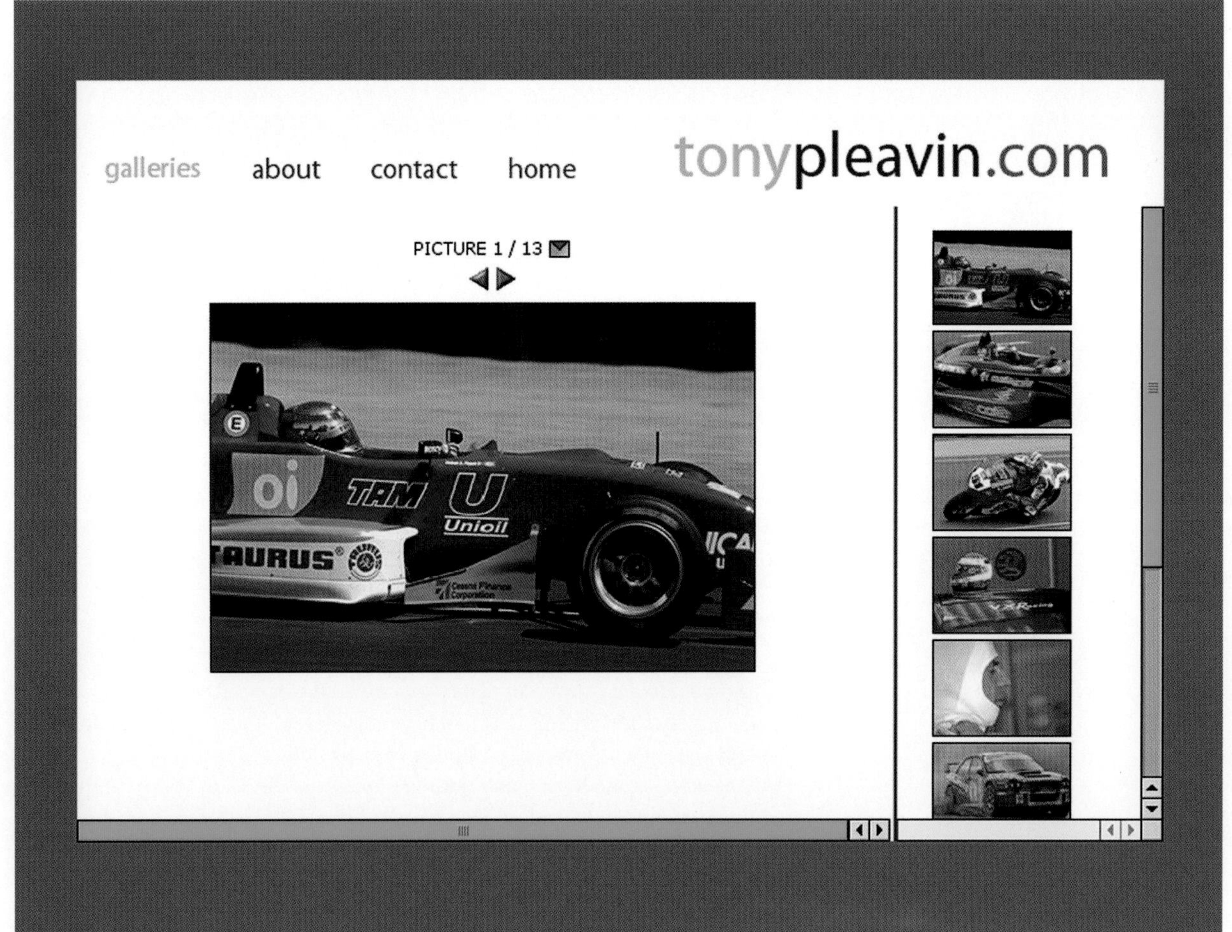

The Internet is a great tool for marketing your images. A professionally designed website, together with a bespoke email template that contains samples of your work, can provide a very cost-effective method of contacting potential customers.

How do you get to the decision maker?

Contact the company to find out the person within the organization who might be willing to buy your work. Once you've done this you will have to decide what is the best way of convincing them to buy from you. This is a marketing issue: you should develop a plan with a clearly identified sales process so that you know how to approach each individual target from first contact to making your first sale and beyond.

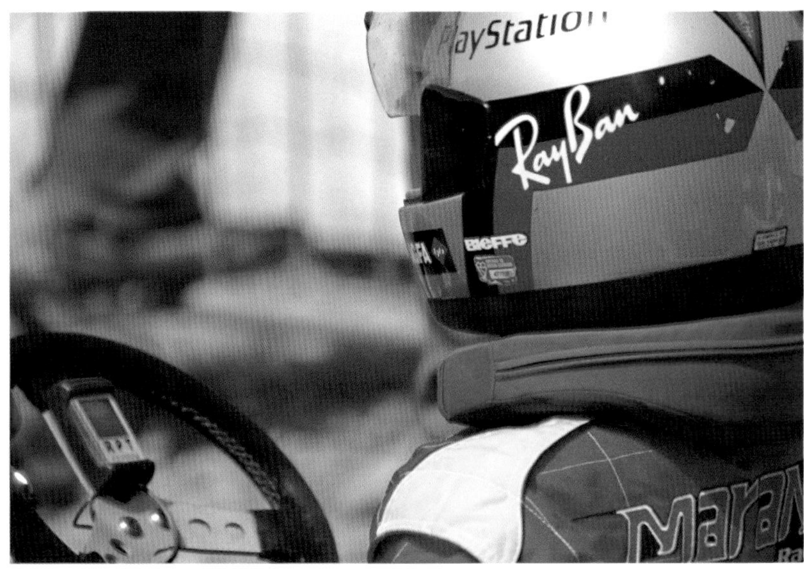

Camera	Pentax *ist D
Focal length	135mm (35mm equivalent: 200mm)
Exposure	1/2000sec at f/4
ISO setting	200

When you set out to sell your racing images it is important that you find a market on which you can cut your teeth. You are unlikely to find it easy to break into the more popular racing series straight away, so try looking at the smaller disciplines such as karting. It's not exactly the big-money end of the market (if in fact there is one), but amateur clubman racers will welcome good pictures of themselves in action.

What marketing tools do you need?

The list of potential marketing tools is endless: business cards, stationery, email templates, brochures, websites, portfolios, promotional CD-ROMs are only the beginning. I would suggest that professional business stationery, a good portfolio and a well-designed website are of paramount importance. Your website will often be the first time a potential client sees your work, and from it they will decide whether to further entertain your advances, so it is vital that this should present your work in a good light.

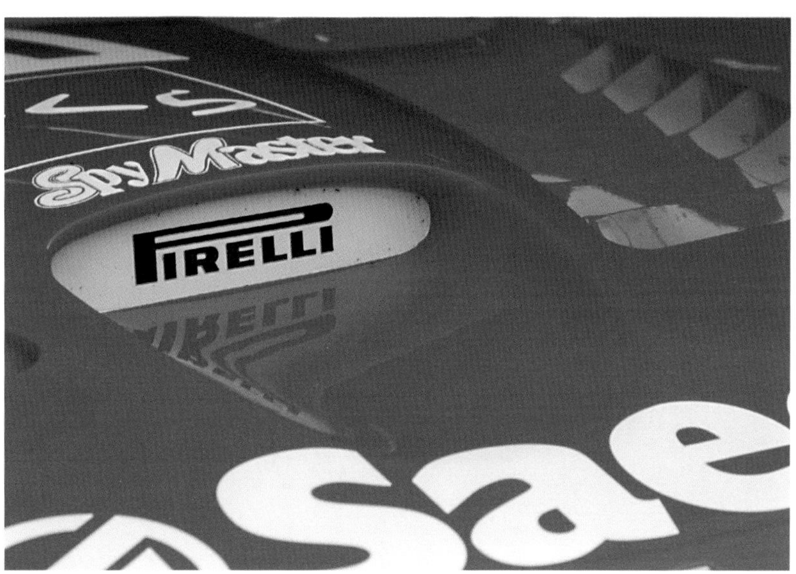

Camera	Pentax *ist D
Focal length	170mm (35mm equivalent: 255mm)
Exposure	1/500sec at f/5.6
ISO setting	200

Team sponsors can provide a lucrative income for the freelance motor sport photographer. However, in a competitive marketplace it is important to give careful consideration to the images you submit. Being aware of the type of images a company has used in the past will help you when it comes to selecting which pictures to send them.

Brand recognition

You can spend a lot of money on marketing, so it is important that whatever you do is well thought out and carefully targeted. There must be consistency between all the elements of your marketing strategy in order to build brand recognition. If you are new to marketing, I would recommend you buy a couple of up-to-date books on the subject – marketing is not rocket science, but the way you market yourself is crucial to your success. You'll probably be a bit nervous about approaching people to begin with, but if the quality of your work is high and you have taken the time to plan and present yourself well, you should be confident in your abilities. Remember, everyone has to start out somewhere.

Camera	***Pentax *ist D***
Focal length	***200mm (35mm equivalent: 300mm)***
Exposure	***1/1000sec at f/5.6***
ISO setting	***200***

If you plan to sell your racing images, it is important to consider how they will be used. Publishers often overlay text onto an image, so you must bear this in mind when arranging your composition. This image is in 'portrait' format, which lends itself to a magazine page; the tarmac area at the bottom is ideal for overlaying text.

Don't undervalue yourself

Pricing is a delicate topic. When working out what to charge for your images, one option is to apply a day-rate fee, for which the client can choose from a range of shots taken that day. Alternatively, if you are selling pictures 'on spec' after you have taken them, it is best to take into consideration the time it took you to get the images, the costs you incurred in taking them (travel, accommodation, film, etc.) and how a client will use the images. You can charge more for a picture if it's going to be used with an advertisement in an international publication than if it's only used in a corporate brochure. If you are working with a new client there will undoubtedly be a degree of negotiating and you'll soon get a feel for what charges the market will accept; but always bear in mind that if you sell your images cheaply to get a foot in the door it will be difficult to increase your prices to a more realistic level at a later date. For this reason I would not recommend that you try to undercut the prices charged by other photographers – this serves only as a short-term gain, and ultimately devalues the work you are doing and makes the market tougher for everyone. By using pricing as the sole differentiator between yourself and your competitors you will only diminish the reputation of your 'brand' and find it harder to be successful in the long term.

There are many ways to present your images. If you have a laptop computer you can easily put together a professional-looking presentation that will allow you to show potential clients a wide range of photographs. If you're doing a face-to-face presentation, make sure you take along a copy of your slide show on a CD (which also contains your contact details) so you can leave it behind for the client to examine at leisure.

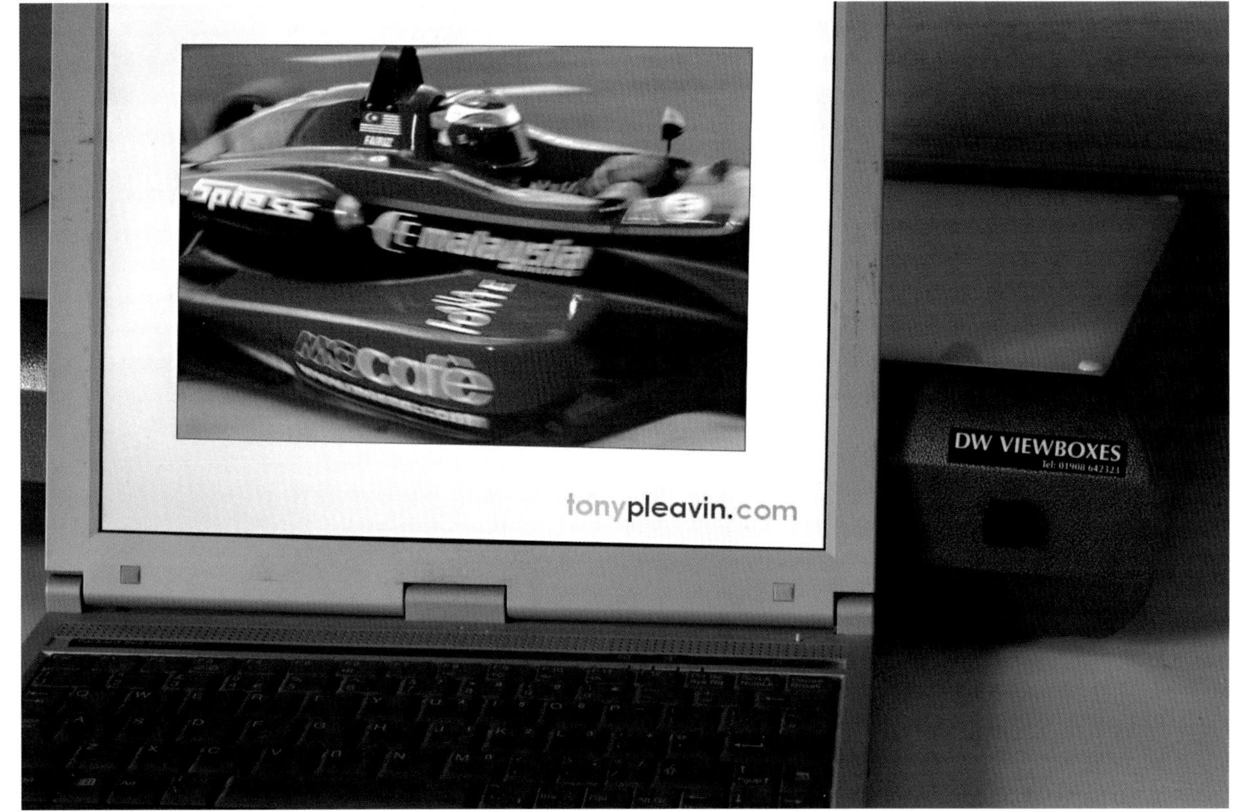

Building a portfolio

A key part of presenting your work is your portfolio. When you've built up a good stock of strong images and gone through all the hard work of making contact with potential clients, it is often your portfolio that will make or break your chances of a commission. The digital revolution has changed the way photographers present their work, and although the word 'portfolio' conjures up images of leather-bound presentation cases containing your best prints, this is not necessarily the way it is done nowadays.

As an alternative to displaying your work in print form, you may opt for a digital presentation using a laptop computer. Due to the pressures of modern working life, marketing people are often very busy. You may find that potential clients will prefer not to meet in person, but will ask you to send them a CD with a presentation of your images on it, or to view images on your website via the Internet. Though both of these are certainly very quick and convenient ways of displaying your work, I prefer, if at all possible, to meet face to face with people. This allows you to 'sell' both yourself and your work. In an actual meeting it is much easier to gauge the mood of the viewer and establish your chances of getting some work.

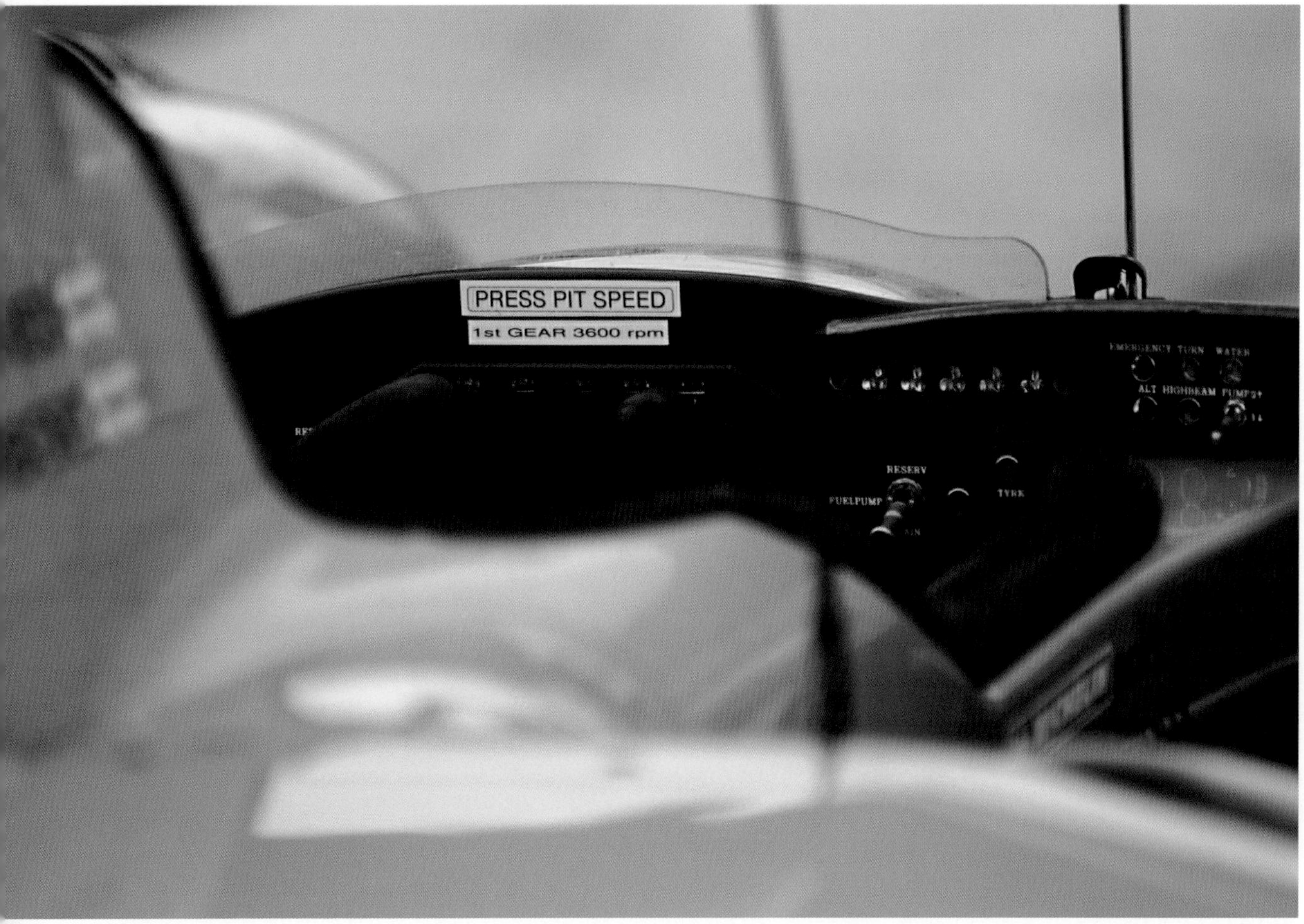

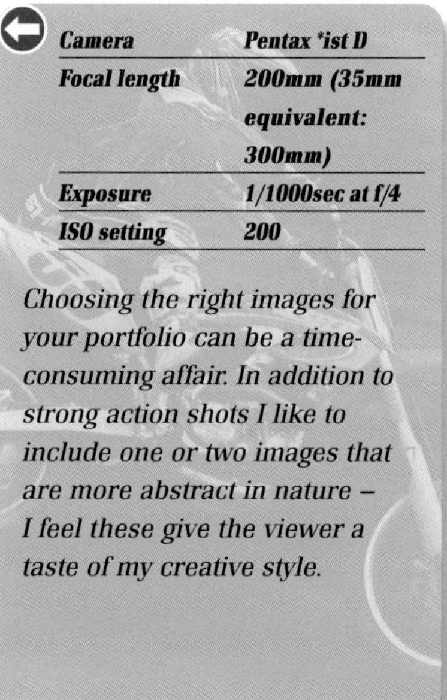

Camera	**Pentax *ist D**
Focal length	**200mm (35mm equivalent: 300mm)**
Exposure	**1/1000sec at f/4**
ISO setting	**200**

Choosing the right images for your portfolio can be a time-consuming affair. In addition to strong action shots I like to include one or two images that are more abstract in nature – I feel these give the viewer a taste of my creative style.

What to include

The choice of images in your portfolio is critical to its success. Rather than simply including 10 or 12 of your favourite images, you should consider the person who will be viewing the work and what they will want to see. By researching each target client to see what images they have used in the past, you can tailor your portfolio to their particular needs, including images which seem to you to complement their requirements but add a different dimension to what they have used before. I like to ensure that 75% of the images I show a client are selected in this way, with the remainder made up of pictures that I can readily talk about, or that show a particular style that differentiates me from the suppliers they have used in the past. The way you 'sell' your images is an important part of any presentation: it is always helpful to arrange your portfolio in a way that allows you to talk about the pictures in a methodical 'flow'.

Once you have chosen which images to use, it is all down to presentation. No matter what medium you choose, it is important that your portfolio is true to your 'brand' – the presentation of a portfolio is almost as important as its contents. Potential clients may see work from many photographers throughout the year, the majority of whom will have presented good-quality images. This is why the presentation of your work deserves careful thought and may help to give you the edge over someone else.

Whichever medium you use to present your work – prints, transparencies or laptop – make sure that you have taken the time to display it as professionally as possible. Prints should be well mounted, transparencies displayed in uniform mounts (don't assume your client will have a lightbox – always take a battery-powered one with you), and laptop presentations should be slick and well designed.

It is also important to consider how you present yourself at a first meeting; whether you choose to look 'businesslike' or more casual may depend on what you feel suits you best, but remember you are representing your 'brand', so it's important that you show it in the best possible light.

Camera	**Pentax *ist D**
Focal length	**175mm (35mm equivalent: 260mm)**
Exposure	**1/500sec at f/9.5**
ISO setting	**200**

Strong action shots like this are a crucial part of any motor sport portfolio, but it is important to show many differing types of image in order to demonstrate the breadth of your abilities. Showing images that vary in composition and style will help potential clients to see how your pictures could work for them.

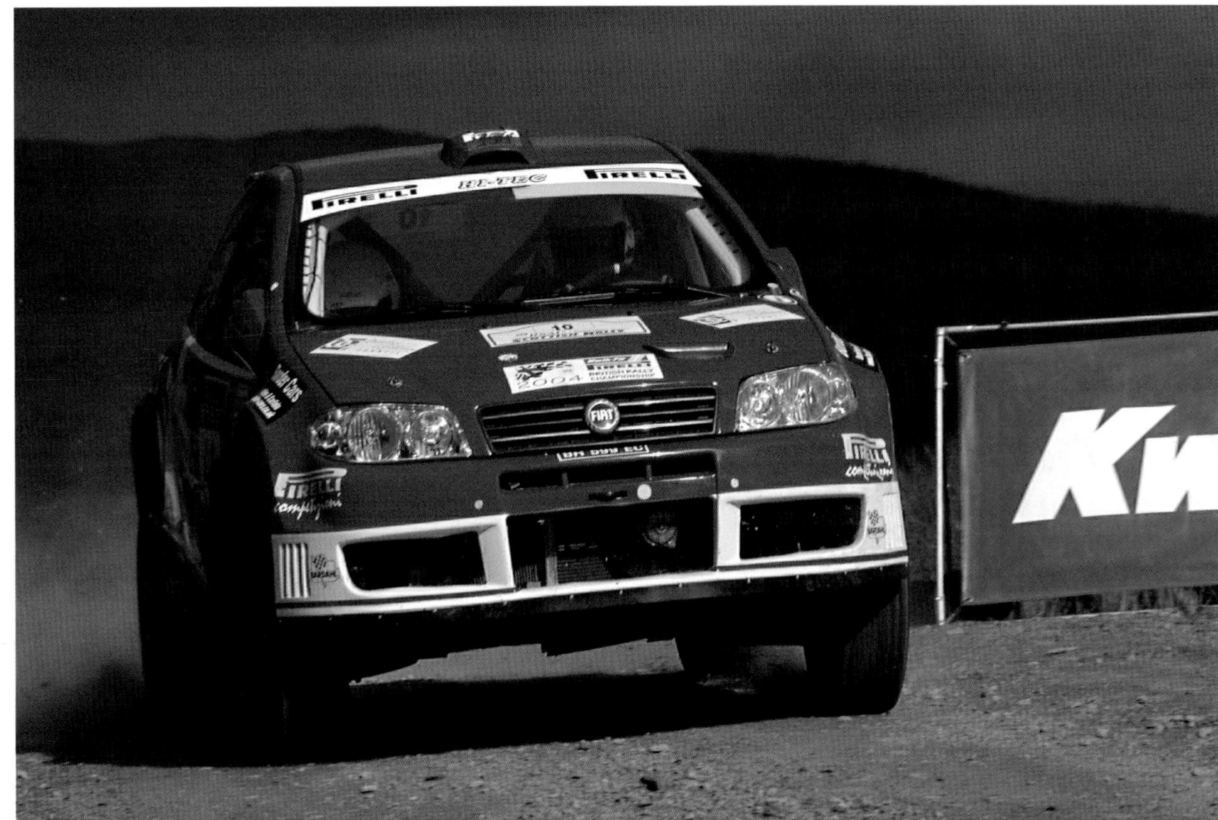

Getting a press pass

Although we have seen that you don't have to have a press pass to take good motor sport photographs, it is a vital asset if you are planning to sell your images professionally. Without media access to an event, you are putting yourself at a serious disadvantage compared to other photographers.

Press passes are generally obtained through the circuit or event organizer; the majority of these have websites where you will find a press section that contains a downloadable application form. In order to qualify for a pass you will need to provide a letter of accreditation from the publication or client for whom you will be working at the relevant event. This may seem a bit of a catch-22, since many people believe that you can't convince a publisher or editor to provide you with accreditation if you can't get access to the press areas in the first place to produce the images you need to show the quality of your work. This is simply not true: applying for a pass is your first opportunity to test the marketing skills you will need further down the line.

Camera	***Pentax *ist D***
Focal length	***200mm (35mm equivalent: 300mm)***
Exposure	***1/125sec at f/11***
ISO setting	***200***

The winners' podium is often located in a restricted area, so you will need a press pass if you want to photograph the victory celebrations.

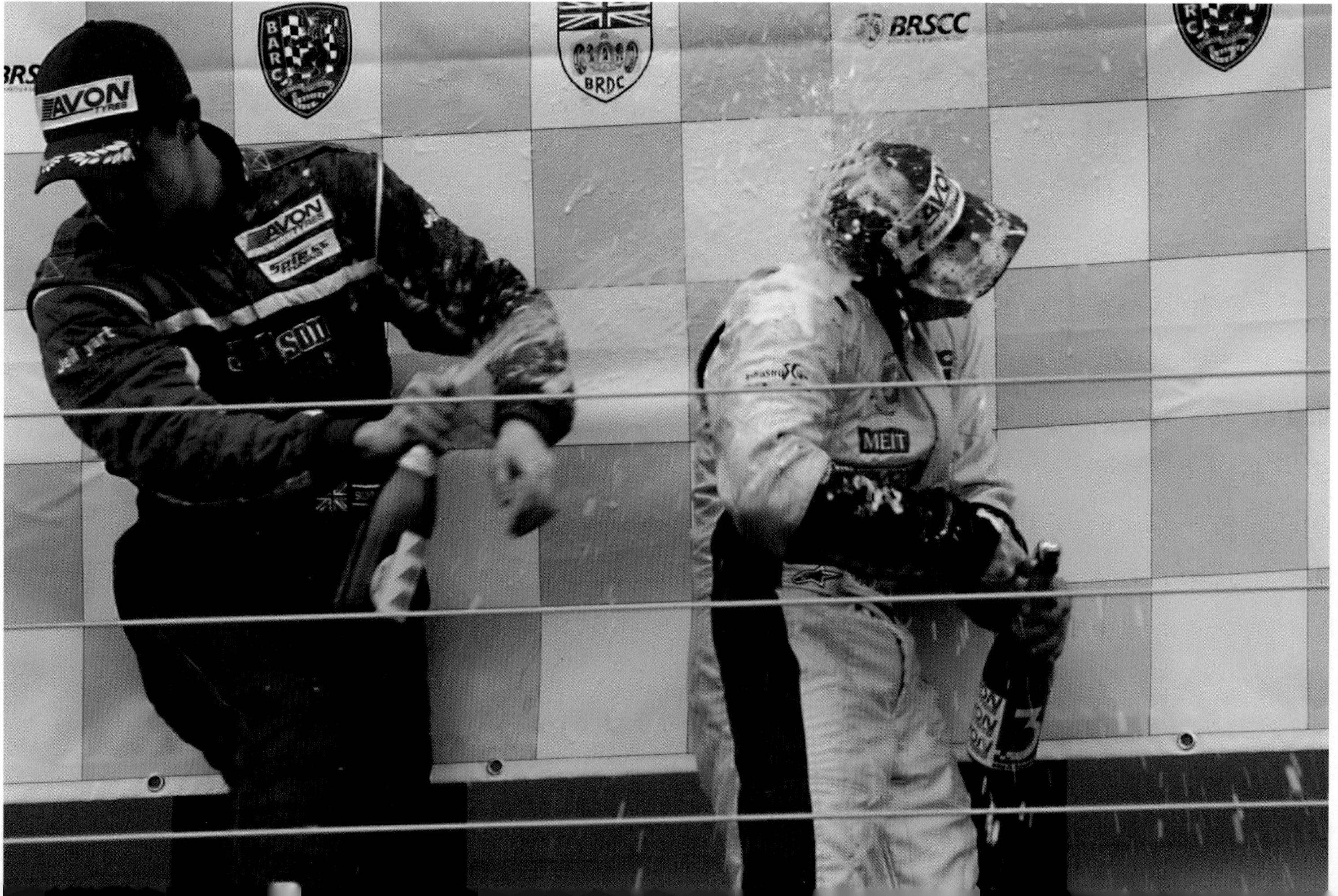

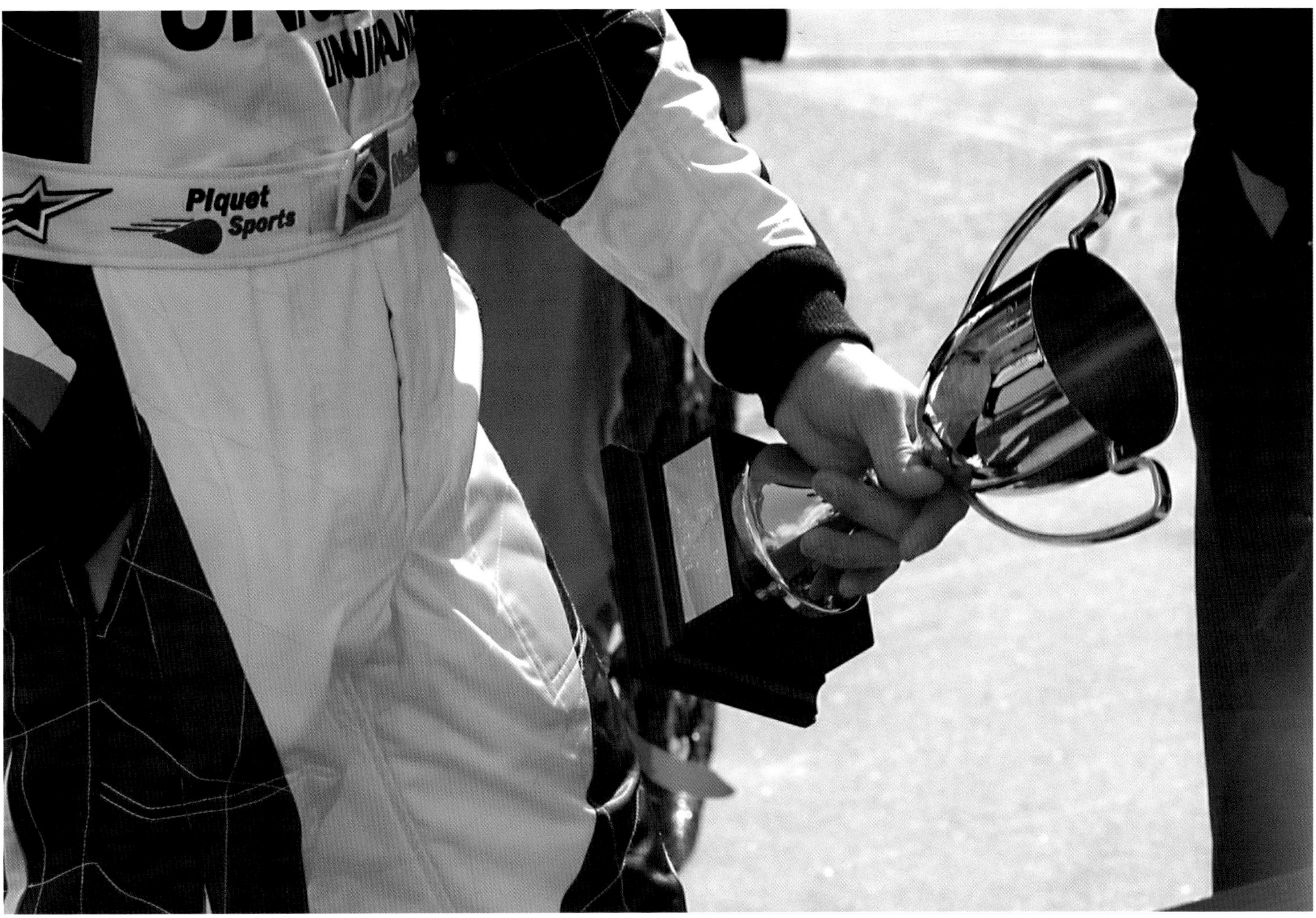

If you think you've got what it takes to sell your racing images, you should already have a good portfolio of work that you have taken from public access areas. I would recommend approaching your local newspaper editor with your portfolio and offering to cover an event at your local circuit. It will help if you have researched any drivers who live locally and are doing well in a championship – you can then offer to provide the editor with photographs of local interest. You might even volunteer to write a few paragraphs to support the images – this would provide the editor with a ready-made story and could well give you your first sale.

Camera	***Pentax *ist D***
Focal length	***140mm (35mm equivalent: 210mm)***
Exposure	***1/350sec at f/8***
ISO setting	***200***

If you can't get access to the podium, why not try getting a shot of the winners' spoils as they return from the podium to their garage in the paddock?

Other routes to a press pass

Alternatively, why not approach a magazine or website that uses racing images? They will doubtless have regular suppliers, but a considerate editor may well provide you with accreditation if you can offer something better or different. Don't discount contacting overseas publishers either – in motor racing there are often competitors from other countries taking part in a championship, and the racing press from their home country may be interested in receiving pictures of their progress.

I had never had a press pass until I was commissioned to write this book. I simply approached the publishers with well-presented examples of my work and a synopsis of my idea for the book, with a covering letter. Once my proposal had been accepted I was provided with a letter of accreditation from the publishers and got busy sending off pass applications (all of them successful) for the races I wanted to cover.

There are no hard and fast rules as to how you can get a press pass, but it is important that you approach it in a professional manner; a little determination, preparation and planning will go a long way.

Camera	**Pentax *ist D**
Focal length	**150mm (35mm equivalent: 225mm)**
Exposure	**1/125sec at f/16**
ISO setting	**200**

Not having press access does restrict the images you can take, but if you're serious about getting accreditation you will need to build a strong portfolio of images. If you choose your events carefully there is no reason why you can't take images of a professional standard.

If you want to sell your images you will have to compete with professional photographers, and you will almost certainly need a press pass. It may not be easy to find a publication that is willing to provide you with the accreditation required. Plan carefully who you are going to approach – if your work is good enough and you present yourself well, you should be able to find an editor who is prepared to give you a chance.

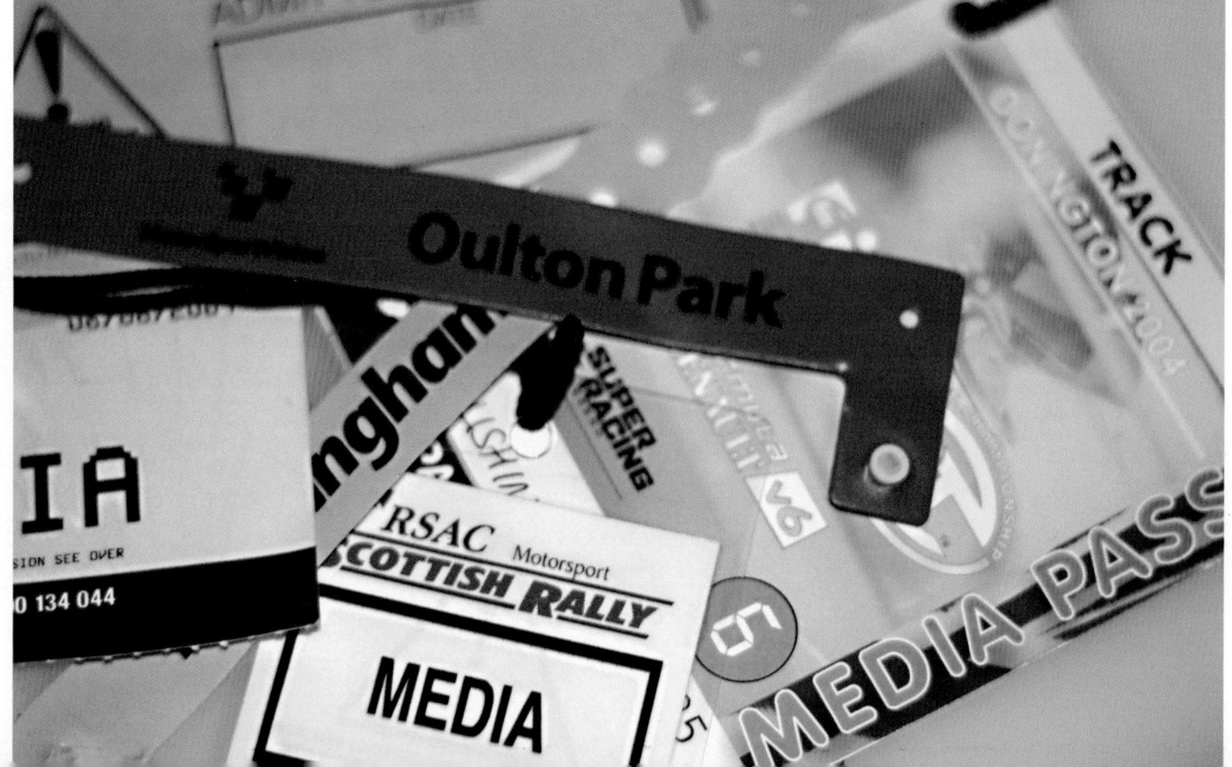

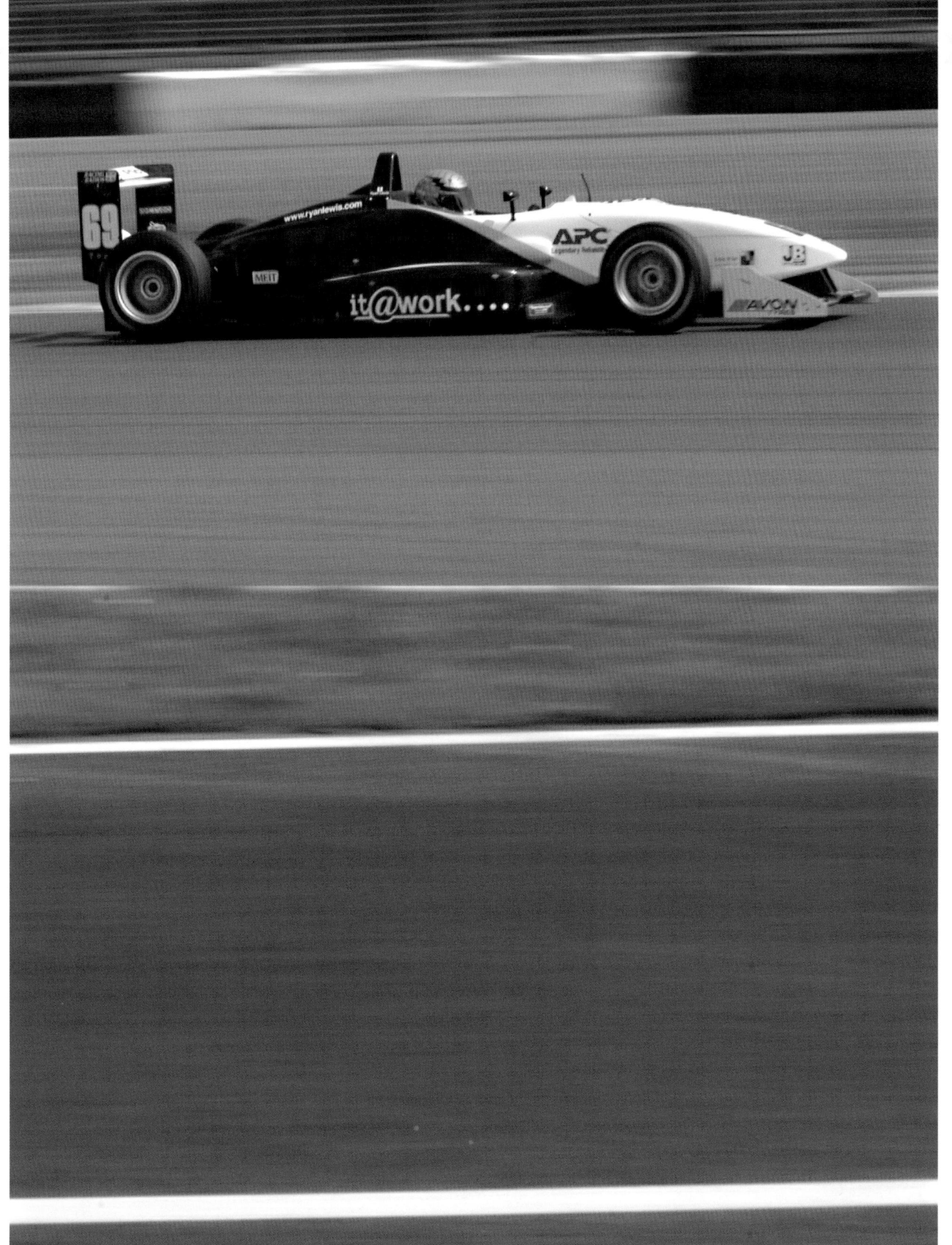
69
www.ryanlewis.com
APC
JB
it@work....
AVON

Finding and keeping clients

The variety of markets available to you is vast, but many are already colonized by contracted or regular suppliers. I would recommend drawing up a list of no more than 30 companies you would like to work for and targeting each of them in a specific way, rather than trying a more general approach to a larger audience. Companies who use motor racing images include the motoring press in print and on the Internet, manufacturers, teams, PR companies, sponsors and many others.

Choosing target clients can be a tricky process, but as a good starting point it is well worth having a look at some of the motor racing business directories. One of the most comprehensive of these that I know of can be found on the Internet by visiting www.autosport.com and following the link to the 'Business' section. Here you will find details of a huge range of companies across all sectors of the motor racing industry. However, you should bear in mind that even this list is not exhaustive and there are many other companies associated with motor sport that can be found with careful research on the Internet.

Finding and approaching new clients is a time-consuming activity, but if you are serious about making money from your photography it is a necessary evil. Don't expect to convert all the people you approach into clients – it simply won't happen. Finding outlets for your work is not an easy process, but with common sense, a professional approach and dogged determination you should be able to begin building a client base.

Camera	*Pentax *ist D*
Focal length	*160mm (35mm equivalent: 240mm)*
Exposure	*1/250sec at f/6.7*
ISO setting	*200*

When you first set out to sell your images you may find it daunting – finding clients can be very time-consuming and often unrewarding. Turning a hobby into a profession can take a lot of the fun out of it if you are ill prepared, so it is important to be realistic about what you expect to achieve. Intense competition means you should plan carefully before giving up your day job.

Once you have put in all the hard effort to find outlets for your work, it is equally important that you keep your clients happy by delivering a level of service that ensures that this relationship continues into the future. It is much easier to lose a client than it is to find a new one, so customer service should be a key part of your plan from the outset.

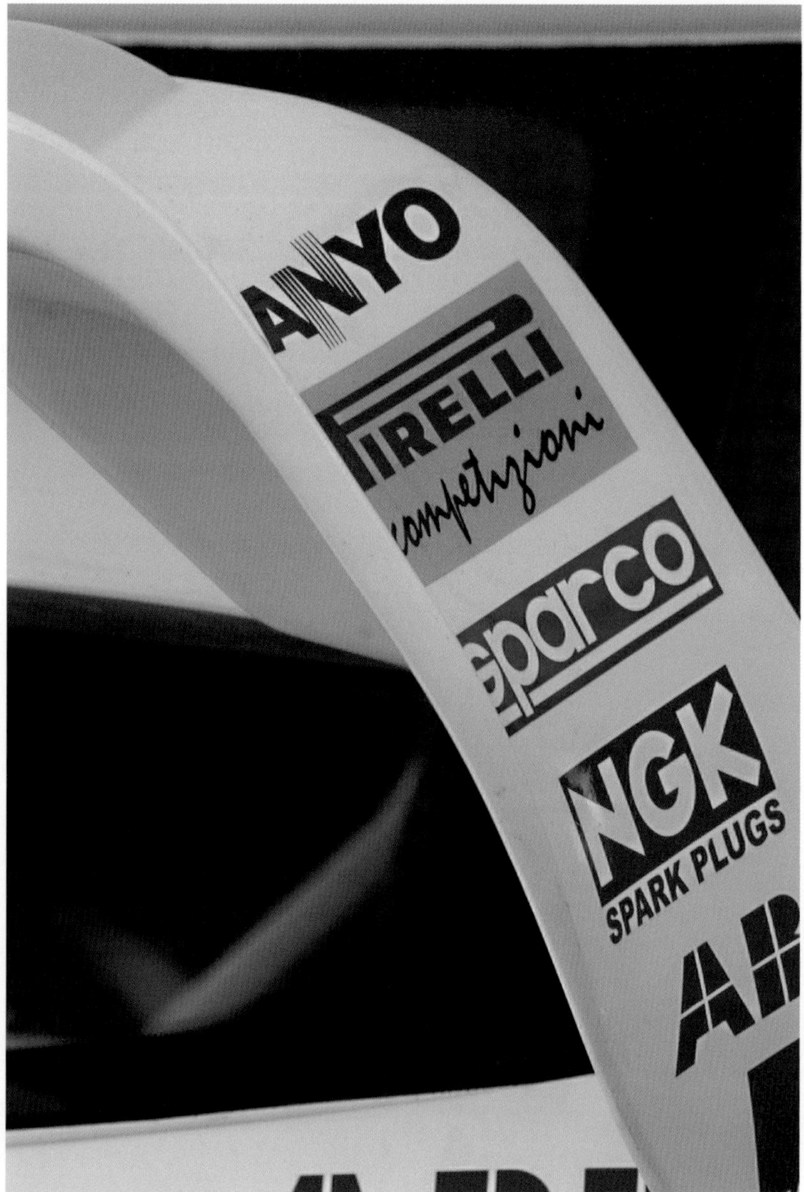

Copyright

For this type of photography copyright issues rarely raise their head, but it is well worth seeking advice before you begin selling your work. I am no legal expert, and always refer to someone who is; it's worth joining a recognized professional photographic association which will be able to give you specific legal advice on such issues.

Generally copyright of an image belongs to the photographer, so for the majority of action shots there should not be any problems. However, if recognizable people appear in the picture it is sometimes necessary to have them sign a model release form giving you permission to use the image, especially if it might be used commercially for advertising purposes.

Camera	**Pentax *ist D**
Focal length	**200mm (35mm equivalent: 300mm)**
Exposure	**1/350sec at f/4**
ISO setting	**200**

There are many different markets for motor sport photographs. Why not try approaching the drivers or teams with images which can be used in the promotional material they develop to attract support from new sponsors? This will also help you get to know the teams and drivers themselves, which will help to get your name known and could lead to further opportunities.

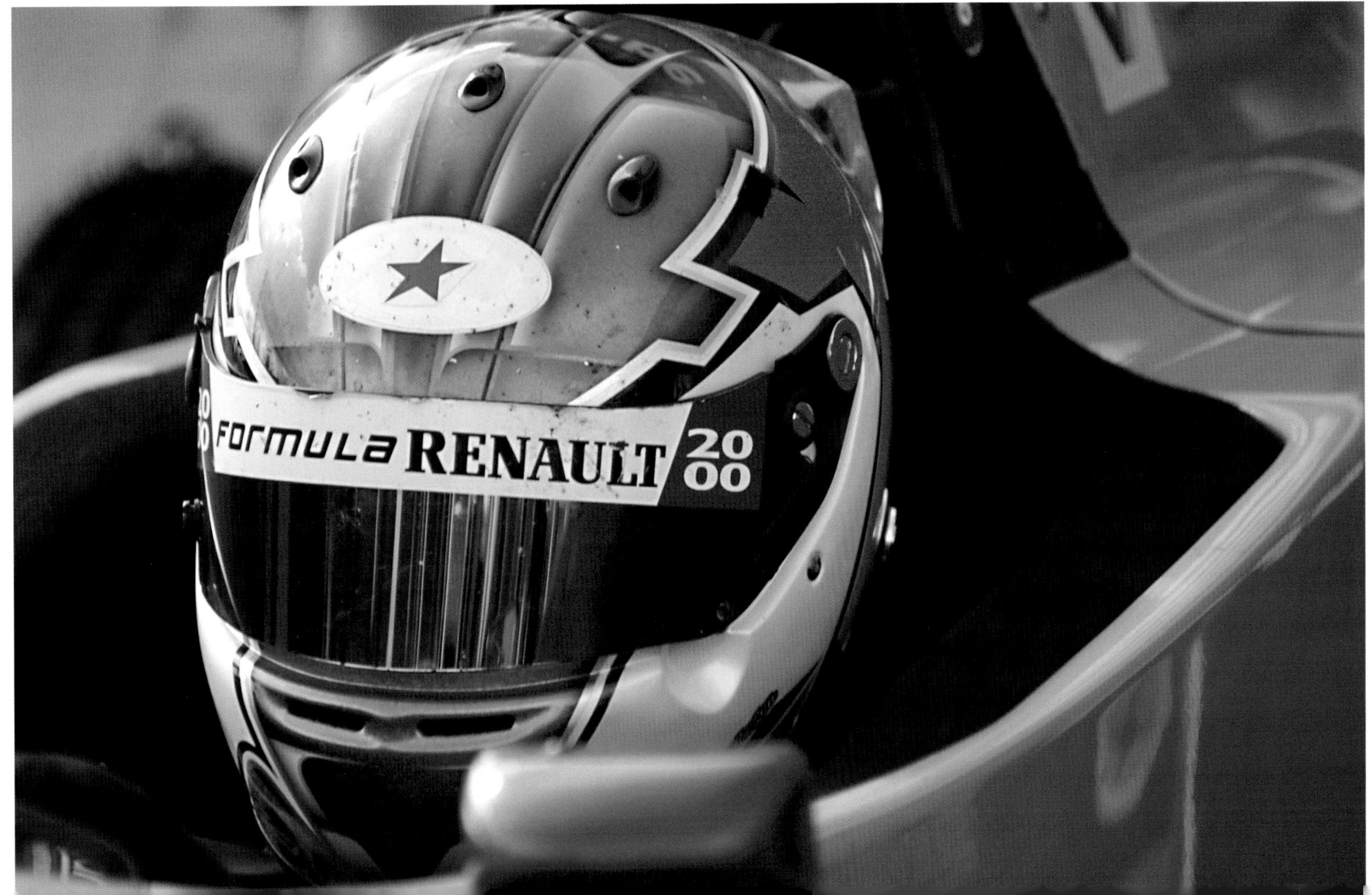

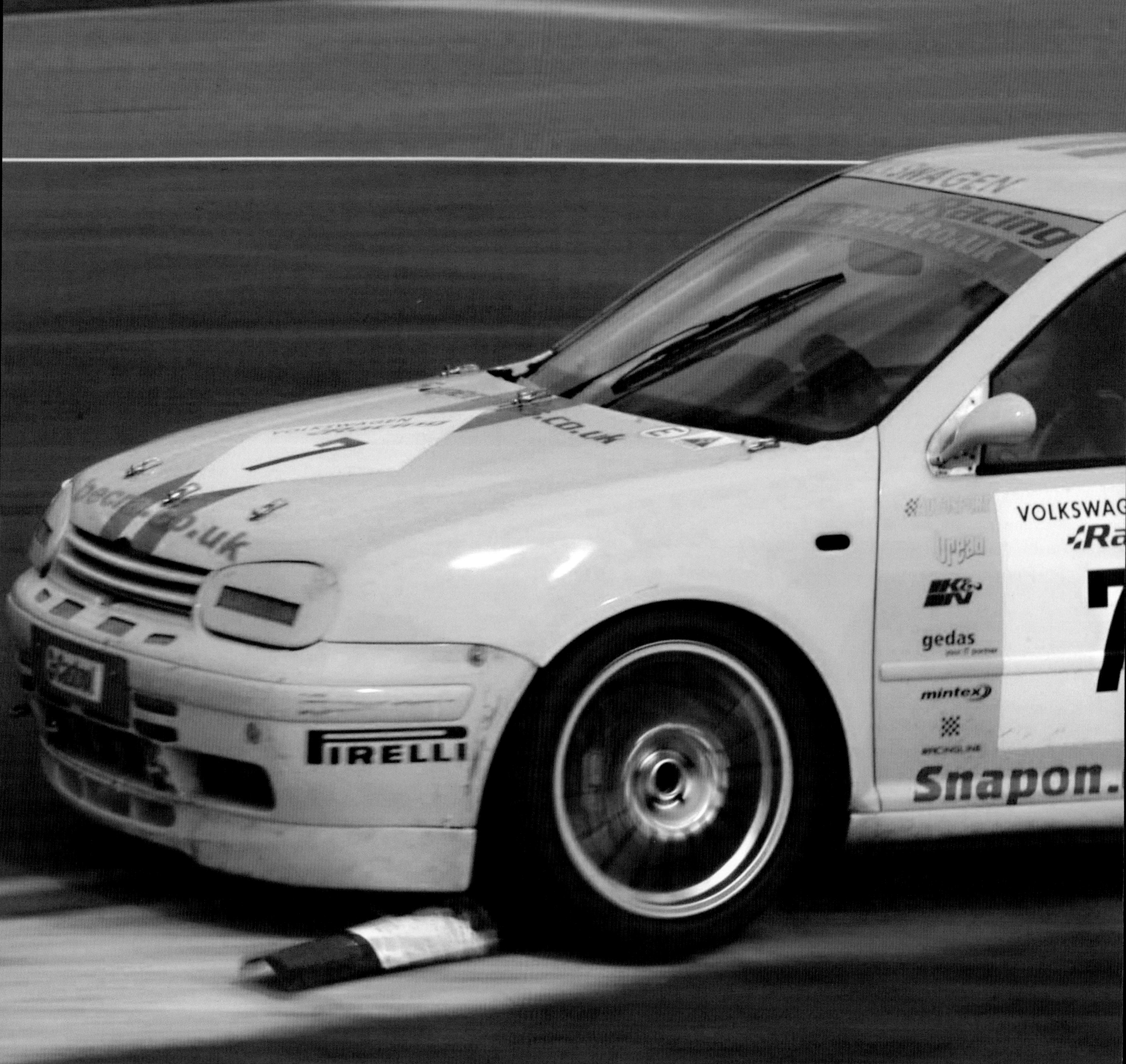

VOLKSWAG
7
gedas
mintex
PIRELLI
Snapon.

CHAPTER 7

At the end of the day

Following a weekend spent shooting an event, you will be faced with the time-consuming process of editing the images you have taken. Whether you shoot on film or digital equipment, the process of evaluating your photographs is much the same.

The key factor is to ensure that you do not allow any substandard images to slip through the editing process for whatever reason. When editing your images it is important to be your own worst critic and try to view your work through the eyes of a disinterested person. I find photography to be a very personal pursuit, and can be quite defensive about criticism of my pictures; the best way to forestall criticism is to make sure that substandard photographs move straight from the lightbox into the waste bin without any public airing at all.

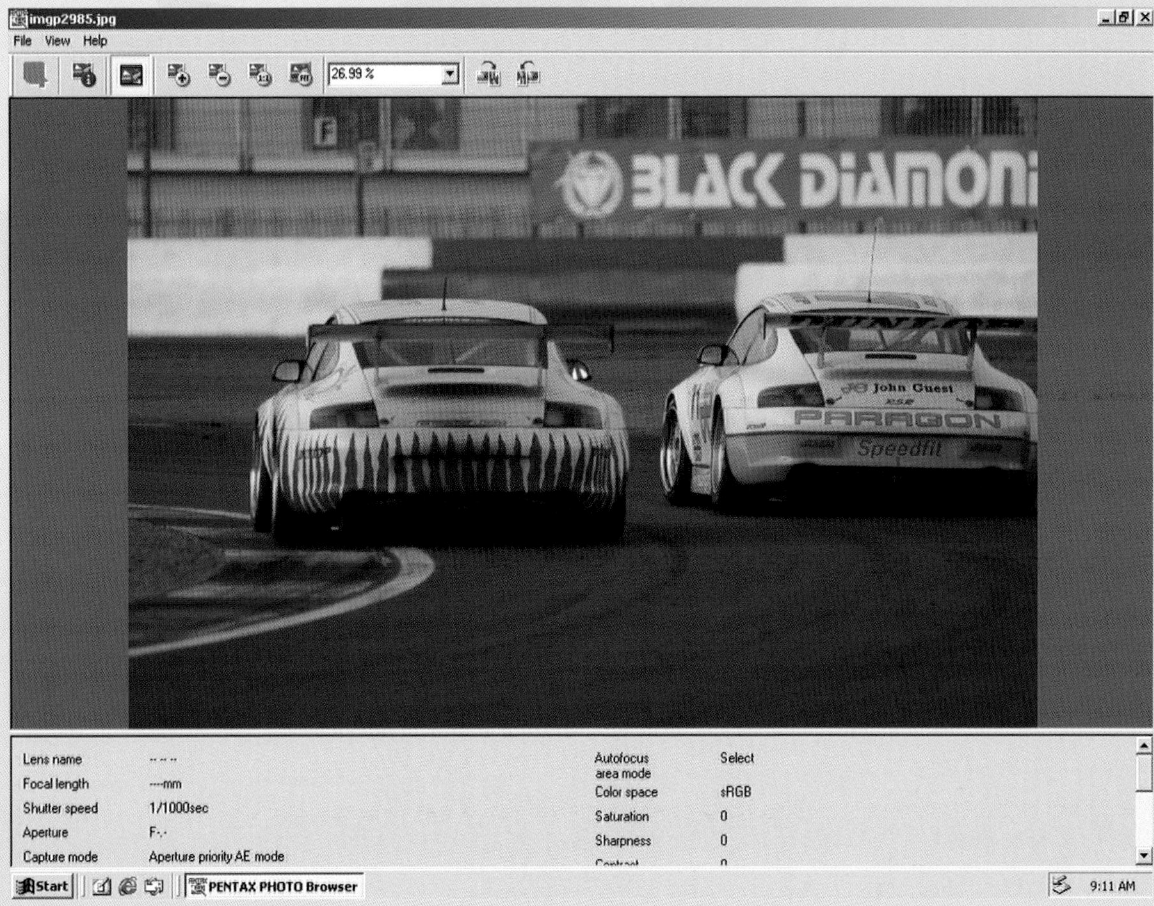

Editing is a time-consuming but vital part of organizing your images. Shooting digitally means that I now edit images on my computer rather than on a lightbox. Whichever process you use, make sure you don't allow substandard images to slip through. Throw them away – they will only take up valuable storage space.

Editing

When I first began photographing motor sports I was far less self-critical and kept every image that I thought was technically acceptable – in focus and correctly exposed – without giving much consideration to composition or style. While I knew that I would be unlikely to use any of these shots, I felt I ought to keep them because throwing them away would drastically reduce the number of successful shots I obtained from a day's photography, and would in some way make me a worse photographer.

Camera	*Pentax *ist D*
Focal length	*135mm (35mm equivalent: 200mm)*
Exposure	*1/125sec at f/16*
ISO setting	*200*

I really wanted this image to make it through the editing process; it's technically competent, but the composition lacks impact due to the position of the car in the frame. Had I used the camera in portrait format and positioned the car at the top or bottom of the frame, there's a good chance it would have been a successful image.

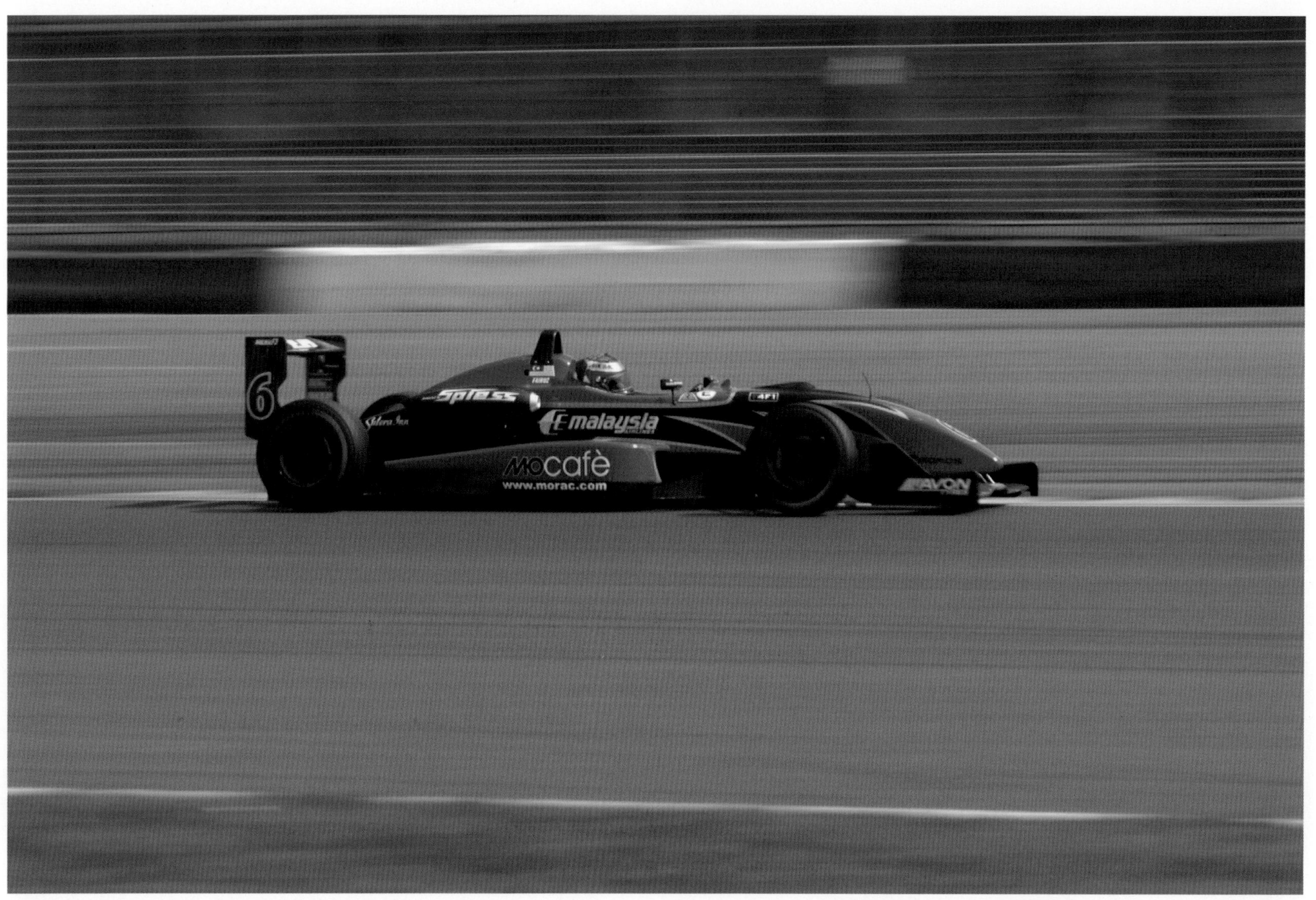

On reflection this was not such a bad thing. The only repercussion was that my filing cabinet contained many images that were simply gathering dust, and the knowledge that I was not consistently producing enough images of an acceptable standard drove me to practise and improve. Keeping substandard images was like having a comfort blanket; but as my photographic skills improved I became much more critical of my images and began to feel comfortable about editing out any such pictures.

Few people like taking criticism – I certainly don't – but learning to ask for and accept it will make you a better photographer. Learn to be critical of your photographs and edit out substandard work – you will find that although you may have a smaller number of images on file, their quality will be much higher.

Camera	**Pentax *ist D**
Focal length	**190mm (35mm equivalent: 285mm)**
Exposure	**1/90sec at f/16**
ISO setting	**200**

Another example of an image that failed to make it through the editing process. The driver of this car clipped the bollards as he came through this chicane on the previous lap, so I decided to watch him on the next lap – when he ran over the bollard altogether. When I reviewed the image in the camera I was pleased to have captured the moment just before the bollard disappeared under the car. On further reflection, while editing the image, I decided that I had not paid enough attention to the composition: there is too much space in front of the car, and the crop is a little too tight – I would like to have had the rear wheel in shot.

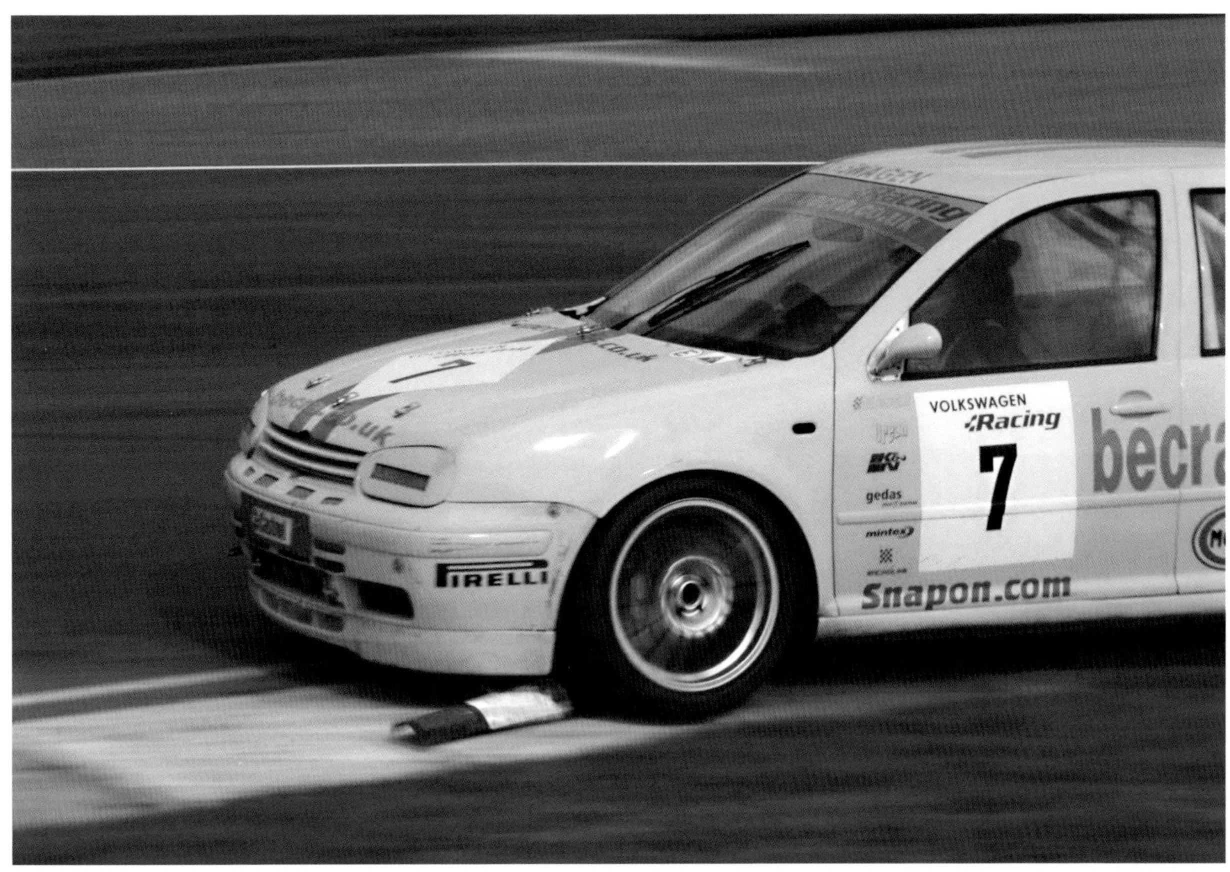

Learning to be ruthless

When editing your images it is important to be truly critical of your work. This picture of a Formula Renault V6 is an example of an image that I really hoped would survive the editing process, but on final analysis it failed to do so. The image is correctly exposed and focused, it captures the brake discs glowing red as the car brakes towards a tight corner, and you can see flames emerging from the exhaust at the rear of the car – all of which surely adds up to a good motor racing image? Not so. At the time of capture I felt that the colour of the car was complemented by the blue and white barrier behind it, so I framed the composition to include this. However, on reflection I found the composition pretty weak and decided to discard it. Pleased though I was to have captured the glowing brake discs and flames at the rear – both of which appear for only a split second – after careful consideration the picture was left out of my archive.

Camera	***Pentax *ist D***
Focal length	***135mm (35mm equivalent: 200mm)***
Exposure	***1/180sec at f/8***
ISO setting	***200***

Being critical of your images is crucial to your development as a photographer. Distancing yourself from the trials and tribulations of the image-taking process can be hard, but at the end of the day you must be objective.

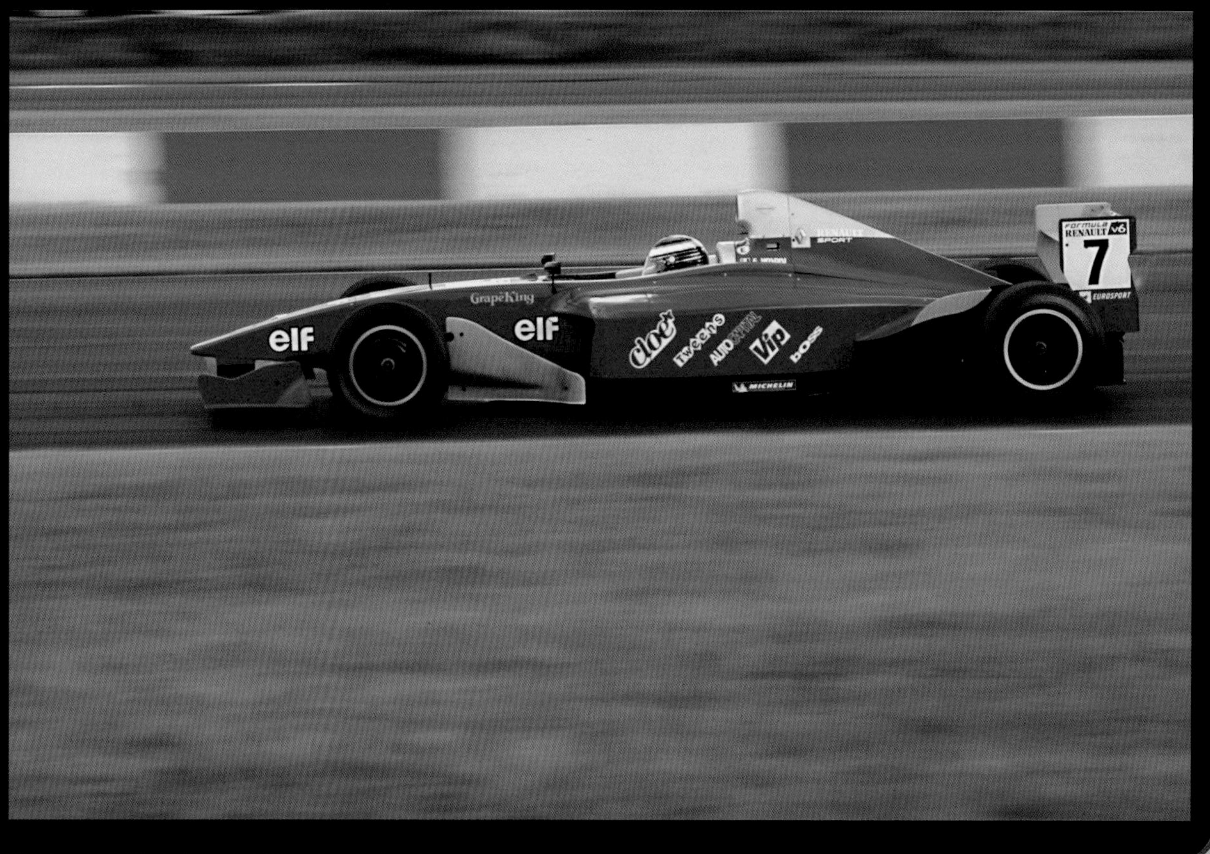

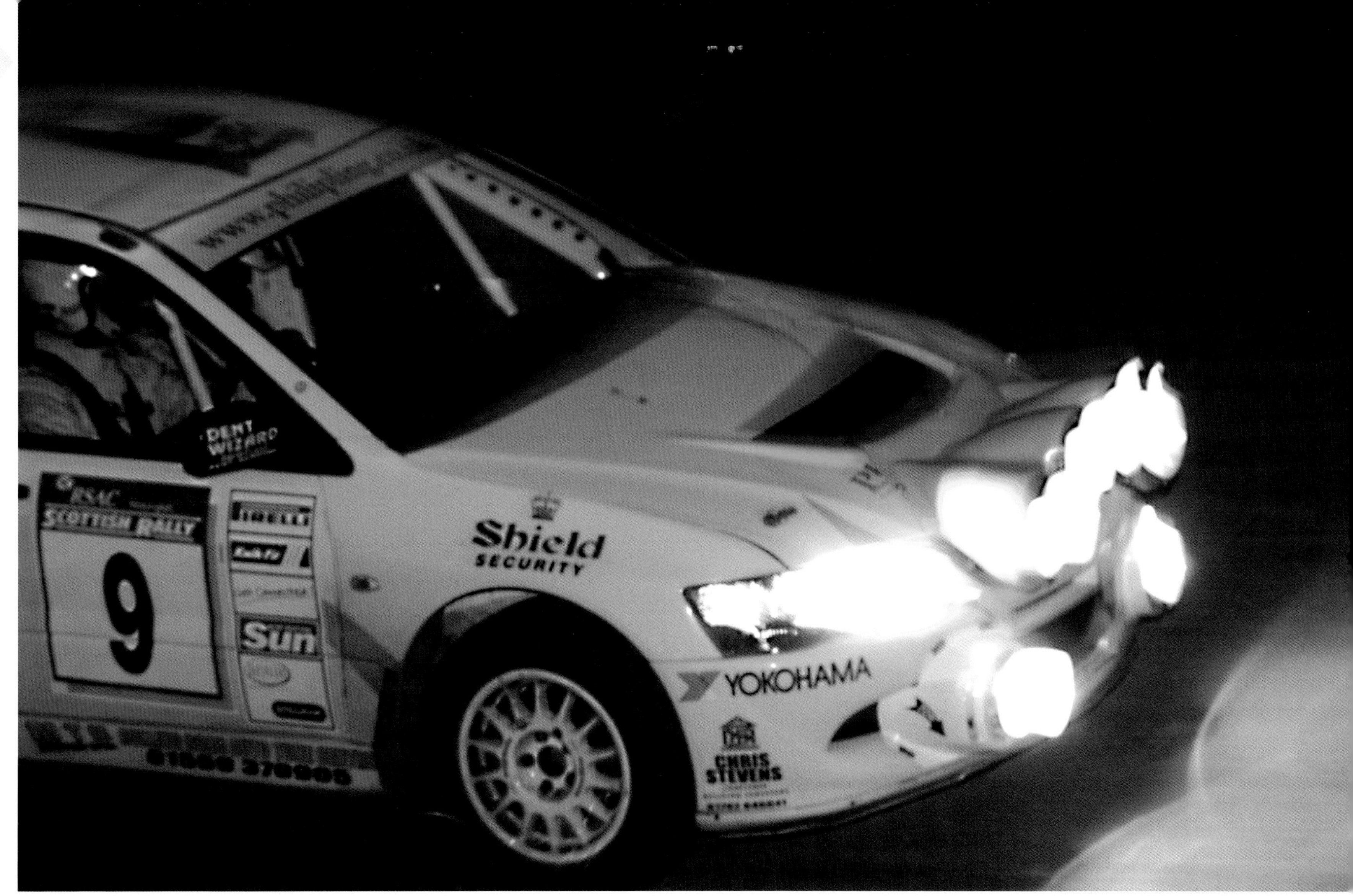

Camera	Pentax *ist D
Focal length	120mm (35mm equivalent: 180mm)
Exposure	1/10sec at f/5.6
ISO setting	200

Though the slow shutter speed has produced a pleasing light trail from the headlights and caught the sparks coming from the brake discs, the lack of light prevented me from focusing correctly. No matter how much you like an image, unless it passes strict editing criteria you should discard it – letting pictures through because you are emotionally attached to them will only devalue your other work.

Storage and archiving: Film

If you're new to photography, the storage and archiving of your images may appear to be fairly straightforward: as long as you don't have large numbers of images you'll be able to find individual pictures quite easily. However, if you're out shooting regularly you'll soon build up a library of hundreds or thousands of pictures which will need to be stored in a practical way – not only for their own protection, but so that you will be able to find pictures quickly without having to trawl through boxes of prints or transparencies to find the image you're looking for.

To store my transparencies I bought a small two-drawer filing cabinet that slides under my desk; I then allocated one drawer to two-wheeled motor sports and the other to four wheels. I placed labelled file holders in each drawer for particular racing disciplines; for example, my 'Four-wheel' drawer was originally set up with only a few categories:

- **Rallying**
- **Karting**
- **Tin-top racing**
- **Slicks-'n'-wings.**

This was fine to start with, but as the number of images grew it became difficult to find pictures quickly. I then subdivided the categories again, providing a folder for each of the classes in each category; for example, 'Slicks-'n'-wings' was split into:

- **Formula 3**
- **Formula Renault**
- **Formula Palmer Audi**
- **Formula Ford**
- **etc.**

At the end of each racing season I would then label each category with the appropriate year and move them to the back of the drawer to make way for the next season's images.

I store my transparencies in clear plastic file pages that contain 20 pockets on a page, each holding a mounted 35mm slide; these fit neatly into the file folders in my cabinet. Not only do these file pages make storing and viewing slides much easier, but they also protect them from scratching.

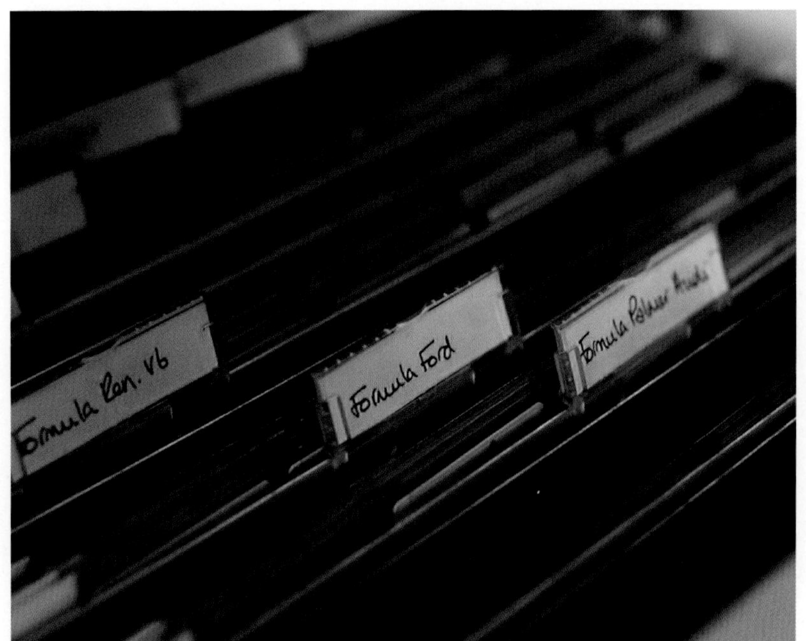

Storing your images in a filing cabinet with a practical and organized layout is essential to enable you to find your images quickly, and at the same time protects them from getting damaged. If you have a large number of transparencies or negatives which either have a commercial worth or are of value to yourself, it is worth scanning all your images with a bespoke film scanner and saving them onto CD or DVD so they can be stored with a friend or relative.

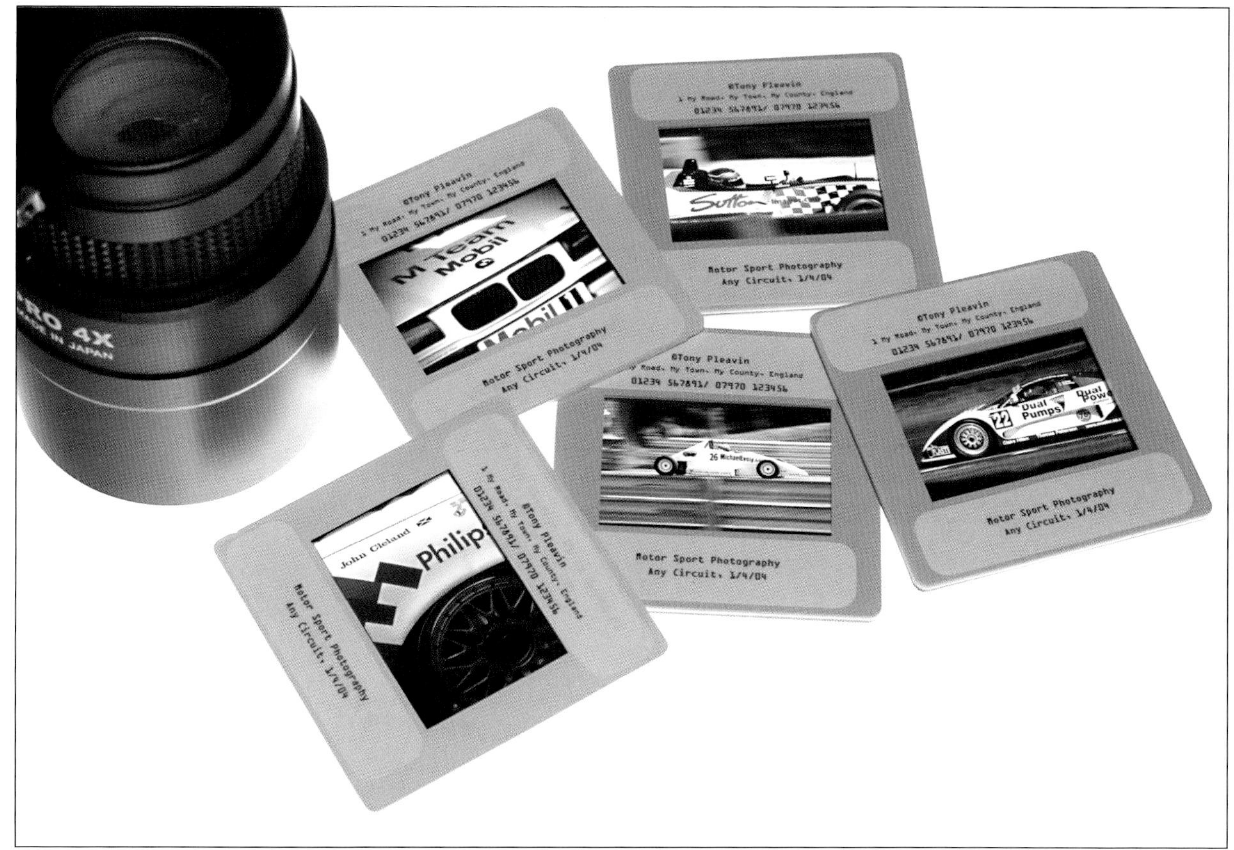

A computer-based system will make it much easier for you to label your slides with relevant information, such as your contact details and a brief description of the subject. Although this is a time-consuming exercise, it should be done before you commit any images to file – this is much easier than trying to remember details at a later date.

Once you've set up your system, storing and archiving can all be done relatively quickly. However, if you are thinking about selling your images or submitting them for publication it is important that each slide or print is labelled with your name and contact details, as well as details of the image. Bearing in mind the size of a 35mm slide mount, it is impossible to write all the relevant information on it by hand in a legible way. There are packages available which allow you to print labels from your computer that you then stick onto the slide mount; not only does this help you to get all the details onto the mount, but it also looks far more professional.

Backing up

As a final point, it is worth considering the safety of your images. As my library increased in size I began to worry about the implications of theft or fire: my precious transparencies could be lost or damaged with little or no chance of my ever seeing them again. With this in mind I decided that it would be wise to have copies of my pictures stored at a separate location.

I found the best solution to this problem was to scan all my images onto CD-ROM as a back-up of the originals. I bought a Nikon film scanner (which is a fairly expensive purchase) and set about scanning all of my slides. This is an extremely time-consuming thing to do, with each slide taking a couple of minutes to scan, but I felt it was worth the effort. I now keep these CDs at a friend's house so that in the event of a disaster I will at least have a record of my images.

Storage and archiving: Digital

With digital images storage can be a little simpler. Once you have decided what method of storage best suits your needs, there are basically three choices available:

- **the hard drive of your computer**
- **CDs or DVDs**
- **external hard drives.**

Each has its pros and cons, and whichever you choose will depend on your own personal requirements.

Computer hard drive

Modern computers have sizeable hard drives, and to begin with you may wish to set up a number of file folders on your hard drive, organized in a similar way to the filing cabinet described on page 170. In the short term this is an easy way to store your images, but as you add more pictures you will begin to use up space on your hard drive, thereby slowing its performance; you will therefore need to look for alternative storage media. I would in any case be slightly nervous of using this as my sole storage method; I would worry that a problem with the computer could result in the loss of all my images, with no back-up copies.

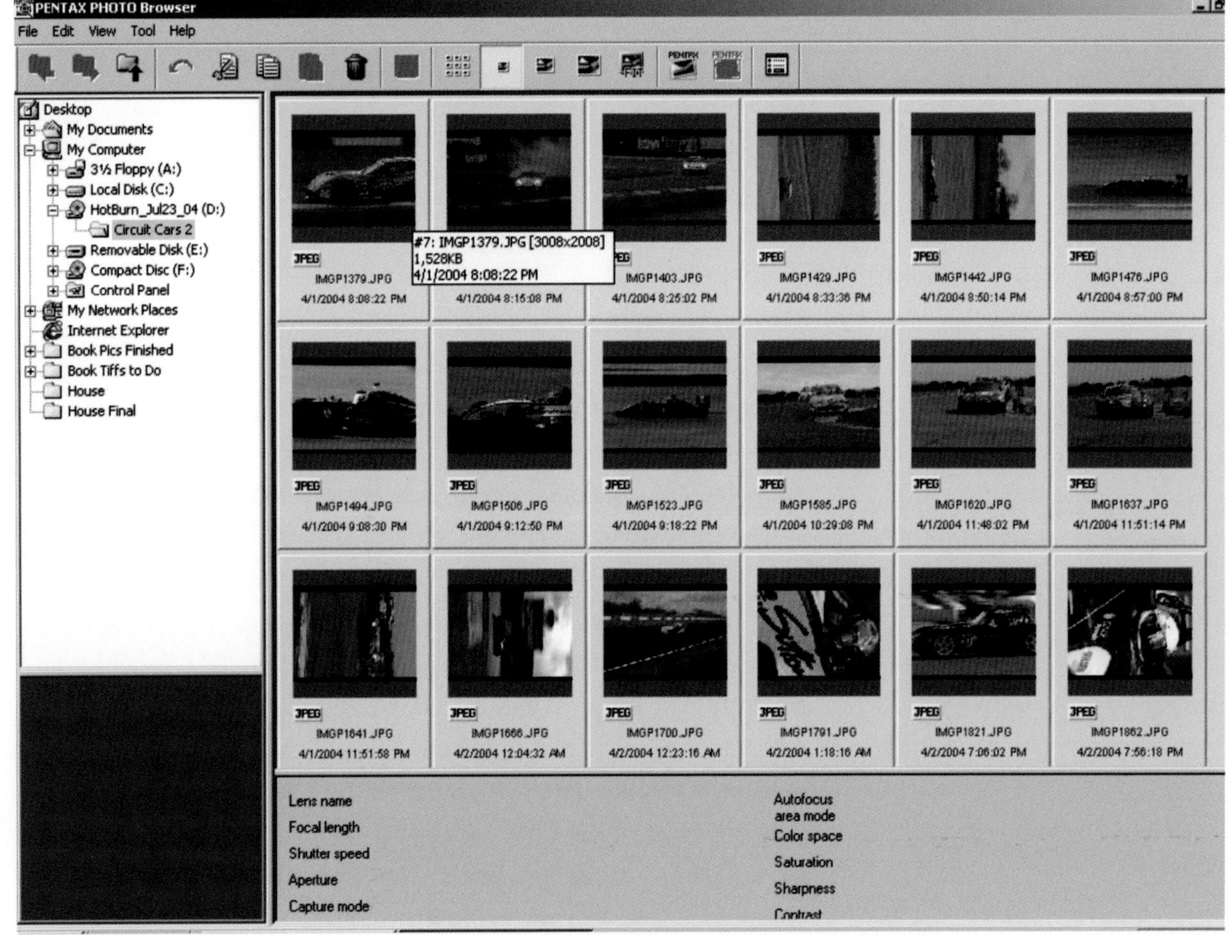

Most digital SLRs come with an image browser software package that allows you to view images on your computer when editing or archiving your work. These are generally very quick and easy to use, allowing you to browse through your images as thumbnails before selecting which ones to look at in greater detail. One function I particularly like is that the digital camera records exposure data which can be viewed using the image browser - so I no longer have to record or remember shutter speeds and apertures.

CD-ROM or DVD-ROM

Archiving your images to CDs or DVDs is an effective way of storing your files. CDs can hold up to 700Mb of information, while DVDs have a much larger capacity of 4.7Gb – over six times the capacity of a CD-ROM.

Once you've edited your shots you can burn the files onto a disc and store them away. I archive my discs by event date, and list on the cover the racing classes contained on the disc, the location and the date of the event. There are different types of CD available; I always use CD-Rs, as I have read that the life expectancy of data on other types of CD (notably rewritable CDs or CD-RWs) can be as short as two years.

CDs have proved not to be the indestructible storage media that they were claimed to be when first launched, and repeated use can cause discs to become corrupted. This is another reason for my choice of CD over DVD: if a disc does fail (which to date has never happened to me) I will only lose a maximum of 700Mb of images, as opposed to the much greater capacity on a DVD. In an effort to combat this risk I always make two copies of every disc I burn: one is for everyday use, while the other is labelled as the 'master'; this acts as a back-up, and is safely stored at a friend's house.

External hard drive

External hard drives are connected to your computer via USB or Firewire ports, and act as a supplement to your computer's internal hard drive. The benefits are that you can store huge amounts of data on them (in some cases over 1,000Gb), and once one is full you simply buy another and add it to your system. Though hard drives can fail, it is often possible to recover the data by using data recovery software. However, if I were to use this method of storage I think my 'belt and braces' attitude would make me want to back up my files onto discs in order to protect my images from failure, theft or fire.

If you shoot digitally and choose to store your images on CDs, you'll need to find space for them - I compiled just over 50 CDs full of images during the production of this book. Also bear in mind how and where you store your CDs: keep them away from sunlight and extreme temperatures to prevent deterioration.

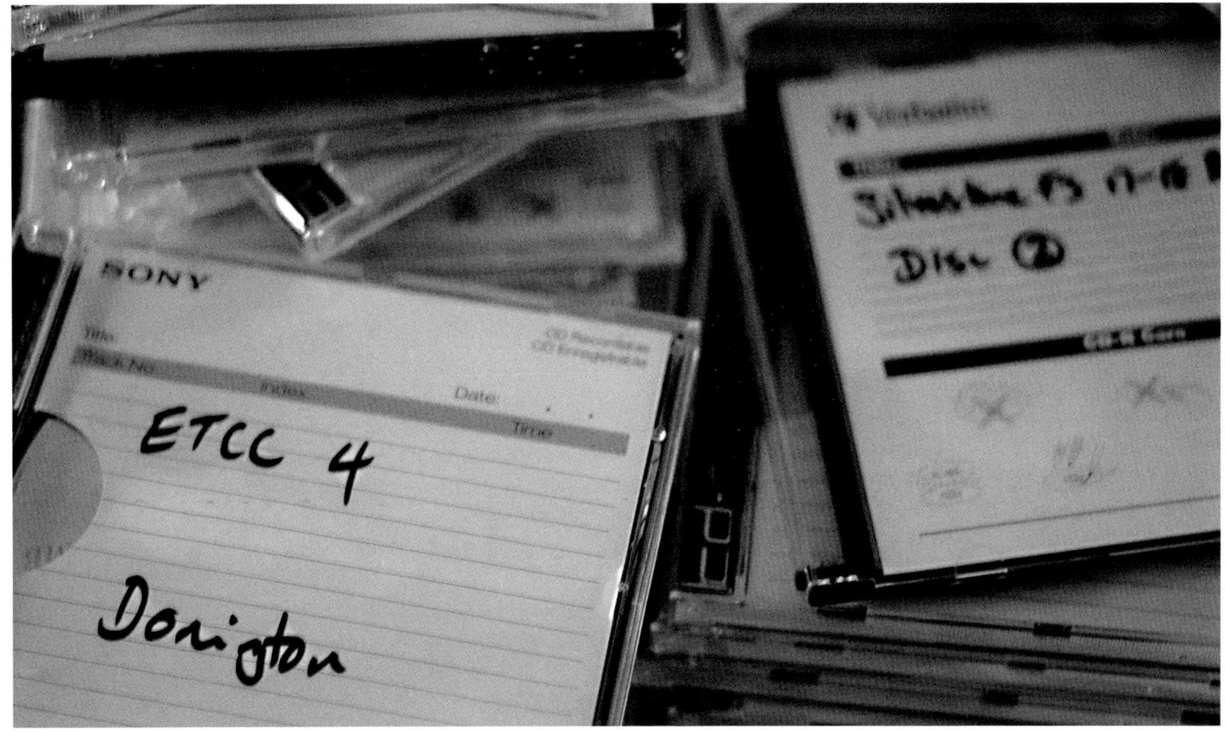

A final word

As the chequered flag falls on this book, I hope it has given you some insight into how you can improve your motor racing photographs. Though much of the book deals with technique and camera-control issues, I think the most valuable lessons for the photographer to learn relate to creativity and the development of a personal style. No matter what your level of ability or photographic ambitions, taking images is first and foremost a way of communicating to others how you see the things around you.

Motor sport photography can be tiring, frustrating, expensive and dangerous, yet all this fades into insignificance when you capture in a split second what you have spent many hours preparing for.

Whether you view your images on a lightbox or a computer screen, there is no substitute for being out there taking photographs, challenging your creativity in the pursuit of a truly enjoyable pastime. I can only hope that in some small way I may have inspired you to do so.

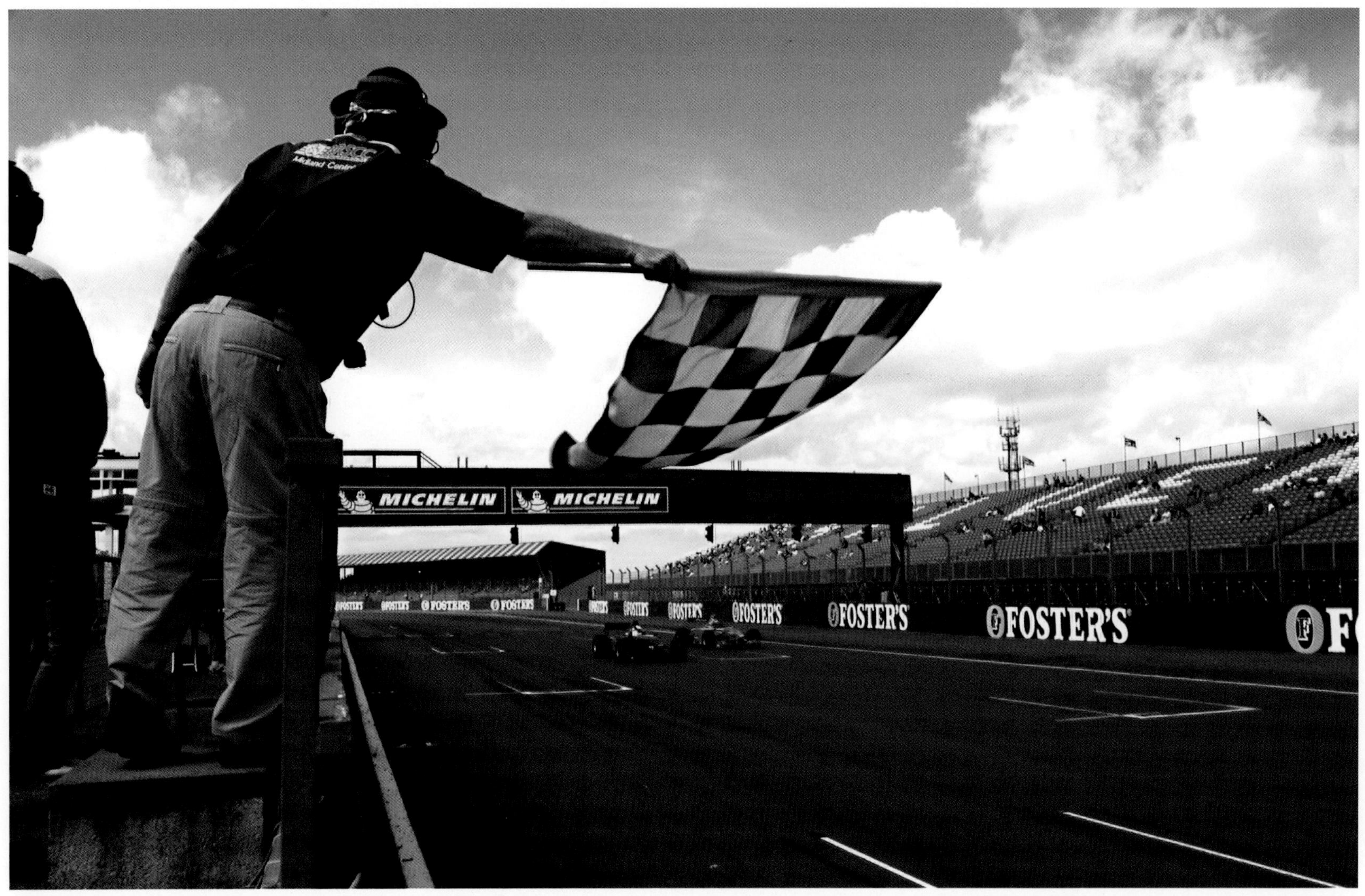

Sources of information

Motor sport websites

www.motorsport.com US-based general racing site covering most international disciplines

www.crash.net UK-based site covering national and international racing

www.racer.com site for one of the leading US racing publications

www.racedates.net UK-based site listing racing events in many disciplines throughout the world

www.autosport.com international site for one of the best racing magazines

www.transworldmotocross.com US-based motocross site

www.ezracer.com US-based site covering all motorcycle disciplines

www.motorcyclenews.com/sport site for one of the UK's weekly motorcycle publications

Motor sport photography sites

www.latphoto.co.uk one of the world's leading motor sport photo agencies

www.sutton-images.com international motor sport photo agency

www.jakobebrey.com UK-based racing photographers

www.doublered.co.uk photographers specializing in superbike racing

www.mcklein.de one of the world's best rallying agencies

Racing circuits

www.etracksonline.co.uk international site listing racing circuits throughout the world

www.motorsportvision.co.uk home of the UK's largest circuit owner

www.donington-park.co.uk well-known UK circuit

www.mallorypark.co.uk well-known UK circuit

www.croftcircuit.co.uk UK racing circuit

www.knockhill.com Scottish racing circuit

Race organizers and governing bodies

www.msauk.org governing body for racing in the UK

www.fia.com governing body of world motorsport

www.scca.org the Sportscar Club of America

www.acu.org.uk governing body for motorcycle racing in UK

www.ama-cycle.org American Motorcycles Association

www.britishf3gt.com home page for British Formula 3 and GT championships

www.tocatour.co.uk British touring car site

www.brcweb.co.uk home of the British Rally Championship

www.imsaracing.net US-based International Motor Sports Association

www.worldsbk.com organizers of the World Superbike Championship

www.amasuperbike.com organisers of the American Superbike Championship

Glossary

aperture an opening within a lens which can be enlarged or reduced to control the amount of light passing through onto the film or digital sensor.

aperture priority an exposure mode in which the photographer selects the aperture size while the camera automatically sets the shutter speed.

automatic flash an on-camera flash unit that regulates its output by reading its own light as it bounces back off the subject.

backlighting the situation in which bright light falls from behind the subject towards the camera, which can cause silhouetting of the subject.

burst length the number of frames that a digital camera can shoot in rapid succession before lock-out occurs.

CD-R a compact disk onto which data can be recorded for storage.

CD-RW a compact disk on which data can be erased and re-recorded.

centre-weighted metering an in-camera light-metering system in which readings are taken chiefly from the central area of the frame.

CompactFlash® card a common type of removable media card used in digital cameras to store image data.

contrast the variety of tones within an image.

dedicated flash an on-camera flash unit, specific to one make or model of camera, that automatically sets exposure.

depth of field the distance between the nearest and farthest points within an image which can be brought into acceptably sharp focus at the same time.

D-SLR digital single-lens reflex camera.

DVD-R a recordable disk which can be used to store image data; it resembles a CD but has a much larger capacity.

exposure the amount of light passing through the lens onto the film or sensor, controlled by the combination of shutter speed and aperture.

fast lens a lens with a wide maximum aperture, such as f/1.4.

fill-in flash flash used as a supplementary light source in daylight to reduce contrast and lighten shadows.

film speed a standard measure of the sensitivity of a film to light, usually expressed as an ISO rating.

filter a transparent or translucent surface placed in front of a lens to control or alter the light which passes through the lens.

flash a device which produces a short, concentrated burst of light to supplement or replace natural light in poorly lit conditions.

flash-sync speed the highest shutter speed at which a camera is designed to synchronize with flash.

focal length the distance between the nodal point of the lens and the focal plane when the lens is focused at infinity.

f-stop the standard unit in which the aperture size of a lens is measured.

gigabyte (Gb) 1,000 megabytes.

grain a visible pattern or texture caused by clumps of metallic silver particles on developed film.

hard drive a computer's internal storage system, or a separate unit with a similar function.

hot shoe a fixture with electrical contacts, usually on the top of a camera, which allows for the attachment of a flash gun or other device.

image buffer a facility in digital cameras which allows for multiple images to be stored before lock-out occurs.

ISO short for International Standards Organization. Film speeds are expressed in ISO ratings, a doubling of the ISO number representing a twofold increase in the sensitivity of the film to light. Sensors on digital cameras can be set to various levels of sensitivity, measured in the same way.

landscape format a rectangular picture format, wider than it is high.

LCD a liquid crystal display screen, as used for reviewing images on a digital camera.

lightbox an electric light source with a diffused screen for viewing transparencies.

lock-out the situation in which a digital camera becomes temporarily inoperable because the image buffer is full; it becomes operational again once the images have been written to the memory card.

manual a metering mode in which the photographer controls both shutter speed and aperture to obtain correct exposure.

medium format any film format that uses rolls of film wider than 35mm – typically 6 x 4.5, 6 x 6 or 6 x 7cm.

megabyte (Mb) a unit of computer memory, around 1,000,000 bytes.

megapixel (Mp) 1,000,000 pixels.

monopod a camera support with a single leg, often used to steady telephoto lenses.

noise in digital photography, an effect resembling grain that occurs in low light or when a high ISO rating is used.

overexpose to admit too much light onto the film or digital sensor by using incorrect aperture or shutter speed, rendering the image overly bright and 'washed out'.

panning moving the camera to follow a moving subject, so that the subject appears relatively sharp and the background blurred.

PhotoShop® an image-manipulation software package widely used by professionals.

pixel one of the minute elements which form the basis of a digital image.

polarizer (polarizing filter) a lens filter used to darken blue skies and reduce reflections from non-metallic surfaces.

portrait format a rectangular picture format, taller than it is wide.

prime lens a lens of fixed focal length.

print film a film that is processed to make negative images, from which positive prints can be made.

program mode a fully automated exposure mode where the camera automatically sets both shutter speed and aperture.

pushing rating a film at a higher ISO setting than recommended, and then compensating for the resultant underexposure by increasing the developing time.

reciprocity the relationship between shutter speed and aperture, such that a one-stop increase in aperture can be compensated for by a one-stop decrease in exposure duration, and vice versa.

reversal film a less common name for slide or transparency film.

rule of thirds a rule of thumb used in photographic composition: the scene is divided by two horizontal and two vertical lines, and focal points are placed where these lines intersect.

shutter the mechanism which admits light to the film or sensor for a controlled length of time.

shutter priority an exposure mode in which the photographer selects the shutter speed while the camera automatically sets the aperture size.

shutter speed the length of time the shutter remains open.

skylight filter a lens filter used to reduce ultraviolet light.

slide film film which is processed to make a positive image (transparency) as opposed to a negative. When suitably mounted, the transparency becomes a slide which can be projected.

slow-sync flash flash used in conjunction with a slow shutter speed so as to combine a sharp image with motion blur.

SLR single-lens reflex camera.

spot metering a light-metering system that measures light levels from only a small area of the scene.

standard lens a lens whose focal length is approximately equal to the diagonal of the film or sensor format; for 35mm film, 50mm is considered standard.

stop (1) same as f-stop. (2) a unit of exposure: exposure increases by one stop when the quantity of light reaching the film or sensor is doubled.

teleconverter a supplementary lens placed between camera body and main lens in order to increase the effective focal length.

telephoto lens a lens of longer than standard focal length.

three-quarter panning panning the camera with a subject that is moving towards or away from the photographer as well as from side to side.

transparency film another term for slide film.

underexpose to allow insufficient light onto the film or sensor because of incorrect aperture or shutter speed, rendering the image overly dark.

UV (ultraviolet) filter a lens filter used to reduce ultraviolet light.

wideangle lens a lens of shorter than standard focal length.

zoom lens a lens of variable focal length.

About the author

Photography has always been Tony Pleavin's passion. He sold his first photograph in 1984 when he was only 15, and has been taking and selling images ever since. Now working as an Internet marketing consultant, he is also a semi-professional photographer with a growing reputation for landscape and travel photography, as well as motor sports. His work has been published in the UK and internationally, and he is a Licentiate of the Royal Photographic Society.

A keen mountain biker and kart racer, he lives in the north-west of England with his wife Jenni.

A further selection of Tony's work can be viewed on his website, www.tonypleavin.com

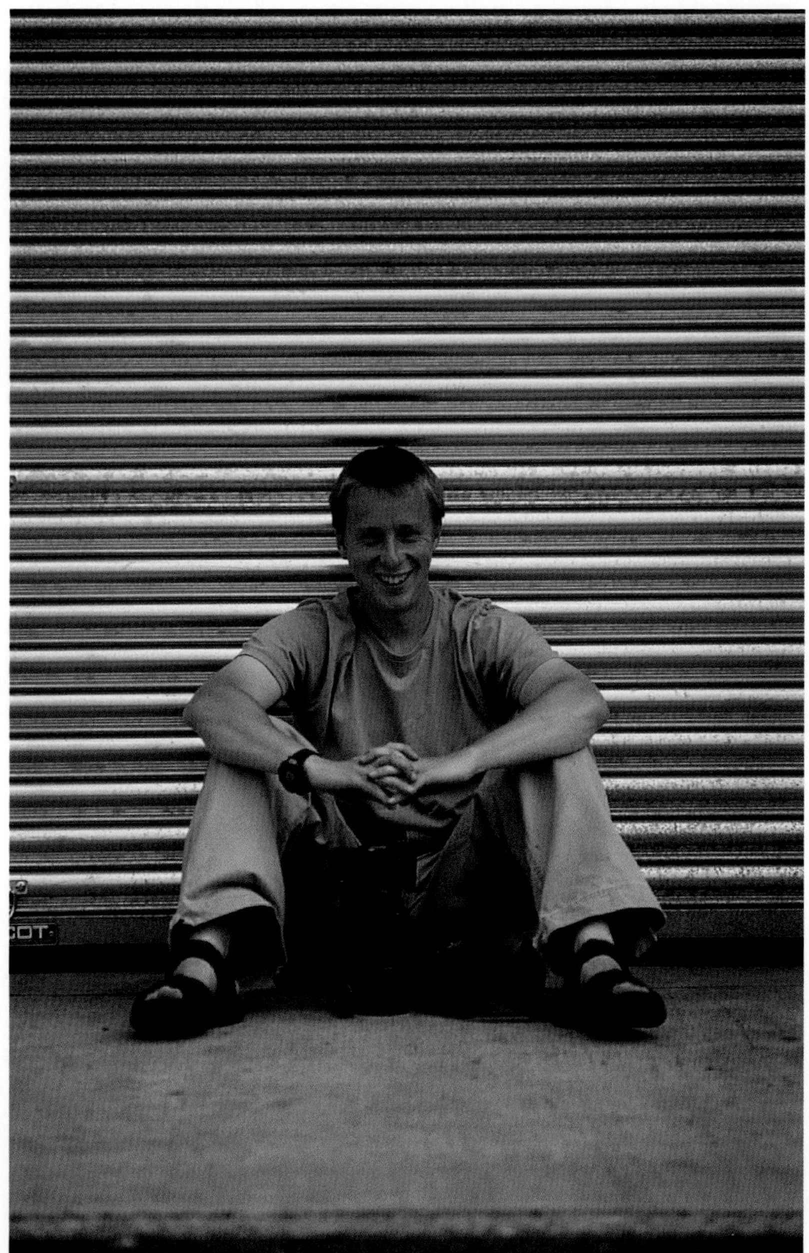

Photo: Pete Gardner

Index

Photographers' Institute Press
Castle Place, 166 High Street, Lewes, East Sussex BN7 1XU, United Kingdom
Tel: 01273 488005 Fax: 01273 402866
E-mail: pubs@thegmcgroup.com
Website: www.gmcbooks.com
Contact us for a complete catalogue, or visit our website. Orders by credit card are accepted.